Pocket Dictionary of Statistics

03/13

Pocket Dictionary of Statistics

Hardeo Sahai
University of Puerto Rico

Anwer Khurshid
University of Karachi

Boston   Burr Ridge, IL   Dubuque, IA   Madison, WI   New York
San Francisco   St. Louis   Bangkok   Bogotá   Caracas   Kuala Lumpur
Lisbon   London   Madrid   Mexico City   Milan   Montreal   New Delhi
Santiago   Seoul   Singapore   Sydney   Taipei   Toronto

McGraw-Hill Higher Education

A Division of The *McGraw-Hill* Companies

POCKET DICTIONARY OF STATISTICS

 This book is printed on acid-free paper.

1 2 3 4 5 6 7 8 9 0 BKM/BKM 0 9 8 7 6 5 4 3 2 1

ISBN 0-07-251693-3

Publisher: *Brent Gordon*
Executive editor: *Richard T. Hercher, Jr.*
Developmental editor: *Lee Stone*
Senior marketing manager: *Zina Craft*
Associate project manager: *Catherine R. Schultz*
Production supervisor: *Carol A. Bielski*
Coordinator of freelance design: *Mary Kazak*
Media producer: *Greg Bates*
Cover design: *Jon Resh*
Typeface: *9/11 Times Roman*
Compositor: *Interactive Composition Corporation*
Printer: *Bookmart Press*

Library of Congress Cataloging-in-Publication Data

Sahai, Hardeo.
    Pocket dictionary of statistics / Hardeo Sahai, Anwer Khurshid.
        p.   cm.
    ISBN 0-07-251693-3 (alk. paper)
    1. Mathematical statistics—Dictionaries. I. Khurshid, Anwer. II. Title.
QA276.14 .S25 2002
519.5$'$03—dc21   2001044248

www.mhhe.com

Contents

Preface

Statistics is the subject of data analysis and data-based reasoning. The study of statistics has become increasingly popular during the last two decades. The widespread availability of high-speed mainframes and microcomputers and myriads of accompanying software has made it much simpler to perform a wide range of statistical analyses, and has enlarged the role of statistics as a tool for empirical research. Today, statistical methods are commonly used in nearly all fields of endeavor; from A(ccounting) to Z(oology). College students in behavioral, engineering, management, life, and other sciences increasingly encounter statistical concepts, terms, notations, and formulas in the current literature in their respective fields of study. Some familiarity with this subject is now an essential component of a college education.

Every field of study has its own terminology, and statistics is no exception. During the last few decades there has been an explosive growth in the coining of many new terms to describe new concepts and techniques. Furthermore, these new developments in the field have caused great changes in the research, teaching, and curriculum of statistics. In all these phases, statistical terminology plays a vital role, and the first step in gaining an understanding of statistical methods is to master the professional terminology of statistics. The purpose of this volume is to provide clear, accurate, and informative definitions of some common statistical terms likely to be encountered in introductory- and intermediate-level statistics courses and in published literature in a variety of substantive fields.

In preparing definitions for the entries, we have relied primarily on our knowledge but have also, when necessary, referred to textbooks, glossaries, and other dictionaries. After considerable editing and revisions of the definitions originally compiled, the final versions of the definitions were prepared. In preparing the final definitions, we have attempted to provide explanations in several different ways, all of which are roughly equivalent. We hope this would help to clarify the meaning of certain terms that are sometimes difficult to comprehend. In addition, in describing many statistical concepts and ideas, we have relied as far as possible on verbal descriptions and have minimized the use of mathematical formulas. However, a list of such formulas has been included in an appendix. Furthermore, in order to facilitate the understanding of many concepts and terms, we have attempted to include a generous supply of illustrations including graphs and tables. Finally, references to many textbooks and specialized works where a more detailed treatment of a topic can be found have been provided in an appendix.

The list of terms was compiled from introductory- and intermediate-level statistics textbooks used in a variety of substantive fields, as well as scientific literature. Some related terms in mathematics, probability, economics, business, decision analysis, demography, epidemiology, clinical trials, biostatistics, public health, quality control, and other related fields have also been included. Although an attempt has been made to include terms from all areas of applications, there is probably greater emphasis from medical and epidemiological statistics because of compilers' special interests in these fields.

The terms are arranged in alphabetical order following the usage of dictionaries published in the United States. Entries are alphabetized using the letter-by-letter rather than word-by-word convention, regardless of the form of the words. When a term contains more than one word, the term's location is usually kept in alphabetical order starting from the first word and is not inverted. Thus, all words and phrases are alphabetized in their natural sequential ordering, without being rearranged, and spaces and hyphens between words are ignored. Thus, **logarithmic transformation** is listed as such and not under **transformation, logarithmic.** Greek letters are alphabetized according to the English transliteration of the letter. The terms containing numbers are spelled out with English words and alphabetized accordingly. Thus, α error is found under **alpha error** and 2×2 table is alphabetized under **two-by-two table.** The reader who encounters unfamiliar terms in a definition or explanation can usually find them defined elsewhere in the book. The major goal has been to provide a quick refresher for terms that may have escaped the student's mind, as well as an explanation in the cases of first-time exposure.

Many of the terms in this dictionary use other statistical terms in their definitions or are closely related to other concepts and terms. In such cases, we have endeavored to indicate as many cross references as possible. When a term used in the definition of a particular entry has an independent entry of its own, it has been highlighted in **bold** for ease of cross-referencing. Cross-references are also used from a term to every other term that is used in contradistinction to it. Such cross-references are usually preceded by the word *compare*. The dictionary also contains an abundant supply of terms that are synonymous to entries already defined and are cross-referred to the relevant entries preceded by the word *same as*. When a term is not completely synonymous but has been implicitly or explicitly defined elsewhere, it has been cross-referred to the relevant entry preceded by the word *see*. The work can be used as a supplement to a textbook or as handy reference source where students and others can find quick definitions of a wide variety of concepts and terms used in statistics and other related fields.

Hardeo Sahai
Anwer Khurshid

Acknowledgments

The authors wish to thank the many colleagues, friends, and students who provided stimulus and insights about what to include and made helpful suggestions and comments concerning the manuscript for this book. Our special thanks go to Dr. S. C. Misra of the U.S. Food and Drug Administration and American University, Washington, D.C., who assisted us in the initial stage of the preparation and processing of the manuscript.

Hardeo Sahai would like to acknowledge two sabbaticals (1978–1979 and 1993–1994) granted by the Administrative Board of the University of Puerto Rico during which period a major portion of the manuscript was compiled and edited. Parts of the manuscript were written and revised during the course of his appointment as the Patrimonial Professor of Statistics at the University of Veracruz (Mexico) and he wishes to thank the Mexican National Council of Science and Technology (CONACYT) for extending the appointment and providing a stimulating environment for research and study. He is especially grateful to Dr. Mario Miguel Ojeda for many helpful discussions and remarks, and for all his kindness and hospitality extended during the author's stay in Mexico. He also wishes to extend his appreciation to members and staff of the Puerto Rico Center for Addiction Research, especially Dr. Rafaela R. Robles, Dr. Hector M. Colon, Ms. Carmen A. Marrero, M.P.H., Mr. Tomás L. Matos, and Mr. Juan C. Reyes, M.P.H., who as an innovative research group provided the necessary stimulus to undertake and complete a project of this magnitude. Finally, he would like to thank his children Amogh, Mrisa, and Pankaj for their enduring patience and understanding throughout the time the work was in progress.

Anwer Khurshid would like to express special thanks to his colleague Muhammad Akram who spent countless hours in the word processing and proofreading the manuscript. He is also indebted to his family: son Sohaib, daughter Sumayya, and wife Shehla—each provided the necessary inspiration to undertake and complete this project, to say the least.

In the course of compiling this dictionary, we frequently consulted numerous other textbooks, dictionaries, glossaries, and encyclopedias that provided the basis for many entries and definitions included here. Our sincere appreciation to all these unnamed authors, too numerous to acknowledge individually, who have unwittingly provided definitions of many of the entries included here. Our special and grateful thanks go to our publisher, especially Mr. Richard Hercher, Executive Editor of Operations and Decision Sciences for his encouragement and support of this project. Equally, we would like to record our thanks to the editorial, marketing, and production staff at McGraw-Hill/Irwin, especially Lee

Stone, Mary Kazak, Cathy Schultz, and Zina Craft, for all of their help and cooperation in bringing the project to its fruition.

We would be grateful to readers for any comments and criticisms regarding inclusion of new terms or any inaccuracies in the definitions that could improve this work in a future edition.

List of Illustrations

A

abacus– A simple mechanical device to facilitate arithmetical operations such as addition, subtraction, multiplication, and division by sliding counters along rods or ingrooves. There are several such instruments currently in use. The one most commonly used at present is depicted below.

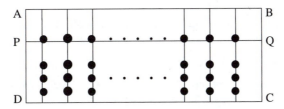

The form of an abacus currently in common use

abortion rate– The number of abortions actually observed during a calendar year divided by the total number of women of childbearing age (expressed per 1000). The childbearing or reproductive age is normally defined as between 15 and 44 years.

abscissa– The **horizontal axis** or *x* **axis** on a graph using the **Cartesian coordinate** system. Generally, it refers to the baseline of most of the graphs used in **statistics.** Compare *ordinate.*

absolute central moment– See *absolute moment.*

absolute class frequency– The actual number of items or **observations** that belong to a particular class as opposed to **relative frequency** or **proportion** of items, namely the ratio of the **frequency** to the total frequency. See also *cumulative class frequency, cumulative frequency.*

absolute deviation– In general, absolute difference between any two quantities. In **statistics,** the term is normally used to denote the **absolute values** of the differences of the observed **scores** from their **mean.** See also *deviation from the mean.*

absolute frequency distribution– A **tabular representation** of a **data set** showing the actual class frequencies in each of several mutually exclusive and exhaustive classes, as opposed to **relative frequencies.** See also *frequency distribution.*

absolute moment– The **moment** of the **absolute value** of a **random variable.** The rth absolute moment about the origin of a random variable X is defined as $E[|X|^r]$. The rth absolute **central moment** of X is given by the quantity $E[|X - E(X)|^r]$.

absolute risk– Same as *incidence rate.*

absolute risk difference– In epidemiological studies, the absolute risk difference (ARD) is defined as the difference of the **risks** of an event, such as a disease or death, between two groups of subjects; for example, between the **intervention** or **exposure group** and the **control.** Algebraically, $\text{ARD} = R_i - R_c$, where R_i and R_c denote the risks in the intervention and **control group** respectively. See also *attributable risk.*

absolute value– The numerical value of a mathematical expression, regardless of its algebraic sign. Thus, the absolute value of a positive number is the number itself and the absolute value of a negative number is the positive of that number. Absolute value marks are two vertical lines (| |), one on each side of the expression under consideration.

acceptable quality level– In **quality control,** the **proportion** of nondefective items in a lot that is considered to be at an acceptable quality level by the consumer. See also *acceptance sampling.*

acceptance error– Same as *type I error.*

acceptance number– In **acceptance sampling,** the number of defective items such that the decision to accept or reject the lot depends on this number.

acceptance region– Same as *region of acceptance.*

acceptance–rejection algorithm– The name of an **algorithm** commonly employed for generating **random numbers** from a **probability distribution.**

acceptance sampling– A type of **sampling** used in **quality control** where a **sample** is taken from a batch of items and the decision to accept or reject the batch is based on the **proportion** of defective items in the sample. See also *acceptance number.*

accrual rate– The rate at which eligible patients are enrolled in a **clinical trial.** It is measured as the number of persons per unit of time.

accuracy– A term used to denote the tendency of an observed **score** to cluster around the true value being measured. The **reliability** of a measuring method depends among other things on its accuracy. In **statistical estimation,** it refers to the **deviation** of an **estimate** from the true **parameter** value. The term is not synonymous to **precision,** though sometimes they are used interchangeably. In general, the term is used for the quality of a **measurement** that is both correct and precise.

acquiescence bias– A term used in **public opinion surveys** to designate a type of **bias** caused by the tendency of certain respondents to give affirmative responses (yes, true, certainly, etc.) to a question.

action branches– In a **decision tree** diagram, branches emanating from an **action point** are called action branches. They represent the possible actions available to the decision maker.

action lines– See *control charts.*

action point– In a **decision tree** diagram, a point of choice represented by a square. This is the point at which the decision maker is in control. It is also called decision fork, decision node, and decision point.

actions– In **decision theory,** the mutually exclusive choices of decision alternatives available to a decision maker.

active controlled trial– A **clinical trial** in which **experimental treatment** is compared with some other active drug rather than an inert substance or **placebo.**

active treatment– Same as *experimental treatment.*

actuarial analysis– See *life table analysis.*

actuarial statistics– The statistical methods and techniques used in the calculation of **risks,** liabilities, insurance premium rates, policy dividends, and many other situations that arise in the insurance business. In addition to **mortality** and **morbidity** data, actuarial methods make use of **statistics** relating to the rates of return on investments and to the rates of expense involved in implementing life, health insurance, or pension programs. In many business applications, actuarial methods are employed to determine the annual retirement of plants and equipment and to provide an **estimate** of the average life facilities on the basis of detailed company records of each unit of plant and equipment.

actuary– A person, often an official of an insurance company, who is trained in the applications of mathematical and statistical procedures in the scientific study of insurance risks and premiums. In Europe, the term is sometimes used to refer to a clerk, especially one employed by a large corporation

acute angle– An angle whose magnitude is less than $90°$.

adaptive sampling– **Sampling designs** in which the procedure for selecting units in the **sample** depends on the values of certain **variables** of interest observed during the **survey.** For example, in a survey designed to estimate the **population** of certain rare species, neighboring sites may be added to **sampling units** whenever the species is encountered in the survey.

addition of matrices– The **matrix** obtained by adding two or more matrices of the same dimension. Given two matrices $\mathbf{A} = (a_{ij})$, $\mathbf{B} = (b_{ij})$, let $\mathbf{C} = (c_{ij})$ be the matrix obtained by adding the matrices $\mathbf{A}$ and $\mathbf{B}$, then $c_{ij} = a_{ij} + b_{ij}$, for all i and j.

addition rule for probability– A **probability law** used to calculate the **probability** for the occurrence of a **union of two** or more **events.** For any two arbitrary events A and B, it is expressed as $P(A \cup B) = P(A) + P(B) - P(A \cap B)$. For two **mutually exclusive events,** when $P(A \cap B) = 0$, it reduces to $P(A \cup B) = P(A) + P(B)$. The rule can be generalized for more than two events.

additive effect– A term used to represent the condition when the **effect** of administering two **treatments** together is the sum of their separate effects. See also *additive model.*

additive model– A **mathematical** or **statistical model** in which the **explanatory variables** have an **additive effect** on the **response measure** of interest. For example, if a **treatment** A has an effect α on some response measure and another treatment B has an effect β on the same measure, then an additive model for A and B has a combined effect of $\alpha + \beta$.

An additive model excludes the possibility of any **interaction** between the two treatments. See also *multiplicative model.*

additive time-series model– A **classical time-series model** that represents the actual value (Y) of a **time series** as the sum of its components comprising **trend** (T), **cycle** (C), **seasonality** (S), and **irregular variation** (I); i.e., $Y = T + C + S + I$. See also *mixed time-series model, multiplicative time-series model.*

additivity– The term used to indicate the property of an **additive model.**

adherence– Same as *compliance.*

adjoint of a matrix– Given a **matrix** A, the matrix obtained by transposing A to obtain A' and then replacing each element a_{ij} by its cofactor A_{ij}. It is written as adj A. The adjoint of a matrix is useful in the evaluation of the **inverse of a matrix.** See also *cofactor of a matrix, transpose of a matrix.*

adjusted death rates– **Death rates** that provide an overview of the general well-being of a community or population when various demographic factors such as age, sex, and education are held constant.

adjusted means– Same as *adjusted treatment means.*

adjusted rate– A **rate** adjusted so that it is independent of the distribution of a possible **confounding variable.** In comparative studies, it refers to rate computed after taking into account a **confounding factor,** which may possibly explain the event. For example, when computing **death rates** in two populations, it may be necessary to take into account any age differences between the two populations so that age-adjusted rates are independent of the age distribution in the population to which they apply. There are a number of methods such as **stratification, standardization,** and **multiple regression** that are used to obtain adjusted rates.

adjusted sample coefficient of multiple determination– A measure, denoted by $\bar{R}^2$ or R^2_{adj}, that is the value of R^2 adjusted for the number of **independent variables** (**degrees of freedom**). It provides an **unbiased estimator** of the corresponding **population coefficient of determination.** See also *coefficient of multiple determination, sample coefficient of multiple determination.*

adjusted treatment means– A term used for **estimates** of the **treatment means** after adjusting them to the **mean** level of any **covariate**(s) that may act as **confounder**(s). Adjusted means are frequently used in **experimental design** when an increase in **precision** is desired and a concomitant **observation** is used (rather than **blocking**). The overall objective is to adjust the **average** response so that it reflects the true **effect** of the **treatment.**

adjusting for baseline– In a **longitudinal study,** the term is used to denote the process of adjusting for the **effects** of **baseline characteristics** on the **response measure** of interest.

adjustment– The process of accounting for the **effects** of **prognostic factors** or **baseline characteristics** when estimating differences attributable to **treatments** or other prognostic factors. Two primary tools for adjustment are **multiple regression** and **stratified analysis.**

age distribution– A **frequency distribution** based on **measurements** of the chronological age of the **population** under study and grouped according to **class intervals** selected to best describe the age profile of the population.

age-specific death rate– The **death rate** in a specified period of time for a given age or age group. See also *cause-specific death rate, standardized death rate.*

age-specific fertility rate– Number of live births per woman in a specified period of time for a given age or age group. See also *fertility rate.*

age-specific incidence rate– The **incidence rate** calculated for a given age or age group.

age-specific mortality rate– Same as *age-specific death rate.*

age-specific rate– The **rate** or **frequency** of occurrence of an event in a given age group.

aggregate index number– An **index number** obtained by calculating the sum of the figures applicable to each period of time under consideration, assigning index number 100 to the period chosen as the base, and determining for each of the other periods a figure that bears the same relation to 100 that the sum of the figures for that period bears to the sum of the **base period.**

aggregative model– A **statistical model** involving **variables** whose individual **observations** represent aggregates.

aleatory variable– Same as *random variable.*

algebra of events– The algebra of events defines rules for some basic operations on **events,** similar to the algebraic operations on real numbers. Some basic operations on events are the so-called union, intersection, and complementation.

algorithm– A set of well-defined rules or a formula that, when applied step by step, permits the solution of any mathematical or computational problem in a finite number of steps, for example, calculation of the roots of an equation through an **iterative procedure** or computing a rate of return on an investment.

alias– In **experimental design, a treatment effect** that is confounded with another **effect.** The term is especially associated with **fractional factorial designs,** in the analysis of which **estimates** of certain **contrasts** have **sums of squares** and **distributions** that reflect the existence of any one, or some, or a number of different effects. See also *confounding.*

alignment chart– Same as *nomogram.*

allocation of a sample– In **stratified random sampling,** the assignment of parts of a **sample** to different **strata** of subpopulations. See also *optimum allocation, proportional allocation.*

allometry– A field of study dealing with the quantitative relationship between size and shape of an organism. An important problem in allometry is concerned with whether one group of individuals or species represents an allometric extension of another.

all subsets regression– A type of **regression analysis** in which **models** with all possible subsets of **predictors** are fitted and the "best" one, selected by comparing the values of some appropriate criterion such as R^2 or **Mallow's** C_p **statistic.**

alpha (α)– Same as *significance level.*

alpha (α) error– Same as *type 1 error.*

alpha (α) level– Same as *alpha (α).*

alphanumeric– The term is generally used in reference to a computer statement pertaining to a character set that includes alphabetic letters, digits, and special characters such as asterisk (*), dollar sign ($), etc.

alpha (α) risk– Same as *alpha (α).*

alpha (α) value– The level of alpha (α) selected by the researcher in a **test of hypothesis.**

alternating logistic regression– A form of **logistic regression** used in the analysis of **longitudinal data** involving a **binary response** variable.

alternative hypothesis– In **hypothesis testing,** the proposition about an unknown **parameter**(s) that the researcher proposes to establish. It is also called the research hypothesis. It always states that the **population parameters**(s) have value(s) different from that specified by the **null hypothesis.** Thus, it is a complement of the null hypothesis to be concluded if the null hypothesis is rejected. In general, it is any admissible hypothesis, alternative to the null hypothesis, that is tentatively assumed to be false. It is usually denoted by H_A or H_I.

amplitude– In **time-series analysis,** the value of the series at its peak or trough measured from some **mean** value or **trend** line.

analysis of covariance– A statistical procedure for comparing the **means** of a quantitative **response variable** while taking into account the **measurements** made on one or more other quantitative **independent variables** that may act as **cofounders.** It is a special type of **analysis of variance** (or **regression**) used to control for the linear effect of a possible **confounding variate.** The confounding variate is often referred to as a **covariate.** The procedure consists of the combined application of the analysis of variance and **linear regression** techniques by using **dummy variables** to represent the groups being compared. In performing analysis of covariance, it is assumed that the covariates are unaffected by **treatments** and are linearly related to the response variable. If this assumption holds, the use of covariates decreases the **error mean square** and thus increases the **power** of the F **test** in testing treatment differences. The use of analysis of covariance allows the researcher to remove the effect of covariates as the source of possible explanations of **variation** in the **dependent variable.** Nowadays the term is used to describe almost any analysis seeking to assess the relationship between a response variable and a set of **explanatory variables.**

analysis of dispersion– A term sometimes used as a synonym for the **multivariate analysis of variance.**

analysis of regression– Same as *regression analysis.*

analysis of repeated measure– Same as *repeated measures analysis.*

analysis of residuals– In an **analysis of variance** or **regression,** an analysis of the differences between the observed and the expected values, known as **residuals,** in order to evaluate the validity of the **assumptions** of the **model.**

analysis of variance– Analysis of variance is a statistical procedure devised by Sir Ronald A. Fisher to analyze the results of complex **experiments** involving several **factors.** It involves a method of comparing any number of **group means** simultaneously, for determining whether or not the **means** of several **populations** are equal, by the use of one or more F **tests.** The F **statistics** are based on **sums of squares** obtained by partitioning the **total sum of squares,** calculated as the sum of squares of **deviations** of response **measurements**

about their mean, into parts on the basis of particular factors. It is an extension of the **two-sample *t* test** for comparing the means of a **quantitative variable** between two or more than two groups. The results of an analysis of variance procedure can be obtained rather conveniently by **regression** methods, by using a **dummy** or **indicator variable** to represent the groups. Like the *t* **test,** analysis of variance is based on a **model** that requires certain **assumptions** for its validity. Three main assumptions of analysis of variance are that: (1) each **treatment group** is selected randomly, with each **observation** independent of all other observations, and the treatment groups independent of each other; (2) the **samples** emanate from populations in which the observations are normally distributed; and (3) the treatment group **variances** all are assumed to be equal to a common variance σ^2. See also *analysis of variance table, multiway analysis of variance, one-way analysis of variance, three-way analysis of variance, two-way analysis of variance.*

analysis of variance *F* test– Same as *F test for analysis of variance.*

analysis of variance table– In an **analysis of variance,** a table used to summarize the results of analysis of variance calculations. It contains columns showing the sources of variation, the **degrees of freedom,** the **sums of squares,** the **mean squares,** and the values of *F* **statistics.**

analytical statistics– Same as *inferential statistics.*

ANCOVA– Acronym for *analysis of covariance.*

Anderson–Darling test– A **test procedure** for testing the **hypothesis** that a given **sample** of **observations** comes from some specified theoretical population. In particular, it is useful for testing the **normality** of a **data set.** It is based on a modified version of the **Cramér–von Mises statistic.** It is an omnibus test in the sense that it is sensitive to all types of deviations from **normality.** In addition, it is somewhat more sensitive to deviations in the tails of the **distribution,** which is frequently the way **nonnormality** makes itself known. The test is competitive with the better known **Shapiro–Wilk *W* test.** Although other tests are sometimes more powerful, they are often more difficult to calculate. The combination of ease of computation and good **power** makes it an attractive procedure for a **goodness-of-fit test.** See also *Cramér–von Mises test, D'Agostino test, Michael's test, Shapiro–Francia test.*

Andrews' plot– These are **graphical representations** of **multivariate data** in which all dimensions of the **data** are displayed. Each **data point** is depicted as a line or function running across the detecting groups of similar **observations** and assessing **outliers** in multivariate data. Statistical properties of the plots enable the **tests of significance** to be made directly from the plot. See also *Chernoff's faces.*

angular transformation– Same as *arc-sine transformation.*

annual rate– A quantity determined to reflect relative annual change for demographic or economic **data.**

annual rate of population increase (growth)– Relative change in a population size per year.

ANOVA– Acronym for *analysis of variance.*

ANOVA *F* test– Same as *F test for analysis of variance.*

Ansari–Bradley test– A **nonparametric procedure** for testing the equality of **variances** of two **populations** having the common **median.** It is assumed that the two populations being compared are of identical **shape** and differing at most in their **scale parameters.** See also *Barton–David test, Conover test, F test for two population variances, Klotz test, Mood test, Rosenbaum test, Siegel–Tukey test.*

antagonistic effect– See *interaction.*

antimode– A term sometimes used to denote the opposite of a **mode** in the sense that it corresponds to a (local) minimum **frequency.**

AOQ– Acronym for *average outgoing quality.*

a posteriori comparison– Same as *post-hoc comparison.*

a posteriori distribution– Same as *posterior distribution.*

a posteriori probabilities– Same as *posterior probabilities.*

apparent limits– The lower and upper limits actually shown for the **class intervals** of a **frequency distribution.**

applied economics– The application of principles and methods of **economics** to the solution of economic problems of a country or region.

approximate test– Often, it is not possible to obtain a test with a **level of significance** exactly equal to α, and then the test is referred to as an approximate test. See also *conservative test, exact test, liberal test.*

approximation– A mathematical result that is not exact but is sufficiently close to the exact value and can be recommended for practical use in many scientific and research applications.

a priori comparison– Same as *planned comparison.*

a priori distribution– Same as *prior distribution.*

a priori probabilities– Same as *prior probabilities.*

arc–sine transformation– The **transformation** of the form $y = \sin^{-1}(x/n)$ designed to stabilize the **variance.** The arc–sine transformation is normally used on **data** in the form of **proportion** and produces values that satisfy the assumption of **homogeneity** required in the application of **analysis of variance** and **regression** techniques. It is also called angular transformation because arc–sine is angle. A modified form of the transformation given as arc–sin $\left(\sqrt{x + \frac{3}{8}} \Big/ \sqrt{n + \frac{3}{4}} \right)$ is somewhat more effective in equalizing variances. See also *logarithmic transformation, power transformation, reciprocal transformation, square-root transformation, square transformation.*

ARE– Acronym for *asymptotic relative efficiency.*

area sample– See *area sampling.*

area sampling– A type of **sampling design** employed when a complete **frame** of **reference population** is not available. The total area under the study is divided into a small number of subareas (e.g., counties, towns, blocks) that are sampled **at random** or by some restricted **random** device. Each of the chosen subareas is then enumerated and may constitute a frame for further **sampling** in the subarea. For example, suppose a **sample** of households within a state is desired, and there does not exist a comprehensive list from which such a sample might be selected. The state in such a case might be divided into a certain geographical units, say counties, and a certain number of counties selected for the sample. Each county included in the sample might then be divided into municipalities and a certain number of municipalities selected for the sample. Each municipality included in the sample might then be divided into blocks and a certain number of blocks selected for the sample. Finally, from each block included in the sample, a certain number of households might be identified and selected in the sample. Area sampling is usually less costly and less reliable than alternative procedures, such as **stratified** or **simple random sampling.** See also *cluster sampling, multistage sampling.*

area under the curve– In pharmacokinetic studies, the term is used to describe the estimated area under a time–concentration curve. It may indicate a predictor of biological or clinical effects such as efficacy or toxicity.

ARIMA– Acronym for *autoregressive integrated moving average.*

arithmetic chart– Same as *arithmetic paper.*

arithmetic mean– Same as *mean.*

arithmetic paper– A graph paper having uniform subdivisions for both *x* and *y* **axes.**

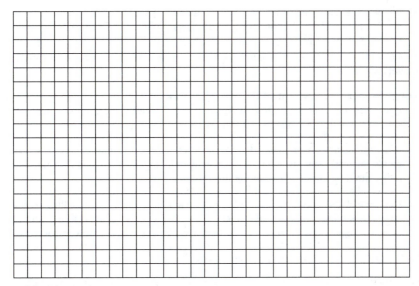

Arithmetic paper

arithmetic probability paper– A graph paper that has uniform subdivisions for the *x* **axis** but the *y* **axis** is ruled in such a way that a plot of the cumulative **normal distribution** appears as a straight line.

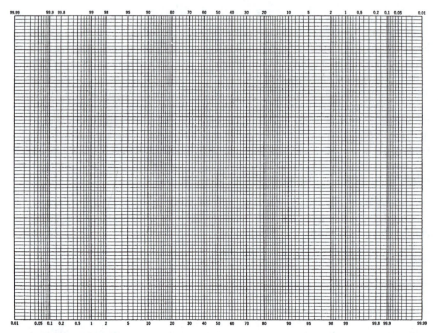

Arithmetic probability paper

arithmetic progression or series– A series of numbers is said to form an arithmetic progression when the difference between any two adjacent numbers is the same. For example, the series 3, 5, 7, 9, 11, 13, . . . is an arithmetic progression. Population sizes over a period of time are in arithmetic progression if the size of the population changes by a **constant** amount each year.

array– A simple arrangement of the individual **observations** or values of a **data set** arranged in order of magnitude, from the smallest to the largest value. For example, for the data set {2, 7, 5, 9, 3, 4, 6}, an ordered array is {2, 3, 4, 5, 6, 7, 9}.

artificial intelligence– A term coined to designate a scientific discipline concerned with investigating the intelligent behavior, i.e., reasoning, thinking, learning, and **decision making,** of machines by means of **computer simulation.**

ascertainment bias– A type of **bias** that arises from a relationship between the **exposure** to a certain **risk factor** and the **probability** of detecting an event of interest. It commonly occurs in many epidemiological studies, particularly in **retrospective case-control studies**.

ASN– Acronym for *average sample number.*

association– The term is more or less synonymous with **correlation**. It is more commonly used to describe the relationship between a pair of **nominal** or **qualitative variables**. See also *measures of association.*

association analysis– Same as *correlation analysis.*

assumptions– The term is most commonly used to refer to certain specific conditions that should be satisfied for the application of certain statistical procedures in order to produce valid statistical results. For example, the usual assumptions for the application of an **analysis of variance** procedure are **normality** of distribution, **homogeneity of variance,** and **independence** of **observations.**

asymmetrical distribution– A **frequency (probability) distribution** that is not symmetrical. A **univariate distribution** is said to be asymmetrical if a vertical centerline divides it into two parts, which are different in **shape** and area. Some examples of an asymmetrical distribution are **exponential distribution** and **lognormal distribution.** Compare *symmetrical distribution.* See also *skewed distribution.*

asymmetrical population– A **population** that is not symmetrical.

asymmetric measure of association– A **measure of association** that is based on conceptual and computational distinctions between the **independent** and **dependent variables.** Compare *symmetric measure of association.* See also *Somer's D.*

asymmetry– The property of the **shape** of a **frequency distribution** that exhibits **skewness.** Compare *symmetry.*

asymptotic– Said of a line on a graph that continually approaches but never reaches the *x* **axis.** For example, the tails of a **normal curve** are asymptotic to the *x* axis. Moreover, lines or curves may be asymptotes to things other than just the *x* axis. In general, any line such that, for any given curve, the shortest distance from a point on the curve to the line approaches zero as the point moves to infinity from the origin. The term is also commonly used as a prefix to denote a large **sample** or a limiting property (as $n \rightarrow \infty$) in expressions such as **asymptotic test** and **asymptotic variance.**

asymptotically efficient estimator– An **estimator** of a **parameter** with a **variance** achieving the **Cramér–Rao lower bound** as the **sample size** approaches infinity.

asymptotically unbiased estimator– An **estimator** of a **parameter** that is biased but tends to become unbiased as the **sample size** increases and becomes infinitely large. For example, the usual **sample variance** (with divisor n) is a **biased estimator** of the **population variance** σ^2, but is asymptotically unbiased.

asymptotic distribution– The limiting form of the **probability distribution** of a **random variable** as the **sample size** approaches infinity.

asymptotic efficiency– The **efficiency** of an **estimator** in the limit as the **sample size** approaches infinity.

asymptotic method– Same as *large sample method.*

asymptotic normality– The exact **distribution** of a **statistic** is usually complicated and difficult to work with. The distribution is said to possess asymptotic normality if its limiting form approaches a **normal distribution.** The **central limit theorem** can often be used to approximate the distribution of a statistic by a normal distribution.

asymptotic relative efficiency– The **relative efficiency** of two **estimators** of a **parameter** as the **sample size** approaches infinity. The term is also used as an asymptotic measure of relative test·efficiency as the sample size (n) increases against alternatives that approach the **null hypothesis** as n increases.

asymptotic technique– See *large sample method.*

asymptotic test– See *large sample method.*

asymptotic variance– The **variance** of a **statistic** as the **sample size** becomes infinitely large.

at random– In a **random** fashion.

attenuation– A term applied to denote the **correlation** between two **variables,** when both variables are subject to **measurement error,** to indicate that the value of the correlation between the true values is likely to be underestimated if both variables were measured with perfect **reliability.**

attributable fraction– See *attributable risk.*

attributable risk– The term is often used as a synonym to **absolute risk difference.** The attributable risk is often expressed as the fraction or **proportion** of the **risk** in the **intervention** or **exposed group,** and then it is known as proportional attributable risk (PAR) or attributable fraction. The PAR is defined as PAR $= (R_i - R_c)/R_i$, where R_i and R_c denote the risks in the **intervention** and **control group,** respectively.

attribute– The qualitatively distinct characteristics such as healthy or diseased, positive or negative. The term is often applied to designate characteristics that are not easily expressed in numerical terms.

attribute sampling– A **sampling procedure** in which the characteristic being measured is simply a quality or **attribute** of the items or individuals included in the **sample.** For example, an item may be classified as defective or nondefective. Compare *variable sampling.*

attrition– A term used to describe the loss of **study subjects** that may occur in a **clinical trial** or any **longitudinal study.**

autocorrelation– In a **time-series analysis,** it is the internal **correlation** between **observations** often expressed as a function of the lag time between them. For example, given the observed values $x_1, x_2, \ldots, x_n$ of a series, the sample autocorrelation of lag ℓ is defined as

$$\frac{\sum_{i=1}^{n-\ell}(X_i - \overline{X})(X_{i+\ell} - \overline{X})}{\sum_{i=1}^{n}(X_i - \overline{X})^2}$$

More generally, autocorrelation can occur when **residual error terms** from observations of the same **variable** at different time intervals are correlated. In **regression analysis,** autocorrelations can be reduced by using generalized rather than **ordinary least squares.** When the **variance** term from the denominator is omitted it is called autocovariance.

autocovariance– See *autocorrelation.*

automation– A term often used to refer to the use of advanced machinery and other modern equipment, especially in combination with high-speed computers.

autoregression– A term used to indicate the possibility that the **error term** in a **regression model** may be correlated with one or more lagged **endogenous variables.**

autoregressive integrated moving average– Same as *Box–Jenkins method.*

average– A medial numerical figure describing the typical or characteristic value of a group of numbers. It is a general term used for all types of averages, variously described as **measures of location** or **measures of central tendency.** When used unqualified, the term can be taken to refer to the **arithmetic mean.** Otherwise, it is a figure describing any **statistical measure** of the center of a **data set,** including arithmetic mean, **median,** or **mode,** among others.

average absolute deviation– A measure of **variability** or **dispersion** obtained by averaging **the absolute values** of the **deviations** about the **mean, median,** or **mode** for a particular set of **data.** Average absolute deviation is called mean deviation from the mean, the median, or the mode, according to the point about which the deviations have been measured. It is also called mean deviation, mean variation, average error, average departure, average variation, mean absolute error, and sometimes mean error.

average departure– Same as *average absolute deviation.*

average deviation– Same as *average absolute deviation.*

average error– Same as *average absolute deviation.*

average outgoing quality (AOQ)– The expected quality of the outgoing product following the use of an **acceptance sampling** plan for a given value of incoming product quality. It is calculated as the ratio of defective items to total items, i.e., the total number of defectives in the lots accepted divided by the total number of items in these lots. The AOQ serves as an index of performance measure associated with an acceptance sampling when the sampling plan is used repeatedly.

average rank– Suppose that x is one of a set of n **observations** that has the same value as (is tied with) some of the other observations. The **average** rank of x, in the **ranking** of the n observations, is the **mean** of those **ranks** that would be assigned to x and the other observations having the same value as x, if these tied observations could be distinguished.

average run length– In **statistical process control,** the length of time the process, on the average, must run before a **control chart** is capable of detecting a shift in the process level. It is usually measured in terms of the number of consecutive points plotted on the control chart.

average sample number– In a **sequential sampling** procedure, the **average** or **expected value** of the **sample size** required to reach a decision to accept or reject the **null hypothesis** and thereby to terminate **sampling.**

average variation– Same as *average absolute deviation.*

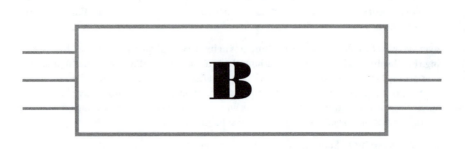

back-to-back stem-and-leaf plot– A method of constructing two sets of leaves, in the **stem-and-leaf plots** involving two sets of **data,** hanging on both sides of the same stem.

A back-to-back stem-and-leaf plot

First data set				Second data set		
		2	28	8		
	3	1	29	2	7	
	7	5	30	6	8	8
		4	31	2	8	
8	6	1	32	6	7	9 9
7	5	3	33	8		
	6	6	34	1		
		9	35			
		1	36	2		

backward elimination procedure– In **multiple regression analysis,** a method for select-ing the "best" possible set of **predictor (independent) variables** of the **criterion (depen-dent) variable.** The method begins by including all the **variables** in the **model equation** and then eliminating them one at a time according to a prechosen criterion of **statistical significance.** The variable with the smallest possible **correlation** is selected first and is eliminated if it meets the criterion. Next, the variables with the second lowest, third lowest, etc. **partial correlations** are examined if they meet the criterion. The process is continued until all the variables are examined and there are no more to be eliminated. Compare *for-ward selection procedure, stepwise regression.*

backward induction– A process by which a decision problem is solved by using a **deci-sion tree** diagram that involves the computation of expected **payoff** values at each fork of the tree. The expected payoff values are calculated with the help of ultimate payoff values and event branch **probability** values. The term is also used to refer to starting a problem with the answer and working back to the question.

backward-looking study– Same as *retrospective study.*

backward solution– Same as *backward elimination procedure.*

Bahadur efficiency– An **asymptotic technique** for assessing the optimality of a **test procedure.** It is basically a concept of theoretical nature and provides a useful optimality criterion for comparing tests in situations where optimal tests based on a finite **sample** may not exist.

balanced data– Same as *orthogonal data.*

balanced design– Same as *orthogonal design.*

balanced incomplete block design– A type of **incomplete block design** having the following properties: (1) each **block** contains the same number of **treatments,** (2) each treatment occurs the same number of times in all the blocks, and (3) each pair of treatments occurs together the same number of times in any block.

**A layout of a balanced
incomplete block design**

Block	Treatment		
1	T_4	T_5	T_1
2	T_4	T_2	T_5
3	T_2	T_4	T_1
4	T_5	T_3	T_1
5	T_3	T_4	T_5
6	T_2	T_3	T_1
7	T_3	T_1	T_4
8	T_3	T_5	T_2
9	T_2	T_3	T_4
10	T_5	T_1	T_2

balanced repeated replications– A procedure for estimating the **standard errors** of **sample estimates** derived for complex **survey designs** that make use of both clustering and **stratification.**

bar chart– A **graphical display** or portrayal, used with **frequency distribution** of **qualitative** or **nominal data,** in which the **frequency** associated with each category is represented by vertical bars proportional to the frequencies with spaces in between them. Each constituent of the bars has its own color or shading in order to facilitate visual comparison between them. The lengths of the bars and areas are pro rata to the absolute magnitudes of the **statistics** they represent. In contrast to **histograms,** bar charts are used for **categorical data** and it is a good practice to separate bars, one from the other, since the values on the **horizontal axis** merely represent labels and do not have any numerical meaning whatsoever. Bar charts are widely used as a method of **graphical representation** in newspapers, magazines, and general publications. See also *component bar chart.*

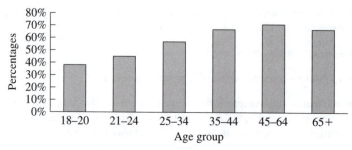

Bar chart showing the percentage of people from various age groups who reported voting in a U.S. presidential election in a hypothetical year

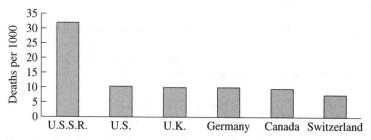

Bar chart for infant mortality rates in selected developed nations in 1980

bar diagram– Same as *bar chart.*

bar graph– Same as *bar chart.*

Bartlett's test– A **test procedure** for testing three or more **independent samples** for **homogeneity of variances** before using an **analysis of variance** procedure. The test may also be used to check the **homogeneity** of high-order **interactions** in **factorial experiments,** and to investigate fluctuations in smoothed periodograms in **time-series analysis.** Bartlett's **test statistic** is a slight modification of the **likelihood ratio statistic** first proposed by Neyman and Pearson. The test is of limited practical utility because of its extreme sensitivity to **nonnormality.** See also *Box's test, Cochran's test, Hartley's test.*

Barton–David Test– A **nonparametric method** for testing the equality of **scale parameters** of two continuous **populations** that have a common **median.** The test is linearly related to the **Ansari–Bradley test.** See also *Conover test, F test for two population variances, Klotz test, Mood's test, Rosenbaum test, Siegel–Tukey test.*

baseline characteristics– A term used to describe sociodemographic characteristics of the subject such as age, sex, race, or any other social and health characteristics likely to be correlated with the **response variable** of interest, taken at the time of entry into a study.

base period– The period from which the changes are measured in the construction of an **index number.** Two methods of selecting the base period are **fixed-base** and **chain-base index numbers.**

BASIC– A programming language widely used for writing programs for microcomputers. It is an acronym for Beginner's All-Purpose Symbolic Instruction Code.

basic outcome– Same as *outcome.*

Bayesian analysis– Same as *Bayesian inference.*

Bayesian inference– A form of **statistical inference** in which **parameters** are considered as **random variables** having a **prior distributions** reflecting the current state of knowledge. The **prior probabilities** are then revised into a set of **posterior probabilities,** by the application of **Bayes' theorem,** which are employed in making inference. Note that Bayesian inference differs from the classical form of **frequentist inference** in terms of its use of the prior distribution, which is characterized by the investigator's prior knowledge about the parameters before collecting the data. During recent decades Bayesian techniques have been greatly developed in the statistical literature, where highly complex models have received systematic and thorough treatment from the Bayesian viewpoint. See also *classical statistical inference, posterior distribution.*

Bayesian interval estimation– A method in which **interval estimates** of a **population parameter** are derived from the **posterior probability distribution** of that parameter.

Bayesian point estimation– A method of **estimation** in which the **estimator** with the minimum expected risk is selected.

Bayesian statistics– The term is used to designate statistical methods and techniques based on the concept of **Bayesian inference.**

Bayes' postulate– Same as *equal-likelihood criterion.*

Bayes' rule– Same as *Bayes' theorem.*

Bayes' strategy– The **optimal strategy** selected in a **decision-making** problem solved by optimizing the **expected value** of the **payoff.**

Bayes' theorem– A **probability** formula for modifying initial **prior probabilities** concerning occurrence of **mutually exclusive events** that include all possible **outcomes** by use of **conditional probability.** The modified probabilities are called **posterior probabilities.** The theorem plays an important role in an approach to **statistical inference** called **Bayesian inference.** In clinical diagnosis, Bayes' theorem forms the basis for the calculation of probability of a disease given the results of a relevant **diagnostic test.** The theorem was developed by Thomas Bayes (1702–1761), an eighteenth century English cleric, and was posthumously published in the form of an essay in 1763.

Behrens–Fisher problem– A **statistical test** for testing the equality of **means** of two **normal populations** with unequal **variances.** It is also referred to as the two-means problem or as the Behrens problem. An essentially equivalent problem is that of finding an **interval estimate** for the difference between two **population means.** The procedure is based on the concept of **fiducial probabilities.** It was first proposed by Behrens and later studied by Fisher. Since then a number of **test procedures** have been proposed, although none are completely satisfactory.

Behrens–Fisher test– See *Behrens–Fisher problem.*

Behrens problem– Same as *Behrens–Fisher problem.*

Bell–Doksum test– A variant of the **Kruskal–Wallis test** obtained by replacing **ranks** by values of ordered **unit normal (random) variables.** It has comparable performance and may even have slightly higher **power** than the Kruskal–Wallis test. It also competes favorably with other **test procedures** for this problem.

bell-shaped curve– Same as *normal curve.*

bell-shaped distribution– A term used to characterize the **shape** of the **normal (Gaussian) distribution.** A bell-shaped distribution is a symmetrical **frequency curve** resembling a vertical cross section of a bell.

benchmarking– A **statistical procedure** for adjusting a **data set** prone to **measurement errors** in order to bring it into conformity with more reliable **measurements** known as benchmarks.

benchmarks– See *benchmarking.*

Berkson's fallacy– In an epidemiological study, a **measure of risk** provides a valid **estimate** of the strength of an **association** only if the **sample observations** from which it is estimated are **random.** In many studies, **samples** of patients are often selected from a particular clinic or hospital out of convenience. Since subjects with severe disease are more likely to be hospitalized than those with moderate illness, our conclusions based on patients who are hospitalized are likely to be biased. As a result, we may observe an association that does not actually exit. **Cases** (with history of a disease and **exposure condition**) more likely to be admitted than **controls** may lead to positive **spurious correlation** between the disease and the **risk factor** while cases that are less likely to be admitted than controls may lead to a negative spurious correlation. This kind of spurious relationship is often known as Berkson's fallacy.

Bernoulli distribution– The **probability distribution** of a **binary (random) variable** X, where $P(X = 1) = p$ and $P(X = 0) = q$ with $p + q = 1$.

Bernoulli process– A sequence of n identical **trials** of a **random experiment** such that each trial (1) results in one of two possible complementary **outcomes** that are conventionally called success and failure and (2) each trial is independent so that the **probability** of success or failure is **constant** from trial to trial. The Bernoulli process is named after the Swiss mathematician James Bernoulli.

Bernoulli trials– Same as *Bernoulli process.*

Bernstein's inequality– A refinement of **Chebyshev's inequality** first stated by S. Bernstein in 1926.

Bessel's correction– A term used to denote a factor by which the **variance** of a small **sample** is multiplied in order to provide an **unbiased estimate** of the **variance of the population.** The factor is equivalent to $n/(n - 1)$, where n is number of **data points** in the sample. The greater the value of n, the closer the correction approaches to unity, so that for very large samples, the correction becomes rather unnecessary.

best linear unbiased estimator– An **unbiased estimator** that is a **linear function** of **observations** and has smaller **variance** than any other **estimator** in this class.

beta (β)– In **hypothesis testing**, the **probability** of accepting the **null hypothesis** when it is false.

beta coefficient– Same as *standardized regression coefficient.*

beta distribution– A **random variable** is said to have beta distribution if its **probability density function** is given by

$$f(x) = \frac{\Gamma(\alpha + \beta)}{\Gamma(\alpha)\Gamma(\beta)} x^{\alpha-1}(1-x)^{\beta-1} \qquad 0 < x < 1, \ \alpha > 0, \ \beta > 0$$

where $\Gamma(x)$ represents the **gamma function.** A beta distribution assumes a **U-shaped distribution** if $\alpha < 1$, $\beta < 1$, and a **J-shaped distribution** if $(\alpha - 1)(\beta - 1) < 0$.

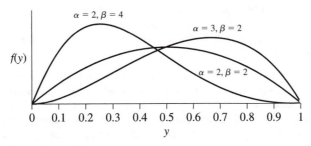

Probability density curves for beta distribution for various values of α and β

beta (β) error– Same as *type II error.*

beta function– The beta function denoted by $B(\ell, m)$ is defined as

$$B(\ell, m) = \int_0^1 x^{\ell-1}(1-x)^{m-1} \, dx, \qquad \ell > 0, \ m > 0$$

A beta function satisfies the relationship

$$B(\ell, m) = \frac{\Gamma(\ell)\Gamma(m)}{\Gamma(\ell + m)}$$

beta (β) risk– Same as *beta (β).*

beta (β) value– The value of beta (β) selected by the researcher in a **test of hypothesis.**

beta weight– Same as *standardized regression coefficient.*

between group mean square– Same as *mean square between groups.*

between group sum of squares– Same as *sum of squares between groups.*

between group variation– The amount of **variation** among **means** in a study with two or more groups.

between mean square– Same as *mean square between groups.*

between patients trial– Same as *clinical trial.*

between subjects design– Same as *independent samples design.*

between sum of squares– Same as *sum of square between groups.*

Bhattacharya's bounds– A set of lower bounds for the **variance** of an **unbiased estimator** of a **parameter** based on a **random sample** of size n. The **Cramér–Rao lower bound** is a special case of these bounds.

bias– The **error** that may distort a statistical result in one direction. Bias is caused by **systematic errors,** which are consistently wrong in one or another direction, as opposed to **random errors,** which tend to balance out the result on the **average.** In general, bias is anything that causes systematic error in a research finding that results in deviation of results or inferences from the truth. In a research study, a bias can occur in the form **of selection bias, information bias,** and **confounding. In statistical estimation,** it is the difference between the **expected value** of a **biased estimator** and the true value of the **parameter** being estimated. In **hypothesis testing** it results in a procedure that does not test the **hypothesis** to be tested.

biased estimator– An **estimator** whose **expected value** does not equal the true value of the parameter being estimated. In other words, the **probability distribution** of a biased estimator has a **mean** value that is different from the value of the parameter being estimated. The motivation for using a biased estimator over an **unbiased estimator** comes from the fact that it is possible for the **variance** of such an estimator to be much smaller than the variance of an unbiased estimator to more than compensate for the **bias** incurred.

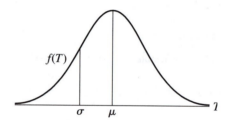

Sampling distribution of a biased estimator

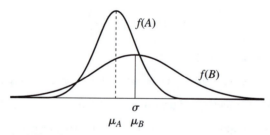

Sampling distribution of a biased estimator A and
an unbiased estimator B of σ

biasedness– A term used to describe the property of a **biased estimator.** Compare *unbiasedness.* See also *bias, unbiased estimator.*

biased sample– A **sample** selected in such a manner that certain units of a **sampled population** are more likely to be included in the sample than others. Thus, the sample is not a representative one of the **population** as a whole. **Nonrandom sampling,** especially **convenience** or **judgment sampling,** often produces a biased sample. For example, suppose a social scientist wishes to survey the opinions of the residents of a city concerning a new ordinance to be passed by the city hall. If she stood on a busy corner of the city at 10:00 a.m. on a given day and interviewed the first 200 people who happened to walk by, her sample would almost surely be biased. The reason being that this type of **sampling** excludes a large part of the city residents who for a number of reasons never visit that corner of the city, especially at 10 o'clock in the morning.

bifactor solution– A method of **factor rotation** in **factor analysis** developed by K. J. Holzinger. Essentially, the method consists of deriving group factors that do not overlap.

bimodal distribution– When a **frequency** or **probability distribution** has two distinct **modes** or peak **frequencies** separated by a definite trough, it is said to have a bimodal distribution. Such a **distribution** probably indicates that **data** come from two different **populations** or sources. It is used in contradistinction to a **unimodal distribution.** See also *multimodal distribution, trimodal distribution.*

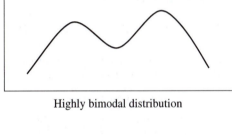

Highly bimodal distribution

Slightly bimodal distribution

Some examples of bimodal distributions

bimodal frequency distribution– See *bimodal distribution.*

binary assay– Same as *quantal assay.*

binary data– Same as *dichotomous data.*

binary measure– Same as *dichotomous measure.*

binary notation– See *binary number.*

binary number– A number that consists of just two numbers, 0 and 1, in contrast to a decimal number that consists of 10 numbers, 0 to 9. In binary, 10 equals 2 of the decimal notation and is described in terms of the decimal system as having a base of 10. For technical reasons, computers employ the binary system internally; however, printouts are invariably produced in decimal notations.

binary response– Same as *dichotomous variable.*

binary response variable– Same as *dichotomous variable.*

binary system– See *binary number.*

binary variable– Same as *dichotomous variable.*

binomial coefficient– The binomial coefficient

$$\binom{n}{x}$$

denotes the number of arrangements or patterns with x successes and $n - x$ failures that can result in n **trials** that satisfy the condition of a **Bernoulli process.** For example, with $n = 5$ and $x = 2$,

$$\binom{5}{2} = 10$$

The patterns (letting S denote success and F failure) are

SSFFF SFSFF SFFSF SFFFS FSSFF FSFSF FSFFS FFSSF FFSFS FFFSS.

Binomial coefficients are referred to as such because of the way they appear in the binomial expansion. See also *multinomial coefficient, Pascal's triangle.*

Binomial coefficients

n	$\binom{n}{0}$	$\binom{n}{1}$	$\binom{n}{2}$	$\binom{n}{3}$	$\binom{n}{4}$	$\binom{n}{5}$	$\binom{n}{6}$	$\binom{n}{7}$	$\binom{n}{8}$	$\binom{n}{9}$	$\binom{n}{10}$
0	1										
1	1	1									
2	1	2	1								
3	1	3	3	1							
4	1	4	6	4	1						
5	1	5	10	10	5	1					
6	1	6	15	20	15	6	1				
7	1	7	21	35	35	21	7	1			
8	1	8	28	56	70	56	28	8	1		
9	1	9	36	84	126	126	84	36	9	1	
10	1	10	45	120	210	252	210	120	45	10	1
11	1	11	55	165	330	462	462	330	165	55	11
12	1	12	66	220	495	792	924	792	495	220	66
13	1	13	78	286	715	1287	1716	1716	1287	715	286
14	1	14	91	364	1001	2002	3003	3432	3003	2002	1001
15	1	15	105	455	1365	3003	5005	6435	6435	5005	3003
16	1	16	120	560	1820	4368	8008	11440	12870	11440	8008
17	1	17	136	680	2380	6188	12376	19448	24310	24310	19448
18	1	18	153	816	3060	8568	18564	31824	43758	48620	43758
19	1	19	171	969	3876	11628	27132	50388	75582	92378	92378
20	1	20	190	1140	4845	15504	38760	77520	125970	167960	184756

binomial distribution– The **probability distribution** of the number of successes in n independent **Bernoulli trials,** where each **trial** has two outcomes (conveniently labeled success and failure), and the **probability** of success p is the same for each trial. If the number of trials refers to the number of items selected **at random** from a batch of articles, where success and failure represent acceptance and rejection, the same kind of reasoning applies. See also *binomial formula.*

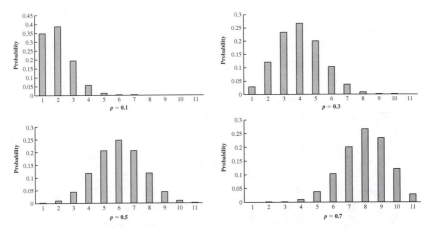

Bar diagrams for binomial distribution for $p = 0.1, 0.3, 0.5,$ and 0.7

binomial experiment– A **probability experiment** involving independent **Bernoulli trials.**

binomial formula– A formula for calculating the **probability** of x successes in n independent **Bernoulli trials.** The probability of x successes in n independent trials is calculated by the formula

$$\binom{n}{x} p^x q^{n-x}$$

See also *binomial distribution.*

binomial function– Same as *binomial formula.*

binomial index of dispersion– An index or **statistic** used to test the **hypothesis** of equality of several **binomial proportions.** Given k **sample proportions** $\bar{p}_1, \bar{p}_2, \ldots, \bar{p}_k$ based on **samples** of sizes $n_1, n_2, \ldots, n_k$, it is calculated by the formula

$$\sum_{i=1}^{k} n_i (\bar{p}_i - \bar{p})^2 / \{\bar{p}(1 - \bar{p})\} \qquad \text{where } \bar{p} = \sum_{i=1}^{k} n_i \bar{p}_i \Big/ \sum_{i=1}^{k} n_i$$

The significance of the index is tested by the fact that under the **null hypothesis** of the **homogeneity** of all **proportions,** the index has approximately a **chi-square distribution** with $k - 1$ **degrees of freedom.** See also *Poisson index of dispersion.*

binomial paper– Same as *binomial probability paper.*

binomial probability– The **probability** that a **binomial random variable** assumes a given value calculated using the **binomial formula.**

binomial probability distribution– Same as *binomial distribution.*

binomial probability function– Same as *binomial function.*

binomial probability paper– A graph paper where both x and y **axes** are ruled in such a manner that the distances from the origin are proportional to the square roots of the coordinates. It is designed to facilitate the analysis of **count data** in the form of **proportions** or percentages. An example of binomial probability paper is given below.

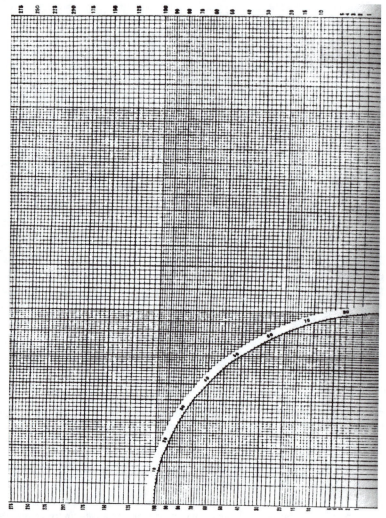

Binomial probability paper

binomial probability tables– Tables that give **binomial probabilities (probabilities** of x successes in n **Bernoulli trials**) for various possible combinations of values of n (number of trials) and p (probability of success) in any one trial. A portion of binomial probability tables is given in the table below.

binomial proportion– The **parameter** in a **binomial distribution** representing the **probability** of success for each **trial**.

binomial random variable– A **discrete random variable** that represents the number of successes realized in a **binomial experiment.**

binomial test– A statistical procedure to test the **hypothesis** that a **sample** with two possible **outcomes** has been drawn from a **population** with a specified **proportion** of each of the outcome. The **test statistic** is based on the **binomial distribution,** but for a large sample can be approximated by a **normal distribution** with **mean** np and **variance** $np(1 - p)$, where n is the **sample size** and p is the specified proportion of the outcome.

Binomial probability table

n	x	.01	.05	.10	.20	.30	.40	.50	.60	.70	.80	.90	.95	.99	x
1	0	.9900	.9500	.9000	.8000	.7000	.6000	.5000	.4000	.3000	.2000	.1000	.0500	.0100	0
	1	.0100	.0500	.1000	.2000	.3000	.4000	.5000	.6000	.7000	.8000	.9000	.9500	.9900	1
2	0	.9801	.9025	.8100	.6400	.4900	.3600	.2500	.1600	.0900	.0400	.0100	.0025	.0001	0
	1	.0198	.0950	.1800	.3200	.4200	.4800	.5000	.4800	.4200	.3200	.1800	.0950	.0198	1
	2	.0001	.0025	.0100	.0400	.0900	.1600	.2500	.3600	.4900	.6400	.8100	.9025	.9801	2
3	0	.9703	.8574	.7290	.5120	.3430	.2160	.1250	.0640	.0270	.0080	.0010	.0001	.0000	0
	1	.0294	.1354	.2430	.3840	.4410	.4320	.3750	.2880	.1890	.0960	.0270	.0071	.0003	1
	2	.0003	.0071	.0270	.0960	.1890	.2880	.3750	.4320	.4410	.3840	.2430	.1354	.0294	2
	3	.0000	.0001	.0010	.0080	.0270	.0640	.1250	.2160	.3430	.5120	.7290	.8574	.9703	3
4	0	.9606	.8145	.6561	.4096	.2401	.1296	.0625	.0256	.0081	.0016	.0001	.0000	.0000	0
	1	.0388	.1715	.2916	.4096	.4116	.3456	.2500	.1536	.0756	.0256	.0036	.0005	.0000	1
	2	.0006	.0135	.0486	.1536	.2646	.3456	.3750	.3456	.2646	.1536	.0486	.0135	.0006	2
	3	.0000	.0005	.0036	.0256	.0756	.1536	.2500	.3456	.4116	.4096	.2916	.1715	.0388	3
	4	.0000	.0000	.0001	.0016	.0081	.0256	.0625	.1296	.2401	.4096	.6561	.8145	.9606	4
5	0	.9510	.7738	.5905	.3277	.1681	.0778	.0312	.0102	.0024	.0003	.0000	.0000	.0000	0
	1	.0480	.2036	.3280	.4096	.3602	.2592	.1562	.0768	.0284	.0064	.0004	.0000	.0000	1
	2	.0010	.0214	.0729	.2048	.3087	.3456	.3125	.2304	.1323	.0512	.0081	.0011	.0000	2
	3	.0000	.0011	.0081	.0512	.1323	.2304	.3125	.3456	.3087	.2048	.0729	.0214	.0010	3
	4	.0000	.0000	.0004	.0064	.0284	.0768	.1562	.2592	.3602	.4096	.3280	.2036	.0480	4
	5	.0000	.0000	.0000	.0003	.0024	.0102	.0312	.0778	.1681	.3277	.5905	.7738	.9510	5
6	0	.9415	.7351	.5314	.2621	.1176	.0467	.0156	.0041	.0007	.0001	.0000	.0000	.0000	0
	1	.0571	.2321	.3543	.3932	.3025	.1886	.0938	.0369	.0102	.0015	.0001	.0000	.0000	1
	2	.0014	.0305	.0984	.2458	.3241	.3110	.2344	.1382	.0595	.0154	.0012	.0001	.0000	2
	3	.0000	.0021	.0146	.0819	.1852	.2765	.3125	.2765	.1852	.0819	.0146	.0021	.0000	3
	4	.0000	.0001	.0012	.0154	.0595	.1382	.2344	.3110	.3241	.2458	.0984	.0305	.0014	4
	5	.0000	.0000	.0001	.0015	.0102	.0369	.0938	.1866	.3025	.3932	.3543	.2321	.0571	5
	6	.0000	.0000	.0000	.0001	.0007	.0041	.0156	.0467	.1176	.2621	.5314	.7351	.9415	6
7	0	.9321	.6983	.4783	.2097	.0824	.0280	.0078	.0016	.0002	.0000	.0000	.0000	.0000	0
	1	.0659	.2573	.3720	.3670	.2471	.1306	.0547	.0172	.0036	.0004	.0000	.0000	.0000	1
	2	.0020	.0406	.1240	.2753	.3177	.2613	.1641	.0774	.0250	.0043	.0002	.0000	.0000	2
	3	.0000	.0036	.0230	.1147	.2269	.2903	.2734	.1935	.0972	.0287	.0026	.0002	.0000	3
	4	.0000	.0002	.0026	.0287	.0972	.1935	.2734	.2903	.2269	.1147	.0230	.0036	.0000	4
	5	.0000	.0000	.0002	.0043	.0250	.0774	.1641	.2613	.3177	.2753	.1240	.0406	.0020	5
	6	.0000	.0000	.0000	.0004	.0036	.0172	.0547	.1306	.2471	.3670	.3720	.2573	.0659	6
	7	.0000	.0000	.0000	.0000	.0002	.0016	.0078	.0280	.0824	.2097	.4783	.6983	.9321	7

Source: Computed by using a software.

bioassay– Statistical methods and techniques used in the evaluation of potency of a stimulus such as drugs, poisons, radiations, and vitamins by analyzing the response of biological organisms such as animals, humans, cells, and tissues. See also *probit analysis.*

bioequivalence– Used to describe the equivalence of certain important clinical outcomes of a new drug and the previous brand name drug already being used for a certain disease or disorder.

bioequivalence trial– A **clinical trial** carried out to compare the pharmacological properties of two or more drugs in order to determine whether they produce the comparable level of physiological effect.

biological assay– Same as *bioassay.*

biological significance– Same as *practical significance.*

biomathematics– Mathematical methods and techniques applied to the study of life sciences. The term is often used to refer to the study of **deterministic models** as opposed to **probabilistic** or **stochastic models.**

biometry– The application of statistical methods and techniques to the study of biological **observations.** The term was coined by W. F. R. Weldon and later popularized by Francis Galton and Karl Pearson, among others.

biostatistics– Statistical methods and techniques applied to the study of agricultural, biological, and medical problems. In the United States the term is more commonly used to refer to the use of **statistics** primarily in the fields of medicine and health.

biplots– A **graphical representation** of **multivariate data** in which all the **variables** are represented by a point. In addition to showing the relationship between variables, the technique is useful in displaying any hidden structure or pattern among the individuals and for displaying results found by more conventional methods of analysis. Biplots can be considered as the multivariate analogue of **scatter plots,** which can approximate the **multivariate distribution** of a **sample** in few dimensions.

Birnbaum–Hall test– A **nonparametric procedure** to test the **homogeneity** of three **independent samples** drawn from three **populations.** It provides an alternative to the **Kruskal–Wallis test** for the three-sample problem.

birth cohort– A **cohort** of persons born in a certain defined period of time.

birth-cohort study– The term is applied to a **longitudinal study** of a **birth cohort.**

birth–death ratio– The **ratio** of number of births to number of deaths occurring during a specified period of time in a certain **population.**

birth rate– Number of live births per 1000 of the **population** occurring during a specified period. It is calculated as the number of births actually observed divided by the population of the area as estimated at the middle of a particular time period or a calendar year (expressed per 1000 population).

biserial coefficient of correlation– The **correlation coefficient** between a **continuous variable** and a **dichotomous variable** with two categories represented by the numbers 0 and 1, but having underlying continuity and **normality.** It is an **estimate** of the **product moment correlation** from two **continuous distributions** if the dichotomized variable were normally distributed. It is a special form of **Pearson's product moment correlation coefficient** and can be calculated by a simple algebraic formula.

biserial correlation– A measure of the relationship between two **variables,** one of which is recorded as **binary response** and the other is measured on a continuous scale. The **binary variable** is actually a **continuous variable** but has been collapsed to two levels.

bivariate analysis– Statistical analysis involving simultaneous **measurements** on two **variables.** See also *multivariate analysis, univariate analysis.*

bivariate association– See *correlation.*

bivariate beta distribution– Two **random variables** X and Y are said to have a bivariate beta distribution if their **joint probability density** function is given by

$$f(x, y) = \frac{\Gamma(\alpha + \beta + \gamma)}{\Gamma(\alpha)\Gamma(\beta)\Gamma(\gamma)} x^{\alpha-1} y^{\beta-1} (1 - x - y)^{\gamma-1} \qquad x, y \geq 0; x + y \leq 1; \alpha, \beta, \gamma > 0$$

The distribution can be derived as the joint distribution of $X = X_1/(X_1 + X_2 + X_3)$ and $Y = X_2/(X_1 + X_2 + X_3)$, where X_1, X_2, X_3 are independent random variables having **gamma distributions** with **parameters** α, β, and γ, respectively.

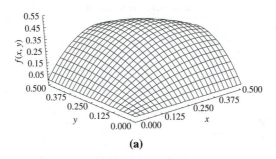

(a)

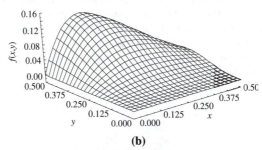

(b)

Plots of two bivariate beta distributions:
(a) $\alpha = 2, \beta = 2, \gamma = 2$; (b) $\alpha = 2, \beta = 4, \gamma = 3$

bivariate correlation– Same as *correlation.*

bivariate data– A **data set** that contains simultaneous **measurements** on two **variables** for each subject or item under study.

bivariate data set– Same as *bivariate data.*

bivariate density function– A bivariate continuous function $f(x, y)$ defined for all possible pairs of values (x, y) in the range of the **random variables** X and Y such that $f(x, y) \geq 0$ and

$$\int_{-\infty}^{\infty} \int_{-\infty}^{\infty} f(x, y) \, dx \, dy = 1$$

See also *joint density function, multivariate density function.*

bivariate distribution– Same as *bivariate frequency* or *probability distribution.*

bivariate frequency distribution– A method of classifying and representing a **bivariate data set** that involves a row × column **contingency table:** rows and columns listing the categories, **score intervals,** or **events,** into which the bivariate data are sorted and **cells** indicating the number of items or **frequency** in each cell. It is also called a **bivariate frequency table.**

bivariate frequency table– A **tabular representation** of a **bivariate frequency distribution.** The term is often used interchangeably with bivariate frequency distribution.

A bivariate frequency distribution for blood pressure and serum cholesterol level

Serum cholesterol in mg/100cc	Blood pressure in mm Hg				
	<127	127–146	147–166	>166	Total
<200	119	124	50	26	319
200–219	88	100	43	23	254
220–259	127	220	74	49	470
>259	74	111	57	44	286
Total	408	555	224	142	1329

bivariate histogram– A generalization of a **histogram** to represent a **bivariate frequency distribution.** A bivariate histogram can be constructed by drawing a horizontal plane containing a pair of perpendicular axes that are divided by ruled lines drawn at points corresponding to the end points of the **class intervals** for the corresponding **marginal distributions.** Finally, a column is erected on each cell of the bivariate distribution proportional in value to the **frequency** of that cell.

Schematic diagram of a bivariate
histogram

bivariate linear relationship– See *linear relationship.*

bivariate normal distribution– Two **random variables** X and Y with **means** μ_1 and μ_2, **variances** σ_1^2 and σ_2^2, and **correlation** ρ are said to have a bivariate normal distribution if their **joint probability density function** is given by

$$f(x, y) = \frac{1}{2\pi\sigma_1\sigma_2\sqrt{1-\rho^2}}$$
$$\times \exp\left\{-\frac{1}{2(1-\rho^2)}\left[\frac{(x-\mu_1)^2}{\sigma_1^2} - 2\rho\frac{(x-\mu_1)(y-\mu_2)}{\sigma_1\sigma_2} + \frac{(y-\mu_2)^2}{\sigma_2^2}\right]\right\}$$

It is a generalization of the **univariate normal distribution** to two random variables. See also *multivariate normal distribution, trivariate normal distribution.*

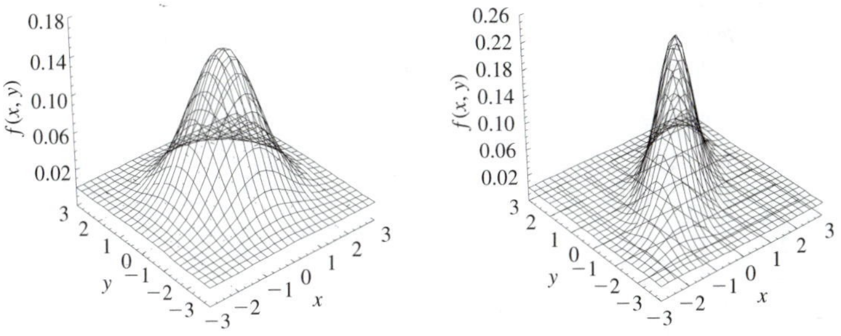

(a) (b)

Two bivariate normal distributions: **(a)** $\sigma_1^2 = \sigma_2^2$, $\rho = 0$; **(b)** $\sigma_1^2 = \sigma_2^2$, $\rho = 0.75$

bivariate plot– A two-dimensional plot of the values of two characteristics measured on the same set of subjects. See also *scatter diagram.*

bivariate polygon– A generalization of **polygon** to represent a **bivariate frequency distribution.**

bivariate prediction– The **prediction** of **scores** on one **variable** based on scores of one other variable.

bivariate probability distribution– The concept of the **probability distribution** of a **random variable** extended to a pair of random variables. A bivariate probability distribution is characterized by a **bivariate probability function** for **discrete random variables** and a **bivariate density function** for **continuous random variables.**

bivariate probability function– A bivariate discrete function $p(x, y)$ defined for all possible pairs of values (x, y) in the range of the **random variables** X and Y such that $p(x, y) \geq 0$ and $\sum_{x,y} p(x, y) = 1$. See also *bivariate density function, joint probability function.*

An example of a bivariate probability function

	y				
x	**1**	**2**	**3**	**4**	
1	0	1/12	1/12	1/12	1/4
2	1/12	0	1/12	1/12	1/4
3	1/12	1/12	0	1/12	1/4
4	1/12	1/12	1/12	0	1/4
	1/4	1/4	1/4	1/4	1

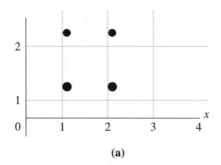

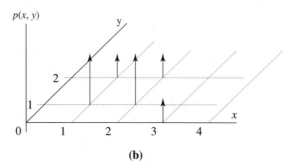

Two graphical representations of a bivariate probability
function: **(a)** $p(x, y)$ is represented by the size of the point;
(b) $p(x, y)$ is represented by the height of the vertical line
erected at the point

bivariate regression– Same as *simple regression.*

bivariate regression coefficient– See *regression coefficient.*

blinding– A procedure used in a **clinical trial** whereby either subjects or investigators or
both subjects and investigators are kept unaware of **treatments** given or received in order
to avoid the possible observer and respondent **biases** that might be introduced if the subjects and/or investigators knew which treatment the patient is receiving. In trials comparing an **active treatment** with no treatment, **placebos** are usually administered to patients
in the **control group** to maintain blinding. See also *blind study.*

blind study– A **clinical trial** or an **experimental study** in which subjects are unaware of
the **treatment** they are receiving. The investigators may also not know the treatment patients are receiving, in which case, it is called a **double blind study.** See also *double blind
trial, single blind trial, triple blind trial.*

block– The name given in an **experimental design** to a group of **experimental units** that
receive the same **treatment.** The purpose of grouping the experimental units in blocks is to
make a block as homogenous as possible by controlling for sources of **variability** due to
extraneous causes. Some examples of blocks are groups of contiguous plots in a field experiment, groups of animals or individuals with common characteristics such as age, sex,

race, or litters. The **variation** in **experimental observations** can then be divided into effects due to differences between blocks and effects due to variation within blocks and thereby provide more precise **estimates** of certain treatment comparisons.

block design– An **experimental design** in which **experimental units** within each **block** (or group) are assigned to a different **treatment.** See also *blocking, completely randomized design, incomplete block design, randomized block design.*

blocking– The process of using the same or similar **experimental units** for all **treatments** by means of grouping of **plots** or experimental units into **blocks** of homogenous units. The purpose of blocking, in an **experimental design,** is to remove the effects of extraneous sources from the **error term.** Blocking on a certain **variable** should decrease **variation** within a block and increase variation between blocks in order to increase **precision** of **estimates** and provide a more powerful or sensitive test for testing difference in **population** or **treatment means.** The effect of using a **block design** is similar to the use of **covariates** in an **ANCOVA** design.

block randomization– A method of constrained **randomization** in which **blocks** of subjects of even size (say 4, 6, or 8) are used to randomize so that half of the patients of each block are assigned to the **treatment group** and the other half to the **control group.** The method ensures that at no point during randomization will the imbalance be large and that there will be exactly equal treatment numbers at equally spaced points in the sequence of subject assignment.

BLUE– Acronym for *best linear unbiased estimator.*

BMDP– A **statistical computing package** for analyzing biomedical **data.** It was initially developed by W. J. Dixon at the University of California at Los Angeles. It is a large and powerful package that allows application of many well-known statistical methods. The programs perform **description** and **tabulation,** most **multivariate techniques, regression analysis, contingency tables, nonparametric methods, robust estimators, analysis of repeated measures, time-series analysis, variance analysis,** and **graphical procedures,** which include **histograms, bivariate plots, normal probability plots, residual plots,** and **factor loading** plots. It is an acronym for Biomedical Data Package.

body mass index– Same as *Quetlet's index.*

Bonferroni correction– Same as *Bonferroni procedure.*

Bonferroni inequality– If $A_1, A_2, \ldots, A_k$ are a set of k **events,** and $\bar{A}_i$ is the **complementary event** of A_i, then the Bonferroni inequality states that

$$P\left(\bigcap_{i=1}^{k} A_i\right) \geq 1 - \sum_{i=1}^{k} P(\bar{A}_i)$$

Bonferroni inequalities are used in simultaneous comparison of **population means** of three or more groups involving an **analysis of variance** or **regression procedure.** See also *Bonferroni procedure.*

Bonferroni procedure– A method for comparing **population means** in an **analysis of variance** procedure. It is also called the Dunn multiple comparison procedure. The procedure is designed to control **type I error** when performing a series of ***t*-tests** for comparing **means** of three or more groups. To control the type I error to a **probability level** α, the procedure performs each of the m tests at a level α/m. For example, if two groups are compared by four different tests, then each test should be performed at α **level** of 0.0125 in order to maintain an overall conventional **cutoff level** of 0.05. For large values of m, the method is highly conservative but for a small number of comparisons, it provides a reasonable solution to the problem of **multiple testing.** See also *Bonferroni inequality, Duncan multiple range test, Dunnett multiple comparison test, Newman-Keuls test, Scheffé's test, Tukey's test.*

Bonferroni test– Same as *Bonefrroni procedure.*

bootstrap– A **nonparametric technique** for estimating **standard error** of a **statistic** by repeated **resampling** from a **sample**. The technique treats a **random sample** of **data** as a substitute for the **population** and resamples from it a large number of times to produce sample bootstrap estimates and standard errors. Thus, given the original sample $x_1, x_2, \ldots, x_n$, the procedure involves **sampling with replacement** to generate a large number of bootstrap samples, each providing a bootstrap estimate and standard error. The sample bootstrap estimates and standard errors are then averaged and used to obtain a **confidence interval** around the **average** of the bootstrap estimates. This average is called a bootstrap estimator. The bootstrap estimate and associated confidence interval are used to assess the goodness of **sample statistic** as an estimate of the **population parameter.** Bootstrap estimates are often used when an appropriate mathematical formula does not exist or when the assumptions underlying an existing formula are not tenable. For example, to calculate a confidence interval for a **median,** the median for each bootstrap sample is calculated. The confidence interval is then based on the **distribution** of these medians. Compare *jackknife.*

bootstrap estimate– See *bootstrap.*

bootstrapping– Same as *bootstrap.*

bootstrap sample– See *bootstrap.*

box-and-whisker diagram– Same as *box-and-whisker plot.*

box-and-whisker plot– A method of **graphical presentation** of the important characteristics of a **data set.** The display is based on a **five-number summary.** A box is drawn with its right located at the **upper hinge** and its left located at the **lower hinge.** Two-dashed horizontal lines are drawn, one connecting the minimum value to the lower hinge and the other connecting the maximum value to the upper hinge. A line is also drawn at the **median** value, dividing the box into two halves. A box-and-whisker plot displays both the **frequencies** and **variability** of the **data,** and is useful for comparing two or more **distributions,** particularly to describe **quantitative variables** that have a **skewed distribution.** See also *stem-and-leaf plot.*

Box–Cox transformation– Same as *power transformation.*

Box–Jenkins method– A statistical method for **forecasting** a **time series** based on its own historical **data.** This is an alternative to **regression forecasting,** which is based on other **independent variables.** The procedure, also called ARIMA (autoregressive integrated moving average), considers the time series as a group of **random variables** following an underlying **probability distribution.** By analyzing the **ratios** among the **variables,** the method aims to estimate the distribution and thereby forecast the series.

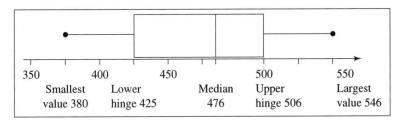

Box-and-whisker plot for hypothetical data

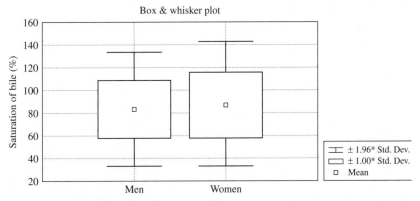

Comparative box-and-whisker plots for percentage saturation of bile for men and women

box plot– Same as *box-and-whisker plot.*

Box's test– A **test procedure** for testing three or more **independent samples** for **homogeneity of variances** before using an **analysis of variance** procedure. The test is less sensitive to departures from **normality** than **Bartlett's test.** See also *Cochran's test, Hartley's test.*

breakeven analysis– An economic analysis used to compute the approximate profit or loss that will be experienced by a firm at various levels of production. In performing this analysis, each expense item is classified as either fixed or variable. The procedure consists of determining the rate of sales in quantity such that the rate of money sales can be equated to the rate of costs, usually expressed in terms of annual rates.

breakeven chart– A **graphical device** for performing **breakeven analysis** in which one curve shows the total of fixed and variable costs and another curve shows the total income, both drawn at various production levels. The intersection of the two curves represents the breakeven point. It is a point indicating specific values of sales at which a firm neither makes any profit nor loses any money. At a value above this point, a firm begins to show a profit, while a value below it results in loss.

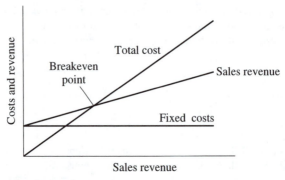

A breakeven chart

breakeven point– See *breakeven chart.*

BRR– Acronym for *balanced repeated replications.*

bulk sampling– A term used to describe the process of **sampling** a heap of objects.

Bureau of the Census– The chief statistical agency of the United States government. It is responsible for conducting a decennial **census** of the **population** as well as other censuses and **surveys.** It also has the mandate for collecting important **statistics** for almost every aspect of the national life; and publishes numerous reports, tabulations, and current bulletins. The bureau is a part of the U.S. Department of Commerce.

business cycles– A recurring sequence of successive changes in business enterprise. Beginning with a period of prosperity, business activity gradually declines until a low point, called depression, is reached. A period of recovery then follows where business conditions become more favorable until prosperity is again restored; and in this manner a **cycle** is completed.

business statistics– The collection, summarization, analysis, and reporting of numerical findings relevant to a business decision or situation.

C

cake diagram– Same as *pie chart*.

canned program– An old term used to describe a **computer program** written and documented so that the user needs only a data deck and the proper calling cards to access and run the particular program of interest.

canonical correlation– See *canonical correlation analysis*.

canonical correlation analysis– A **multivariate statistical technique** for examining the relationships between two sets of numerical measurements made on the same set of subjects. The technique involves grouping the two sets of **independent** and **dependent variables** into linear composites which are a weighted combination of **predictor variables** and a weighted combination of **criterion variables.** It then calculates a **bivariate correlation** known as a canonical correlation between the two composites. The technique can be considered an extension of **multiple regression analysis** to situations involving more than a single dependent variable. It can also be viewed as an analogue of **principal components analysis** where a **correlation** rather than a **variance** is maximized. Canonical correlation analysis is a useful and powerful technique for exploring the relationships among multiple predictor (independent) and multiple criterion (dependent) variables.

capture–recapture sampling– A **sampling** scheme especially designed for the **estimation** of size of a wildlife population such as fish in a lake or birds in a sanctuary. The procedure involves the selection of an initial **sample** of animals that are marked and then released and allowed to mix with the population. Subsequently, a second sample is taken and the **proportion** of marked animals is determined. From this proportion the total number of animals is estimated by using the relation between the **parameters** of a **hypergeometric distribution.** For example, let n_1 be the size of the first sample, n_2 be the size of the second sample, and m the number of marked animals in the second sample. Then an estimator of the total number of animals is given by $\hat{N} = n_1 n_2 / m$. The estimator is sometimes known as the Petersen estimator.

carryover effect– In **crossover studies,** a carryover effect occurs when the **treatment** given in one period of the **trial** continues to exert its effect into the following period.

Carryover effects may lead to **treatment-period interactions,** and it is generally important to assess the relative importance of the effects attributable to the treatment given in a period compared to the period given in the previous period. In order to minimize the influence of carryover effects, **washout periods** of appropriate length must be allowed between two consecutive treatments.

Cartesian coordinate– A point that is located by measuring the distances from the coordinate axes (*x* **axis** and *y* **axis**) on a two-dimensional graph.

Cartesian graph– A graph drawn in a *cartesian plane.*

Cartesian plane– A plane whose points are labeled with **Cartesian coordinates.**

Cartesian product– The set of ordered pairs (*x, y*) of real numbers.

Cartesian space– Same as *cartesian plane.*

case– A term used most frequently in **epidemiology** to designate an individual in a **study population** having a certain disease or condition of interest.

case-control study– An **observational study** that entails **patient cases** who have a certain outcome or disease under investigation and comparable **control subjects** who do not have the outcome or disease. It then examines backward to identify possible **etiologic** or **risk factors.** Such a study is also called a **retrospective study** because it starts after the onset of disease and looks retrospectively to identify **risk** or **causal factors.** Case-control studies are often used to investigate the relationship between an **exposure** or risk factor and one or more **outcomes.** They are particularly useful in the study of rare disorders and infectious disease outbreaks. However, case-control studies are prone to some common sources of **bias,** such as **selection bias** and **recall bias,** among others. See also *Berkson's fallacy, cohort study, cross-sectional study, prospective study.*

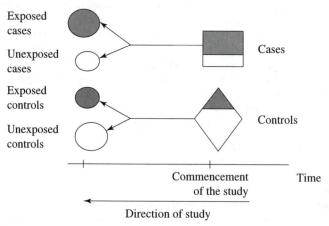

Schematic diagram of a case-control study

case-fatality rate– This **rate** is designed to measure the **probability** of death among diagnosed **cases** of a disease. It is obtained as the **proportion** of cases of the disease who die during the same time period. More specifically, it is given by the number of deaths from a disease in a given period divided by the number of diagnosed cases of that disease in the same period.

case report– Published report describing a detailed clinical case history of **cases** which are unique or rare in certain aspects.

case-series study– A simple narrative description or **case report** of certain interesting or intriguing observations that occurred in a small group of patients. Case-series studies frequently lead to generation of **hypotheses** that are subsequently tested in a **case-control, cross-sectional,** or **cohort study.** See also *retrospective study.*

categorical data– See *categorical variable.*

categorical observations– Same as *categorical data.*

categorical variable– A **variable** whose values are categories or groups of objects as **measurements.** Examples of categorical variables are sex (male or female), marital status (married, single, divorced, etc.), and blood group (A, B, AB, O). For convenience of data collection and analysis, the categories are often assigned numerical labels, but they have no quantitative significance whatsoever. The values of a categorical variable are known as categorical data or observations. See also *qualitative variable, quantitative variable.*

Cauchy–Schwartz inequality– Given two **random variables** X and Y having finite second **moments,** the Cauchy–Schwartz inequality states that

$$[E(XY)]^2 \leq E(X^2)E(Y^2)$$

As a corollary to the above inequality it follows that $|\rho| \leq 1$ where ρ is the **correlation coefficient** between X and Y. In general, if a_i's and b_i's are real integers, then it follows that

$$\left(\sum_{i=1}^{n} a_i^2\right)\left(\sum_{i=1}^{n} b_i^2\right) \geq \left(\sum_{i=1}^{n} a_i b_i\right)^2$$

causal analysis– A method, such as **path analysis** or **latent variable modeling,** that analyzes **correlations** among a group of **variables** in terms of predicted patterns of **causal relations** among them.

causal diagram– A **graphical representation** of the **cause–effect relationship** between **variables.** In a causal diagram, paths in the form of unidirectional or bidirectional arrows are drawn from the variables taken as causes (independent) to the variables taken as effects (dependent). The **correlation** between two **exogenous variables** is depicted by a curved line with an arrowhead at both ends.

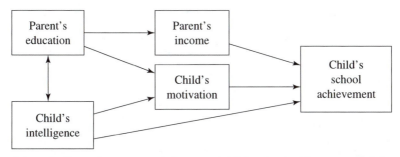

Schematic illustration of a causal diagram of child's school achievement via links between the child's intelligence, child's motivation, parent's education, and parent's income

causal factor– Same as *causal variable.*

causal inference– A form of **inference** used for assessing a **causal relationship** by designing a valid **experiment.**

causality– The term is most commonly used to describe a **cause–effect relationship** between **variables.** Many investigations in social, medical, and health sciences purport to establish causality between certain **events;** for example, cigarette smoking and lung cancer. See also *causal analysis, causal diagram, causal model, causal modeling, causal variable.*

causal model– A **mathematical model** describing **causal relations** among sets of **exogenous** and **endogenous variables.** See also *path analysis, structural equation model.*

causal modeling– A method of analysis of **causal relations** among sets of **exogenous** and **endogenous variables. Path analysis** and **structural equation models** are examples of causal modeling.

causal relation– Same as *cause–effect relationship.*

causal relationship– Same as *cause–effect relationship.*

causal variable– A **variable** that brings about changes in a given variable. A causal variable is treated as an **independent variable.** See also *causal diagram, causal model, causal modeling.*

cause-and-effect diagram– A **graphical device** that is used to identify, display, and examine possible causes of a poor quality or an undesirable condition present in a system or process. It is also known as an Ishikawa diagram, after K. Ishikawa, who first popularized its use during the mid-40s. The five common causes of a poor quality are environment, materials, manpower, machines, and methods. The steps in constructing a cause-and-effect diagram can be summarized as follows: (1) Identify the quality characteristic for which a cause-and-effect relationship is to be established. (2) Using the experience of knowledgeable people, generate several major categories of causes that can affect the quality. (3) For each of those major categories of causes, identify the possible causes that fall within that category and insert these subcauses into the diagram via horizontal lines emanating from the major category names.

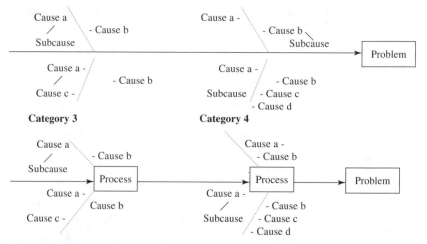

Schematic illustration of two hypothetical cause-and-effect diagrams

Categories of causes   Categories of causes, subcauses, subsubcauses, etc.

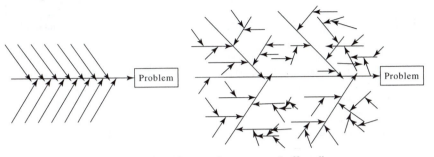

Schematic illustration of a simple and a complex cause-and-effect diagram

cause–effect relationship– A term used to describe the **association** between two **variables** whenever it can be established that one of the variables causes the other. Statistical analysis has a long way to go toward establishing the existence of a cause–effect relationship between any two variables. It cannot establish the nature of any causal relationship, nor can it be used for proving that any two variables are not causally related. Statistical analysis may show that two variables X and Y are related; however, it cannot show X causes Y or that Y causes X. It is just possible that the relationship shown to exist may be the effect of a third variable Z; i.e., it may be that X and Y represent joint effects of Z. There are several criteria, such as biological plausibility, **dose–response relationship,** temporal relationship, consistency with other studies, lack of **bias,** and **confounding** effect, among others, that must be met before reaching such a conclusion.

cause-specific death rate– The **death rate** in a specified period of time and place due to a specific disease, source, or cause. This **rate** is designed to measure the **probability** of death from a particular disease. It is obtained as the total number of deaths due to the specified cause during a calendar year divided by the midyear population of the region (expressed per 1000). See also *standardized death rate.*

Death rates and percent of total deaths for the 15 leading causes of death: United States 1980 (rates per 100,000 population)

Rank	Cause of death	Rate	Percent of total deaths
	All causes	878.3	100.0
1.	Heart diseases	336.0	38.2
2.	Malignant neoplasm, including neoplasm of lymphatic and hematopoietic tissues	183.9	20.9
3.	Cerebrovascular diseases	75.1	8.6
4.	Accidents and adverse effects	46.7	5.3
5.	Chronic obstructive pulmonary diseases and allied conditions	24.7	2.8
6.	Pneumonia and influenza	24.1	2.7
7.	Diabetes mellitus	15.4	1.8
8.	Chronic liver disease and cirrhosis	13.5	1.5
9.	Atherosclerosis	13.0	1.5
10.	Suicide	11.9	1.4

(Continued)

(Continued)

Rank	Cause of death	Rate	Percent of total deaths
11.	Homicide and legal intervention	10.7	1.2
12.	Certain conditions originating in the perinatal period	10.1	1.1
13.	Nephritis, nephrotic syndrome, and nephrosis	7.4	0.8
14.	Congenital anomalies	6.2	0.7
15.	Septicemia	4.2	0.5
	All other causes	95.6	10.9

Source: National Center of Health Statistics, U.S. Department of Health, Education & Welfare.

cause-specific mortality rate– Same as *cause-specific death rate.*

***c* chart–** A **graphical device** used to control a process by inspecting the number of defectives (c) taken from various batches or subgroups. The values of c computed from each batch are plotted on the **vertical axis** and can then be used to control the quality of the batch. The **center line** of the c chart is the **average** number of defectives ($\bar{c}$) taken from a pilot set (about 20 rational subgroups). **Control lines** are fixed at three **standard deviations** from the center line (based on the **normal approximation** to the **Poisson distribution,** i.e., $\bar{c} \pm 3\sqrt{\bar{c}}$). See also *control chart, p chart, run chart, s chart, x-bar chart.*

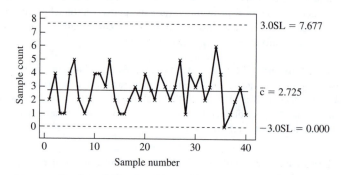

An example of a *c* chart

cell– A category of counts or values in a **contingency table.** It is formed by the intersection of a row and column in a **statistical table.** In an **analysis of variance** design, a cell represents any single group.

cell count– Same as *cell frequency.*

cell frequency– Frequency counts relating to a particular **cell** in a **contingency table.**

cell mean– The **mean** of all the **observations** in a particular **cell** or **level** of a **factor.**

censored data– Same as *censored observations.*

censored observations– An **observation** whose value is unknown simply because the subject or item has not been in the study a sufficient time for the outcome of interest, such as death or breakdown, to occur or the observation is less than the **measurement** limit of detection (LOD) or it is purposely ignored. Censored observations frequently arise in many **longitudinal studies** where the **event** of interest has not occurred to a number of subjects at the completion of the study. Moreover, the **loss to follow-up** often leads to censoring since the outcomes remain unknown.

censored regression analysis– A form of **regression** where the values of the **dependent variable** are censored or truncated.

censored sample– A **sample** that has some of its values, usually the largest and/or smallest, censored because they are unobservable.

censoring– See *censored observations.*

census– The complete count (enumeration) or **survey** involving the observation of every member of a **population** or a group of items at a point in time with respect to certain well-defined characteristics of interest. A census of the human population is a counting of the people within the boundaries of a country. More generally, it is the total process of collecting, compiling, and publishing demographic, economic, and social **data** pertaining, at given time period, to all persons in a country or delimited territory. The use of information derived from a census has become indispensable to any modern government. In modern times, censuses have come to include many topics other than just counting people. Some of the areas independent of the census of human population are agriculture, housing, business establishments, and industries.

census area– The well-defined geographical area in which the **census** is undertaken.

census unit– The smallest geographical area into which the entire **census area** is divided for administrative and data collection purposes.

center line– See *control charts.*

centile charts– Same as *percentile charts.*

centiles– In a series of **observations** arranged in ascending order of magnitude, centiles are those values that divide the observations into 100 equal parts. It is an abbreviated form of **percentile** not commonly used but is frequently encountered in psychological and educational testing literature. See also *deciles, quartiles.*

centralized database– In a **multicenter clinical trial,** a term sometimes used to refer to a **database** that is located and maintained in a central coordinating office.

central limit theorem– A mathematical theorem that states that, regardless of the **distribution** form of the **parent population,** the **sampling distribution** of the **sample mean** approaches the **normal distribution** as the **sample size** n becomes very large. More specifically, if a **random variable** X has **population mean** μ and **population variance** σ^2, then the sample mean $\overline{X}$, based on n **observations,** has an approximate normal distribution with **mean** μ and **variance** σ^2/n for sufficiently large n. It enables us to use the normal probability distribution to approximate the sampling distribution of the mean whenever the sample size is large. The central limit theorem generally applies whenever the sample size exceeds 30. This theorem is of great importance in **probability** and **statistics** since it justifies the use of normal distribution for a great variety of statistical applications.

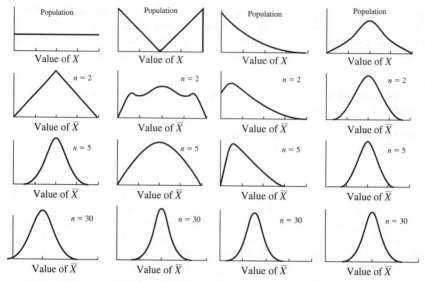

Diagram illustrating central limit theorem

central location– Same as *central tendency.*

central moments– See *moments.*

central range– The range of values that contains the central 90 percent of **observations** of a **data set.**

central tendency– Central tendency refers to the property of clustering of the data points in a distribution around a more or less central value. It is central or typical value of a given **data set** and provides an indication of the center or middle of a **distribution.** It is also referred to as **location.** See also *measures of central tendency.*

centroid method– A method of **factor analysis** developed by L. L. Thurstone, which mathematically designates a center point, from which all reference axes extend. **Principal components analysis,** the most common method of factor analysis, employs this method.

certainty equivalent– The figure that a decision maker would be indifferent to receiving for certain as compared to participating in a particular gamble.

chain-base index number– A type of **index number** which changes its base and its pattern of weights from one period to the other. Both **Laspeyres'** and **Paasche's index** numbers can be easily converted to chain-base index.

chance– A complex system of cause and effect leading to the occurrence of an **event** or phenomenon which cannot be explained otherwise. The term is loosely used as a synonym for **probability.**

chance agreement– A measure of the **proportion** of times two or more observers would agree in their **measurement** or assessment of a phenomenon under investigation simply by chance. See also *kappa statistic.*

chance error– Same as *random error.*

chance variable– Same as *random variable.*

chaos theory– A term coined to designate a scientific discipline concerned with investigating the apparently **random** and chaotic behavior of a system or phenomenon by use of **deterministic models.**

Chapman's estimator– In **capture–recapture sampling,** a modification of the **Petersen estimator** made to avoid the possibility of zero in the denominator. More specifically, the Chapman estimator of the total number of animals is given by

$$\hat{N} = \frac{(n_1 + 1)(n_2 + 1)}{m + 1} - 1$$

where n_1 and n_2 are the sizes of the first and second samples, respectively, and m is the number of marked animals in the second sample.

characteristic function– A function of a **variable** t associated with the **probability distribution** of a **random variable** X, defined by

$$\phi_X(t) = E(e^{itX})$$

where $i = \sqrt{-1}$. If $\phi_X(t)$ is expanded as a power series in t, the coefficient of $(it)^k/k!$ gives the kth **moment** of X about the origin. For some **distributions,** the **moment generating function** does not exist. However, the characteristic function always exists and plays an important role in the characterization of a probability distribution.

Chebyshev's inequality– Same as *Chebyshev's theorem.*

Chebyshev's theorem– A theorem in **probability theory** that allows the use of the knowledge of the **standard deviation** and **mean** to determine the fraction of a **population** within k standard deviations of the mean. It states that, regardless of the **shape** of a population's frequency distribution, the **proportion** of **observations** falling within k standard deviation of the mean is at least $(1 - 1/k^2)$ given that k is 1 or more. Thus, according to this theorem, at least $(1 - 1/2^2)$, i.e., 75% of the observations fall within two standard deviations of the mean.

Chernoff's faces– A statistical technique for representing **multivariate data** in which each **data point** is represented by a computer-generated graphic resembling a human face, and the shape, size, and feature of each face is determined by the values taken by particular **variables.** The **sample data** are then arranged or grouped according to similarities among faces and thus may be used to assess similarities or differences between **observations.**

chi distribution– The **probability distribution** of a **random variable** $\chi = +\sqrt{X}$ where X has a **chi-square distribution.**

child death rate– The number of deaths of children aged 1 to 4 years observed in a given year divided by the total number of children in this age group (expressed per 1000).

child mortality rate– Same as *child death rate.*

chi (random) variable– A **random variable** that has a **chi distribution.**

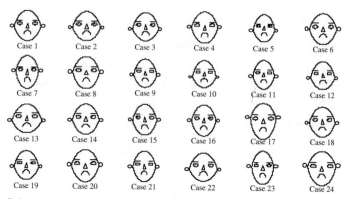

Schematic diagram illustrating Chernoff's faces

chi-square distribution– The **distribution** may be considered as a sum of squares of k independent variables, where each variable follows a **normal distribution** with **mean 0** and **standard deviation** 1. The **parameter** k is known as the number of **degrees of freedom.** The distribution is frequently used in many applications of **statistics,** for example, in testing the **goodness of fit** of **models** and in analyzing count data in **frequency tables.** The **chi-square test** is based on it. The following table gives the **critical values** of a **chi-square variable,** which denotes the value for which the area to its right under the chi-square distribution with v degrees of freedom is equal to α. The entries in this table are values of $\chi^2_{v,\alpha}$ for which the area to their right under the chi-square distribution with v degrees of freedom is equal to α.

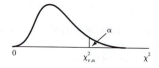

Chi-square table

$\alpha \rightarrow$ $v\downarrow$	0.995	0.99	0.975	0.95	.05	0.025	0.01	0.005	$\leftarrow\alpha$ $\downarrow v$
1	.0000393	.000157	.000982	.00393	3.841	5.024	6.635	7.879	1
2	0.011	0.0201	0.051	0.103	5.991	7.378	9.210	10.597	2
3	0.072	0.115	0.216	0.352	7.815	9.348	11.345	12.838	3
4	0.207	0.297	0.484	0.711	9.488	11.143	13.277	14.860	4
5	0.412	0.554	0.831	1.145	11.071	12.833	15.086	16.750	5
6	0.676	0.872	1.237	1.635	12.592	14.449	16.812	18.548	6
7	0.989	1.239	1.690	2.167	14.067	16.013	18.475	20.278	7
8	1.344	1.646	2.180	2.733	15.507	17.535	20.090	21.955	8
9	1.735	2.088	2.700	3.325	16.919	19.023	21.666	23.589	9
10	2.156	2.558	3.247	3.940	18.307	20.483	23.209	25.188	10
11	2.603	3.053	3.816	4.575	19.675	21.920	24.725	26.757	11
12	3.074	3.571	4.404	5.226	21.026	23.337	26.217	28.300	12

(*Continued*)

$\alpha \rightarrow$ $v\downarrow$	0.995	0.99	0.975	0.95	.05	0.025	0.01	0.005	$\leftarrow\alpha$ $\downarrow v$
13	3.565	4.107	5.009	5.892	22.362	24.736	27.688	29.819	13
14	4.075	4.660	5.629	6.571	23.685	26.119	29.141	31.319	14
15	4.601	5.229	6.262	7.261	24.996	27.488	30.578	32.801	15
16	5.142	5.812	6.908	7.962	26.296	28.845	32.000	34.267	16
17	5.697	6.408	7.564	8.672	27.587	30.191	33.409	35.719	17
18	6.265	7.015	8.231	9.390	28.869	31.526	34.805	37.156	18
19	6.844	7.633	8.907	10.117	30.144	32.852	36.191	38.582	19
20	7.434	8.260	9.591	10.851	31.410	34.170	37.566	39.997	20
21	8.034	8.897	10.283	11.591	32.671	35.479	38.932	41.401	21
22	8.643	9.542	10.982	12.338	33.924	36.781	40.289	42.796	22
23	9.260	10.196	11.689	13.091	35.172	38.076	41.638	44.181	23
24	9.886	10.856	12.401	13.848	36.415	39.364	42.980	45.559	24
25	10.520	11.524	13.120	14.611	37.653	40.646	44.314	46.928	25
26	11.160	12.198	13.844	15.379	38.885	41.923	45.642	48.290	26
27	11.808	12.879	14.573	16.151	40.113	43.195	46.963	49.645	27
28	12.461	13.565	15.308	16.928	41.337	44.461	48.278	50.993	28
29	13.121	14.256	16.047	17.708	42.557	45.722	49.588	52.336	29
30	13.787	14.953	16.791	18.493	43.773	46.979	50.892	53.672	30

Source: Computed by using software.

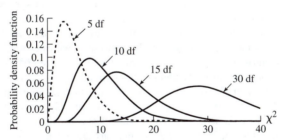

Probability density curves for chi-square distributions with
5, 10, 15, and 30 degrees of freedom

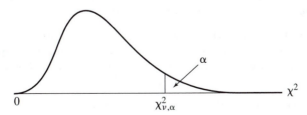

For v degrees of freedom, χ^2 value such that area in the
right tail is α

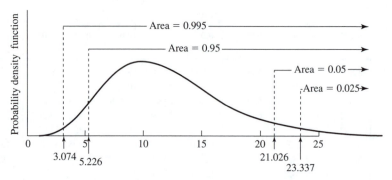

Probability density curve of the chi-square distribution with 12 degrees of freedom (area to the right of 5.226 is 0.95 and so on)

chi-square (random) variable– A **random variable** that has a **chi-square distribution.**

chi-square statistic– In general, any **statistic** that has a **chi-square distribution.** There are many statistical applications of the chi-square statistic. One of the most common procedures involves testing the **hypothesis** of **independence** for the **two-way classifications** of a **contingency table.** In this case, the chi-square statistic is obtained as the sum of all the quantities obtained by taking the difference between each **observed** and **expected frequency,** squaring the difference, and dividing this squared deviation by the expected frequency. See also *goodness of fit statistic.*

chi-square test– A test of **statistical significance** based on the **chi-square distribution.** This test is used in many situations. Some of the more common uses are: (1) an overall **goodness-of-fit test** for comparing the **frequencies** of **events** that are classified in **nominal categories** with hypothetical frequencies falling into specified categories; (2) testing the **association** in a **contingency table** by comparing the observed **cell frequencies** with the frequencies that would be expected under the **null hypothesis** of no association; (3) testing the **hypothesis** that a **sample** comes from a hypothetical **normal population** with known **variance.** For the validity of a chi-square test, it is generally assumed that **expected frequencies** of all the **cells** be greater than 1 and at least 80% of the cells have expected frequencies greater than 5. When these assumptions are not met, other tests, such as **Fisher's exact test,** are more appropriate.

chi-square test for independence– A **chi-square test** used in a **contingency table** by comparing the observed **cell frequencies** with the **frequencies** that would be obtained under the **null hypothesis** of **independence** of row and column categories.

chi-square test for trend– A **chi-square test** used in a $2 \times k$ **contingency table** with k ordered categories to test the **hypothesis** of a difference in the trend of the k **proportions** in the two groups. The test is generally more powerful than the usual **chi-square test for independence.**

circle chart– Same as *pie chart.*

circular distribution– The **probability distribution** of a **random variable** defined as the value of an angle confined to be on the unit circle. It ranges in value from 0 to 2π. It is used to model the phenomena that have a period of 2π so that the **probability density** at any point θ is the same that any point $\theta + 2\pi k$ for any integral value of k. The **probability mass** may be regarded as distributed around the circumference of a circle.

class boundary– Same as *class limit.*

class frequency– Same as *absolute class frequency.*

classical inference– Same as *classical statistical inference.*

classical probability– A definition of **probability** that assumes that all the experimental **outcomes** of a **random phenomenon** are equally likely or is based on some other objective or theoretical considerations. It is equal to the number of equally likely outcomes favorable to the occurrence of an **event** of interest divided by the total number of equally likely basic outcomes possible. See also *empirical probability, objective probability, subjective probability.*

classical statistical inference– Same as *statistical inference.* The term is sometimes used to distinguish it from the so-called **Bayesian inference.**

classical statistics– Same as *classical statistical inference.*

classical time-series model– A **time-series model** that attempts to explain the pattern or **variation** observed in an actual **time-series data** by the sum/product of the four components: **trend, cyclical, seasonal,** and **irregular components.** See also *additive time-series model, multiplicative time-series model, mixed time-series model.*

classification– The process of subdividing the range of values of a **variable** into classes or groups.

classification errors– Errors in assigning or classifying persons, objects, or **events** into separate classes, categories or groups.

classification techniques– A general term applied to any of the techniques used in **cluster** and **discriminant analysis.**

class interval– One of the intervals into which the entire range of the **variable** values has been divided. It represents the length of a class or the range of values covered by a class of a **frequency distribution.**

class limits– In a **frequency distribution,** the **variable** values that demarcate each **class interval.** For example, 2.1 and 2.4 are, respectively, the lower and upper class limits of the class interval 2.1–2.4.

class mark– Same as *midpoint.*

class midpoint– Same as *midpoint.*

class midvalue– Same as *midpoint.*

class width– The length or difference between the numerical values of the **upper real limit** of a class and the **lower real limit** of that class.

clinical decision making– Same as *medical decision making.*

clinical significance– Same as *practical significance.*

clinical trial– An **experimental study** of a medical treatment or procedure on human beings, designed to investigate the efficacy of the treatment. It generally entails comparison between two or more **study groups,** by administering treatments/interventions to at least one of the study groups to assess the relative efficacy of treatments. The paradigm of a clinical trial is a **randomized controlled trial.** See also *phase I trial, phase II trial, phase III trial, phase IV trial.*

cluster– A cluster is a subset of the **population** of objects. Generally, the clusters consist of natural groupings of the individuals or objects such as residents in a city block, a family, hospital, school, etc.

cluster analysis– An advanced statistical technique in **multivariate analysis** that determines a **classification** or taxonomy from multiple measures of an initially unclassified set of individual or objects. The procedure is designed to determine whether individuals or objects are similar enough to belong to the same or separate groups or **clusters.** The sets of **measurements** pertaining to individuals being studied, known as profiles, are compared and individuals that are close or similar are classified as being in the same cluster or group. During recent decades, applications of cluster analysis have grown at rapid pace. Programs for carrying out cluster analyses are now included in much of the widely used **statistical software.**

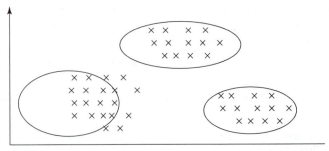

Schematic diagram for clusters of data

clustering– The division of a **population** into a number of subpopulations commonly known as **clusters.** Clustering makes use of natural groupings; for example, employees in a firm may be divided into work groups, children in a school may be grouped into designated classes, and dwellings of a city may be organized into blocks.

cluster randomization– A method of **randomization** in which groups or **clusters** of individuals rather than individuals themselves are randomly assigned to **treatment groups.** Although the method is not as efficient as the individual randomization, it is useful in terms of certain economic, ethical, and practical considerations.

cluster sampling– A **two-stage sampling** procedure in which the **population** is divided into groups of units known as **clusters.** A **random sample** of clusters is drawn, and then random samples of subjects within the clusters are selected. A one-stage cluster random sample entails a complete enumeration of all randomly chosen clusters. Typically, entire households, schools, or hospitals are sampled. Generally, the clusters consist of natural groupings of individuals or objects. Cluster sampling is usually employed when the researcher cannot obtain a complete list of the elements of a population under study but can get a complete list of groups of individuals (all persons in a city block, a family, hospital, school, etc.) of the population. In the determination of the **sample size** required in a study, where the clusters are the **sampling units,** it is necessary to modify the commonly used formulas for this purpose. See also *multistage sampling*.

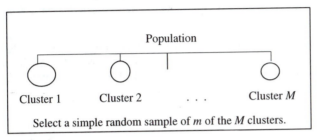

Schematic diagram for cluster sampling

COBOL– An acronym for Common Business Oriented Language. A business-oriented programming language used for writing programs.

Cochran's *C* test– **A test procedure** for testing three or more **independent samples** for **homogeneity of variances** before using an **analysis of variance** procedure. It is based on the ratio of the largest **sample variance** to the sum of all the sample variances and was proposed by W. G. Cochran in 1941. See also *Bartlett's test, Box's test, Hartley's test*.

Cochran's *Q* test– **A nonparametric procedure** for comparing several correlated **proportions** arising from **dependent** or **matched groups** to determine whether **frequencies** or **correlations** differ significantly among themselves. It is a generalization of **McNemar's chi-square test** for more than two matched groups and is best suited for nominal or dichotomized **ordinal data.**

coding– A term used to refer to a **variable** with arbitrary origin or possibly transforming it in some other unit.

coefficient– A **constant** multiplier that measures some property of a **variable** or functions of a variable.

coefficient of alienation– A term sometimes used to denote a measure of the **proportion** of **variability** in the **response variable** that is not explained by the **estimated regression equation.** It is obtained as the **ratio** of the **sum of squares due to residuals** to the **total sum of squares.** It can be considered as a measure of the lack of fit of the estimated regression equation. It is interpreted as the amount of error in predicting values of the **dependent variable** that could not be eliminated by using values of the **independent variables.** It is equivalent to $1 - R^2$ where R^2 is the **coefficient of multiple determination.**

coefficient of concordance– Same as *Kendall's coefficient of concordance*.

coefficient of contingency– Same as *contingency coefficient*.

coefficient of correlation– Same as *correlation coefficient*.

coefficient of cross-elasticity– The mathematical relationship between a percentage change in the price of a certain commodity or service and the resulting percentage change in the sales of a substitute commodity or service.

coefficient of determination– Same as *coefficient of multiple determination.*

coefficient of elasticity– The mathematical relationship between the percentage change in the quantity of a commodity or service acquired or offered and the percentage change in the price.

coefficient of kurtosis– A measure of **kurtosis** of a **distribution** defined by $\beta_2 = \mu_4/\mu_2^2$ where μ_2 and μ_4 denote the second and fourth **central moments** of the distribution. For a **normal** or **mesokurtic distribution** $\beta_2 = 3$, for a **leptokurtic distribution** $\beta_2 > 3$, and for a **platykurtic distribution** $\beta_2 < 3$.

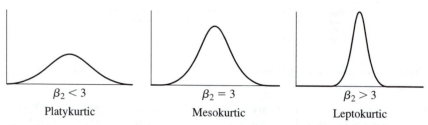

$\beta_2 < 3$	$\beta_2 = 3$	$\beta_2 > 3$
Platykurtic	Mesokurtic	Leptokurtic

The relationship between the coefficient of kurtosis and the degree of peakedness

coefficient of linear correlation– Same as *coefficient of correlation.*

coefficient of multiple correlation– Same as *multiple correlation coefficient.*

coefficient of multiple determination– It is a measure of the **proportion** of **variability** in the **response variate** that is explained by the **estimated regression equation.** It is obtained as the **ratio** of the **sum of squares due to regression** to the **total sum of squares.** It can be interpreted as a measure of how well the estimated regression equation fits the **data** or explains the **variation** in the data. It is equivalent to R^2 where R is the **multiple correlation coefficient.** See also *adjusted sample coefficient of multiple determination, sample coefficient of multiple determination.*

coefficient of part correlation– See *part correlation.*

coefficient of partial determination– In **multiple regression analysis,** a **measure of association** between the **dependent variable** and one of the **independent variables,** after adjusting for the **effects** of one or more other independent variables. See also *sample coefficient of partial determination.*

coefficient of regression– Same as *regression coefficient.*

coefficient of relative variation– Same as *coefficient of variation.*

coefficient of skewness– A measure of **skewness** of a **distribution** defined by $\beta_1 = \mu_3^2/\mu_2^3$ where μ_2 and μ_3 denote the second and third **central moments** of the distribution. The size of μ_3 relative to $\mu_2^{3/2}$ indicates the extent to which the distribution departs from **symmetry.** Thus $\sqrt{\beta_1}$ gives a measure of the relative skewness of a distribution, or its skewness normalized by its **spread.** It can be used to compare the symmetry of two distributions with different values of scales. For a **symmetrical distribution,** $\sqrt{\beta_1} = 0$. For a distribution having right tails, $\sqrt{\beta_1} > 0$. For a distribution having left tails, $\sqrt{\beta_1} < 0$. See also *coefficient of kurtosis, kurtosis.*

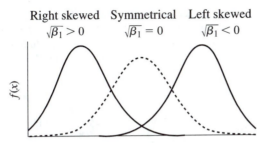

Right skewed   Symmetrical   Left skewed
$\sqrt{\beta_1} > 0$ $\sqrt{\beta_1} = 0$ $\sqrt{\beta_1} < 0$

The relationship between the coefficient of skewness
and concentration of tails of a distribution

coefficient of variation– A measure of relative **dispersion** for a **data set.** It is calculated by dividing the **standard deviation** by the **mean.** It is generally represented as percentage by multiplying it by 100. It expresses the magnitude of the **variation** relative to its **average** size and is used for comparing the **variability** in different **distributions.** The standard deviation provides an absolute **measure of dispersion** of a data set expressed in the same units of **measurements,** for example, tons, yards, or pounds. However, the coefficient of variation provides a means of comparing the variability in two or more data sets measured in different units and can be considered a statistical measure of the relative dispersion, variability, or **scatter** of a data set or **frequency distribution.** It is a purely statistical entity free of any units of measurement. Coefficient of variation is also often used as a measure of the repeatability of a measurement method by taking repeated measurements with the method in question and calculating its coefficient of variation.

cofactor of a matrix– The ijth cofactor of an $n \times n$ **matrix** A denoted by A_{ij} is given by

$$A_{ij} = (-1)^{i+j} \left| M_{ij} \right|$$

where M_{ij} is the ijth minor of A.

cohort– A group composed of individuals of the same generation, age, occupation, geographical area; or any designated group of persons with some common characteristics who are followed or traced over a period of time, as in a **cohort analysis** or **study.**

cohort analysis– The study of the same cohort over an extended period of time. See also *cohort study.*

cohort study– An **observational study** that includes a group of subjects who have a **risk factor** or have been exposed to an agent and a second group of subjects who do not have the risk factor or **exposure.** Both groups are followed prospectively through time to determine and compare the **outcomes** of interest in the two groups. The alternative terms for a cohort study are **follow-up, longitudinal,** and **prospective study.** In investigating the relationship between an exposure or risk factor and the **incidence** of disease, cohort studies generally yield more precise results and are less prone to **biases** of different sources than **case-control studies.** However, the cohort study generally entails the study of a large population for a prolonged period of time. Since the cohort studies can take a long period of time to complete, they may be very costly to conduct. They are usually unsuitable for investigating rare outcomes since it would require that an extremely large number of subjects be followed in order to get an adequate number of **events** of interest. Moreover, in many cohort studies, some subjects may not be followed for the full length of the study since they may move to another area or may even die. Thus, **loss to follow-up** and surveillance bias are two common sources of bias in this type of study. See also *cohort analysis, cross-sectional study.*

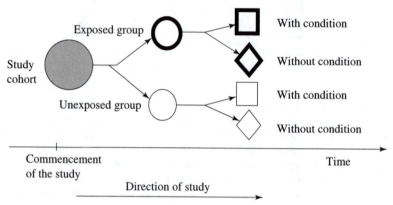

Schematic diagram of a cohort study

collectively exhaustive events– Same as *exhaustive events.*

collinearity– Same as *multicollinearity.*

column chart– Same as *bar chart.*

column marginals– In a **cross-tabulation,** the **frequencies** of the **variable** appearing across the columns. Compare *row marginals.*

column sum of squares– Same as *sum of squares for columns.*

combination– A combination is a nonrepeating arrangement or selection of distinguishable elements or objects in which the order is ignored. Thus, the arrangement ABC is the same combination as BCA, CAB, CBA, or ACB. The number of possible combinations, each containing r objects, that can be formed from a set of n distinct objects is given by

$$\binom{n}{r} = \frac{n!}{r!(n-r)!}.$$

community controls– In **case-control studies,** the selection of **controls** from the same population from which **cases** are drawn. The use of community controls is appropriate if the source population is well defined and the cases in the **study sample** are considered representative of all the cases in this population. See also *hospital controls.*

comparative experiment– An **experimental study** designed to make comparisons between a **control group** and one or more **treatment groups.** In a **clinical trial,** the term is synonymous with **phase III trial.**

comparative study– A study designed to make comparisons between one or more groups of subjects.

comparative treatment trial– Same as *phase III trial.*

comparative trial– Same as *controlled trial.*

comparison group– Same as *control group.*

comparisonwise error rate– In a **multiple comparison** procedure, one is concerned with individual comparisons as well as sets of such comparisons. In individual comparisons, the **significance level** is referred to as comparisonwise error rate. See also *experimentwise error rate.*

compatible events– Different **random events** that have at least some basic **outcomes** in common.

complementary event– Same as *complement of an event.*

complement of an event– The complement of an **event** A is the event containing all **sample points** that are not in A. It is an event contrary to the one of interest. It is denoted by $\overline{A}$, A', or A^C.

completely randomized design– An **experimental design** in which the **treatments** are allocated to the **experimental units** randomly without any restriction. This type of design controls **extraneous variables** by creating one **treatment group** for each treatment and assigning each experimental unit to one of these groups by a **random process.** Thus, a completely randomized design assigns the experimental units to the treatments in such a way that any one allocation of experimental units to the treatments is just as probable as any other. See also *block design, blocking, randomized block design.*

compliance– A term used in **clinical trial** to indicate the extent of adherence of patients to the study **protocol.**

component bar chart– A **bar graph** in which each bar is divided into sections proportional in size to the components of the total they represent. The various components are usually colored or shaded to enhance the overall appearance and effectiveness of the graph.

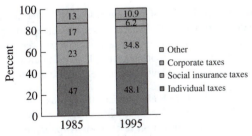

Component bar charts showing percent
distributions for the sources of federal income
for hypothetical data: 1985 and 1995

component bar graph– Same as *component bar chart.*

composite event– Any **event** comprising two or more **basic outcomes.**

composite hypothesis– A **hypothesis** that specifies a range of values for an unknown **parameter**—for example, the hypothesis that the **mean** of a **population** is different than some given value.

composite sampling– A relatively inexpensive method of **sampling** used for items that require an expensive and time-consuming process of **measurements.** For example, to estimate the moisture content of a trainload of corn, one could take a bushel of corn from each wagon, mix these in a blender, and measure the moisture content of the resulting composite sample. In this manner, every part of the trainload can be sampled but only one expensive measurement need to be taken.

compound distribution– A type of **probability distribution** where a **parameter** of the **distribution** is also a **random variable** having a given probability distribution. For example, the **negative binomial distribution** can be expressed as a **Poisson distribution** where the **mean** is a random variable having a **gamma distribution.**

compound event– An **event** that comprises two or more **simple events** that are not necessary **mutually exclusive.**

computational formula– An algebraic formula that is mathematically equivalent to the **definitional formula** and is easier to use for manual computations but does not directly display the meaning of the procedure it symbolizes. Compare *definitional formula.*

computer-aided diagnosis– The use of computers to assist clinicians in approaching the diagnostic task by compiling available **data** and developing a list of one or more diagnostic possibilities. The basic idea behind computer-aided diagnosis is to use the historical data gathered from the clinical study of previously examined patients to determine the likely diagnosis in a new patient exhibiting another set of data on symptoms, signs, or laboratory results. A computer-aided diagnosis thus requires a **mathematical** and **statistical model** and the use of a computer to store, organize, and process vast quantities of information related to symptoms, common clinical findings, and laboratory results. Several mathematical and statistical models have been proposed to assist the computer-aided diagnosis and prognosis. Among the procedures employed are **Bayes' theorem, discriminant analysis, likelihood ratio statistic, logistic regression,** and **numerical taxonomy.**

computer-assisted survey– The use of a computer to aid the interview and **data** collection process during a **survey.** Typically, the computer presents the question text on the screen, along with the available response categories, and the interviewer or respondent answers directly into the computer. The computer can also be used to undertake various forms of data processing at the time of interview, including electronic transfer of data files.

computer-intensive statistical methods– Statistical methods that require recomputing the **test statistic** for many (typically 100 to 5000) artificially constructed **data sets.** Examples of these methods include **randomization tests, bootstrap,** and other **resampling** procedures. However, these methods are very general; for example, practically every **nonparametric procedure** is a special case of one of these methods. Computer-intensive methods are easy to use, do not make the usual assumptions about the data set, and can be used to assess the significance in a **hypothesis test.**

computer package– A set of **computer programs** for storing, retrieving, and analyzing data using commonly used statistical procedures and techniques. Some widely used computer packages are **SAS, SPSS, BMDP,** and **MINITAB,** among others.

computer program– A set of instructions written in a language that a computer can read.

computer simulation– See *Monte Carlo method.*

computer software– Same as *computer package.*

conceptual model– The process of conceiving or defining **outcomes** of a phenomenon on the basis of theoretical considerations.

concordant pairs– See *Kendall's tau.*

concurrent control group– Same as *concurrent controls.*

concurrent controls– In a **clinical trial,** concurrent controls are subjects assigned to a **placebo** or **control group.** The most widely used method of assigning subjects to a **treatment** or control group is to use **random allocation** to determine which treatment each patient receives.

conditional distribution– Same as *conditional probability distribution.*

conditional logistic regression– A type of **logistic regression** used for paired **binary data.** It is commonly used in the analysis of **case-control studies** where **cases** and **controls** have been individually matched.

conditional mean of Y– In a **regression analysis,** the **mean** $\mu_{Y|x}$ of a **conditional probability distribution** of the **dependent variable** Y, for a given value of the **independent variable** X. For example, if two **random variables** X and Y with means μ_1 and μ_2, **variances** σ_1^2 and σ_2^2, and **correlation** ρ have a **bivariate normal distribution,** then the conditional probability distribution of Y given X is normal with mean $\mu_2 + \rho(\sigma_2/\sigma_1)(x - \mu_1)$ and variance $(1 - \rho^2)\sigma_2^2$.

conditional probability– The **probability** of an **event** given that another event has occurred. The conditional probability of A given that another event B has occurred is denoted as $P(A|B)$. It is calculated by the formula $P(A|B) = P(A \cap B))/P(B)$, where $P(A \cap B)$ is the probability of intersection of A and B. The formula assumes that $P(B) > 0$. The conditional probability is a measure of the likelihood that a particular event will occur, given that another event has already occurred. The notion of conditional probability plays a fundamental role in the postulation of **Bayes' theorem.** Compare *unconditional probability.*

conditional probability distribution– In a **bivariate** or **multivariate distribution,** the **probability distribution** of a **random variable** (or the **joint distribution** of several random variables) when the values of one or several other random variables are held constant.

conditional standard deviation– In a **bivariate analysis,** the **standard deviation** of a **conditional probability distribution** of Y given X.

confidence bands– In **regression analysis,** dashed lines on each side of an **estimated regression** line or curve that have a specified **probability** of including the line or curve in the **population.** The confidence bands can be constructed by determining **confidence intervals** for the **regression line** for the entire range of X values. One can then plot the upper and lower **confidence limits** obtained for several specified values of X and sketch the two curves that connect these points. Confidence bands are also known as confidence belts.

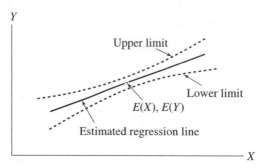

Confidence bands showing how the confidence
intervals for $\mu_{\hat{y}}$ become larger as the distance
between X and $E(X)$ increases

confidence belts– Same as *confidence bands.*

confidence coefficient– The confidence coefficient of a **confidence interval** for a **parameter** is the **probability** that the interval contains the value of the parameter of interest. It is the percentage of intervals (obtained from repeated **samples,** each of size n, taken from a given **population**) that can be expected to include the actual value of the parameter being estimated. For example, if an **interval estimation** procedure yields an interval such that 95% of the time the value of the **population mean** is included within the interval, the **interval estimate** is said to be constructed at the 95% confidence coefficient and 0.95 is referred to as the confidence coefficient.

confidence interval– The interval computed from **sample data** that has a specified **probability** that the unknown **parameter** of interest is contained within the interval. For example, a $1 - \alpha$ confidence interval for an unknown parameter μ is an interval computed from the sample data having the property that, in repeated **sampling,** $100(1 - \alpha)$ percent of the intervals obtained will contain the value μ. Thus, a 95% confidence interval implies that in repeated sampling 95% of the intervals would be expected to contain the true parameter value. It should be noted that the stated probability level refers to the property of the interval in repeated sampling and not to that of the parameter. Some common confidence intervals are 90%, 95%, and 99%. Note that a 99% confidence interval will be wider than the 95% confidence interval, which in turn will be wider than the corresponding 90% confidence interval. The width of a confidence interval is also related to **sample size** and measurement **variability.** The width is decreased by increasing the sample size, but is increased with the increasing variability. Wide confidence intervals reflect considerable uncertainty about the true parameter values and stem from small sample sizes, large variability, and a high **confidence coefficient.** The confidence intervals are very useful in assessing the **practical significance** of a given result.

confidence level– Same as *confidence coefficient.*

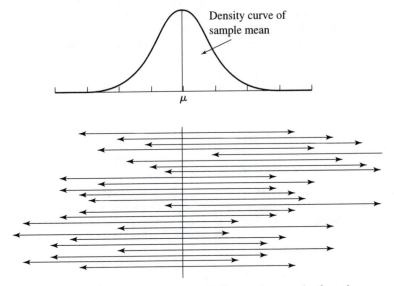

Empirical illustration of confidence intervals: Twenty-five samples from the same population generated these 95% confidence intervals. In the long run, 95% of all samples produce an interval that contains μ

confidence limits– The lower and upper limits of a **confidence interval** that define the interval within which a **population parameter** being estimated presumably lies. These limits are computed from **sample data** and have a known **probability** that the unknown parameter of interest is contained between them.

confirmatory data analysis– A term used to designate statistical procedures of **inferential statistics** in contrast to the methods and techniques of **exploratory data analysis.**

confirmatory factor analysis– See *factor analysis.*

confluent hypergeometric function– The confluent hypergeometric function denoted by $M(\alpha, \beta, x)$ is defined as

$$M(\alpha, \beta, x) = 1 + \frac{\alpha}{\beta.1!}x + \frac{\alpha(\alpha+1)}{\beta(\beta+1).2!}x^2 + \frac{\alpha(\alpha+1)(\alpha+2)}{\beta(\beta+1)(\beta+2).3!}x^3 + \cdots$$

Confluent hypergeometric functions have been found very useful in the solution of many statistical problems.

confounded– A term used to describe an **experiment** or study that has one or more **extraneous variables** present that may lead to biased **estimates** and incorrect interpretations of the results. The term is also used to refer to two or more processes whose separate **effects** cannot be determined.

confounder– Same as *confounding variable.*

confounding– A term used to describe a condition in a **factorial design** where certain comparisons can be made only for **treatments** in combinations and not for separate treatments; for example, **main effects** and **interactions** cannot be estimated separately. This is so since the **contrast** that measures one of the effects is exactly the same that measures the other. The two effects that are **confounded** are usually referred to as **aliases.** In **epidemiology,** the term is used to refer to **bias** arising from comparing groups that are different with regard to important **risk** or **prognostic factors** other than the **factor** under investigation. For example, in comparing the **incidence** of heart disease between smokers and nonsmokers any observed difference between the two groups could well be due to one group being older than the other. Here, age is acting as a **confounder** and the effect of smoking on heart disease cannot be properly assessed, as a result of important age differences between the two groups.

confounding factor– Same as *confounding variable.*

confounding variable– A **variable** more likely to be present in one group of subjects than another that is related to the **outcome** of interest and thus potentially confuses or "confounds" the results. A confounding variable is associated with both **treatment** and outcome and can affect both. The term is generally used in the context of epidemiologic and other **observational studies.**

confounding variate– Same as *confounding variable.*

congruential method– A method for generating **random numbers** based on a congruence relationship. Although the method is found to generate a good sequence of random numbers with satisfactory statistical properties, in certain cases its behavior is too erratic.

Conover test– A **nonparametric test** procedure for testing the equality of **variances** of two **populations** having different **medians.** The test has rather a low **power;** its **asymptotic relative efficiency** compared to the traditional F **test** for **normal distribution** is only 76 percent, which is slightly higher than the Siegel-Tukey efficiency measure of 0.61. See also *Ansari-Bradley test, Barton-David test, F test for two population variances, Klotz test, Mood test, Rosenbaum test, Siegel-Tukey test.*

conservative confidence interval– A term used to describe a **confidence interval** in which the actual **confidence coefficient** exceeds the nominal or stated level.

conservative test– A term used to describe a **statistical test** in which the **probability** of a **Type I error** is smaller than the nominal or stated level. Conservative tests are often preferred when only **approximate tests** are available. See also *exact test, liberal test.*

consistency– A term used to describe the property of a **consistent estimator.**

consistency checks– A term sometimes used to describe the checks being performed to assess the internal consistency of a set of **observations** in a **database.**

consistent estimator– A **sample estimator** or **statistic** such that the **probability** of its being close to the **parameter** being estimated gets ever larger (and, therefore, approaches unity) as the **sample size** increases. A consistent estimator is said to converge in probability, as the sample size increases, to the parameter being estimated.

consistent test– A test of a **hypothesis** is said to be consistent with respect to a particular **alternative hypothesis** if the **power** of the test approaches unity as the **sample size** tends to infinity.

constant– A mathematical term or a value that does not change; that is, it remains the same for all units of analysis. There are the universal mathematical constants such as π and e, and the so-called physical constants such as the velocity of light. The opposite of a constant is **variable.**

consumer price index– An **index number** designed to measure the **variations** in prices of the goods and services. It includes changes in prices of a fixed market basket of hundred of goods and services, including such items as milk, lettuce, rent, and doctor's visit, among others. The index is compiled by the U.S. Bureau of Labor Statistics and is based on about 125,000 monthly quotation prices.

contingency– A chance occurrence, i.e., an **event** incidental to another. In a **contingency table,** it is the difference between the **observed frequency** and the **expected frequency** under the assumption that the two characteristics are independent.

contingency coefficient– In a **contingency table,** a measure of the strength of the **association** between two **categorical** or **qualitative variables.** The contingency coefficient is a function of the **chi-square statistic** and is never negative, but has a maximum value less than one. It is calculated by the formula

$$C = \sqrt{\frac{\chi^2}{n + \chi^2}}$$

where χ^2 is the usual chi-square statistic for testing the **independence** of the two **variables** and n is the **sample size.** See also *phi (ϕ) coefficient, Sakoda coefficient, Tschuprov coefficient.*

contingency table– A contingency table is a table that cross-classifies **bivariate data** where two **variables** are **nominal** or **categorical.** The **cells** in the table contain the **observed frequencies** of the combinations of the **levels** of two variables. The cells are mutually exclusive where each **observation** can be included in one and only one of the cells. In general, a contingency table classifies **data** according to two or more categories associated with each of two **qualitative variables.** For example, if the characteristic A is r-fold and the characteristic B is c-fold, the contingency table will have r rows and c columns. It is then often called an $r \times c$ contingency table, or simply an $r \times c$ table. The objective of an analysis of a contingency table is to determine whether two directions of classifications are dependent on each other.

Column / Row	1	2	...	c	Row totals
1	n_{11}	n_{12}	...	n_{1c}	n_1
2	n_{21}	n_{22}	...	n_{2c}	n_2
$\vdots$	$\vdots$	$\vdots$		$\vdots$	$\vdots$
r	n_{r1}	n_{r2}	...	n_{rc}	n_r
Column totals	$n_{.1}$	$n_{.2}$	...	$n_{.c}$	n

General $r \times c$ contingency table

contingency table analysis– Methods and techniques for analyzing relationships between **categorical variables** forming a **contingency table** using the familiar **chi-square test.** Three- and higher-dimensional tables are analyzed by using **log-linear models** and related procedures.

continuity correction– Same as *correction for continuity.*

continuous data– **Data** obtained on measures of a **continuous variable,** i.e., using interval and ratio **scales of measurement.** See also *discrete data, nominal data, numerical data, qualitative data.*

continuous distribution– Same as *continuous probability distribution.*

continuous probability distribution– It is the **probability distribution** of a **continuous random variable.** A continuous probability distribution is represented by a continuous function called a **probability density function.** Compare *discrete probability distribution.*

continuous quantitative variable– Same as *continuous variable.*

continuous scale– A scale used to measure a numerical characteristic with values that occur on an entire continuum.

continuous stochastic process– See *stochastic process.*

continuous (random) variable– A **(random) variable** that can theoretically assume any real value between the two points on a **measurement scale** with no gaps or spaces between possible values. When recording an **observation** on a continuous variable, it is not restricted to a particular value, except by the accuracy of the **measurement,** and a refinement of the measuring instrument yields a more precise observation. Some examples of continuous variables are height and weight. See also *categorical variable, discrete variable, ordinal variable.*

inches

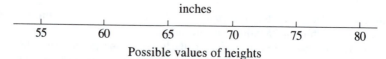

Possible values of heights

Illustration of a continuous random variable

contrast (in population means)– A **linear combination** of the **population means** such that the **coefficients** of the population means sum to zero. Thus, the statement that

$$\sum_{i=1}^{k} \ell_i \mu_i = \ell_1 \mu_1 + \ell_2 \mu_2 + \cdots + \ell_k \mu_k$$

is a contrast in the k populations means $\mu_1, \mu_2, \ldots, \mu_k$ if the ℓ_i's sum to zero; that is, if

$$\sum_{i=1}^{k} \ell_i = \ell_1 + \ell_2 + \cdots + \ell_k = 0$$

Two such contrasts are said to be orthogonal if the sum of the pairwise products of their coefficients is equal to zero. Contrasts are used in making **post-hoc comparisons** of population means.

contrast (in sample means)– A **linear combination** of the **sample means** such that the **coefficients** of the sample means sum to zero. Thus, the statement that

$$\sum_{i=1}^{k} \ell_i \bar{x}_i = \ell_1 \bar{x}_1 + \ell_2 \bar{x}_2 + \cdots + \ell_k \bar{x}_k$$

is a contrast in the k sample means $\bar{x}_1, \bar{x}_2, \ldots, \bar{x}_k$ if the ℓ_i's sum to zero; that is, if

$$\sum_{i=1}^{k} \ell_i = \ell_1 + \ell_2 + \cdots + \ell_k = 0$$

Two such contrasts are said to be orthogonal if the sum of the pairwise products of their coefficients is equal to zero.

control– In a **case-control study,** the term is used to refer to an individual who does not have the disease or condition of interest. In a **clinical trial,** the term is used for a subject assigned to the **placebo** or **control condition.** See also *control group.*

control charts– **Graphs** that highlight the **average** performance values and the **variation** around this average so that average and variation of the past become standards for controlling performance in the present. A control chart is made up of three horizontal lines; one, called the center line, is drawn at the **mean** value, and the other two, called action lines or control lines, are drawn at appropriate and equal distance above and below the center line. The center line corresponds to the mean value of the characteristic under investigation. Control charts are used to decide whether a process is in statistical control. The process is judged to be "in control" as long as the plotted points lie between the two lines, and is considered "out of control" if any one of the points falls outside the control limits. Central to the idea of a control chart is the concept of **variance.** Walter Shewhart, an engineer working at Bell Laboratories, devised control charts. See also *c-chart, p-chart, R-chart, run chart, statistical quality control, x-bar chart.*

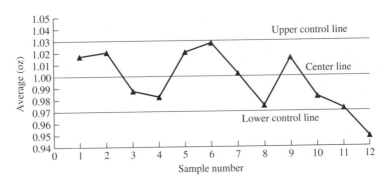

Figure showing a control chart

control condition– Placebo or any other standard **treatment** assigned to a **control group.**

control group– The subjects in an experiment that do not receive an **intervention.** In a **clinical trial,** these are subjects assigned to the **placebo** or any other **control condition.** A control group can be concurrent or historical, depending on whether subjects are investigated concurrently or taken from some historical records. In crossover trials, there is usually a single group of subjects where each individual acts as its own control. In a **case-control study,** the subjects without the disease or outcome are called a control group. See also *community controls, controlled clinical trial, crossover study, historical controls, hospital controls.*

controlled (for)– A term used to describe an extraneous **factor** or **variate** that is adjusted for its **confounding** effect either in the design or the analysis of the study.

controlled clinical trial– A **phase III clinical trial** in which subjects are allocated to a **control group** as well as to an experimental **treatment group.** A control group may be either the current standard **treatment** or a **placebo.** The most widely used method of unbiased treatment allocation is to use **random allocation** to determine which treatment each patient receives. Controlled trials provide direct comparison between the treatment and control groups. See also *clinical trial, phase I trial, phase II trial, phase III trial, phase IV trial, randomized controlled clinical trial.*

controlled trial– Same as *controlled clinical trial.*

control lines– See *control charts.*

controls– Same as *control group.*

control subjects– Same as *control group.*

control treatment– The **placebo** or any other **control condition** being assigned to the **control group.**

control variable– Same as *covariate.*

convenience sample– A **sample** selected in such a manner that convenience and expediency is the main consideration in selecting **elementary units** for **observation,** and usually the most easily accessible units are taken in the study. Some examples of convenience samples are workers in an office, houses in block, a group of people interviewed on a street corner, or the top items in a carton. Since **probability theory** is not employed in drawing a convenience sample, **standard errors** of the **sample estimates** cannot be determined. See also *judgment sample, nonprobability sample, probability sample, random sample.*

convenience sampling– See *convenience sample.*

conventional levels of significance– The **levels of significance** ($p < 0.05, p < 0.01$) that are widely used in scientific research and other statistical applications.

convolution– A mathematical procedure used to determine the **probability distribution** of the sum of two or more **random variables.**

Cook's distance– A diagnostic measure commonly used in **regression analysis** to detect the presence of an **outlier.** It is designed to measure the shift (change) in the estimated **parameter** values from fitting a **regression model** when a particular **observation** is omitted. The values of measure greater than 1 suggest the undue influence of the observation on the corresponding **regression coefficients.** See also *DFBETA, DFFIT.*

cooperative clinical trial– Same as *multicenter clinical trial.*

corner test– A **graphical procedure** designed to measure the **association** between two **variables.** The procedure involves drawing a **scatter plot** for the pairs of **observations,** and dividing it into four quadrants by lines parallel to x and y **axes,** passing through the

medians of the **bivariate data sets.** The **test statistic** is based on the outlying members in each quadrant.

corrected chi-square test– A **chi-square test** for a 2×2 **table** that uses **Yates' correction for continuity.** The corrected test, however, results in a more **conservative test.**

correction for continuity– When a **statistic** is discrete, but its **distribution** is being approximated by a **continuous distribution** (such as the **normal distribution**), **probabilities** can sometimes be more accurately obtained by using the tables of the continuous distribution, not with the actual values of the statistic, but with slightly corrected values. The corrected values are obtained generally by adding or subtracting a value $\frac{1}{2}$. The correction is known as 'correction for continuity.' See also *Yates' correction for continuity.*

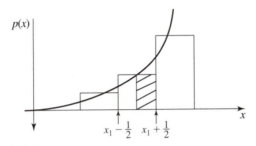

Schematic diagram illustrating correction for continuity

correlated groups– Same as *dependent groups.*

correlated samples– Same as *dependent samples.*

correlated samples *t* test– Same as *paired t test.*

correlation– A general term denoting **association** or relationship between two or more **variables.** More generally, it is the extent or degree to which two or more quantities are associated or related. It is measured by an index called **correlation coefficient.** See also *intraclass correlation, Kendall's rank correlation, Spearman's rank correlation.*

correlation analysis– A technique for measuring the **association** or relationship between sets of **data** involving two or more **variables.** When the two sets of scores increase and decrease simultaneously (or vary directly), the variables are said to be positively correlated. Conversely, when the sets of scores change in opposite directions so that one set decreases as the other set increases (or vary inversely), the variables are said to be negatively correlated. See also *correlation, correlation coefficient.*

correlation coefficient– A numerical measure of the **linear relationship** between two sets of **measurements** made on the same set of subjects. It is also known as the Pearson product moment correlation coefficient. It is denoted by the letter r and its value ranges from -1 to $+1$. A value of $+1$ denotes that two sets are perfectly related in a positive sense and a value of -1 indicates that two sets are perfectly related in a negative sense. A value close to zero indicates that they are not linearly related. See also *rank correlation coefficient.*

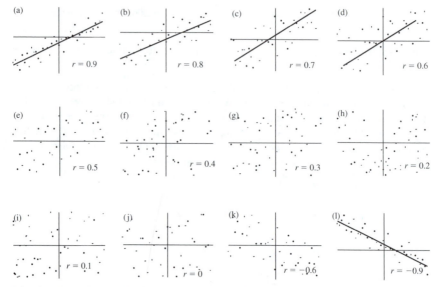

Bivariate data with correlation coefficient r of various magnitudes

correlation difference test– A **statistical test** for testing the **hypothesis** concerning the difference between two **population correlation coefficients.**

correlation for attenuation– Same as *attenuation.*

correlation matrix– A square array that represents all pairs of **correlations** of a set of **random variables.** The correlation matrix is a **square matrix** with as many rows as columns. Each **cell** of the **matrix** is occupied by a **correlation coefficient** between the **variables** represented by the particular row and column that the cell occupies. The element r_{ij} of the matrix is the correlation coefficient between the variables x_i and x_j. The diagonal elements, those going from the upper left-hand corner to the lower right-hand corner of the matrix, are each equal to 1, i.e., $r_{ii} = 1$ for all i. Moreover, the correlation matrix is symmetrical about the diagonal, i.e., $r_{ij} = r_{ji}$ for $i \neq j$.

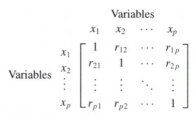

Correlation matrix

correlation ratio– Same as *eta.*

correlation research– Studies that do not control and manipulate **variables.** Correlation research examines the covariation among variables.

correlogram– A plot of the **sample values** of the **autocorrelation** against the lag.

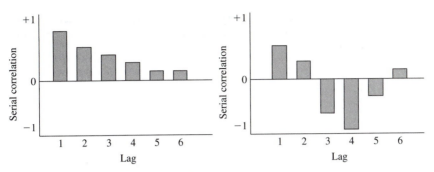

Sample correlograms of the serial correlation coefficient

correspondence analysis– A **multivariate statistical technique** used to describe the relationship between two **variables** measured on a **nominal scale.** The method uses a set of coordinate values to represent the rows and columns of a **contingency table** and thus allows the **association** in the table to be displayed graphically. For each variable, the distance between category points in a plot reflects the relationship between categories with similar ones plotted in proximity to each other. The horizontal and vertical coordinates are analogous to those derived from **principal components analysis.** The technique, however, differs from principal components analysis in that it involves a partition of a **chi-square statistic** rather than the total **variance.**

cost–benefit analysis– An economic analysis in which costs and benefits of various alternative decisions and actions (treatments/interventions/procedures, etc.) and the associated risks and uncertainties (loss of net earnings due to illness, death or disabilities, etc.) are evaluated. The preferred action is one that provides the greatest benefit for a given cost or requires the least cost for a given level of benefit.

cost–effectiveness analysis– An economic analysis of costs and effectiveness of alternative decisions and actions.

cost–minimization analysis– An economic analysis of the costs and outcomes of alternative actions when these actions can be shown to have comparable results or impact.

cost–utility analysis– An economic analysis of costs and outcomes of alternative actions in which outcomes are measured in terms of their personal or social utility.

count data– Data relating to **frequency counts** of occurrences of certain **random events** or phenomena in contrast to **continuous data** that are obtained by taking **measurements** on some scale. Count data arise frequently in demographic **sampling,** in **survey research,** in learning experiments, and in almost every other branch of social, engineering, and life sciences.

covariance– The first product moment of two **variables** about their **mean** values. It is calculated as the sum of the product of **deviations** of the x's and y's about their respective means divided by $n - 1$ in a **sample** and N in the **population.** It is a measure of the joint **variance** of two variables. It ranges from $-\infty$ to $+\infty$. A positive value indicates that two variables are directly related and a negative value indicates that they are inversely related. See also *correlation, covariance matrix, sample covariance.*

covariance matrix– A square array that represents all pairs of **covariances** of a set of **random variables.** A covariance matrix is a **square matrix** in which main diagonal elements represent **variances** of the **variables** and off-diagonal elements are the covariances. Moreover, like the **correlation matrix,** a covariance matrix is also symmetrical about the diagonal.

$$
\begin{array}{c}
\text{Variables}\\
\begin{array}{cccc}
x_1 & x_2 & \cdots & x_p
\end{array}\\
\text{Variables}\;
\begin{array}{c}
x_1\\ x_2\\ \vdots\\ x_p
\end{array}
\left[
\begin{array}{cccc}
\sigma_1^2 & \sigma_{12} & \cdots & \sigma_{1p}\\
\sigma_{21} & \sigma_2^2 & \cdots & \sigma_{2p}\\
\vdots & \vdots & \ddots & \vdots\\
\sigma_{p1} & \sigma_{p2} & \cdots & \sigma_p^2
\end{array}
\right]
\end{array}
$$

Covariance matrix

covariance structure model– Same as *structural equation model.*

covariate– The term used for a **confounding variate** as a source of possible explanation of **variation** in the **dependent variable.** This is a **variable** that the researcher seeks to control by use of techniques such as **analysis of covariance** and **regression.** The value of a covariate is held constant in an analysis in order to observe its **effect** on the original **association** between two or more variables. The term is also used simply as an alternative name for an **explanatory variable.** It is also sometimes employed to refer to a variable that is not of primary interest in an investigation but is thought to be related to the **response variable** of interest and probably should be taken into account in any analysis and **model building.** It is also known as a control variable.

covariation– Joint variation in **observations** involving a **bivariate data set.** See also *covariance.*

Cox regression– Same as *proportional hazards regression.*

Cox–Mantel test– A **nonparametric statistical test** for comparing two **survival curves.** If the survival experience of the two groups is the same, then the **test statistic** can be approximated by a **standard normal distribution.**

Cramér–Rao inequality– An inequality giving a lower bound of the **variance** of any **unbiased estimator** of a **parameter** θ, or more generally a given parametric function $g(\theta)$, in the **probability density function** $f(x, \theta)$ of the observed **random variable.** The inequality states that

$$
\text{Var }(T) \geq \frac{[g'(\theta)]^2}{nE\left[\left(\dfrac{\partial}{\partial\theta}\log_e f(x,\theta)\right)^2\right]}
$$

where T is an unbiased estimator of $g(\theta)$, $g'(\theta)$ is the derivative of $g(\theta)$ with respect to θ, and n is the **sample size.**

Cramér–Rao lower bound– See *Cramér–Rao inequality.*

Cramér's V– Same as *Cramer's V coefficient.*

Cramér's V coefficient– A **measure of the association** or relationship between two **nominal** or **categorical variables** whose **data** are cross-classified in a 2×2 or higher-order

contingency table. It is based on the usual **chi-square statistic** for testing the **independence** and is calculated by the formula

$$V = \sqrt{\frac{\chi^2}{n \times \min(r-1, c-1)}}$$

where χ^2 is the usual chi-square statistic, r and c are the number of rows and columns of the table and n is the **sample size.** It is related to the **phi coefficient** by the formula, $V = \phi / \sqrt{\min(r-1, c-1)}$.

Cramér–von Mises statistic– A **goodness-of-fit statistic** for testing the **hypothesis** that the **cumulative distribution** of a **random variable** has a specified form. It was proposed by Harold Cramér in 1928 and independently by von Mises in 1931.

Cramér–von Mises test– A test of **normality** based on **order statistics** from **sample data.** See also *Anderson–Darling test, D'Agostino's test, Michael's test, Shapiro–Francia test, Shapiro–Wilk W test.*

criterion variable– The **dependent variable** that is being predicted in a **regression analysis.** In such usage the **independent variable** is known as the **predictor variable.**

critical bounds– Same as *critical values.*

critical ratio– The term for the z or t **score** and other **test statistics** that define the **critical region** of a **statistical test.**

critical region– In **hypothesis testing,** the range of possible values of the area in the **sampling distribution** of a **test statistic** that leads to rejection of the **null hypothesis.** It is also known as the rejection region. The value of the test statistic must fall in this region in order for the null hypothesis to be rejected. Compare **region of acceptance.**

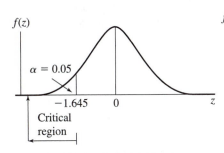 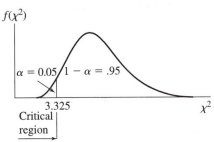

Examples of left-tailed critical regions

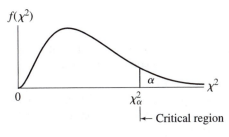 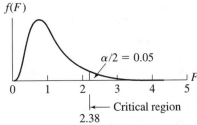

Examples of right-tailed critical regions

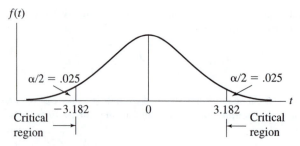

Example of a two-tailed critical region

critical value– The theoretical value of a **test statistic** that leads to rejection of the **null hypothesis** at a given **level of significance.** It provides a cut off point for the **region of rejection** and the **region of acceptance** of the null hypothesis. Thus, in a **statistical test,** the critical value divides the rejection and the acceptance regions. The **decision rule** for the test can be stated in terms of the critical value or values. The critical value is related to the level of significance chosen.

Cronbach's alpha– A measure of **reliability** or internal consistency of the items or **variables** in a composite index developed on a summation scale. For binary test items, it is calculated by the formula

$$\alpha = \frac{n}{n-1} \left[1 - \frac{1}{\sigma^2} \sum_{j=1}^{n} \sigma_j^2 \right]$$

where n is the number of items, σ^2 is the **variance** of the total score, and σ_j^2 is the variance of binary score (0 or 1) on item j. It is commonly used to measure the reliability of multiple item scales employed in psychological and mental health tests. A multiple item instrument is internally consistent if its items are highly intercorrelated, and Cronbach's alpha measures this internal consistency.

crossbreak table– Same as *cross-tabulation.*

cross-classification– Same as *cross-tabulation.*

crossed model– An **analysis of variance** model in which the **levels** of one or more **factors** cut across the levels of one or more other factors. Compare *crossed-nested model, nested model.*

crossed-nested model– An **analysis of variance** model in which the **levels** of some **factors** are crossed while of some other factors are nested. Compare *crossed model, nested model.*

crossover design– See *crossover study.*

crossover rate– The **proportion** or percent of subjects who switch over from the **treatment** to which they were initially allocated to the alternative treatment. See also **crossovers, intention-to-treat analysis.**

crossovers– In **clinical trials,** the term is used for patients who, for some reason, do not take or receive the **treatment** to which they were allocated, but instead take or receive the alternate treatment. See also *intention-to-treat analysis.*

crossover study– A **study design** in which patients act as their own **controls** by receiving both the **treatment** being assessed and the **control treatment** in an alternate random sequence. The study uses two groups of subjects where one group is assigned to **experimental treatment** and the other to **placebo** or **control group.** After a certain period of time, both groups are withdrawn for a waiting or **washout period** without receiving any treatment. After the washout period, the **experimental group** receives the placebo and the control group receives the experimental treatment. The analysis of a crossover design is complicated because of the possibility of **carryover effects,** that is, the residual effects of the treatment administered on the first occasion that may remain present into the second occasion. Thus, it is important to introduce appropriate washout periods. In the presence of a strong **treatment period interaction,** the data for the second period are usually discarded, resulting in a **parallel design** trial lacking in sufficient **power.** The use of this type of design is not recommended if there is the possibility of strong carryover effects. In addition, this type of design is not appropriate for studies involving acute conditions or when treatment periods are too long, since patients are prone to drop out.

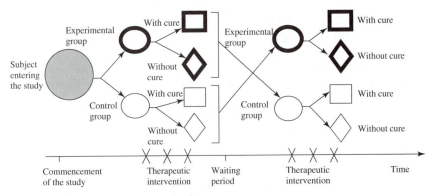

Schematic diagram of a crossover study

crossover trial– Same as *crossover study.*

cross-product ratio– Same as *odds ratio.*

cross ratio– An abbreviated form for the cross-product ratio.

cross-sectional data– **Data** relating to units of different subjects that have been observed simultaneously at a particular point in time or during a particular period of time. See also *cross-sectional study.*

cross-sectional design– See *cross-sectional study.*

cross-sectional study– An **observational study** that explores the characteristics of interest in a group of subjects at a single point in time. In contrast to a **follow-up study,** a cross-sectional study gathers data on subjects on just one occasion. A cross-sectional study provides a "snapshot" of the characteristics or conditions of interest. In epidemiological studies, a cross-sectional design yields **estimates** of **prevalence** rather than **incidence.** A cross-sectional study offers only indirect evidence about the effects of time and must be interpreted with extreme caution concerning any inference regarding change. However, such a study may be suggestive of an **association** that should be investigated more thoroughly later, say, by a **prospective** or **retrospective study.** It is also called a **survey** or **poll** in social science research. Some common problems with this type of study are the selection of an adequate **sampling design** and **nonresponse** and **volunteer bias.** See also cross-sectional data.

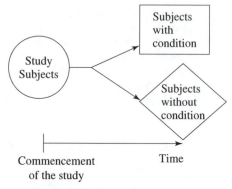

Schematic diagram of a cross-sectional study

cross-section series– A series that relates to different things or places at the same time, as distinct from a **time series** which relates to the same thing or place at different times.

cross-tabulation– A **frequency table** involving at least two **variables** that have been cross-classified. It is a way of presenting **data** about two variables in a table so that their relations are more clearly understood. It is also called a **contingency table** or crossbreak table. See also *cross-tabulation analysis.*

cross-tabulation analysis– Analysis of **data sets** involving two or more **qualitative variables** by cross-classifying in the form of **contingency tables.** See also *cross-tabulation.*

cross-validation– A procedure for applying the results of statistical analysis from one **sample** of subjects to a new sample of subjects in order to assess the **reliability** of the estimated **parameters.** It is frequently used in **regression** and other **multivariate statistical procedures.**

crude annual death rate– Same as *crude death rate.*

crude birth rate– Same as *birth rate.*

crude death rate– A measure or **rate** of **mortality** in which no adjustments are made to take into account social, demographic, economic, or other factors that may contribute to mortality. It is calculated as the number of deaths actually observed divided by the population of the region as estimated at the middle of particular time period, usually the calendar year (expressed per 100,000 of population). See also *age-specific death rate, cause-specific death rate, standardized mortality rate.*

crude estimates– A term used for **estimates** obtained from a **study population** without taking into account the **effects** of **confounding factors.** If the study involves some strong confounding effects, then the results obtained from the crude estimates will be biased and must be adjusted for the effects of confounding factors.

crude mortality rate– Same as *crude death rate.*

crude rate– A **rate** for the total population that is not specific for any given segment of the population or adjusted to take into account other factors. If different populations have different age structures, a direct comparison of crude rates will be biased if age is not taken into account.

cumulant generating function– The function $\Psi_X(t) = \log_e \phi_X(t)$ is known as the cumulant generating function, where $\phi_X(t)$ is the **characteristic function** of a **random variable** X. If $\Psi_X(t)$ is expressed as a power series in t, the coefficient of $(it)^k/k!$ gives the kth cumulant of X. See also *moment generating function*.

cumulants– The cumulants of a **probability distribution** are defined by the following identity in t:

$$\exp\left(\sum_{r=1}^{\infty} \frac{\kappa_r t^r}{r!}\right) = \sum_{r=0}^{\infty} \frac{\mu'_r t^r}{r!}$$

where κ_r is the rth cumulant and μ'_r is the rth **moment about the origin**. Like **moments**, cumulants are used to characterize the **distribution** of a **random variable**. However, cumulants have certain mathematical properties that make them more useful for theoretical work.

cumulative class frequency– The number of **observations** belonging to a particular class or the ones below it. It is obtained by summing all the **frequencies** (absolute or relative) of previous classes including the class in question. See also *absolute class frequency, cumulative frequency*.

cumulative distribution– Same as *distribution function*.

cumulative distribution function– Same as *distribution function*.

cumulative frequency– For a given **value** or **outcome,** the total number of cases in a **data set** that are less than or equal to that value. See also *cumulative class frequency*.

cumulative frequency distribution– A **tabular representation** of a **frequency distribution** that shows the total number of **data values** with a value less than or equal to the real upper limit for the class. See also *cumulative relative frequency distribution*.

Cumulative frequency/percentage distribution for student grades: hypothetical data

Class	Frequency	Cumulative Frequency	Cumulative Percentage
50–54	4	4	4.0
55–59	8	12	12.0
60–64	11	23	23.0
65–69	20	43	43.0
70–74	18	61	61.0
75–79	15	76	76.0
80–84	11	87	87.0
85–89	6	93	93.0
90–94	5	98	98.0
95–99	2	100	100.0

cumulative frequency polygon– A **frequency polygon** expressed in terms of the **cumulative class frequency.** At the right-hand endpoint of each **class interval,** at a height equal to the cumulative class frequency of that interval, a dot is placed on a graph. Then the successive dots or points are joined by straight-line segments to form the cumulative frequency polygon. The term is more or less synonymous with **ogive curve.**

cumulative hazard– In **survival analysis,** the **risk** of an **event** over a specified period of time.

cumulative meta-analysis– A special type of **meta-analysis** which combines the results from individual studies, as these studies are carried out and the results gradually become available.

cumulative percentage– See *cumulative relative frequency.*

cumulative percentage distribution– See *cumulative relative frequency distribution.*

cumulative probability distribution– A **probability distribution** that shows the **probability** of a **random variable** being less than or equal to any given value of the random variable.

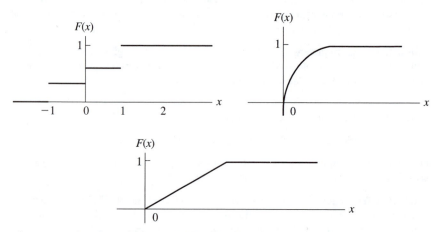

Some examples of cumulative probability distributions

cumulative relative class frequency– The **cumulative class frequency** expressed as a **proportion** or percentage of the total number of values.

cumulative relative frequency– The **cumulative frequency** expressed as a **proportion** or percentage of the total number of values.

cumulative relative frequency distribution– A **cumulative frequency distribution** expressed in terms of **proportions** or percentages of **cumulative relative frequency.**

cumulative relative frequency polygon– A **cumulative frequency polygon** expressed in terms of the **cumulative relative class frequency.**

Current Population Survey– The **sample survey** conducted annually by the **U.S. Bureau of the Census** to obtain estimates of income, employment, and other characteristics of the general labor force and of the population as a whole or of various subgroups of the population. The survey is based on about 60,000 households, which are sampled by a complex multistage stratified cluster design.

curvilinear regression– Same as *nonlinear regression.*

curvilinear relationship– A relationship between two variables that forms a curve rather than a straight line.

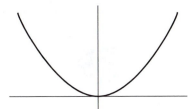

Figure showing a curvilinear relationship

cutoff level– Same as *significance level.*

cutoff point– See *critical value.*

cycle– A term used in **time-series analysis** to denote the period of the series resulting in one complete up-and-down and down-and-up movement. See also *cyclical component, trend.*

cycle plot– A method of **graphical representation** for investigating the behavior of a seasonal **time series.** It provides a powerful visual aid for assessing the overall pattern of the seasonal change.

cyclical component– In a **time-series analysis,** up-and-down fluctuations of the **variable** of interest around the **trend,** with the swings lasting from one to several years each and typically of different length and amplitude from one to the next. These are long-term periodic **variations** caused by forces generating a **business cycle,** as distinct from **seasonal components.** There are a number of statistical procedures currently available for estimating cyclical components. See also *cycle, time series.*

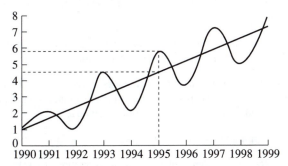

Figure showing a cyclical component in a time series: hypothetical data

cyclical fluctuation– Same as *cyclical component.*

cyclical variation– Same as *cyclical component.*

D

D'Agostino's test– A test of **normality** based on **order statistics** from **sample data.** It is a modification of the **Shapiro–Wilk W test,** and it is readily calculated without the **coefficients** of the order statistics. It is based on the **ratio** of a linear **unbiased estimator** of the **standard deviation** (using order statistics) to the usual mean square estimator. The test was originally proposed for moderate **sample sizes** and can detect departures from normality both for **skewness** and **kurtosis.** See also *Anderson–Darling test, Cramér–von Mises test, Michael's test, Shapiro–Francia test.*

Darling test– A test that a **random sample** is drawn from an **exponential distribution.**

data– Numerical **observations** collected in some systematic manner by assigning numbers or **scores** to **outcomes** of a **variable(s).** The term "data" is a plural form of "datum" and usually takes a plural verb. Sometimes the word is used informally as a synonym for "information."

data analysis– Usually, the process of reducing accumulated **data** to a manageable size, developing summaries, looking for patterns, and performing statistical analysis.

Database– A structured collection of information comprising numeric and nonnumeric values about any topic that can be used for storage, modification, editing, and retrieval, and can be readily accessed by a variety of applications **software.**

data dependent stopping rule– Same as *stopping rule.*

data editing– A term used to denote the process of correcting any **errors** from **data** or modifying the data structure.

data elements– The items of information extracted for some statistical purposes, e.g., sex and age.

data matrix– A **rectangular array** that represents a collection of **measurements** taken on several **variables** for a number of subjects. Let x_{ij} be the **observation** corresponding to the *i*th individual and the *j*th variable. Then the data matrix is displayed in the form

$$\begin{bmatrix} x_{11} & x_{12} & \cdots & x_{1p} \\ x_{21} & x_{22} & \cdots & x_{2p} \\ \vdots & \vdots & \vdots & \vdots \\ x_{n1} & x_{n2} & \cdots & x_{np} \end{bmatrix}$$

Data matrix

where *n* is the number of subjects and *p* is the number of variables.

data mining– The term used to describe the concepts of discovering knowledge from **databases.** The idea behind data mining is to identify valid, useful, and recognizable patterns in **data.**

data points– Same as *data values.*

data reduction– The process of summarizing a large quantity of **data** by means of **tables, charts,** and **descriptive statistics.**

data screening– An initial examination of a **data set** to check for any **errors** or discrepancies in the **data.** The technique is also useful for checking the quality of the data and identifying any possible **outliers.** See also *exploratory data analysis, initial data analysis.*

data set– A collection of **observations** about one or more characteristics of interest, for one or more **elementary units** during any type of scientific investigation. A general term used to refer to any set of observations.

data transformation– The use of algebraic **transformation** on the **data values** in order to make them appear more normally distributed and make the **variances** of the **error terms** constant. Data transformations are used to correct for the violations of **assumptions** of a statistical procedure. Conclusions derived from the statistical analyses performed on the transformed data are generally applicable to the original data. See also *arc-sine transformation, logarithmic transformation, power transformation, reciprocal transformation, square-root transformation, square transformation.*

data validation– See *validity checks.*

data values– The values assigned to all the **observations** in a **data set.**

datum– A single numerical **observation** about a particular characteristic of interest measured on an **elementary unit.**

death rate– Same as *crude death rate.*

deciles– The deciles divide a **data set** into 10 equal parts, each of which contains 10% of the total **observations.** The **percentile points** at the 10th, 20th, 30th, ..., and 90th **percentiles** are called the first decile (D_1), second decile (D_2), third decile (D_3), ..., and ninth decile (D_9), respectively. See also *quartiles.*

The data arranged in increasing order of magnitude

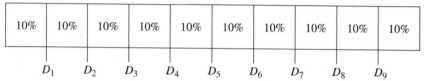

Schematic representation of deciles of a data set

decision analysis– A formal and systematic procedure for describing and analyzing a process for making a decision by **ranking** several possible mutually exclusive courses of actions in order of merit, in accordance with some criterion such as profitability, and in choosing one of them. An important concept in decision analysis is that of decision maker's **payoff,** i.e., of the relative value of each **outcome.** It is commonly known as decision making. A decision analysis is usually carried out with the help of a **decision tree.**

decision branches– Same as *action branches.*

decision fork– Same as *action point.*

decision making– See *decision analysis.*

decision-making under uncertainty– Any situation in which the ultimate **outcome** of a decision maker's choice depends on **chance.**

decision node– Same as *action point.*

decision point– Same as *action point.*

decision rule– In **hypothesis testing,** a decision rule states the values of the **test statistic** at which the **null hypothesis** is to be rejected or not rejected. For all possible values of a test statistic, a decision rule specifies in advance when the null hypothesis should be rejected or not rejected.

decision theory– A variety of quantitative methods and techniques employed in the formulation, analysis, and solution of decision-making problems that arise because **uncertainty** exists about future course of **events** over which the decision maker has no control, but which will affect the ultimate **outcome** of a decision. It is based on the concept of forming a decision as to what action to take for each possible outcome. Statistical decision theory was introduced by Abraham Wald in 1939 as a generalization of the classical statistical theories of **estimation** and **hypothesis testing.** It has extended the scope of **statistics** to embrace the science of **decision-making under uncertainty.** It provides a unified approach to all problems of estimation, hypothesis testing, and **prediction.**

decision tree– A **graphical representation** of a set of possible **actions,** their corresponding **probabilities,** and the values of the **outcomes** as foreseen by the decision maker. It shows graphically in chronological order from left to right every potential action, outcome, and **payoff.** It is used to analyze a decision process and gives a concise summary of a **decision-making** situation under **uncertainty.** The analysis is carried out by starting from the outcomes and working back to the expected payoffs of different courses. Different possible courses of actions represented by squares and circles show the resulting outcomes. The expected payoff is attached to each one of the outcomes. The probabilities of the different outcomes are calculated from the historical data and are shown on the branches of the tree. To give an example of a decision tree, consider a hypothetical case where a physician must choose between two courses of action—surgery and no surgery. The patient is known to have one of two diseases, *A* or *B*, with a probability of 0.3 and 0.7, respectively. A simple decision tree for this problem is depicted below.

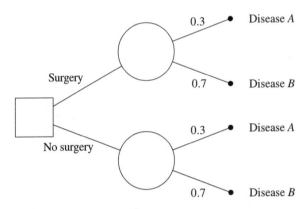

Illustration of a simple decision tree

deduction– An act or process of deriving a conclusion from a known principle to an unknown or from the general to the particular. Compare *induction.*

deductive inference– The drawing of **inference** about the particular proposition based on information about the general. Compare *inductive inference.*

deductive reasoning– Same as *deductive inference.*

definitional formula– The algebraic formula that directly displays the meaning of the procedure it symbolizes. Compare *computational formula.*

degrees of freedom– The number of independent units of information in a **sample** that are free to vary in calculating a **statistic** when certain restrictions are imposed on the **data set.** Degrees of freedom measure the quantity of information available in **sample data** for estimating the **population parameters.** It is a characteristic of the statistic being employed and is equal to the number of values that can be freely chosen when calculating the statistic. The appropriate degree of freedom for each statistical procedure appears with the formula defining the **test statistic.** For example, in a **2 × 2 contingency table** with fixed **marginals,** only one of the four **cell frequencies** is free to vary, and therefore the table has single degree of freedom associated with it. Similarly, whenever the *t* **distribution** is used to make **inferences** about a **population mean** with unknown **variance,** the required *t* distribution has $n - 1$ degrees of freedom, where *n* is the **sample size.** Although many people find the concept of degree of freedom a bit difficult to understand, the practical application is relatively easy.

Delphi method– A qualitative **forecasting** method that obtains forecasts through a group consensus.

demand function– An equation used in economic analysis that expresses the quantity of a commodity in demand as a function of price by $Q = Cp^{-e}$ where Q is the quantity in demand, p is the price, e is the price elasticity, and C is the constant.

demographic transition– The process by which continuous changes in **fertility, mortality,** and migratory rates, over a number of years in the population, produce changes in the characteristics and structure of the population under study.

demography– The study of human populations with respect to age, sex, size, density, migration, **fertility, mortality,** and other **vital statistics** by statistical methods, and techniques. Demographic studies are based on **data** from **population censuses** and increasingly from **sample surveys.** The methods of demography are **empirical** and statistical and frequently make use of advanced mathematical techniques.

DeMoivre–Laplace theorem– A form of **central limit theorem** that establishes large sample **normality** of a **binomial distribution.** More specifically, the theorem states that if X is a **binomial random variable** with **parameters** n and p, then as n increases the **distribution** of X can be approximated by a **normal distribution** with **mean** np and **variance** $np(1 - p)$.

density– Same as *probability density.*

density curve– Same as *probability density curve.*

density estimation– Any of several **nonparametric procedures** for estimating **density function** of a **probability distribution.** Some of the simplest and classical methods for density estimation are **histogram** and **frequency polygon.** More modern and sophisticated procedures include kernel methods and spline techniques for smoothing histograms. Density estimates provide valuable information regarding characteristics and features of a **distribution,** such as **skewness** and multimodality.

density function– Same as *probability density function.*

dependent events– Two **outcomes** or **events** are said to be dependent when the occurrence of one affects the **probability** of occurrence of another. For two dependent events A and B, $P(A) \neq P(A|B)$ or $P(B) \neq P(B|A)$. Compare *independent events.* See also *conditional probability.*

dependent groups– Groups of one or more *samples* in which the values in one sample are related to the values in the other sample. **Paired** or **matched samples** are examples of dependent groups.

dependent-groups *t* **test–** Same as *paired t-test.*

dependent samples– Same as *dependent groups.*

dependent variable– The **variable** in an **experiment** or study that is affected by the **treatment(s)** or the choice of the **independent variable(s).** In a **regression analysis,** it is usually a response that is being predicted by the **regression equation.** It is a variable of primary importance since one of the objectives of many research investigations is to predict the values of the dependent variable in terms of the known values of the independent variables. See also *criterion variable, predictor variable.*

description– Same as *statistical description.*

descriptive statistics– (1) The type of **statistics** used to organize and describe the **sample data** and not for inferring any characteristics of a **parent population** or **universe** from which they are derived. Some of the descriptive statistics procedures include calculating **means, proportions,** and **variance** and plotting **histograms, scatter diagrams,** and other graphs and charts. (2) Statistical methods and techniques that deal with the collection, organization, description, and presentation of numerical information. See also *exploratory data analysis, inferential statistics, initial data analysis.*

design of experiment– A statement of the purpose of and proposed approach to an **experiment** or investigation involving statistical analysis. More specifically, it refers to a set of rules or restrictions for allocating **treatments** to **experimental units.** Each rule or restriction for allocating treatments has a definite purpose. Some general principles of a good design are **control group, randomization,** and **replication.**

detection bias– Same as *ascertainment bias.*

deterministic model– A **mathematical model** based on a **deterministic relationship.** A deterministic model does not involve any **random** or probabilistic term. Compare *probability model.*

deterministic relationship– A relationship between any two **outcomes** or **variables,** such that the value of one is uniquely determined whenever the value of the other is specified.

deviance– A **statistic** used to assess the **goodness of fit** of a **regression model** fitted by the **method of maximum likelihood.** Larger values of deviance indicate that the **model** in question provides a poor fit while smaller values support the adequacy of the model. The importance of a given set of **predictor variables** is tested by the difference in deviance between any two **hierarchical models,** one with the set of predictors included and the other without the predictors. The deviance has asymptotically a **chi-square distribution** with **degrees of freedom** equal to the difference in the number of **parameters** in the two hierarchical models. The term "deviance" was originally proposed by M. G. Kendall to denote the **sum of squares of observations** about their **mean.** See also G^2 *statistic, likelihood ratio statistic.*

deviate– The value of a **score** measured from its group **average,** usually the **mean.** It is generally expressed as a **standardized score,** i.e., as a multiple of the **standard deviation.**

deviation– The distance or difference between a **score** and its respective group **average** such as **mean, median,** or **mode.** In general, the difference between any two quantities. See also *deviation from the mean.*

deviation from the mean– The difference (positive or negative) between an individual observed value and the **mean** of the group. The total of all such deviations from the mean is equal to zero. Deviations may also be measured from the **median** or the **mode.** Algebraically, the deviation of the ith **observation** from the **sample mean** $\bar{x}$ is given by $x_i - \bar{x}$ and $\sum_{i=1}^{n}(x_i - \bar{x}) = 0$. The **absolute value** of $x_i - \bar{x}$, namely $|x_i - \bar{x}|$, is known as an **absolute deviation.** See also *average absolute deviation.*

deviation score– Same as *deviation.*

DFBETA– A **diagnostic measure** commonly used in **regression analysis** to detect the presence of an **outlier.** It is designed to measure the standardized change in a **regressional**

coefficient when a certain observation is deleted from the analysis. See also *Cook's distance, DFFITS.*

DFFITS– A **diagnostic measure** commonly used in **regression analysis** to detect the presence of an **outlier.** It is closely related to **Cook's distance** and is designed to measure the **influence** of an **observation** on the predicted **response value.** See also *DFBETA.*

diagnostic measure– A **goodness-of-fit statistic** that indicates how well a **regression** or any other **statistical model** fits a given set of **data.**

diagnostic procedure– Same as *diagnostic test.*

diagnostic testing– See *diagnostic tests.*

diagnostic tests– Medical procedures, such as clinical, laboratory, or other tests, that are performed to establish an actual diagnosis as regards to the presence or absence of a disease. A diagnostic test may result in a positive or negative finding. An ideal diagnostic test should classify all the cases with the disease as positive and all those without the disease as negative. Two measures of performance of a test to determine how often the test leads to correct classification are **sensitivity** and **specificity.** See also *predictive value negative, predictive value positive.*

diagram– A general term that now appears to be used generically to refer to all types of charts and graphs employed in the representation of **statistical data.**

dichotomous attribute– A characteristic classified into only two categories or groups, usually defined by the presence or absence of a certain condition (e.g., sick or not sick; improved or not improved). Some characteristics are inherently dichotomous by nature (e.g., male/female, alive/dead), but all characteristics, whether or not inherently dichoto-mous, can be made dichotomous by defining and identifying one category and putting all other observations into a second category. See also *dichotomous variable.*

dichotomous data– These are **data** arising from **measurements** that can assume only one of two values. The values are conventionally represented as 0 and 1 but they need not be a number. Dichotomous data can arise in many different forms and generally require specialized techniques for their analysis.

dichotomous measure– Same as *dichotomous variable.*

dichotomous variable– A **qualitative variable** or **nominal measure** that has only two **outcomes** or about which **observations** can be made in only two categories. Some exam-ples are gender: male or female; marital status: married or not married. Dichotomous vari-ables are frequently encountered in many medical and health studies. **Data** involving dichotomous **response variable** often require specialized techniques for their analysis. Often the **response values** are coded as zero or one for the purpose of analysis. See also *dichotomous attribute.*

dichotomy– A division into two mutually exclusive subclasses or categories.

diffuse prior– Same as *vague prior.*

digital computer– A computer that stores, retrieves, and processes information in digital form, using the familiar Arabic numerals from 0 to 9. Electronic digital computers usually employ **binary notation** and perform operations at high speeds by making repeated use of the conventional arithmetic process of addition, subtraction, multiplication, and division.

directional hypothesis– An **alternative hypothesis** that specifies the direction of the possible differences from the **parameter** value being tested under the **null hypothesis.** It is also referred to as one-sided or one-tailed hypothesis.

directional test– Same as *one-tailed test.*

directly standardized rate– See *standardization.*

direct relationship– A relationship between any two **variables,** such that the values of one increase or decrease according to increase or decrease in the values of the other. Compare *inverse relationship.*

direct standardization– See *standardization.*

Dirichlet distribution– The **random variables** $X_1, X_2, \ldots, X_q$ are said to have a Dirichlet distribution if their joint probability density function is given by

$$f(x_1, x_2, \ldots, x_q) = \frac{\Gamma(\ell_1 + \ell_2 + \cdots + \ell_{q+1})}{\Gamma(\ell_1)\Gamma(\ell_2)\cdots\Gamma(\ell_{q+1})} x_1^{\ell_1-1} x_2^{\ell_2-1} \cdots$$
$$x_q^{\ell_q-1}(1 - x_1 - x_2 - \cdots - x_q)^{\ell_{q+1}-1}$$

where $x_i \geq 0$, $\ell_i > 0$, $i = 1, 2, \ldots, q$, and $x_1 + x_2 + \cdots + x_q \leq 1$. It is a multivariate extension of the **beta distribution.** The distribution has many important applications in statistics.

Dirichlet function– The Dirichlet function denoted by $D(\ell_1, \ell_2, \ldots, \ell_q, \ell_{q+1})$ is defined as

$$\int_{\substack{x_i \geq 0, i=1,2,\ldots,q \\ x_1+x_2+\cdots+x_q \leq 1}} \cdots \int x_1^{\ell_1-1} x_2^{\ell_2-1} \cdots x_q^{\ell_q-1}(1 - x_1 - x_2 - \cdots - x_q)^{\ell_{q+1}-1} dx_1 dx_2 \ldots dx_q$$

It is a multivariate extension of the **beta function.** Dirichlet functions have been found useful in the solution of many statistical problems.

discordant pairs– See *Kendall's tau.*

discrete data– **Data** obtained on measures of a **discrete variable,** i.e., using a **discrete scale** of measurement. See also *continuous data, nominal data, numerical data, qualitative data.*

discrete distribution– Same as *discrete probability distribution.*

discrete probability distribution– A table, graph, or algebraic equation showing the values of a **discrete random variable** and the associated **probabilities.**

Probability distribution of the number of dots when a pair of fair dice is tossed

x	2	3	4	5	6	7	8	9	10	11	12
$p(x)$	$\frac{1}{36}$	$\frac{2}{36}$	$\frac{3}{36}$	$\frac{4}{36}$	$\frac{5}{36}$	$\frac{6}{36}$	$\frac{5}{36}$	$\frac{4}{36}$	$\frac{3}{36}$	$\frac{2}{36}$	$\frac{1}{36}$

Some examples of other discrete probability distributions

x	0	1
p(x)	0.5	0.5

x	-2	-1	0	-1	2
p(x)	0.2	0.2	0.2	0.2	0.2

x	1	2	3	4	5	6
p(x)	0.1	0.1	0.3	0.3	0.1	0.1

discrete scale– A scale used to measure a numerical characteristic that entails only integer values.

discrete stochastic process– See *stochastic process.*

discrete uniform distribution– See *uniform distribution.*

discrete (random) variable– A quantitative (random) variable that can be measured only in terms of a whole number (integer) such as the number of children per family, the number of cars per household, and so on. A discrete variable can assume only a finite or, at most, a countable number of possible values. The scales of discrete random variables contain gaps where no real values of the variable, such as "1.65 children," occur.

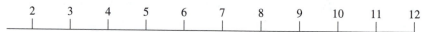

Possible values of the sum of the number of dots of two dice

Figure illustrating a discrete random variable

discriminant analysis– A **multivariate technique** for predicting a nominal outcome that has two or more values. It uses two or more continuous **independent variables,** known as **predictors,** to classify subjects or objects into different groups with minimal **probability** of misclassification. It is also called discriminant function analysis. When subjects are to be classified into more than two groups, it is known as multiple discriminant analysis. In the case of two groups, the most commonly used procedure is Fisher's linear discriminant function in which a **linear function** of the **variables** resulting in maximum separation between the two groups is determined. This provides a classification rule that may be used to allocate a new object into one of the two groups. In cases involving more than two groups, there are several possible linear functions of the variables that can be used for separating them. In a discriminant analysis, it is important to assess its misclassification rate, i.e., the **proportion** of cases that are incorrectly classified. Ideally a **sample** of new cases should be used in order to assess the **error rate.** When there are many predictors, the search for the best subset of predictors is usually done by a **stepwise procedure.**

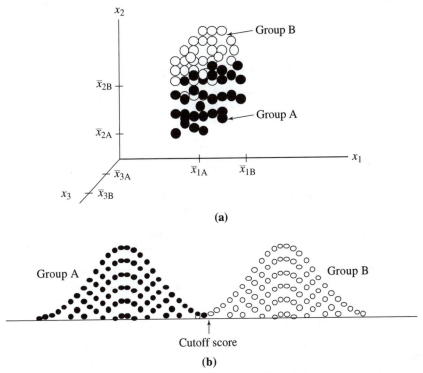

(a)

(b)

Schematic illustration of discriminant analysis: two groups compared on **(a)** three predictor variables and **(b)** the derived discriminant function

discriminant function analysis– Same as *discriminant analysis.*

disjoint events– Same as *mutually exclusive events.*

disjoint sets– In **set theory,** two or more **sets** are said to be disjoint if they have no common elements between them.

dispersion– Same as *variability.*

distance sampling– A method of **sampling** employed to determine the number of certain species of plants or animals in a given geographic area.

distribution– The values of a characteristic or **variable** along with the **frequency** or **probability** of their occurrence, often plotted on a graph. Distributions may be based on **empirical** results or may be theoretical **probability distributions.** Examples of some well-known theoretical distributions are **normal, binomial,** and **Poisson,** among others. Classical statistical procedures are based on the assumption that the **data** have an empirical distribution, which is closely approximated by the theoretical ones. See also *frequency distribution.*

distribution-free methods– A term sometimes used for **nonparametric methods,** since they usually do not require assumptions about the underlying population distributions (such as the **normal**), but will work for a wide range of different distributions.

distribution function– For any **random variable** X, the distribution function of X, denoted by $F(x)$, is defined by $F(x) = P(X \leq x)$; that is, the distribution function is equal to the **probability** that a random variable assumes a value less than or equal to x for $-\infty < x < \infty$.

Dixon's test– A **test procedure** based on **order statistics** used to test for an **outlier.**

dominant action– In **decision** or **game theory,** an action that is undoubtedly superior to an alternative action because it generates **payoffs** that are as good as or superior to those of the alternative action under any condition.

dominant strategy– Same as *dominant action.*

Doolittle method– A computational **algorithm** employed in solving a system of linear equations. The procedure is fairly straightforward to implement and enables one immediately to detect any arithmetic errors being made. Its use is recommended whenever there are more than two **variables** involved in the equations.

dose-finding trial– A pharmaceutical trial with a primary objective of identifying the optimal dose of a drug. The term is synonymous with **phase I trial.**

dose–response curve– A two dimensional graph displaying the relationship between the values of dose of a drug plotted on the horizontal x **axis** and the corresponding values of a **response variable** plotted on the vertical y **axis.**

dose–response relationship– See *dose-response curve.*

dot-plot– A **graphical procedure** for displaying the **frequency distribution** of numerical **observations** for one or more groups of **data** in which each dot (.) designates one observation. It is usually a more effective method for displaying **quantitative data** that are labeled.

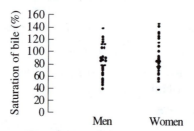

Two dot plots for percentage saturation of
bile for men and women

double-blind study– Same as *double-blind trial.*

double-blind trial– A **clinical trial** in which neither the physician nor the investigator nor the patient have any knowledge of the particular **treatment** being assigned to patients in the study, so that subjective **biases** are avoided. See also *blind study, single-blind trial, triple-blind trial.*

double-entry table– A **statistical table** requiring two entries, such as two values of **degrees of freedom,** one for columns and one for rows, is referred to as a double-entry table. The value at the intersection of the appropriate column and row is the **critical value** of the **statistic.** The percentiles of the **F distribution** require a double-entry table.

double exponential distribution– A **continuos probability distribution** defined by the **probability density function** of the form

$$f(x) = \frac{1}{2\beta} \exp\left(-\frac{|x - \alpha|}{\beta}\right) \qquad -\infty < x < \infty, \alpha > x, \beta > 0$$

It can be derived as the distribution of the difference between two **random variables** each having an identical **exponential distribution.**

double-logarithmic chart– See *logarithmic chart.*

double-masked study– Same as *double-blind trial.*

double-masked trial– Same as *double-blind trial.*

double Poisson distribution– A **Poisson distribution** in which the **parameter** λ is itself regarded a **random variable** having a Poisson-type distribution.

double sampling– A **sampling** procedure in which first a preliminary **sample** is selected for the purpose of obtaining certain auxiliary information only; and subsequently a second sample, usually a subsample of the first, is selected for measuring the **variable** of interest in addition to the auxiliary information. The purpose of this type of sampling is to increase the **precision** of the **estimate** by exploiting the **correlation** between the auxiliary variable and the variable of interest. The procedure is particularly useful when the information on the auxiliary variable can be obtained by an inexpensive and easy-to-use procedure. Such a sampling is also known as two-phase sampling.

double-tailed test– Same as *two-tailed test.*

doubly censored data– A term sometimes applied to **survival data** to indicate that both the time of the originating **event** of interest and the failure of the event (relapse, death, etc.) are **censored.**

doubly ordinal contingency table– See *ordinal contingency table.*

drop-ins– Same as *crossovers.*

drop-outs– In a **clinical trial,** drop-outs are patients who decide to withdraw from the study, for whatever reason, either voluntarily or because asked to do so by the physician conducting the study, possibly because of an adverse side effect associated with the **intervention.** The drop-outs have important implications in terms of how the **data** should be analyzed, and whenever possible such cases should be located and their **outcome** ascertained.

D^2 **statistic–** Same as *Mahalanobis D^2.*

Duckworth test– A quick and simple test, proposed by John W. Tukey in 1959, for comparing the **medians** of two **populations** that does not require any table of **critical values.** Suppose that the smallest **observation** is from the x population having m observations and the largest from the y population having n observations. The **test statistic** D is the sum of the following two overlaps: (1) The number of x observations that are smaller than the smallest y and (2) the number of y observations that are larger than the largest x. If either $3 + 4n/3 \leq m \leq 2n$ or vice versa, the statistic D is reduced by one. The table of critical values consists of three numbers, *7, 10* and *13*, corresponding to $\alpha = 0.05, 0.01$, and 0.001

respectively. The **null hypothesis** of equal medians is rejected if D exceeds the critical values at respective **levels of significance.**

dummy coding– A procedure in which a code of 0 or 1 is assigned to a nominal response and **predictor** or **independent variable** used in a **regression analysis.**

dummy variable– A **dichotomous variable** that is coded as 1 to indicate the presence of an attribute and 0 to indicate its absence. In performing a **regression analysis,** a dummy variable is created to incorporate a **binary variable** into a **model** by means of **dummy coding. Categorical variables** with more than two categories are incorporated by a series of dummy variables.

Duncan multiple range test– A type of **multiple comparison** procedure for making **pairwise comparisons** between **means** following a significant F **test** in the **analysis of variance.** The procedure involves a step-by-step approach where the **sample ranges** are tested in exactly the same way as the **Newman–Keuls test** except that the observed ranges are based on Duncan's multiple range distribution. The procedure has been found to be somewhat more conservative than the Newman–Keuls test. See also *Bonferroni procedure, Dunnett multiple comparison test, Scheffe's test, Tukey's test.*

Dunnett multiple comparison test– A **multiple comparison** procedure for comparing several **treatment groups** in which each of a number of treatment groups is compared with a single **control group** following a significant F **test** in an **analysis of variance.** See also *Bonferroni procedure, Duncan multiple range test, Newman–Keuls test, Scheffe's test, Tukey's test.*

Dunnett's test– Same as *Dunnett multiple comparison test.*

Dunn multiple comparison procedure– Same as *Bonferroni procedure.*

Durbin–Watson test– A procedure for testing **independence** of **error terms** in **least squares regression** against the alternative of **autocorrelation** or **serial correlation.** The **test statistic** d is a simple **linear function** of **residual autocorrelations,** and its value decreases as the autocorrelation increases. It is calculated by dividing the sum of the squared first differences of **residuals** by the sum of the squared residuals. Exact **significant levels** for d are not available, but Durbin and Watson have tabulated lower and upper **critical bounds** for various values of n (the number of **paired observations**) and k (the number of **explanatory variables**). If the computed value of d falls below the lower limit (d_1), there seems to be evidence for the presence of autocorrelation. If it falls above the uper limit (d_2), there is lack of any autocorrelation. And if it lies between the lower and upper limits, then the test is inconclusive.

EC50– Acronym for *effective concentration 50.*

ecological correlation– Same as *geographic correlation.*

ecological fallacy– See *geographic correlation.*

ecological statistics– Statistical methods and techniques used in the study of the dynamics of natural habitats and their interaction to environment. See also *environmental statistics.*

econometrics– A branch of **economics** concerned with the **empirical** study of economic laws by application of mathematical and statistical techniques, usually modeling economic phenomena involving stochastic elements. It expresses economic principles and theories in mathematical terms in order to verify them by statistical methods. It is mainly concerned with the empirical **measurement** and testing of economic relations that are expressable in mathematical form.

economic model– A set of mathematical equations designed to provide a quantitative explanation of the behavior of economic **variables.**

economics– The field of study concerned with production, distribution, and consumption of goods and services. Theoretical economics is concerned with the study of economic principles and laws while **applied economics** employs theoretical principles in developing economic programs and policies.

EDA– Acronym for *exploratory data analysis.*

effect– In a **factorial experiment,** a quantity representing a change in response caused by a change in **level** of one or more of the **factors.** In **analysis of variance** and **regression,** a change in **response variable** caused by a change in one or more **explanatory variables.**

effective concentration 50– Same as *median lethal dose.*

effective sample size– The final **sample size** after taking into account losses due to **attrition, nonresponse, drop-outs,** and any other causes.

effect size– The magnitude of a difference or relationship between two **treatments** or **variables** considered of importance to be detected in a study. To obtain the effect size, the magnitude of the difference is generally divided by the **standard deviation** of the **measurement.** It is the basis for statistical methods used in **meta-analysis** and the computation of **power** and **sample size.**

efficiency– A term most commonly used in the context of comparing **variances** of two **unbiased estimators;** an **estimator** being regarded more efficient than another if it has smaller variance. If T_1 and T_2 are two unbiased estimators of the same **parameter** with variances V_1 and V_2, then the efficiency of T_1 with respect to T_2 is defined by the **ratio** V_2/V_1. In an **experimental design,** a design is said to be more efficient if its **error mean square** is less than that of another design applied to the same number of experimental units. The term is also used for **power efficiency** of one test with respect to the other.

efficient estimator– The **sample estimator** or **statistic,** among the entire class of **unbiased estimators,** that has the smallest **variance** for a given **sample size.**

elementary event– In **probability theory,** the single elementary result of an **experiment** or **trial** that rules out the occurrence of all the alternative results. Observing a 7 for the total of face values when throwing a pair of dice and drawing an ace from a deck of cards are examples of an elementary event.

A	2	3	4	5	6	7	8	9	10	J	Q	K
♣	♣	♣	♣	♣	♣	♣	♣	♣	♣	♣	♣	♣
A	2	3	4	5	6	7	8	9	10	J	Q	K
♦	♦	♦	♦	♦	♦	♦	♦	♦	♦	♦	♦	♦
A	2	3	4	5	6	7	8	9	10	J	Q	K
♥	♥	♥	♥	♥	♥	♥	♥	♥	♥	♥	♥	♥
A	2	3	4	5	6	7	8	9	10	J	Q	K
♠	♠	♠	♠	♠	♠	♠	♠	♠	♠	♠	♠	♠

Elementary events for an experiment consisting of drawing a card from a deck of cards

elementary unit– A person or object possessing a certain characteristic of interest to an investigator. It is the smallest unit yielding information concerning the characteristic under investigation.

eligibility– A term used in a **clinical trial** to describe the criteria each patient must satisfy before entering a study.

empirical– A term commonly used to denote results based on **experimental data** rather than deduced from theoretical considerations.

empirical Bayes method– A form of **Bayesian inference** in which the **prior distribution** is determined from some **empirical** evidence rather than the investigator's prior knowledge about the **parameters.** The empirical evidence is generally derived from the use of **data** previously collected by the same selection procedure as now proposed for use in a new **experiment** to be conducted on the same **study population.**

empirical probability– An **estimate** of **probability** based on past **experimental data** with the **outcomes** of an **experiment** or some other phenomenon. It is equal to the number of times an **event** did occur in a large number of experimental **trials** divided by the maximum number of times the event could have occurred during these trials. See also *classical probability, objective probability, subjective probability.*

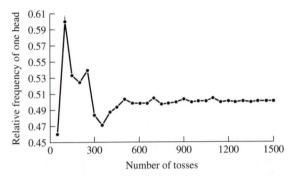

The relative frequency approaches the true probability of 0.5

Empirical probability as the relative frequency of obtaining a head; from a computer simulation

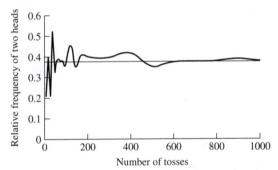

The relative frequency approaches the true probability of 0.375

Empirical probability as the relative frequency of obtaining two heads in many tosses of four coins; from a computer simulation

empirical rule– A rule that is useful in interpreting the **variability** of a **bell-shaped distribution.** The rule states that approximately 68% of the **observations** in a **data set** will be within one **standard deviation** of their **mean,** 95% of the observations will be within two standard deviations of the mean, and 99.7% of the observations will be within three standard deviations of the mean. See also *normal distribution.*

endogenous variable– A **variable** whose **variability** is assumed to be determined by variables in the causal system. In other words, an endogenous variable is a variable that is caused by variables internal to a causal system. For example, price and demand are considered endogenous to an **economic model.** Similarly, consumption, savings, investment, private wage payments, and profit are generally considered endogenous variables in studies of a nation's aggregate economic activity. Compare *exogenous variable.*

endpoint– A term commonly used in medical and health science investigation to describe a well-defined **event** or **outcome,** such as infection, myocardial arrest, death, or relapse.

Sometimes **surrogate outcomes** are used as endpoints because of their strong relationship with more definitive outcomes of interest.

enumerator– The person who carries out the enumeration of the households in a **census** or **survey** operation.

environmental statistics– Statistical methods and techniques used in the study of environment, especially in environmental pollution and monitoring involving soil, air, water, solid wastes, and hazardous substances. See also *ecological statistics*.

epidemiology– The study of the distribution and causes of disease in a **population** and the methods and techniques for acquiring such knowledge.

equal ignorance principle– Same as *equal-likelihood criterion*.

equal-likelihood criterion– In **decision theory,** the assignment of equal **prior probabilities** to all possible outcomes in the absence of any information about the likelihood of occurrence of any of these **outcomes.**

error– A general term used to describe any mistake associated with any action such as transcribing error, judgment error, or **observation** error. In statistics the term is used in a very limited context to describe the difference between the "true" or "expected" value and the observed value with no implication of any mistake. See also *random error, unexplained variation*.

error effect– In a **statistical model** the **effect** attributable to the **error term.**

error mean square– The **mean square** used in the denominator of an *F* **test** in an **analysis of variance** procedure. It is obtained by dividing the **error sum of squares** by its **degrees of freedom**. It provides an **unbiased estimator** of the common **error variance.**

error of acceptance– Same as *type II error.*

error of estimation– Same as *estimation error.*

error of rejection– Same as *type I error.*

error of the first kind– Same as *type I error.*

error of the second kind– Same as *type II error.*

error rate– A term sometimes used to designate the **rate** at which the **error of the first kind** will be allowed to occur. In general the rate at which any type of error can occur, for example, the **proportion** of cases misclassified by a classification rule derived from a **discriminant analysis.**

errors of classification– Same as *classification errors.*

error sum of squares– In an **analysis of variance,** the sum of squared deviations of all individual **observations** from the **sample means** of their respective **treatment groups**. It is algebraically equal to the **total sum of squares** minus **treatment sum of squares**. It is also called residual sum of squares or **within** group sum of squares.

error term– In a **statistical model** the term representing the contribution from various other variables, known or unknown, which are omitted from the model.

error variance– In an **analysis of variance,** the contribution to the **variance** that is not ascribed to **treatment** or **block** effects. It may be due to many causes such as individual differences between subjects, inconsistencies in the experimental conditions, **measurement errors,** or any uncontrolled or **unexplained variation.** It is also referred to as the error variance of the **error term.**

establishment survey– A **survey** of business and commercial enterprises usually conducted monthly by a government agency of a country. In the United States such surveys are carried out by the **Bureau of the Census.**

estimate– An estimate is the particular numerical value yielded by an **estimator** for a given **sample data.** An estimate can be a **mean, proportion, correlation coefficient** or any other **parameter value** derived from a **sample.** An estimate is used to make **inference** about a **target population** whose true parameter value is unknown. See also *estimation.*

estimated partial regression coefficient– The **estimated regression coefficient** of an **independent variable in a multiple regression model;** it is interpreted as an **estimate** of the net change in the **dependent variable** for a unit change in the independent variable, while other independent variables are kept **constant.** See also *partial regression coefficient.*

estimated regression coefficient– An **estimate** of the **regression coefficient** obtained by **sample data,** using the **least squares** or any other method of **estimation.**

estimated regression equation– An **estimate** of the **regression equation** obtained by **sample data** using the **least squares** or any other method of **estimation.**

estimated regression line– An **estimate** of the **regression line** obtained by **sample data,** using the **least squares** or any other method of **estimation.** A **graphical representation** of the estimated regression line drawn through the pattern of points on a **scatter diagram** summarizes and averages out the relationship between the **dependent** and **independent variables.**

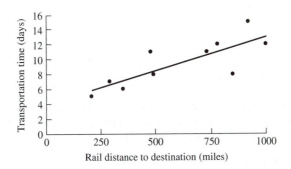

An estimated regression line

estimated regression model– Same as *estimated regression equation.*

estimation– The process of using information from **sample data** in order to estimate the numerical values of unknown **parameters** in a **population.** If a single value is calculated to estimate a parameter, the process is called **point estimation.** If an interval is calculated, the process is called **interval estimation.** See also *confidence interval, inferential statistics, least squares estimation, maximum likelihood estimation.*

estimation error– The difference between an **estimate** and the true value of the **parameter** being estimated.

estimation of parameter– Same as *estimation*.

estimator– The **sample statistic** used to make **inferences** about an unknown **parameter.** For example, one might use **sample mean** to estimate the value of the **population mean.** An estimator is usually given as algebraic formula. See also *estimation*.

eta– The **correlation** between two **variables** measured on an **interval scale** that is an index of the nonlinear relationship between the variables. It is also known as correlation ratio.

etiological fraction– Same as *attributable risk.*

etiologic factor– Same as *risk factor.*

Euclidean distance– A measure of the distance between two points as determined by the location of their coordinates. The Euclidean distance between two points: $(x_1, x_2, \ldots, x_n)$ and $(y_1, y_2, \ldots, y_n)$ is determined by the formula

$$\sqrt{|x_1 - y_1|^2 + |x_2 - y_2|^2 + \cdots + |x_n - y_n|^2}$$

where $|x_i - y_i|$ represents the **absolute value** of $(x_i - y_i)$ for $i = 1, 2, \ldots, n$. Note that $|x_i - y_i|^2 = (x_i - y_i)^2$ when the coordinates are real numbers. It is a special case of the **Minkowski distance.**

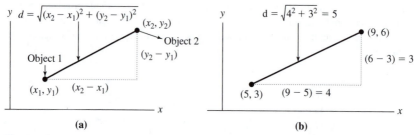

(a)   **(b)**

The Euclidean distance between two objects measured on two variables:
(a) general definition and **(b)** specific example

event– A set consisting of a collection of **sample points** or **outcomes** of an **experiment.** In **probability theory,** an event is a subset of the **sample space.** In general, the term is used to represent any outcome, condition, or eventuality.

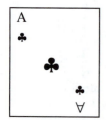 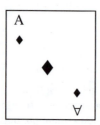 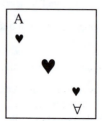 

Illustration of the event "an ace card is selected"

event branches– In a **decision tree** diagram, branches emanating from an **event point** and representing the possible **outcomes** confronting the decision maker.

event point– In a **decision tree** diagram, a point representing a **random event** over which the decision maker has no control. It is usually symbolized by a circle.

exact hypothesis– A **hypothesis** that specifies a single value for an unknown **parameter.** See also *simple hypothesis.*

exact test– A **statistical test** is called exact if its **level of significance** is exactly equal to the nominal or stated level. See also *approximate test, conservative test, liberal test.*

exhaustive– A set of conditions, **events,** or values is said to be exhaustive if, taken together, the components account for all the possible **outcomes.**

exhaustive events– A set of **events** is said to be exhaustive if the components jointly contain all the **outcomes** in the **sample space,** that is, there are no other possible outcomes. The sum of the **probabilities** of the exhaustive events equals 1.

exogenous variable– A **variable** whose **variability** is assumed to be determined by causes outside the causal system. In other words, an exogenous variable is a variable that is caused by variables external to a causal system. For example, rainfall and natural disasters are considered exogenous to an **economic model.** Similarly, export statistics are usually considered an exogenous variable in a study of a nation's aggregate economic activity. Compare *endogenous variable.*

expanded safety trial– A type of surveillance trial designed primarily for estimating the frequency of unusual side effects as a consequence of administering a treatment. In drug development studies, the term is synonymous with **phase II trial.**

expectation– Same as *expected value.*

expectation of life at birth– The number of years a newborn child is expected to live, under the prevailing social, economic, and health conditions in the population. See also *life table.*

expected frequency– The **frequency** expected for an **event** if certain **probability laws** were exactly followed as distinct from the actual frequency that may be observed in a **sample.** In a **contingency table,** the frequency expected for each **cell** if the **null hypothesis** of **independence** or **homogeneity** were true. The expected frequency for a cell is obtained by multiplying its row total by its column total and dividing the result by the grand total. Compare *observed frequency.*

expected mean square– In an **analysis of variance,** the **expected value** of a **mean square** derived under a given set of **assumptions** of the **model** being postulated.

expected monetary gain– Same as *expected monetary value.*

expected monetary return– Same as *expected monetary value.*

expected monetary value– The **weighted average** of the **payoffs** associated with an action, the weights being the **probabilities** of the alternative **outcomes** that give rise to the various possible payoffs.

expected monetary value criterion– One of several probabilistic criteria for making decisions under **uncertainty.** According to this criterion, a decision maker determines an

expected monetary value for each possible action and selects the action that maximizes expected monetary value.

expected opportunity loss– The **weighted average** of the **opportunity loss** values associated with an action, the weights being the **probabilities** of the alternative **outcomes** that give rise the various possible opportunity losses.

expected opportunity loss criterion– One of several probabilistic criteria for making decisions under **uncertainty.** According to this criterion, a decision maker determines an **expected opportunity loss** for each possible action and selects the action with the smallest of these values.

expected regret value– Same as *expected opportunity loss.*

expected utility– The **weighted average** of the **utilities** associated with an action, the weights being the **probabilities** of the alternative **outcomes** that give rise to the various possible utility **payoffs.**

expected utility criterion– One of several probabilistic criteria for making decisions under **uncertainty.** According to this criterion, a decision maker determines the **expected utility** for each possible action and selects the action that maximizes the expected utility.

expected value– The expected value of a **random variable** is the **weighted mean** of its **probability distribution.** It can be interpreted as the value of the random variable one can expect to obtain, on the **average,** in successive repetitions of the **random experiment** that generates the values of the random variable.

expected value of perfect information– The maximum amount a decision maker can be expected to pay for obtaining complete information about future **outcomes** and, thus, for eliminating **uncertainty** entirely.

expected value of sample information– The maximum amount a decision maker can be expected to pay for obtaining supposedly incomplete information about future **outcomes** and, thus, for reducing, rather than eliminating, **uncertainty.**

experiment– In **probability theory,** any process or operation that generates well-defined **elementary events** or **outcomes;** for example, tossing a coin or casting a die. In **statistics,** any study undertaken in which the researcher has control over some of the experimental conditions under which the study is undertaken and **measurements** or **observations** of possible outcomes are obtained. In particular, the investigator controls the conditions applied to the subjects and then carefully records the observations on outcomes of interest. The experiment is one of the distinctive tools of the scientist. It enables the scientist to put questions to nature and test **hypotheses** under controlled conditions.

experimental data– **Data** obtained from an **experiment.**

experimental design– Same as *design of experiment.*

experimental error– A term used to refer to the **errors** introduced into an **experiment** by the lack of uniformity in the conduct of the experiment and failure to standardize the use of materials and techniques. Results of an experiment are affected not only by the **treatments** (experimental procedures whose effects are being evaluated and compared) but also by the presence of experimental errors. The presence and cause of experimental error need not concern the investigator provided the results are sufficiently accurate to permit definite conclusions. Often, however, the results of an experiment can be greatly influenced by presence of large experimental errors, making it difficult to draw any valid **inferences.**

experimental group– A group that receives a **treatment** or **intervention** and is compared to a **control group.**

experimental observations– Same as *experimental data.*

experimental planning– A term used to refer to the details of the proposal for and objectives of an **experiment,** including definitions of **treatments,** experimental materials and techniques, and other related **variables** and procedures. See also *experimental design.*

experimental study– A **comparative study** involving an **intervention** or manipulation of experimental conditions by the investigator. It is called a **clinical trial** when human subjects are used. See also *experiment, observational study.*

experimental treatment– The active **treatment** or **intervention** being assigned to the **treatment group.**

experimental unit– The object or item of interest in an **experiment.** It is the smallest independent unit of study assigned to a particular **treatment.**

experimentwise error rate– The experimentwise error rate is the **probability** that at least one (i.e., one or more) of the inferences to be drawn from the same set of **data** will be wrong. It is equivalent to the probability of incorrectly rejecting at least one of the **null hypotheses** in an **experiment** involving one or more tests or comparisons. In a **multiple comparison** procedure, it is the **significance level** associated with the entire set of comparisons of interest to the investigator. See also *comparisonwise error rate.*

explained deviation– In a **regression analysis,** the difference between the regression estimate of an individual **observation** and the **mean** of all the observations of the **dependent variable.**

explained variable– Same as *dependent variable.*

explained variance– Same as *explained variation.*

explained variation– The amount of shared **variation** between two correlated **variables.** In a **regression analysis,** it is the sum of the squares of all the **explained deviations,** also called the **regression sum of squares.** It is obtained by subtracting the **mean** of a set of **observations** from the value predicted by the **linear regression** and squaring and summing these values. It is interpreted as the variation in the **dependent variable** that can be accounted for by variation in the **independent variables.** See also *coefficient of multiple determination.*

explanatory analysis– In a **clinical trial,** a term used to refer to the analysis performed to compare two **treatments** under the assumption that patients remain on their treatment to which they were initially randomized. See also *intention-to-treat analysis.*

explanatory trial– A **clinical trial** designed to explain the process of a **treatment.**

explanatory variable– See *independent variable, predictor variable.*

exploratory analysis– Same as *exploratory data analysis.*

exploratory data analysis– Any of several modern **graphical techniques,** pioneered by John W. Tukey, often by presenting **quantitative data** visually by the use of simple arithmetic and easy-to-draw **diagrams** with a view to examine the **data** more effectively and to discover unanticipated patterns and relationships. It emphasizes the use of informal graphical procedures rather than formal **models** based on prior assumptions. The development of exploratory data analysis has been greatly aided by the widespread availability of modern electronic computers for calculation and for efficient **graphical display.** The **stem-and-leaf plot** and **box-and-whisker diagram** are two well-known examples of exploratory data analysis. Compare *confirmatory data analysis.*

exploratory factor analysis– See *factor analysis.*

exponent– The power to which a number is raised.

exponential distribution– A **continuous probability distribution** defined by the **probability density function** of the form

$$f(x) = \theta e^{-\theta x} \quad \text{for } x \geq 0 \quad \text{and} \quad \theta > 0$$

The **parameter** θ determines the **shape** of the **distribution** and is related to the **mean** and **standard deviation,** which are both equal to $1/\theta$. The distribution has important applications in life testing, **reliability** studies, **queuing theory,** and in many other areas of scientific investigation.

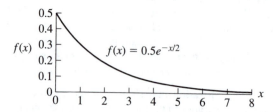

Exponential density function when $\theta = 0.5$

exponential family of distributions– A family of **probability distributions** that includes the **normal, binomial, Poisson,** and **gamma distributions** as special cases. The general form of the **density function** of an exponential family is given by

$$f(x) = \exp[p(\theta)k(x) + q(\theta) + s(x)]$$

where θ is a real **parameter** and $p(\theta)$, $q(\theta)$, $k(x)$, and $s(x)$ are known functions.

exponential regression– A type of **regression** in which the **prediction equation** between a continuous **dependent variable** y and a continuous **independent variable** x is represented by a **model** of the form $y_i = \alpha + \beta e^{\gamma x_i} + \epsilon_i$ where α, β, and γ are **constants** and ϵ_i is a random **error term.**

exponential smoothing– A **forecasting** technique that generates self-correcting **forecasts** by means of a built-in mechanism that adjusts for earlier forecasting errors. It makes use of exponentially weighted **moving averages** and continuously corrects for the amount by which the actual and estimated forecasts for a given period fail to conform. An essential feature of exponential smoothing for forecasting is that later periods are given greater weights than earlier periods.

exponential trend– A **trend** in **time-series data** that can be expressed as an exponential function. It is expressed by an equation of the form $y = ab^t$, where a and b are **constants** and t is time.

exposed– Same as *exposure group.*

exposed group– Same as *exposure group.*

exposure– Same as *exposure factor.*

exposure condition– Same as *risk condition.*

exposure factor– Same as *risk factor.*

exposure group– In epidemiology, a group of individuals who have been exposed to a certain **risk factor,** or possess a characteristic that is a determinant of certain health outcomes of interest.

external validity– The extent to which the findings of a study can be generalized-to-some **target population** of potential subjects beyond the **study population.** The external validity depends on the composition of the **study sample** and usually involves subject-matter judgment and nonstatistical considerations. Compare *internal validity.*

extraneous variable– A loosely used synonym for **confounding variable.**

extrapolation– The technique of estimating or predicting a value that falls outside the range of a series of known values. For example, in **regression analysis,** the value of the **response variable** may be estimated for a value of the **predictor variable** beyond the range of values used in estimating the **regression equation.** It is a practice that theoretical **statisticians** do not favor, and, indeed, it should be used with utmost care and discretion. The further the relationship is extended beyond the observed range, the more risky the procedure becomes. Compare *interpolation.*

extreme observations– Same as *extreme values.*

extreme values– The minimum and maximum values of a **data set.** See also *range.*

factor– In an **analysis of variance** or **regression analysis,** a factor is an **independent variable** that is presumed to influence the **response variable.** In an **experimental design,** a factor is a **variable** that represents a possible source of **variation** of a quantity under investigation and must be controlled. In **factor analysis,** a factor is a **linear combination** of related variables that are expected to have some special affinity among them.

factor analysis– An advanced **multivariate technique** for analyzing the relationships among a large set of items or indicators to delineate the **factors** or dimensions that underlie the **data.** Factor analysis is performed by expressing **observed variables** as a **linear combination** of a smaller number of **variables,** known as factors or **latent variables,** which are of special relevance in the context of the investigation. In its initial stages, the

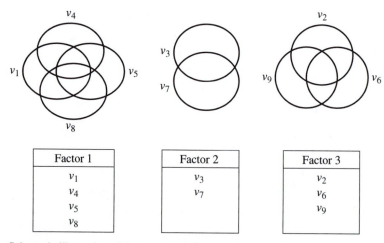

Schematic illustration of factor analysis where nine variables are reduced to three factors

analysis is known as exploratory factor analysis, in contrast to the confirmatory factor analysis that is performed to test a set of common factors for consistency with the **correlations** of the observed variables. Thus, an exploratory factor analysis assesses adequacy of the number of factors postulated in the **model** in order to provide an explanation of the observed correlations between the items while a confirmatory factor analysis assesses whether the correlations between the items can be adequately explained by a given factor model. It is frequently used in the analysis of rating scales and questionnaires.

factorial– A mathematical operation in which an integer is multiplied by all the integers equal and smaller than it up to the integer 1. It is symbolized by an exclamation point (!). For example, $3! = 3 \times 2 \times 1 = 6$, $5! = 5 \times 4 \times 3 \times 2 \times 1 = 120$. Also, by convention, $0! = 1$.

$$1! = 1$$
$$2! = 1 \cdot 2 = 2$$
$$3! = 1 \cdot 2 \cdot 3 = 2! \cdot 3 = 6$$
$$4! = 1 \cdot 2 \cdot 3 \cdot 4 = 3! \cdot 4 = 24$$
$$5! = 1 \cdot 2 \cdot 3 \cdot 4 \cdot 5 = 4! \cdot 5 = 120$$
$$6! = 1 \cdot 2 \cdot 3 \cdot 4 \cdot 5 \cdot 6 = 5! \cdot 6 = 720$$
$$7! = 1 \cdot 2 \cdot 3 \cdot 4 \cdot 5 \cdot 6 \cdot 7 = 6! \cdot 7 = 5{,}040$$
$$8! = 1 \cdot 2 \cdot 3 \cdot 4 \cdot 5 \cdot 6 \cdot 7 \cdot 8 = 7! \cdot 8 = 40{,}320$$
$$9! = 1 \cdot 2 \cdot 3 \cdot 4 \cdot 5 \cdot 6 \cdot 7 \cdot 8 \cdot 9 = 8! \cdot 9 = 362{,}880$$
$$10! = 1 \cdot 2 \cdot 3 \cdot 4 \cdot 5 \cdot 6 \cdot 7 \cdot 8 \cdot 9 \cdot 10 = 9! \cdot 10 = 3{,}628{,}800$$

The first 10 factorials

factorial analysis of variance– The **analysis of variance** from an **experiment** involving two or more **independent variables** that have been cross-classified.

factorial design– A design involving two or more **factors,** each being investigated at two or more **levels.** In a factorial design, all levels of a factor occur with all levels of the others. The simplest factorial design involves the use of two factors, each at two levels, resulting in four treatment combinations. The main goal in a factorial design is to determine whether the factors do or do not interact with each other so that any possible **interactions** can be evaluated. The factors being included may be either qualitative or quantitative, and either independent or dependent. Compare *nested design.*

factorial experiment– Same as *factorial design.*

factorial moment– The rth factorial moment about an arbitrary origin a of a **discrete random variable** X with **probability function** $p(x)$ is defined by

$$\mu'_{[r]} = E(X - a)^{[r]} = \sum_{x=-\infty}^{\infty} (x - a)^{[r]} p(x)$$

where $x^{[r]} = x(x - 1)(x - 2) \cdots (x - \overline{r - 1})$. Factorial moments are used almost entirely for **discrete distributions,** or **continuous distributions** grouped in intervals of a finite length. In statistical theory they are not very useful, but they provide very concise formulas for moments of certain discrete distributions, such as the binomial, which have **probability mass** distributed at equally spaced values.

factorial moment generating function– A function of a **variable** t associated with the **probability distribution** of a **discrete random variable** X distributed at equally spaced values, taken to be 0, 1, 2, . . . , and defined by

$$\eta_x(t) = E(t^X) = \sum_{x=0}^{\infty} t^x p(x)$$

Although not of much theoretical interest, it is useful in the calculation of **factorial moments.**

factorial product– See *factorial.*

factorization theorem– A theorem in mathematical statistics that is based on the concept of the **likelihood function** and **sufficient statistic.** It provides a necessary and sufficient condition that a **statistic** be sufficient for a **parameter** of interest.

factor level– In **experimental design,** a term used to denote the **level** of a **factor** being studied.

factor loading– In a **factor analysis** the term is used to refer to the **coefficients** of the **observed variables** on the common **factors.** They are analogous to **regression coefficients** in **multiple regression analysis** and can be interpreted as **correlations** between each variable and each factor.

factor rotation– In a **factor analysis** the term is used to describe the process of transforming the **factors** initially extracted in order to make the common factors more clearly defined and simplify their interpretation. The procedure consists of turning axes about the origin until an alternate position is reached. The factors being rotated can be either orthogonal and oblique while taking into account the nature of the resulting solution and case of their interpretation. In orthogonal rotation, loadings are uncorrelated while oblique rotation involves correlated loadings.

failure time– Same as *survival time.*

fair gamble– In **theory of games,** a game of chance in which the **expected monetary value** of what is being lost is exactly equal to the expected monetary value of what is being received. In a large sequence of such games, the player with larger capital has greater **probability** of winning over his opponent. Compare *unfair gamble.*

fair game– Same as *fair gamble.*

false acceptance error– Same as *type II error.*

false negative– An **error** in a **diagnostic test** that gives a disease-free indication to a person who really has the disease. Compare *false positive.* See also *screening, sensitivity, specificity.*

false-negative rate– In a **screening** or **diagnostic test,** the **probability** that the test will yield a negative result when administered to a person who has the disease or condition in question. Compare *false-positive rate.* See also *sensitivity, specificity.*

false positive– An error in a **diagnostic test** that gives a disease indication to a person who does not have the disease. Compare *false negative.* See also *screening, sensitivity, specificity.*

false-positive rate– In a **screening** or **diagnostic test,** the **probability** that the test will yield positive result when administered to a person who does not have the disease or condition in question. Compare *false-negative rate.* See also *sensitivity, specificity.*

false rejection error– Same as *type I error.*

F distribution– A theoretical **distribution** which can be described as the distribution of the statistic $F = S_1^2 / S_2^2$, where S_1^2 is the **variance** of a **sample** of size m from a **normal population** with variance σ_1^2 and S_2^2 is the variance of an independent sample of size n from a normal population with variance σ_2^2. The statistic F is said to have an F distribution with $m - 1$ **degrees of freedom** in the numerator and $n - 1$ degrees of freedom in the denominator. In general, an **F statistic** is obtained as the **ratio** of two independent **random variables** each having a **chi-square distribution,** divided by their respective degrees of freedom. The distribution of F involves a family of curves each adjusted for the degrees of freedom associated with the two variances being compared. The F distribution is also known as the variance ratio distribution. It was first studied by R. A. Fisher, and the ratio F was denominated by G. W. Snedecor after the first letter of the originator's name. The distribution is related to the **beta distribution** with $\alpha = v_1/2$ and $\beta = v_2/2$ where $v_1 = m - 1$ and $v_2 = n - 1$. The distribution is of fundamental importance in **analysis of variance.** The accompanying tables give **critical values** of the distribution, which denote the values for which the area to its right under the F distribution with v_1 and v_2 degrees of freedom is equal to α.

F distribution table

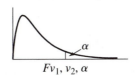

$$Fv_1, v_2, \alpha$$

The entries in this table are values of $Fv_1, v_{2,\,0.01}$ for which the area to their right under the F distribution with v_1, v_2 degrees of freedom is equal to 0.01

→v_1 ↓v_2	1	2	3	4	5	6	7	8	9	10	12	15	20	24	30	40	60	120	∞
1	4052	4999.5	5403	5625	5764	5859	5928	5982	6022	6056	6106	6157	6209	6235	6261	6287	6313	6339	6366
2	98.5	99.00	99.17	99.25	99.30	99.33	99.36	99.37	99.39	99.40	99.42	99.43	99.45	99.46	99.47	99.47	99.48	99.49	99.50
3	34.12	30.82	29.46	28.71	28.24	27.91	27.67	27.49	27.35	27.23	27.05	26.87	26.69	26.60	26.50	26.41	26.32	26.22	26.13
4	21.20	18.00	16.69	15.98	15.52	15.21	14.98	14.80	14.66	14.55	14.37	14.20	14.02	13.93	13.84	13.75	13.65	13.56	13.46
5	16.26	13.27	12.06	11.39	10.97	10.67	10.46	10.29	10.16	10.05	9.89	9.72	9.55	9.47	9.38	9.29	9.20	9.11	9.02
6	13.75	10.92	9.78	9.15	8.75	8.47	8.26	8.10	7.98	7.87	7.72	7.56	7.40	7.31	7.23	7.14	7.06	6.97	6.88
7	12.25	9.55	8.45	7.85	7.46	7.19	6.99	6.84	6.72	6.62	6.47	6.31	6.16	6.07	5.99	5.91	5.82	5.74	5.65
8	11.26	8.65	7.59	7.01	6.63	6.37	6.18	6.03	5.91	5.81	5.67	5.52	5.36	5.28	5.20	5.12	5.03	4.95	4.86
9	10.56	8.02	6.99	6.42	6.06	5.80	5.61	5.47	5.35	5.26	5.11	4.96	4.81	4.73	4.65	4.57	4.48	4.40	4.31
10	10.04	7.56	6.55	5.99	5.64	5.39	5.20	5.06	4.94	4.85	4.71	4.56	4.41	4.33	4.25	4.17	4.08	4.00	3.91
11	9.65	7.21	6.22	5.67	5.32	5.07	4.89	4.74	4.63	4.54	4.40	4.25	4.10	4.02	3.94	3.86	3.78	3.69	3.60
12	9.33	6.93	5.95	5.41	5.06	4.82	4.64	4.50	4.39	4.30	4.16	4.01	3.86	3.78	3.70	3.62	3.54	3.45	3.36
13	9.07	6.70	5.74	5.21	4.86	4.62	4.44	4.30	4.19	4.10	3.96	3.82	3.66	3.59	3.51	3.43	3.34	3.25	3.17
14	8.86	6.51	5.56	5.04	4.69	4.46	4.28	4.14	4.03	3.94	3.80	3.66	3.51	3.43	3.35	3.27	3.18	3.09	3.00
15	8.68	6.36	5.42	4.89	4.56	4.32	4.14	4.00	3.89	3.80	3.67	3.52	3.37	3.29	3.21	3.13	3.05	2.96	2.87
16	8.53	6.23	5.29	4.77	4.44	4.20	4.03	3.89	3.78	3.69	3.55	3.41	3.26	3.18	3.10	3.02	2.93	2.84	2.75
17	8.40	6.11	5.18	4.67	4.34	4.10	3.93	3.79	3.68	3.59	3.46	3.31	3.16	3.08	3.00	2.92	2.83	2.75	2.65
18	8.29	6.01	5.09	4.58	4.25	4.01	3.84	3.71	3.60	3.51	3.37	3.23	3.08	3.00	2.92	2.84	2.75	2.66	2.57
19	8.18	5.93	5.01	4.50	4.17	3.94	3.77	3.63	3.52	3.43	3.30	3.15	3.00	2.92	2.84	2.76	2.67	2.58	2.49
20	8.10	5.85	4.94	4.43	4.10	3.87	3.70	3.56	3.46	3.37	3.23	3.09	2.94	2.86	2.78	2.69	2.61	2.52	2.42
21	8.02	5.78	4.87	4.37	4.04	3.81	3.64	3.51	3.40	3.31	3.17	3.03	2.88	2.80	2.72	2.64	2.55	2.46	2.36
22	7.95	5.72	4.82	4.31	3.99	3.76	3.59	3.45	3.35	3.26	3.12	2.98	2.83	2.75	2.67	2.58	2.50	2.40	2.31
23	7.88	5.66	4.76	4.26	3.94	3.71	3.54	3.41	3.30	3.21	3.07	2.93	2.78	2.70	2.62	2.54	2.45	2.35	2.26
24	7.82	5.61	4.72	4.22	3.90	3.67	3.50	3.36	3.26	3.17	3.03	2.89	2.74	2.66	2.58	2.49	2.40	2.31	2.21
25	7.77	5.57	4.68	4.18	3.85	3.63	3.46	3.32	3.22	3.13	2.99	2.85	2.70	2.62	2.54	2.45	2.36	2.27	2.17
26	7.72	5.53	4.64	4.14	3.82	3.59	3.42	3.29	3.18	3.09	2.96	2.81	2.66	2.58	2.50	2.42	2.33	2.23	2.13
27	7.68	5.49	4.60	4.11	3.78	3.56	3.39	3.26	3.15	3.06	2.93	2.78	2.63	2.55	2.47	2.38	2.29	2.20	2.10
28	7.64	5.45	4.57	4.07	3.75	3.53	3.36	3.23	3.12	3.03	2.90	2.75	2.60	2.52	2.44	2.35	2.26	2.17	2.06
29	7.60	5.42	4.54	4.04	3.73	3.50	3.33	3.20	3.09	3.00	2.87	2.73	2.57	2.49	2.41	2.33	2.23	2.14	2.03
30	7.56	5.39	4.51	4.02	3.70	3.47	3.30	3.17	3.07	2.98	2.84	2.70	2.55	2.47	2.39	2.30	2.21	2.11	2.01
40	7.31	5.18	4.31	3.83	3.51	3.29	3.12	2.99	2.89	2.80	2.66	2.52	2.37	2.29	2.20	2.11	2.02	1.92	1.80
60	7.08	4.98	4.13	3.65	3.34	3.12	2.95	2.82	2.72	2.63	2.50	2.35	2.20	2.12	2.03	1.94	1.84	1.73	1.60
120	6.85	4.79	3.95	3.48	3.17	2.96	2.79	2.66	2.56	2.47	2.34	2.19	2.03	1.95	1.86	1.76	1.66	1.53	1.38
∞	6.63	4.61	3.78	3.32	3.02	2.80	2.64	2.51	2.41	2.32	2.18	2.04	1.88	1.79	1.70	1.59	1.47	1.32	1.00

(Continued)

(Continued)

The entries in this table are values of $F_{\nu_1, \nu_2, 0.05}$ for which the area to their right under the F distribution with ν_1, ν_2 degrees of freedom is equal to 0.05

$\rightarrow \nu_1$ $\downarrow \nu_2$	1	2	3	4	5	6	7	8	9	10	12	15	20	24	30	40	60	120	∞
1	161.4	199.5	215.7	224.6	230.2	234.0	236.8	238.9	240.5	241.9	243.9	245.9	248.0	249.1	250.1	251.1	252.2	253.3	254.3
2	18.51	19.00	19.16	19.25	19.30	19.33	19.35	19.37	19.38	19.40	19.41	19.43	19.45	19.45	19.46	19.47	19.48	19.49	19.50
3	10.13	9.55	9.28	9.12	9.01	8.94	8.89	8.85	8.81	8.79	8.74	8.70	8.66	8.64	8.62	8.59	8.57	8.55	8.53
4	7.71	6.94	6.59	6.39	6.26	6.16	6.09	6.04	6.00	5.96	5.91	5.86	5.80	5.77	5.75	5.72	5.69	5.66	5.63
5	6.61	5.79	5.41	5.19	5.05	4.95	4.88	4.82	4.77	4.74	4.68	4.62	4.56	4.53	4.50	4.46	4.43	4.40	4.36
6	5.99	5.14	4.76	4.53	4.39	4.28	4.21	4.15	4.10	4.06	4.00	3.94	3.87	3.84	3.81	3.77	3.74	3.70	3.67
7	5.59	4.74	4.35	4.12	3.97	3.87	3.79	3.73	3.68	3.64	3.57	3.51	3.44	3.41	3.38	3.34	3.30	3.27	3.23
8	5.32	4.46	4.07	3.84	3.69	3.58	3.50	3.44	3.39	3.35	3.28	3.22	3.15	3.12	3.08	3.04	3.01	2.97	2.93
9	5.12	4.26	3.86	3.63	3.48	3.37	3.29	3.23	3.18	3.14	3.07	3.01	2.94	2.90	2.86	2.83	2.79	2.75	2.71
10	4.96	4.10	3.71	3.48	3.33	3.22	3.14	3.07	3.02	2.98	2.91	2.85	2.77	2.74	2.70	2.66	2.62	2.58	2.54
11	4.84	3.98	3.59	3.36	3.20	3.09	3.01	2.95	2.90	2.85	2.79	2.72	2.65	2.61	2.57	2.53	2.49	2.45	2.40
12	4.75	3.89	3.49	3.26	3.11	3.00	2.91	2.85	2.80	2.75	2.69	2.62	2.54	2.51	2.47	2.43	2.38	2.34	2.30
13	4.67	3.81	3.41	3.18	3.03	2.92	2.83	2.77	2.71	2.67	2.60	2.53	2.46	2.42	2.38	2.34	2.30	2.25	2.21
14	4.60	3.74	3.34	3.11	2.96	2.85	2.76	2.70	2.65	2.60	2.53	2.46	2.39	2.35	2.31	2.27	2.22	2.18	2.13
15	4.54	3.68	3.29	3.06	2.90	2.79	2.71	2.64	2.59	2.54	2.48	2.40	2.33	2.29	2.25	2.20	2.16	2.11	2.07
16	4.49	3.63	3.24	3.01	2.85	2.74	2.66	2.59	2.54	2.49	2.42	2.35	2.28	2.24	2.19	2.15	2.11	2.06	2.01
17	4.45	3.59	3.20	2.96	2.81	2.70	2.61	2.55	2.49	2.45	2.38	2.31	2.23	2.19	2.15	2.10	2.06	2.01	1.96
18	4.41	3.55	3.16	2.93	2.77	2.66	2.58	2.51	2.46	2.41	2.34	2.27	2.19	2.15	2.11	2.06	2.02	1.97	1.92
19	4.38	3.52	3.13	2.90	2.74	2.63	2.54	2.48	2.42	2.38	2.31	2.23	2.16	2.11	2.07	2.03	1.98	1.93	1.88
20	4.35	3.49	3.10	2.87	2.71	2.60	2.51	2.45	2.39	2.35	2.28	2.20	2.12	2.08	2.04	1.99	1.95	1.90	1.84
21	4.32	3.47	3.07	2.84	2.68	2.57	2.49	2.42	2.37	2.32	2.25	2.18	2.10	2.05	2.01	1.96	1.92	1.87	1.81
22	4.30	3.44	3.05	2.82	2.66	2.55	2.46	2.40	2.34	2.30	2.23	2.15	2.07	2.03	1.98	1.94	1.89	1.84	1.78
23	4.28	3.42	3.03	2.80	2.64	2.53	2.44	2.37	2.32	2.27	2.20	2.13	2.05	2.01	1.96	1.91	1.86	1.81	1.76
24	4.26	3.40	3.01	2.78	2.62	2.51	2.42	2.36	2.30	2.25	2.18	2.11	2.03	1.98	1.94	1.89	1.84	1.79	1.73
25	4.24	3.39	2.99	2.76	2.60	2.49	2.40	2.34	2.28	2.24	2.16	2.09	2.01	1.96	1.92	1.87	1.82	1.77	1.71
26	4.23	3.37	2.98	2.74	2.59	2.47	2.39	2.32	2.27	2.22	2.15	2.07	1.99	1.95	1.90	1.85	1.80	1.75	1.69
27	4.21	3.35	2.96	2.73	2.57	2.46	2.37	2.31	2.25	2.20	2.13	2.06	1.97	1.93	1.88	1.84	1.79	1.73	1.67
28	4.20	3.34	2.95	2.71	2.56	2.45	2.36	2.29	2.24	2.19	2.12	2.04	1.96	1.91	1.87	1.82	1.77	1.71	1.65
29	4.18	3.33	2.93	2.70	2.55	2.43	2.35	2.28	2.22	2.18	2.10	2.03	1.94	1.90	1.85	1.81	1.75	1.70	1.64
30	4.17	3.32	2.92	2.69	2.53	2.42	2.33	2.27	2.21	2.16	2.09	2.01	1.93	1.89	1.84	1.79	1.74	1.68	1.62
40	4.08	3.23	2.84	2.61	2.45	2.34	2.25	2.18	2.12	2.08	2.00	1.92	1.84	1.79	1.74	1.69	1.64	1.58	1.51
60	4.00	3.15	2.76	2.53	2.37	2.25	2.17	2.10	2.04	1.99	1.92	1.84	1.75	1.70	1.65	1.59	1.53	1.47	1.39
120	3.92	3.07	2.68	2.45	2.29	2.17	2.09	2.02	1.96	1.91	1.83	1.75	1.66	1.61	1.55	1.50	1.43	1.35	1.25
∞	3.84	3.00	2.60	2.37	2.21	2.10	2.01	1.94	1.88	1.83	1.75	1.67	1.57	1.52	1.46	1.39	1.32	1.22	1.00

Source: Computed by software.

feasibility study– Same as *pilot study.*

fertility– In **demography,** fertility is used in the sense of actual production or bearing of offspring.

fertility rate– Number of live births occurring in a specified period per 1000 women of child-bearing age, i.e., 15 to 49 years. In some countries the child-bearing age is taken as 15 to 44 years. It is calculated as the number of live births actually observed by the female population of child-bearing age (expressed per 1000). It is more refined than the **crude birth rate,** which takes into account the whole population. Further refinements can be made by reporting **ratio** of births for various age groups within 15 to 49 years. See also *age-specific fertility rate.*

fiducial distribution– Same as *fiducial probability distribution.*

fiducial inference– A term first used by R. A. Fisher in 1930 to describe a type of **statistical inference** based on **fiducial probability distribution.** Its objective is to make statistical inference about an unknown **parameter** by deriving its **probability distribution** from the **distribution** of its **estimator** without having first assigned the parameter any **prior distribution.** Many **statisticians** find it a problematic form of **inference** and have commented adversely about it. See also *fiducial interval.*

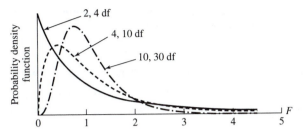

Probability density curves for F distributions with (2, 4), (4, 10) and (10, 30) degrees of freedom

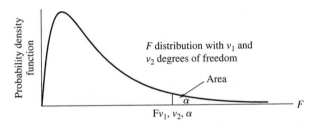

An F value having an area equal to α in the right tail

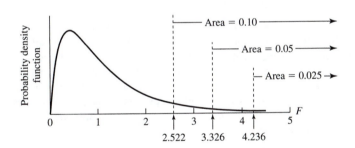

Area to the right of 2.522 is 0.10, etc.

Probability density curve for F distribution with (5, 10) degrees of freedom

fiducial interval– In the theory of **estimation,** an interval similar to **confidence interval** that can be expected, with a specified **probability,** to contain the value of some unknown **parameter.** The term is also used as a synonym of confidence interval but its conceptual origin is different. Whereas in a confidence interval, the limits of the interval are the **random variables,** in a fiducial interval the parameter is assumed to have a (fiducial) distribution.

fiducial limits– The limits of a **fiducial interval** that define the interval.

fiducial probability– See *fiducial probability distribution.*

fiducial probability distribution– A term used to describe the **probability distribution** of a **parameter** being used in a **fiducial inference.** It is not a probability distribution in the usual sense of the term, but is constructed from the **distribution** of **estimators** and contains all the relevant information in the **sample.**

field plot– Same as *plot.*

finite population– A **population** of items or individuals that are finite in number.

finite population correction– If a **sample** of size n is drawn without replacement from a **finite population** of size N, the **standard error** of the **sample mean** $\overline{X}$ can be written as

$$\sigma_{\overline{X}} = \sqrt{\left(\frac{N-n}{N-1}\right)} \frac{\sigma}{\sqrt{n}}$$

where σ is the **population standard deviation.** The multiplier term $(N-n)/(N-1)$ in the above formula is sometimes called the finite population correction; whenever $n/N \leq 0.05$, the finite population factor is close to 1 and hence $\sigma_{\overline{X}} = \sigma/\sqrt{n}$.

finite population factor– See *finite population correction.*

first quartile– The 0.25 **fractile** or 25th **percentile point** in a **data set** below which a quarter of all observations lie. See also *median, quartiles, second quartile, third quartile.*

Fisher information matrix– It is the **matrix** obtained as the inverse of the **variance–covariance matrix** of a set of **estimators.**

Fisher's discriminant function– See *discriminant analysis.*

Fisher's exact test– An "exact" conditional test for analyzing data in a **2 × 2 contingency table.** It is used when the **sample size** is too small (<30) to use the **chi-square test.** It is based on the exact **hypergeometric distribution** of the observed **cell frequencies** within the table. The procedure consists of evaluating the sum of exact hypergeometric probabilities associated with observed cell frequencies and of those deviating more than the observed frequencies under the **hypothesis** of **independence.** The procedure leads to a **conservative test** and has been the subject of controversy among **statisticians.** See also *Yates' correction for continuity.*

Fisher's ideal index number– A **consumer price index** obtained as the **geometric mean** of **Laspeyres' index number** and **Paasche's index number.** Laspeyres and Paasche index numbers are biased, if at all, in opposite directions. For example, if the index is one of prices, the former is usually biased upward and the latter downward. Taking the geometric mean provides an **index number** free from the **bias** inherent in them. It is named in honor of the American economist Irwing Fisher (1867–1947). It is calculated by the formula

$$\sqrt{\frac{\sum_{i=1}^{n} p_1^i q_0^i}{\sum_{i=1}^{n} p_0^i q_0^i} \times \frac{\sum_{i=1}^{n} p_1^i q_1^i}{\sum_{i=1}^{n} p_0^i q_1^i}}$$

where p_0^i = price at base period, q_0^i = quantity at base period, p_1^i = price at first time period, and q_1^i = quantity at first time period.

Fisher's LSD test– Same as *least significant difference test.*

Fisher's scoring method– Same as *scoring method.*

Fisher's transformation of the correlation coefficient– Same as *Fisher's z transformation.*

Fisher's z transformation– A **transformation** applied to the **correlation coefficient** r so that it is normally distributed with **mean** zero and **standard deviation** of one. It is given by the formula

$$z = \frac{1}{2} \log_e \frac{1+r}{1-r}$$

The **statistic** z has mean

$$\frac{1}{2} \log_e \frac{1+\rho}{1-\rho}$$

and **variance**

$$\frac{1}{n-3}$$

where ρ is **the population correlation** and n is the **sample size.** The transformation may be used to test a **hypothesis** or construct a **confidence interval** for ρ.

five-number summary– An **exploratory data analysis** technique that uses the following five numbers to summarize the **data set:** minimum value, **first quartile** (lower hinge), **median, third quartile** (upper hinge), and maximum value. The five-number summary forms the basis for constructing a **box-and-whisker plot.** See also *stem-and-leaf plot.*

fixed-base index number– An **index number** with a common base. The base is usually taken as one of the periods, times, or places within the series, not necessarily the first one. It provides a mechanism for a common standard of comparison.

fixed effects– A term used to denote **effects** attributable to the collection of **levels** of a **factor** or **treatment** where all the levels of interest are included in a given **experiment** or study. Compare *random effects.*

fixed-effects analysis of variance– See *fixed-effects model.*

fixed-effects model– An **analysis of variance** or **regression model** in which the **treatment levels** associated with a **factor** are considered to have fixed or **constant** effects. This model is also referred to as **Model I.** In a fixed-effects model all the **treatments** of interest to the researcher are included in the **experiment** or study under consideration. In the context of **meta-analysis,** the term is used to describe a model that assumes that the number of studies being summarized are the only ones of interest to the investigator. In a meta-analysis with fixed-effects model, the results of the combined estimate can be applied to any subject from the **target population** represented by the individual studies. See also *mixed-effects model, random-effects model.*

fixed factors– Factors in an **analysis of variance** or **regression model** thought to have a **fixed effect.** Some examples of factors that are usually considered fixed are: type of disease, treatment therapy, gender, and marital and economic status. Compare *random factors.* See also *random effects.*

flowchart– A pictorial representation of a system or process that uses certain symbols and conventions to outline all the steps in the process, interrelationships between different steps, and the order in which they are to be executed.

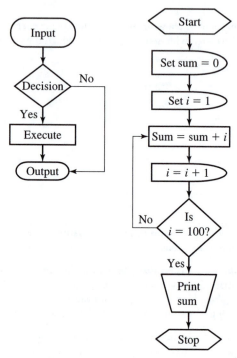

Figures illustrating a flowchart

folded normal distribution– Same as *half-normal distribution.*

folded standard normal distribution– The **probability distribution** of a **random variable** $Z = |X|$, where X has a **standard normal distribution.** Its **probability density function** is given by

$$f(z) = \sqrt{2/\pi}\, e^{-z^2/2}$$

folded t distribution– The **probability distribution** of a **random variable** $t' = |X|$ where X has a t **distribution** with ν **degrees of freedom.** It can be shown that the **folded standard normal distribution** is a limiting form of the folded t distribution as $\nu \to \infty$. The folded t distribution is also related to the **chi distribution** by the relation $t' = x/(\sqrt{\nu}y)$ where X and Y are independent **chi variables** with 1 and ν degrees of freedom respectively.

follow-up– The process of locating individuals participating in a **longitudinal study** in order to determine outcome measures and other pertinent characteristics at regular intervals of time in the future. In a field **experiment** or **sample survey,** the term is used to describe a further attempt to obtain information on individuals who could not be located in the initial attempt.

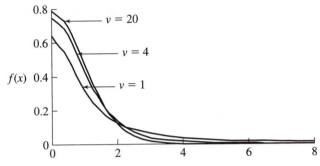

Probability density curves for the folded t distribution

follow-up period– The length of time individuals participating in a **longitudinal study** are kept under observation in order to record outcome measures and other pertinent characteristics.

follow-up study– Same as *prospective study.*

forecast– See *forecasting.*

forecasting– Making statements or **predictions** about an unknown, uncertain, and, generally, future **outcome** or quantity, such as the inflation or interest rate. Forecasting is generally based on past values and employs statistical methods based on **regression model** or **time-series analysis.** The specific value most likely to provide an accurate prediction of a future value is known as the forecast.

FORTRAN– An acronym for Formula Translation. A mathematically oriented programming language used for writing **computer programs.**

forward-looking study– Same as *prospective study.*

forward selection procedure– In **multiple regression analysis,** a method for selecting the best possible set of **predictors** of the **criterion variable.** The method proceeds by introducing the **variables** one at a time according to a prechosen criterion of **statistical significance.** The variable that has the highest **sample correlation** with the criterion variable is selected first and is included in the **model equation** if it meets the criterion. Next, the variable with the highest correlation with the criterion variable, after adjusting for the effect of the first variable included in the model (i.e., the variable with the highest sample correlation coefficient with the **residuals** from step 1) is examined and is included if it meets the criterion. The selection of third, fourth, etc. variables to be included in the **model** proceeds in the same way. The process is continued till the last variable entering the equation does not meet the criterion, or all the variables are included in the model. Compare *backward elemination procedure, stepwise regression.*

forward solution– Same as *forward selection procedure.*

fourfold table– Same as *2 × 2 contingency table.*

fractile– A value in a **data set** below which a certain specified **proportion** of all values lies. Fractiles divide a data set into groups with known proportions of **observations** in each group. It is also called **quantile.** See also *deciles, percentiles, quartiles, quintiles.*

fractional factorial design– In a **factorial design** if there are large number of **treatment factors** and the available resources are limited, it may be necessary to use a **replication** of only a fraction of the total number of treatment combinations. In a design involving a fractional replication, some of the **effects** cannot be estimated since they are **confounded** with one or more other effects. Usually, the choice of a fractional replication is made such that the effects considered to be of importance are confounded only with the effects that can be assumed to be negligible. Thus, the design is likely to be useful only when certain high-order **interactions** can be regarded as negligible.

frame– A list, map, or other record of the **sampling units** that constitute the available information relating to the population designated for a particular **sampling design.**

Freeman–Tukey test– A **test procedure** for testing the **goodness of fit** of a specified **model** or a theoretical **distribution.** The procedure is usually applied on **count** or **frequency data** by comparing the **observed** and the **expected frequencies** under the assumed model. See also *chi-square statistic, goodness-of-fit statistic, goodness-of-fit test, G^2-statistic, likelihood ratio statistic.*

Freeman–Tukey transformation– A **transformation** of the form $\sqrt{x} + \sqrt{x+1}$ proposed by Freeman and Tukey, in order to stabilize its **variance.** It is normally used to a **random variable** having a **Poisson distribution.**

frequency– The number of times a given value of an **observation** or a particular type of **event** occurs, or the number of elements of a **population** that belong to a specified group or class. It is also called count. See also *relative frequency.*

frequency count– Same as *frequency.*

frequency curve– A **graphical representation** of a continuous **frequency distribution** by a smooth curve. The **variate** is marked as the **abscissa,** and **frequency** is shown as the **ordinate.** The frequency curve may be considered a limiting form of the **frequency polygon** as the number of **observations** tends to infinity and the **class width** tends to zero.

frequency data– Same as *count data.*

frequency density– In a **frequency distribution,** the **ratio** of a **class frequency** to the **class width.** See also *probability density.*

frequency distribution– The method of classifying and representing **statistical data** that involve two columns: one listing the categories, **score intervals,** or **events** into which the **data** are sorted and the other indicating the number of items or members in each category. It is customary to list **scores** in descending order, from the highest to the lowest. When values in a **data set** are arranged in ascending or descending order of magnitude, the frequency distribution shows the number of times (**frequency**) that each value occurs. See also *cumulative frequency distribution, cumulative relative frequency distribution.*

frequency function– A mathematical function that gives the **frequency** of a **variate** value x as a function of x. For a continuous **random variable** X, it is the frequency in an elemental range dx. A frequency function is used to describe a **frequency curve.** See also *probability density function, probability function.*

frequency histogram– Same as *histogram.*

Frequency distribution for student grades: hypothetical data

Class	Midpoint	Frequency
50–54	52	4
55–59	57	8
60–64	62	11
65–69	67	20
70–74	72	18
75–79	77	15
80–84	82	11
85–89	87	6
90–94	92	5
95–99	97	2

frequency polygon– A **graphical representation** of a **frequency distribution** in which the **horizontal axis** represents score values or **midvalues** and the **vertical axis** represents **frequency** of occurrence. A dot is placed over each score value at the height representing its frequency of occurrence. These dots are then joined by straight lines to form a polygon. It is useful in comparing two or more frequency distributions.

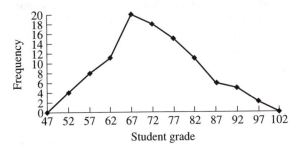

A frequency polygon of the frequency distribution for student grades

frequency table– A **tabular representation** of a **frequency distribution.** See also *cumulative frequency distribution, cumulative relative frequency distribution.*

frequency theory of probability– Same as *empirical probability.*

frequentist– A believer in the **frequency theory of probability** and **classical statistical inference.**

frequentist inference– Same as *classical statistical inference.*

Friedman's rank test– A **nonparametric test** procedure used to compare three or more correlated or **matched samples** of **observations** that cannot be compared by means of an *F* **test** in a **randomized block design** either because the **scores** are ordinal in nature or because the **normality** or **homogeneity of variance** assumptions cannot be satisfied. The method consists of ranking observations separately within each **block,** and the **test statistic** is based on the sum of the **ranks** assigned to the individual **treatment groups.** See also *Kruskal–Wallis test.*

Friedman's two-way analysis of variance– Same as *Friedman's rank test.*

***F* statistic**– In general, any **statistic** that has an *F* **distribution.** In an **analysis of variance,** the **ratio** of two **mean squares** known as **mean square ratio** follows an *F* distribution. The *F* statistic is also used to compare **variances** from two **normal populations.**

***F* test**– A **statistical test** based on an *F* **statistic.** Two commonly used *F* tests are *F* **test for analysis of variance** and *F* **test for two population variances.**

***F* test for analysis of variance**– The **statistical test** for comparing the **means** of several **populations** used in the **analysis of variance.** Under the **null hypothesis** of no difference between the **population means,** the two **mean squares** (between and within) are approximately equivalent and their **ratio** (*F* **statistic**) is nearly equal to 1. In comparison of the means of two **independent groups,** the *F* **test** is equivalent to the **two-sample *t* test.** In **regression analysis,** the *F* statistic is used to test the joint significance of all the variables in the **model.**

***F* test for two population variances**– A test devised by R. A. Fisher to compare the **variances** of two **populations.** It makes its comparisons directly in the form of a **ratio,** with the larger **sample variance** serving as the numerator and the smaller serving as the denominator. This is the simplest use of the *F* **statistic** for testing the difference between the variances of two independent **normal populations.** The *F* test for two **population variances** may be used to compare two **distributions** for **homogeneity of variances** before proceeding to perform *t* **test.** See also *Ansari–Bradely test, Barton–David test, Conover test, F distribution, Klotz test, Mood test, Rosenbaum test, Siegel–Tukey test.*

G

gambler's fallacy– The belief that if a certain event has not occurred for a long period of time, it is sure to occur sometime very soon.

game theory– A mathematical theory involving analysis of decisions that deals with the theory of contests between two or more players involving **random** strategies in which each player wants to play the best way under the rules of the game. The game strategy usually involves a series of **events,** each of which may have a finite number of distinct results. For each event, it is known which player is to make the decision and how much that player knows about the results of the earlier events at the time of the decision. Game theory has applications in diverse fields such as systems analysis, war gaming, disease surveillance and control, and clinical decision analysis.

gamma– A **symmetric measure of association** for **observations** measured on an **ordinal scale.** The measure ranges from -1 to $+1$ and takes into account only the number of untied pairs. It is denoted by the Greek letter Γ. It is more fully known as Goodman–Kruskal gamma.

gamma distribution– A **probability distribution** with **parameters** α and β given by a **density function** of the form

$$f(x; \alpha, \beta) = \begin{cases} \dfrac{1}{\beta^{\alpha}\Gamma(\alpha)} x^{\alpha-1} e^{-\alpha/\beta} & x > 0 \\ 0 & \text{elsewhere} \end{cases}$$

The distribution has many important applications and includes the **chi-square distribution** and the **exponential distribution** as special cases.

gamma function– The gamma function (Γ) is defined by

$$\Gamma(p) = \int_0^\infty e^{-x} x^{p-1} \, dx \qquad p > 0$$

A gamma function satisfies the recursive relationship $\Gamma(p+1) = p\Gamma(p)$. If p is any integer, it follows that $\Gamma(p+1) = p!$.

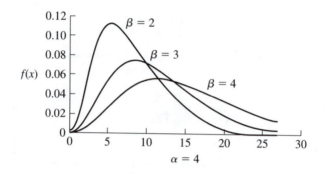

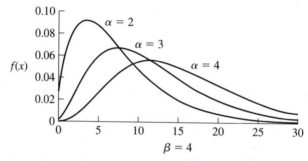

Probability density curves for gamma distribution for various values of α and β

GAUSS– A high-level programming language popular for writing programs in mathematical and scientific computations.

Gaussian distribution– Same as *normal distribution.*

Gaussian quadrature– An **algorithm** for performing numerical integration by approximating the function via a series expansion.

Gauss–Markov theorem– A theorem in mathematical statistics that states that the **least squares estimators** of the **parameters** in a **linear model** have uniformly smaller **variance** than any other **unbiased linear estimator.**

Geary's ratio– Same as *Geary's test.*

Geary's test– A test of **kurtosis** of a **distribution** based on the **statistic** G, defined as

$$G = \frac{\text{mean deviation}}{\text{standard deviation}}$$

In **samples** from a **normal population,** the value of G, when determined for the whole **population,** is 0.7979. Positive kurtosis yields higher values and negative kurtosis yields lower values of G.

Gehan's generalized Wilcoxon test– Same as *Gehan's test.*

Gehan's test– A **nonparametric statistical test** for comparing two **survival curves.** It is a version of the **Wilcoxon rank-sum test** applicable to **survival data** containing **censored observations.**

general fertility rate– Same as *fertility rate.*

generalized linear model– A class of **linear models** that allows the theory and methodology to be applicable to a much more general class of linear models, of which the normal theory is a special case. Such models allow the use of **sample data** that follow a **non-normal probability distribution** such as **Bernoulli** and **Poisson distributions. Estimates** of **parameters** in such models are generally determined by the method of **maximum likelihood estimation.**

generalized p value– A procedure for determining p **value** in the presence of **nuisance parameters.**

generalized Wilcoxon test– Same as *Gehan's test.*

general linear model– A class of **linear models** that includes both **regression** and **analysis of variance** models. Thus, a general linear model is used to study the effect of a continuous **dependent variable** on one or more **independent variables** whether continuous or categorical.

geographic correlation– The **correlation** between quantities determined as **averages** over a geographic region, such as state, country, or continent. These correlations generally give values that are very different from those that would be obtained from an analysis of unit level **data.** The phenomenon is often referred to as the ecological fallacy. It is also known as ecological correlation.

geometric distribution– The **probability distribution** of the number of **trials** required to obtain the first success in a series of **Bernoulli trials.** The **probability** of conducting n trials up to and including the first success is determined by the formula

$$P(n) = p\,(1-p)^{n-1} \qquad n = 1,\,2,\,\ldots$$

where p is the probability of success at each trial.

geometric mean– The geometric mean, symbolized as GM or G, is the nth root of the product of n **observations.** Given $x_1, x_2, \ldots, x_n$, a set of n numbers, it is defined by the formula $\text{GM} = (x_1 \cdot x_2 \cdots x_n)^{1/n}$. It is generally used with characteristics measured on a logarithmic scale or with **skewed distributions.** It is calculated as the antilog of the **mean** from observations that have been transformed to logarithmic scale. The geometric mean lies between the **harmonic mean** and the **arithmetic mean.** It is not very useful as a **measure of location** and has a downward **bias** compared with the arithmetic mean. It is more suitable for averaging **ratios** and is therefore frequently used in the computation of **index numbers** that measure ratios of change in prices and other **data.**

geometric progression– A series of ordered numbers is said to form a geometric progression if the **ratio** of any two adjacent numbers is the same. For example, the series 2, 4, 8, 16, ... is in geometric progression. Population size over a period of years is said to follow a geometrical pattern of growth if the change within a particular year is proportional to the population size at the beginning of that year.

gold standard– In medical diagnosis, the term is used to refer a **diagnostic procedure** that is highly accurate and reliable and generally gives correct diagnosis. Such procedures are generally expensive and are used in studies to assess the performance of a screening procedure. In **clinical trials** the term is applied to a randomized double-blind control clinical trial.

Goodman–Kruskal gamma– Same as *gamma.*

Goodman–Kruskal lambda– Same as *lambda.*

Goodman–Kruskal measures of association– Measures of association between two **qualitative variables** measured on **nominal scale.** Two such measures in common use are the so-called **gamma** and **lambda.**

goodness of fit– A term used to refer to the quality of a **model** or a theoretical **distribution** fitted to a given set of **data.**

goodness-of-fit statistic– An index or number that indicates how well a specified **model** or a theoretical **distribution** fits a given set of **data.** It is usually based on the comparison between the **observed** and **expected frequencies.** See also *chi-square statistic, G^2 statistic, likelihood ratio statistic.*

goodness-of-fit test– A **statistical procedure** performed to test whether to accept or reject a hypothesized **probability distribution** describing the characteristics of a **population.** It is designed to ascertain how well the **sample data** conform to expected theoretical values. It involves testing the fit between an observed **distribution** of **events** and a hypothetical distribution based on a theoretical principle, research findings, or other evidence by means of a **Pearson chi-square statistic** or any other **test statistic.** See also *chi-square test, goodness-of-fit statistic, Kolmogorov-Smirnov test.*

Graeco–Latin square– An **experimental design** involving the allocation of *p* **treatments** in $p \times p$ square array of Roman and Greek letters where each Roman and Greek letter appears once in each row and in each column, and each Roman letter appears once in combination with each Greek letter. A Graeco–Latin square is used to control three sources of **variation** which may be identified with rows, columns, and Greek letters. The design is also useful for investigating simultaneous **effects** of four **factors:** rows, columns, Latin letters and Greek letters in a single **experiment.** The following is an example of a 4 × 4 Graeco–Latin square. See also *hyper-Graeco–Latin square, hyper square, Latin square.*

Aα	Bβ	Cγ	Dδ
Bγ	Aδ	Dα	Cβ
Cδ	Dγ	Aβ	Bα
Dβ	Cα	Bδ	Aγ

Layout of a 4 × 4 Graeco–Latin square

grand mean– The overall **mean** of all the **observations** in all the groups involved in an **analysis of variance** procedure.

graphical device– See *graphical methods.*

graphical display– See *graphical methods.*

graphical methods– A class of methods and techniques that make use of graphs and visual displays to represent the **data** or the results of an analysis. Some examples of graphical methods include **histograms, bivariate plots,** and **residual plots,** among others.

graphical presentation– See *graphical methods.*

graphical procedures– Same as *graphical methods.*

graphical representation– See *graphical methods.*

graphical techniques– Same as *graphical methods.*

graphing– A general term for plotting numbers and fitting a graph to the **scatter** of **data values.**

Greenwood's formula– In **survival analysis,** an algebraic formula for calculating the **variance** of the **Kaplan–Meier estimator.**

gross reproduction rate– Average number of female children that a synthetic cohort of women would have at the end of child-bearing years, assuming the absence of **mortality.** This **rate** gives a measure of replacement of **fertility** in the absence of mortality. See also *net reproduction rate.*

grouped data– Data values that have been sorted and grouped into **class intervals,** in order to reduce the number of scoring categories to a manageable level when the data range very widely. Data available in class intervals are then summarized by a **frequency distribution.** Individual values of the original data are not retained. Thus, with grouped data, one may not know the exact values of the **observations** falling within the class intervals. Compare *ungrouped data.* See also *grouped frequency distribution.*

grouped frequency distribution– A **frequency distribution** that lists **frequencies** for **class intervals** rather than individual **scores.** The **data** are grouped in intervals of equal range and each frequency represents the number of **data values** in one of the intervals. Compare *ungrouped frequency distribution.*

grouping– Same as *classification.*

group mean– The **mean** of all the **observations** in a particular group in an **analysis of variance** design.

group sequential trial– A **clinical trial** in which comparisons are made every time a group of patients has been enrolled in the study. These trials terminate early when **treatment** differences are large. See also *sequential sampling.*

growth curve analysis– The study of correlated **measurements** over time in individuals and groups. For example, in a study of height and weight of a group of children at a particular age, a graph of the height against the weight gives the individual's growth curve. The analysis of growth curve usually involves the problems of **repeated measures designs.**

G^2 **statistic–** A **statistic** based on the likelihood ratio used to test the **goodness of fit** of a specified model or a theoretical **distribution.** It is based on the comparison between the **observed** and **expected frequencies** and is calculated by the formula $G^2 = 2\sum_i O_i \log_e(O_i/E_i)$ where O_i and E_i are observed and expected frequencies in the ith class. See also *chi-square statistic, deviance, goodness-of-fit statistic, likelihood ratio statistic.*

Haldane estimator– In a **2 × 2 contingency table**, an **estimator** of the **odds ratio** obtained by adding $\frac{1}{2}$ to each **cell frequency** in order to avoid the possibility of division by zero. It is calculated by the formula:

$$\frac{\left(a + \frac{1}{2}\right)\left(d + \frac{1}{2}\right)}{\left(b + \frac{1}{2}\right)\left(c + \frac{1}{2}\right)}$$

where a, b, c, and d are the four **cell counts**. See also *Jewell's estimator.*

half-normal distribution– The **probability distribution** of a **random variable** $Z = |X|$ where X has a **normal distribution** with **mean** zero and **variance** σ^2. Its **probability density function** is given by

$$f(z) = \frac{1}{\sigma}\sqrt{\frac{2}{\pi}}\, e^{-z^2/2\sigma^2}$$

The half-normal distribution has its **probability mass** distributed to the positive half of the real line.

half-normal plot– A **graphical method** for assessing the adequacy of a specified **model** and/or detecting the presence of **outliers**. The method involves plotting the **residuals** against the **quantiles** of the **standard normal distribution**.

half-normal probability paper– A **normal probability paper** where the negative **abscissa** is omitted, leaving only the positive half of the x **axis**.

haphazard selection– A method of selecting a **sample** of individuals by taking whoever is available or happens to be first on a list. It should not be confused with a true **random selection**.

hardware– The physical components or units making up a computer system. The term is used in contrast to **programs** and **software** which make up the operating instructions.

harmonic analysis– In **time-series analysis,** a procedure for calculating the period of the **cyclic component**.

harmonic mean– An **average** calculated by using the reciprocals of a set of numbers. It is obtained as the reciprocal of the **arithmetic mean** of the reciprocals. Given $x_1, x_2, \ldots, x_n$, a set of n numbers, it is defined by the formula

$$\text{HM} = n \Big/ \sum_{i=1}^{n} 1/x_i$$

It is generally used to average **data sets** involving unequal **sample sizes.** It is useful in the averaging of certain **ratios,** such as miles per hour or miles per gallon of fuel. In many economic applications, it is used in averaging such **data** as time rates and rate-per-dollar prices. The harmonic mean is either smaller than or equal to the arithmetic mean.

Hartley's test– A **test procedure** for testing three or more **independent samples** for **homogeneity of variances** before using an **analysis of variance** procedure. It is based on the **ratio** between the largest and smallest **sample variances** and was proposed by Hartley in 1950. Like **Bartlett's test,** however, it is found to be sensitive to any departures from **normality.** See also *Box's test, Cochran's test.*

hazard– The instantaneous **risk** of failure or death.

hazard function– The **probability** that an individual dies in a certain time interval, given that the individual has survived until the beginning of the interval. Its reciprocal is equal to the **mean** survival time. The hazard function at time t, known as hazard rate, is determined as the limit of the probability of nearly immediate death for an individual known to be alive at time t. See also *survival function.*

hazard rate– See *hazard function.*

hazard ratio– In **survival analysis,** a measure of the **relative risk,** calculated as

$$\text{HR} = \frac{O_1/E_1}{O_2/E_2}$$

where O_i and E_i $(i = 1, 2)$ denote the observed and expected number of subjects experiencing the **event** of interest in the ith group. An HR of 1 suggests that the two groups being compared have the same **hazard** or **risk** of experiencing the event. An HR of greater than 1 suggests that the group 1 is more likely to experience the event while an HR of less than 1 indicates just the contrary. The **clinical significance** of a high hazard ratio depends on other information including the **absolute risk,** the **significance level,** and the clinical context.

heterogeneity of effects– In **meta-analysis,** the term is used to indicate that the individual studies being combined have effects of different magnitude. In the presence of substantial heterogeneity, it is not advisable to synthesize the individual results of different studies with a view to produce a single summary index. There are formal **statistical tests** to test for heterogeneity of effects; however, they lack sufficient **power** and their use can be misleading.

heterogeneity of effect size– Same as *heterogeneity of effects.*

heterogeneity of variances– When **samples** differ markedly in terms of magnitude of their **variances,** they are said to exhibit heterogeneity of variances. This property of **data sets** is known as heteroscedasticity. Compare *homogeneity of variances.*

heterogeneous– A term used to describe the **variability** in the composition of different groups or within the elements of the same group.

heteroscedasticity– Compare *homoscedasticity.* Same as *heterogeneity of variances.*

hierarchical cluster analysis– Same as *hierarchical clustering.*

hierarchical clustering– An **algorithm** used for implementing one of the techniques of **cluster analysis.** The algorithm proceeds by either combining or dividing clusters.

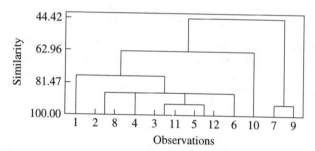

Schematic illustration of hierarchical clustering

hierarchical design– Same as *nested design.*

hierarchical models– A series of **models** where each model is nested within the preceding one or the one immediately following it.

hierarchical regression– Same as *multilevel regression.*

hinge– See *five-number summary.*

histogram– A **graphical presentation** of **frequency distribution** of a **quantitative variable** constructed by placing the **class intervals** on the **horizontal axis** of a graph and the **frequencies** on the **vertical axis.** Each class corresponds to a rectangle whose base is the real class interval and whose height is the **class frequency.** It differs from a **bar chart** in that bars are continuous and no spaces are left between the rectangles, indicating that the scoring categories represent a continuum of values that have been categorized into class intervals. A histogram can be viewed as a **bar diagram** for quantitative variables. In a histogram, the areas of the rectangles correspond to the frequencies being displayed.

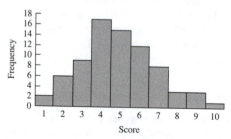

Histogram of some hypothetical data

historical cohort study– A **cohort study** based on **data** about persons at a time, or times, in the past. This method uses existing records or historical data about the health to determine the effect of a **risk factor** or **exposure** on a group of patients. Exposure to different levels of risk factors is then identified for subgroups of the population.

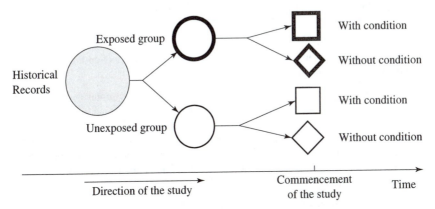

Schematic diagram of a historical cohort study

historical controls– In **clinical trials,** historical controls are **control subjects** for whom **data** were collected at a time previous to that at which the data are gathered on the **treatment group** being studied. Historical controls are generally obtained from clinical records or from the literature. Because of differences in exposures in the treatment group and historical controls, use of historical controls can lead to biased results.

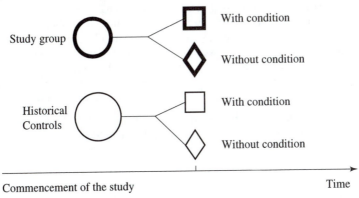

Schematic diagram of a trial with historical controls

historical prospective study– Same as *historical cohort study.*

homogeneity– The extent to which the members of the group tend to be the same on the variables being investigated. The term is also used as a clipped form of **homogeneity of variances.**

homogeneity analysis– A **multivariate statistical technique** used to describe the relationships between two or more **variables** measured on a categorical or **nominal scale.** It is similar to **correspondence analysis,** but is not limited to two variables. Like correspondence analysis, it uses a set of coordinate values to display the relationship graphically. Objects within the same category are plotted close to each other whereas objects in different categories are plotted far apart. Homogeneity analysis is also known as multiple correspondence analysis; it can also be viewed as **principal components analysis** for **nominal data.**

homogeneity of regression– In **analysis of covariance,** the assumption that the **regression lines** within each group are equal.

homogeneity of variances– In an **analysis of variance,** when **samples** are assumed to have been drawn from **populations** with equal **variances,** they are said to exhibit homogeneity of variances. Many of the parametric **tests of significance** require that the variances of the underlying populations, from which the samples are drawn, should be homogeneous. In **regression analysis,** the condition in which the variance of the **dependent variable** (Y) is the same for all the values of the **independent variable** (X). Compare *heterogeneity of variances.*

homogeneous variance– Same as *homogeneity of variances.*

homoscedasticity– Compare *heteroscedasticity.* Same as *homogeneity of variances.*

honestly significant difference (HSD) test– Same as *Tukey's test.*

horizontal axis– The **abscissa** or baseline in a two-dimensional graph. It is also called the x axis.

Hosmer–Lemeshow statistic– A **statistic** used to assess the **goodness of fit** or predictive ability of a **logistic regression.** The procedure consists of computing the **probability** of a particular **event** for each **observation** by using the **model** being fitted. Subsequently, the **data** are grouped into "risk of event" categories (e.g., 0 to 10%, 10 to 20%, 20 to 30%, . . . , 90 to 100%) leading to an $r \times 2$ **contingency table** with the columns representing yes/no outcome and the rows representing risk-of-event categories as indicated above. The tabular entries in each **cell** contain the **observed** and **expected frequencies** for each **crosstabulation.** The **chi-square statistic** is computed from the differences between observed and expected frequencies in each cell and is based on $r - 2$ **degrees of freedom.**

hospital controls– In **case-control studies,** the selection of **controls** from the same clinical source (hospital) from which **cases** are taken so that they represent the same catchment population and are subject to the same type of **selection biases.** See also *community controls.*

hot deck– A widely used and popular method of imputing **missing values** in **survey data.** See also *imputation.*

Hotelling–Lawley trace– See *multivariate analysis of variance.*

Hotelling's T^2– A generalization of **Student's t distribution** to the case of **multivariate observations.** Like Student's t, T^2 can be used to test **hypotheses** involving a broad class of multivariate **statistics,** including **means** and differences of means, **regression coefficients** and their differences. **Tests of significance** involving T^2 can be carried out by using **variance ratio distribution.**

household survey– A **sample survey** conducted by interviewing people in their own homes. These surveys generally employ complex **sampling** methodology involving several stages of sampling. For each geographical unit sampled, there are additional levels of successive subsampling of smaller geographic areas; for example, census tracks, blocks within census tracks, and households within blocks. Finally, the individuals within a household may also be sampled.

HSD test– Acronym for *honestly significant difference test.*

hybrid series– A statistical series consisting of mixture of **time series** and **cross-section series.**

hypergeometric distribution– The **probability distribution** of a set of n elements randomly selected without replacement from a set of N elements, with D elements of one type and $N - D$ elements of a second type, such that the **sample** selected contains x elements of the first type and $n - x$ elements of the second type. The hypergeometric probability distribution is given by the formula

$$p(x) = \frac{\binom{D}{x}\binom{N-D}{n-x}}{\binom{N}{n}} \qquad x = 0, 1, \ldots, \min(n, D)$$

When N is large and n is small compared to N, the hypergeometric distribution can be approximated by the **binomial distribution.** A hypergeometric distribution is frequently used in **quality control, sample surveys,** and in estimating the size of a wildlife population.

hypergeometric function– The hypergeometric function denoted by $F(\alpha, \beta, \gamma, x)$ is defined as

$$F(\alpha, \beta, \gamma, x) = 1 + \frac{\alpha.\beta}{1.\gamma}x + \frac{\alpha(\alpha+1).\beta(\beta+1)}{1.2.\gamma(\gamma+1)}x^2$$

$$+ \frac{\alpha(\alpha+1)(\alpha+2).\beta(\beta+1)(\beta+2)}{1.2.3.\gamma(\gamma+1)(\gamma+2)}x^3 + \cdots$$

Hypergeometric functions have been found useful in the derivation of **characteristic functions** of **probability distributions.**

hyper-Graeco–Latin square– An **experimental design** that is an extension of **Latin** and **Graeco–Latin squares** to control for four sources of **variation.** It can also be used to investigate simultaneous **effects** of five **factors:** rows, columns, Latin letters, Greek letters, and Hebrew letters. It is obtained by juxtaposing or superimposing three Latin squares, one with treatments denoted by Greek letters, the second with treatments denoted by Latin letters, and the third with treatments denoted by Hebrew letters, such that each Hebrew letter appears once and only once with each Greek and Latin letter.

hyper square– A design obtained by superimposing three or more orthogonal **Latin squares.** In general a $p \times p$ hyper square is a design in which three or more orthogonal $p \times p$ Latin squares are superimposed. In using such a design, the researcher must assume that there would be no **interactions** between different **factors.** See also *Graeco–Latin square, hyper-Graeco–Latin square.*

hypothesis– A proposition or conjecture, tentatively advanced as being possibly true, that a researcher intends to test from **observations.** It is a working theory that forms the basis of a scientific investigation. Experience shows that a carefully and well-prepared hypothesis may ultimately save a great deal of time, effort, and money.

hypothesis test– See *hypothesis testing.*

hypothesis testing– In **inferential statistics,** a procedure for testing **hypotheses** about a **population parameter** of interest. The process begins with the choice of the so-called **null hypothesis** and an **alternative hypothesis.** A null hypothesis is usually tested and either rejected in favor of an alternative hypothesis or not rejected, in which case the alternative hypothesis cannot be sustained. Hypothesis testing is a scientific approach to assessing beliefs about a reality or phenomenon under investigation. The following are general steps in hypothesis testing:

1. State a null hypothesis (H_0) based on the specific question or phenomenon to be investigated.
2. State an alternative hypothesis. This may be one-sided or two-sided depending on the problem being investigated as defined in the null hypothesis.
3. Specify the **level of significance** (α). This is commonly taken as 0.05 and represents the maximum acceptable **probability** of incorrectly rejecting the null hypothesis.
4. Determine an appropriate **sampling distribution** of the **sample statistic** of interest. Select a one-tailed or two-tailed test, depending on the alternative hypothesis.
5. Evaluate the **standard error** or, more generally, an **estimate** of the standard error of the sample statistic; the formula for the standard error depends on the sample statistic in question.
6. Compute the true value of the **test statistic** and locate its value on the sampling distribution.
7. Reject or do not reject H_0, depending on whether or not the sample statistic is located on the sampling distribution at or beyond the value of the test statistic at a given α. It is now a standard convention to report a **p-value** as justification for rejecting H_0, which is the probability of obtaining a result equal to or more extreme than the observed value of the test statistic if the null hypothesis were true.

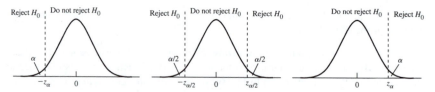

Graphical illustration of hypothesis testing based on the z statistic

See also *composite hypothesis, simple hypothesis, statistical test, type I error, type II error.*

identity matrix– A **square matrix** in which the elements along the main diagonal each have the value 1 and all other elements are 0. It is denoted by the symbol **I**.

IED– Acronym for *individual effective dose.*

improper prior– A term employed in **Bayesian statistics** to refer to a prior whose **probability distribution** does not integrate to 1. For example, if $p(\theta)$ denotes the **probability density function** of a **parameter** θ involving an improper prior, then $\int_{-\infty}^{\infty} p(\theta)\, d\theta$ is not finite. Improper priors are widely used in **Bayesian inference** when little is known about the nature of the unknown parameter, e.g., $p(\theta) \propto \theta, -\infty < \theta < \infty$.

imputation– A general term employed to describe the process of estimating **missing values** by using the available **data** for a subject or item. There are currently many such methods including **computer software** available for this purpose.

inadmissible action– In **decision theory,** an action that is inferior to an alternative action because it generates **payoffs** that are at most as good as and often worse than those of the alternative actions no matter which **outcome** occurs.

incidence– The total number of new **cases** of illness or disease that develop over a given time interval in a given population. More generally, the number of new cases of a disease in a certain population within a specified period of time. The term incidence is sometimes used to denote **incidence rate.** See also *prevalence.*

incidence rate– The **proportion** of people in a population who develop new **cases** of illness or disease over a given time interval. The incidence rate is calculated from the formula:

$$\frac{\text{Number of new cases of disease in a given period}}{\text{Total number of individuals exposed to the risk during this period}} \times 100$$

The incidence rate measures the new cases or appearance of disease and can be characterized as an index of **morbidity** or disease occurrence. For **person–time** data, it is calculated with reference to the person–time at risk during the same period where the denominator is time, not persons. It is usually expressed as per 100, 1000, 10,000, or 100,000 person-time at risk. See also *prevalence rate.*

inclusion probability– In **sampling design** the term is used to denote the **probability** of including a given element or population unit into a **sample.**

incompatible events– Same as *mutually exclusive events.*

incomplete block design– An **experimental design** used in **experiments** involving a large number of **treatments,** but the number of homogenous **experimental units** that can be grouped in a **block** is rather small. Thus, the design consists of blocks of experimental units that are smaller than a complete replication involving all the treatments. For example, suppose in tests of mosquito repellents, which involve exposure of treated arms to mosqui-toes, the blocks consist of two arms of a subject at one time. The incomplete block design given below provides for testing six repellents for each of five subjects (A, B, C, D, and E) to submit two arms to treatment three times. See also *balanced incomplete block design, randomized block design.*

Day	Individuals				
	A	B	C	D	E
1	1, 2	1, 3	6, 2	3, 6	4, 5
2	6, 5	4, 6	4, 1	5, 1	2, 3
3	3, 4	5, 2	3, 5	2, 4	6, 1

Layout of an incomplete block design

incubation period– An interval of time from the onset of an infection to the appearance of given symptoms of a disease.

independence– A characteristic of **observations** or **random events.** Essentially, the term is used to describe the property of independence of events or sample observations. It is an assumption required by many **statistical tests.** See also *independent events, independent observations.*

independent events– In **probability theory,** two **events** or **outcomes** are said to be inde-pendent when the occurrence of one event has no effect on the **probability** of occurrence of another event. Thus, two events are independent if the probability of occurrence of one is the same whether or not the other event has occurred. Using the notation of **conditional probability,** two events A and B are independent when $P(A|B) = P(A)$ or $P(B|A) = P(B)$. If two events are independent, the probability that they will both occur equals the product of their individual probabilities. If two events are not independent, they are said to be dependent. Compare *dependent events.*

independent groups– Same as *independent samples.*

independent observations– Observations obtained at different points in time or by dif-ferent individuals in such a manner that the value of one observation does not affect the value of the other observations.

independent random variables– A set of **random variables** whose **joint probability distribution** (or **density function**) is equal to the product of their **marginal probability**

distributions (or density functions). Random variables that are not independent are said to be dependent.

independent samples– Samples selected from two (or more) **populations** such that all the **observations** of one sample are chosen independently of the observations of the other sample(s). Samples are considered independent with respect to one another when there can be no way in which the observations in one group are related to the observations in the other group. **Independence** is often achieved in **experiments** by assigning the subjects to the **treatment groups** by a random scheme called **randomization.** Samples that are not independent are known as **dependent** or **correlated samples.**

independent-samples design– An **experimental design** in which the scores of one experimental condition are unrelated to (independent of) the scores in any other experimental condition.

independent-samples *t* test– Same as two sample *t* test.

independent trials– A sequence of **trials** of an **event** are said to be independent if the **probability** of occurrence of the **outcome** of any trial is independent of the outcome of the other trials.

independent variable– The **variable** in an **experiment** that is under the control of and may be manipulated by the experimenter. In **regression analysis,** it is the variable being used to regress or predict the value of the **dependent variable.** It is also commonly known as regressor, predictor, or explanatory variable.

index number– A statistical measure designed to give an indication of the change in the values of a **variable** such as prices of commodities over two different periods of time. The base period usually equals 100 and any changes from it represent percentages. Comparisons are usually made over periods of time; however, indices may also be used for comparison between places or categories of items. By use of an index number, a large or unwieldy set of business data, such as sales in millions of dollars, is reduced to a form in which it can be more readily used and understood. Some 200 to 300 formulas have been proposed over the years for the construction of an index number. Many important index numbers show changes in various economic variables and are published regularly by the government or other organizations. See also *chain-base index number, fixed-base index number, Fisher's ideal index number, Laspeyres' index number, Paasche's index number, price index number.*

index of dispersion– See *binomial index of dispersion, Poisson index of dispersion.*

index of industrial production– A quantity index that is designed to measure changes in the physical volume or production levels of industrial goods over time.

index plot– A **graphical representation** of a **diagnostic measure** or **statistic** based on **residuals** for testing the **assumptions** of a **model** being fitted.

indicator variable– Same as *manifest variable.*

indirectly standardized rate– See *standardization.*

indirect standardization– See *standardization.*

individual effective dose– In **biological assay** the amount of stimulus or quantity of dose needed in order to produce a desired response in a subject.

induction– An act or process of deriving a conclusion from the particular to the general. Compare *deduction.*

inductive inference– The drawing of **inference** about the general or whole on the basis of information about the particular or part. Compare *deductive inference.*

inductive reasoning– Same as *inductive inference.*

inductive statistics– Same as *inferential statistics.*

inexact hypothesis– Same as *composite hypothesis.*

infant death rate– The number of deaths under one year of age actually observed during a given calendar year divided by the total live births in the area occurring during the calendar year (expressed per 1000). The neonatal rate is based on deaths occurring during the first 28 days of life.

infant mortality rate– Same as *infant death rate.*

infection period– A term used to describe the time interval of the development of an epidemic during which an infected individual is capable of transmitting the disease to other persons.

inference– The process of drawing conclusions. The term is often used as a clipped form for **statistical inference.** See also *deductive inference, inductive inference.*

inferential statistics– A branch of **statistics** that is concerned with the development and applications of methods and techniques for drawing inferences about a **population** on the basis of **observations** obtained from a **random sample,** usually with a certain degree of **uncertainty** associated with it. See also *descriptive statistics.*

influence– Same as *influential observation.*

influence statistics– A term used to refer to a number of **diagnostic measures** or **statistics** designed to evaluate the effect of an **observation** on the results of fitting a **multiple regression model.** See also *Cook's distance, DFBETA, DFFITS.*

influential observation– A **data value** that exercises undue influence on the results of fitting a **multiple regression model.** An influential observation has a high leverage and is situated far from the **regression equation** that would be fitted if it were omitted. See also *influence statistics, leverage point.*

information bias– A term used to refer to **systematic errors** which may occur during the process of measuring and gathering information. Information bias can be caused by observer or interviewer error, respondent error due to failure to recall factual information or fear and embarrassment, instrument or **measurement error,** lack of **blinding** in **clinical trials,** among others.

information theory– A branch of applied mathematics devoted to the study of problems such as storing and transmitting information, arising in communication and signal processing. It is particularly concerned with the nature, effectiveness, and accuracy of storing and transmitting information.

informative prior– A term used in **Bayesian statistics** to describe a prior whose **probability distribution** contains **empirical** or theoretical information regarding the unknown

parameters. The term is used in contrast to **noninformative prior** where little or no information about the parameter is available. See also *Bayesian inference, improper prior.*

initial data analysis– A term used to describe a preliminary **data analysis** involving checking the quality and consistency of **data,** computing simple **descriptive statistics,** and making appropriate graphs and charts before performing any complex statistical analysis.

instantaneous death rate– Same as *hazard rate.*

institutional surveys– **Sample surveys** in which primary sampling units (PUSs) are institutions or establishments such as hospitals and schools. The **sampling design** for such surveys usually entails complex multistage **cluster sampling** in order to avoid constructing a **sample frame.** See also *multistage sampling.*

integer programming– A mathematical technique designed to choose the best course of action from among various available alternatives. It is similar to **linear programming.** The main difference between the two methods is that solutions to integer programming problems are usually expressed in terms of integers, that is, whole numbers. It is especially useful in situations where input and output variables are indivisible.

intention-to-treat analysis– A term used in **clinical trials** to refer to a practice of analyzing all the patients who were randomly allocated to a **treatment** as representing that **treatment group** irrespective of whether or not they received the prescribed treatment to which they were randomized or withdrew or dropped out from the study. This practice is adopted in order to minimize the **bias** arising from disturbances in the prognostic balance achieved by **randomization.** If the patients are included in the treatment group in which they were actually assigned treatment or are excluded from the analysis altogether, it may lead to serious bias adversely affecting the result of the analysis. Although clinicians sometimes disagree with this type of analysis, the clinical trial literature supports the validity of intention-to-treat principle, because it yields valid tests of the **null hypothesis** of no treatment difference. If a large fraction of patients do not receive the treatments to which they were assigned, neither the intention-to-treat nor treatment-received analyses will yield valid clinical conclusions, since many patients switch treatments for reasons associated with the efficacy of the treatments. See also *explanatory analysis.*

interaction– A term applied to designate a relationship between two or more **independent variables** or **factors** such that they have a different combined **effect** on the **dependent variable.** Thus, the two **variables** are said to interact if the effect of one variable is not **constant** across the **levels** of the other; i.e., the effect of a given level of one factor depends on the level of the other factor. For example, it is known that smoking and obesity are two independent **risk factors** for heart disease. In a study designed to investigate the **association** between obesity and heart disease, it may happen that the **risk** of smoking is greater among obese than nonobese people. In this situation, smoking and obesity are said to interact and their combined effect may be greater than the sum of the two separate effects. When the combined effect of two risk factors is greater than the sum of the two effects, the two factors are said to have synergistic effect. On the other hand, when the combined effect may result in an effect that is smaller than the sum of the two effects, the two effects are said to have antagonistic effect. In a **multiple regression analysis** involving two independent variables that interact with each other, the **regression coefficient** for the interaction term will normally be positive if the interaction is synergistic or negative if it is antagonistic. In a **factorial experiment,** it is the measure of the degree, to which the changes in the levels

of one or more factors depend on the levels of the other factors. See also *additive effect,*
additive model.

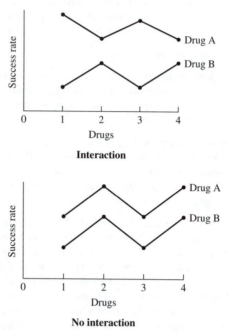

Figures showing presence and absence of
interaction between two factors

interaction effect– See *interaction.*

interaction sum of squares– Same as *sum of squares for interaction.*

intercensal period– Time period between two censuses–usually a 10-year period for national population censuses in many countries.

intercept– The value at which a plotted line crosses the **y axis.** In **regression analysis,** it is the predicted value of the **dependent variable** when the value of the **independent variable** is equal to zero. See also *x intercept, y intercept.*

interfractile range– A **measure of dispersion** in a **data set** based on the difference or distance between two **fractiles.** See also *interquartile range.*

interim analysis– In **clinical trials,** an analysis carried out before the end of the study period in order to detect beneficial effect of one **treatment** compared to the other with sufficient accuracy and certainty. The goal of the interim analysis is to prevent as many patients as possible from being randomized to or receiving an inferior treatment. If the interim analysis is carried out in a haphazard or unplanned manner, it may lead to increased **risk** of **false positive** findings due to **multiple significance testing.** In order to overcome this problem, sequential trials are used where, depending on the number of interim analyses planned, **nominal significance levels** are specified so that the overall **probability** of **type**

I error is kept at an acceptable level. Interim analyses are often problematic and should be planned carefully.

internal validity– The extent and degree to which the inferences drawn from a study can be attributed to the observed differences between the comparison groups under study, apart from **sampling error.** The internal validity of a study is increased by **random allocation** of subjects to comparison groups. Compare *external validity.*

interpenerating sampling– A **sample** in the form of $k(k \geq 2)$ samples using the identical **sampling design** from the same **population.** The procedure has been widely used in assessing **nonsampling errors** such as interviewing errors. For example, if k interviewers are assigned to collect information from k samples, then the interviewer effects can be studied and compared. Samples may or may not be drawn independently and the sampling design can be a complex design, such as multistage stratified, and with equal or unequal **inclusion probability.** The technique was originally introduced by P. C. Mahalanobis in connection with a jute and rice acreage survey in India.

interpolation– The technique of determining a value of a function between two known values by using its position among a series of known values, the increments of which are proportional to the increments of the series for which an intermediate value is desired. An example is the estimation of population of a city or country in say 1996 from the census figures of 1990 and 2000. Compare *extrapolation.*

interquartile range– A **measure of variability** or **dispersion** for a **data set** calculated as the difference or distance between the **third** and **first quartiles.** It comprises the range of values of a **variable** between which the middle 50% of the **scores** of a **distribution** lie. It provides a simple measure of dispersion that is useful in **descriptive statistics,** when the **standard deviation** is not an appropriate measure of **variability.** It is used as a **measure of spread** in conjunction with **median** as a measure of the center of the distribution. It is a robust measure that is not affected by **extreme observations.** See also *semi-interquartile range.*

interrater reliability– The **reliability** between **measurements** made by the same person (or rater) at two different points in time or two different persons (or raters). It is measured by the **kappa statistic.**

intersection of events– The intersection of two **events** A and B, denoted by $A \cap B$, is the event containing all **sample points** or elements that are common to both events A and B.

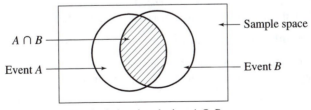

The shaded region depicts $A \cap B$

Figure showing intersection of two events A and B

interval data– **Observations** measured on an **interval scale.**

interval estimate– See *interval estimation.*

interval estimation– The process of **estimation** of a **parameter** in terms of an interval, called an interval estimate, that contains the actual value of the parameter with a given **probability.** The method for calculating an interval estimate from the **sample data** is known as an interval estimator. See also *confidence interval, fiducial interval, point estimation.*

interval estimator– See *interval estimation.*

interval scale– The process of measuring with a scale that has equal units throughout its range. An interval **scale of measurement** has three properties: it sorts **observations** into classes, orders them in terms of differences in magnitude, and specifies the amount of difference between the observations. An interval scale has no true zero and thus produces **measurements** for **quantitative variables** that permit arithmetic operations, but their **ratios** are meaningless. The measure assigned conforms to a fixed numerical unit of measurement and each measure is expressed as a quantity of those units. A well known example of an interval scale is temperature measured in degrees Fahrenheit or Celsius.

interval variable– A **quantitative variable** measured using an **interval scale.** The term is essentially synonymous with **continuous variable.**

interval width– Same as *class width.*

intervention– The maneuver or **treatment** employed in an **experimental study.** It may be a drug, a therapeutic agent, or any other procedure.

intervention group– Same as *treatment group.*

intervention study– Same as *experimental study.*

interviewer bias– A term used to refer to **errors** introduced by interviewers in misunderstanding answers and information provided by respondents to survey questions and recording erroneous responses reflecting their own misunderstandings and mistakes in some systematic manner.

intraclass correlation– A statistical measure of **homogeneity** or similarity within the elements of a group, class or **cluster.** It also serves as the measure of **reliability** for quantitative **measurements** involving repeated **observations.** When the measurement in question involves **binary data,** it is equivalent to the **kappa statistic.** The term was originally introduced in genetics to measure sibling **correlations.** It is calculated as the **product moment correlation coefficient** between two series of **paired data.**

intraclass correlation coefficient– Same as *intraclass correlation.*

intrinsic error– A term normally employed in clinical laboratory analyses to describe the **error** introduced in the **measurements** by the imprecision of analytical methods used in the analysis.

invariance– A term used to describe the property or condition of a **variable** or **statistic** that does not change under certain types of mathematical transformations of the **data.**

inverse binomial trials– A sequence of **Bernoulli trials** that are continued until a given number of successes have been observed. See also *negative binomial distribution.*

inverse J-shaped distribution– See *J-shaped distribution.*

inverse of a matrix– A **square matrix** derived from a given **matrix** in such a manner that the product of the two matrices is the **identity matrix.** Given a square matrix $\mathbf{A}$ of order n, the inverse of $\mathbf{A}$, denoted by $\mathbf{A}^{-1}$, is the matrix of order n such that $\mathbf{AA}^{-1} = \mathbf{I}$.

inverse probabilities– Same as *posterior probabilities.*

inverse relationship– A relationship between any two **variables** such that the values of one decrease with an increase in the values of the other. Compare *direct relationship.* See also *negative correlation, positive correlation.*

inverse sampling– A method of **sampling** commonly used in **quality control** to investigate the events that take a long period of time to occur, such as failures of a device at room temperature. The sampler tests the devices until a previously determined number of devices fail. The number of devices thus tested serve as a basis for any **inferences** on **population parameters.**

inverse-sine transformation– Same as *arc-sine transformation.*

inversion theorem– A theorem in mathematical statistics that states that the **probability distribution** of a **random variable** is uniquely determined by its **characteristic function.** More specifically, let $f(x)$ and $\phi_x(t)$ denote the **density function** and the characteristic function of a random variable X. Then the inversion theorem states that

$$f(x) = \frac{1}{2\pi} \int_{-\infty}^{\infty} e^{itx} \phi_x(t)\, dt$$

irregular component– In **time-series analysis, random** fluctuations in the values of a **variable** of interest after accounting for the **trend, cyclical,** and **seasonal components.** The irregular components tend to average in the long run.

irregular fluctuation– Same as *irregular component.*

irregular variation– Same as *irregular component.*

Ishikawa diagram– Same as *cause-and-effect diagram.*

Ishikawa's seven tools– These are simple **graphical devices** proposed by K. Ishikawa in 1976 for extracting all relevant information from a given **data set.** The proposed devices are: (1) **tally sheets,** (2) **histograms,** (3) **stratification,** (4) **Pareto diagrams,** (5) **scatter plots,** (6) **cause-and-effect diagrams,** and (7) graphs.

item nonresponse– A term used in **sample surveys** to denote the lack of response on the part of the respondent to a particular item or question. See also *nonresponse.*

iteration– A computational procedure in which a set of mathematical operations is repeated and where each step is based on the results obtained in the preceding step.

iterative procedure– Same as *iteration.*

J

jackknife– A **nonparametric technique** for estimating **standard error** of a **statistic.** The procedure consists of taking repeated subsamples of the original **sample** of n **independent observations** by omitting a single observation at a time. Thus, each subsample consists of $n - 1$ observations formed by deleting a different observation from the sample. The jackknife estimate and its standard error are then calculated from these truncated subsamples. For example, suppose θ is the **parameter** of interest and let $\hat{\theta}_{(1)}, \hat{\theta}_{(2)}, \ldots, \hat{\theta}_{(n)}$ be **estimates** of θ based on n subsamples each of size $n - 1$. The jackknife estimate of θ is given by

$$\hat{\theta}_J = \frac{\sum\limits_{i=1}^{n} \hat{\theta}_{(i)}}{n}$$

The jackknife estimate of the standard error of $\hat{\theta}_J$ is

$$\hat{\sigma}_{\hat{\theta}_J} = \left[\frac{n-1}{n} \sum\limits_{i=1}^{n} (\hat{\theta}_{(i)} - \hat{\theta}_J)^2 \right]^{1/2}$$

See also *bootstrap.*

jackknife residuals– A method of assessing the **assumptions** or **goodness of fit** of a **model** by examination of its **residuals.** Each residual is calculated from a model that includes all but the **observation** corresponding to the residual in question. Jackknife residuals are also known as Studentized residuals.

Jensen's inequality– Given a **discrete random variable** X having a finite number of points, the inequality states that $g[E(X)] \geq E[g(X)]$, where g is a concave function.

Jewell's estimator– In a **2 × 2 contingency table,** an **estimator** of the **odds ratio** obtained by adding 1 to each **cell frequency** that appear in the denominator. It is calculated by the formula $ad/\{(b + 1)(c + 1)\}$, where $a, b, c,$ and d are the four **cell counts.** See also *Haldane estimator.*

Johnson's system of distributions– A class of **frequency distributions** based on **transformations** of **variables.** The distributions can be used to summarize a set of **data** by means of mathematical functions, that will fit the data. It was elaborated by Norman L. Johnson in 1949.

joint confidence intervals– Same as *simultaneous confidence intervals.*

joint contingency table– A **contingency table** involving two or more **independent variables** jointly affecting a **dependent variable.**

joint density function– A generalization of the concept of a **probability density function** to two or more **continuous random variables.** Joint density function is also known as a joint probability density or a **multivariate density function.** See also *bivariate density function.*

joint distribution– Same as *joint probability distribution.*

joint probability– The **probability** of two or more **events** occurring simultaneously. It is a measure of the likelihood of the simultaneous occurrence of two or more events.

joint probability density– Same as *joint density function.*

joint probability distribution– The concept of the **probability distribution** of a **random variable** extended to two or more random variables. It is also known as a multivariate probability distribution. A multivariate probability distribution is characterized by a **multivariate probability function** involving **discrete random variables** and a **multivariate density function** for **continuous random variables.**

joint probability function– A generalization of the concept of a **probability function** to two or more **discrete random variables.** Joint probability function is also known as a **multivariate probability function.** See also *bivariate probability function.*

Jonckheere *k*-sample test– Same as *Jonckheere–Terpstra k-sample test.*

Jonckheere–Terpstra *k*-sample test– A **nonparametric procedure** for testing the equality of *k* **location parameters** against an **ordered alternative hypothesis.** For an **ordered alternative,** the test is more powerful than the **Kruskal–Wallis test,** which is an omnibus test of differences between **locations.**

Jonckheere–Terpstra test– A **nonparametric procedure** for testing a specific type of departure from independence in a **contingency table** where both rows and columns represent ordered categories.

Jonckheere test– Same as *Jonckheere–Terpstra k-sample test.*

J-shaped distribution– An asymmetrical **frequency distribution** having general resemblance to the shape of the letter J. The **distribution** has highest **frequency** at one end of the distribution, which rapidly declines at first and then declines more slowly.

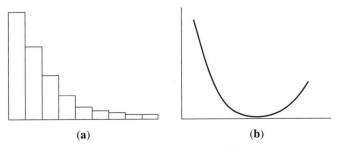

(a)   **(b)**

Inverse J-shaped distribution: **(a)** histogram and **(b)** continuous curve

judgmental errors– Errors caused by differences in the criteria used in classification based on individual judgments.

judgment sample– Unlike a **probability sample,** a **sample** selected in such a manner that an "expert" judgment plays a major role in selecting **elementary units** for **observations.** In general, any sample that is not a probability sample. Although judgment samples may lead to satisfactory results, they lack the **reliability** of a **scientific sample.** See also *convenience sample, nonprobability sample, random sample.*

judgment sampling– See *judgment sample.*

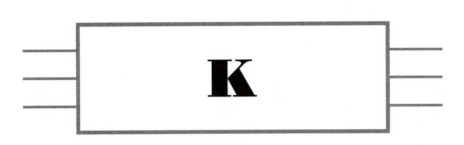

Kaplan–Meier estimator– A method for analyzing **survival data** containing **censored observations.** It uses exact survival times in the calculation of **probabilities** and provides an **estimate** of the **proportion** $S(t)$ of patients whose age at death would exceed t if no patients had been censored. The **estimator** consists of the product of a number of **conditional probabilities** resulting in an estimated **survival function** $\hat{S}(t)$ in the form of a step function. This is used to construct a **survival curve** in which the probability of survival remains **constant** between **events,** but drops at the time of occurrence of a new event. Censored observations are generally marked on the curve at the time of their occurrence. The Kaplan–Meier estimator is used to calculate an estimate of cumulative survival that can then be used to calculate the cumulative **hazard rate.** The Kaplan–Meier estimator differs from the method of **life table analysis** by grouping censored observations into intervals, in contrast to using exact end points in time when an event of interest has occurred. The procedure is also known as the product limit estimator. See also *survival analysis.*

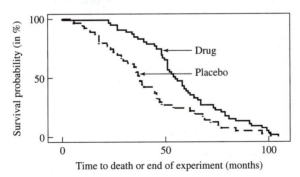

Kaplan–Meier survival curves for a placebo and an active drug

kappa coefficient– Same as *kappa statistic.*

kappa statistic– A **statistic** used to measure agreement or **reliability** between two observers or raters for **nominal data.** It can also be used to assess the agreement between two alternative methods of diagnosis. It is defined as the agreement beyond **chance** divided by the amount of agreement possible beyond chance. Thus, the kappa statistic measures proportional agreement corrected for chance, that is, the **proportion** of agreements over and above what might be expected by chance alone. The formula for kappa statistic (κ) is

$$\kappa = \frac{p_0 - p_e}{1 - p_e}$$

where p_0 is the **probability** of observed occurrence and p_e is the probability of expected or chance agreement. It takes the value 1 when there is perfect agreement and 0 when observed agreement is equal to chance agreement. When the **data** involve **measurements** on **ordinal variables,** a modified procedure known as ordinal kappa statistic is employed.

Kendall's coefficient of concordance– A measure of agreement among two or more raters who rank a number of individuals according to certain criteria.

Kendall's rank correlation– Same as *Kendall's tau.*

Kendall's tau– A nonparametric **measure of association** between two **ordinal variables** proposed by M. G. Kendall in 1938. It is based on the number of inversions (interchanges of **ranks**) in one **ranking** compared with another. It is calculated as $P - Q$ where P is the number of concordant pairs, i.e., pairs with rankings in the same direction, and Q is the number of discordant pairs, i.e., pairs with rankings in the reverse direction. It is especially appropriate for small **sample sizes.** There are a number of modifications of τ introduced in the literature for measuring **associations** in a **contingency table** where both rows and columns represent natural ordered categories.

kernel density estimator– Same as *kernel estimator.*

kernel estimator– A **nonparametric method** for estimating the **density function** of a **probability distribution.** It is calculated from a **sample** of size n by replacing each **data value** by a "kernel" of area $1/n$ resulting in a curve similar to a smoothed **frequency polygon.**

Khinchin theorem– A theorem in mathematical statistics that states that the **sample mean** converges in **probability** to the **population mean** as the **sample size** tends to infinity.

Klotz test– A **nonparametric procedure** for testing the equality of **variances** of two **populations** having the same **median.** It is based on inverse **normal scores** and was developed by Jerome Klotz in 1962. If the populations are symmetrical, its **asymptotic relative efficiency** compared to the classical *F* **test** is one. In many cases its **efficiency** exceeds one. See also *Ansari–Bradley test, Barton–David test, Conover test, F test for two population variances, Mood test.*

Kolmogorov–Smirnov one-sample test– See *Kolmogorov-Smirnov tests.*

Kolmogorov–Smirnov tests– **Nonparametric tests** for testing significant differences between two **cumulative distribution functions.** The one sample test is used to test whether the **data** are consistent with a given **distribution function** and the two sample test is used to test the agreement between two observed **cumulative distributions.** The test is based on the maximum absolute difference between the two cumulative distribution functions. See also *goodness-of-fit test.*

Kolmogorov–Smirnov two-sample test– See *Kolmogorov–Smirnov tests.*

Kruskal–Wallis one-way analysis of variance by ranks– Same as *Kruskal-Wallis test.*

Kruskal–Wallis test– A **nonparametric procedure** used to compare three or more **independent samples** of **observations** that cannot be compared by means of an *F* **test for analysis of variance** either because the **data** are measured on **ordinal scale** or because the **normality** or **homogeneity of variance** assumptions cannot be satisfied. The method consists of **ranking** observations in all **samples** combined and the **test statistic** is based on the sum of the **ranks** assigned to the individual **treatment groups.** The test is a direct generalization of the **Wilcoxon rank-sum test** to three or more independent samples. When the **null hypothesis** is true, the test statistic can be approximated by a **chi-square distribution.** See also *Friedman's rank test.*

***k* statistics–** A set of symmetric functions calculated from the **sample data,** originally proposed by R. A. Fisher to determine the **moments** of **sample statistics.** The univariate *k* statistic of order *r* is defined as the **statistic** whose **mean** value is the *r*th **cumulant** of the **parent population.** The *k* statistics possess semi-invariant properties and their sampling cumulants can be determined directly from combinatorial methods.

kurtosis– The degree of "flatness" or "peakedness" of a univariate **frequency distribution.** A measure of kurtosis is obtained as the product moment ratio μ_4/μ_2^2, where μ_4 is the fourth **central moment** and μ_2 is the **variance.** For the **normal distribution,** it takes the value of 3. See also *coefficient of skewness, coefficient of kurtosis, leptokurtic, mesokurtic, platykurtic.*

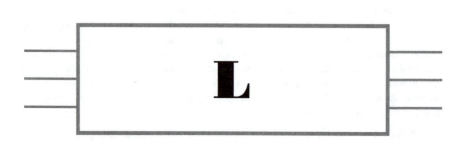

L

lambda– An **asymmetric measure of association** between the two **variables** forming a **contingency table.** The measure is designed for the situation in which one variable is considered explanatory and the other the response. It is more fully known as Goodman–Kruskal lambda. It ranges in value from zero to one.

Laplace criterion– Same as *equal-likelihood criterion.*

Laplace distribution– Same as *double exponential distribution.*

large sample method– A statistical procedure that makes the assumption of a large sample for its validity; that is, its **sampling distribution** is derived under the assumption of large sample theory. The procedure is based on an approximation to a **normal** or other **probability distribution** whose accuracy increases as the **sample size** increases.

large-scale trial– A **multicenter clinical trial** that enrolls a larger number of patients than the typical trial. The term is more or less synonymous with multicenter clinical trial.

Laspeyres' index number– A weighted aggregative price index named after a German economist named Etienne Laspeyres which is based on a combination of several items, with base period quantities employed as weights. If p_0^i, q_0^i ($i = 1, 2, \ldots, n$) denote the prices and quantities sold of a set of n commodities in a **base period** and p_1^i ($i = 1, 2, \ldots, n$) denote the corresponding prices in a given period, then the Laspeyres' index is defined as

$$
L_{01} = \frac{\sum\limits_{i=1}^{n} p_1^i q_0^i}{\sum\limits_{i=1}^{n} p_0^i q_0^i}
$$

The formula assigns to each current price a quantity weight that is appropriate for the base year. The quantity weight for each commodity is held constant for a number of years' computations. Laspeyres' index number is the most widely used throughout the world for making **price index numbers.** It is based on the basket of goods principle; that is, if a basket of goods costs $20 in the based period and if the same basket costs $25 in the given period, then the price index in the given period compared to the base is $25/20 = 1.25$. Price indices derived by this method usually have an upward **bias** because they allow for shifts in quantity in response to price increases.

latent factor– Same as *latent variable.*

latent variable– A **variable** representing a theoretical construct that cannot be measured directly. A latent variable is also called a true or unobserved variable. Many of the variables used in social and behavioral sciences are latent variables, for example, ambition, anxiety, aspiration, attitude, motivation, intelligence, and so forth.

latent variable modeling– See *structural equation model.*

Latin square– An **experimental design** involving the allocation of p **treatments** in a $p \times p$ square array such that each treatment occurs exactly once in each row or column. A Latin square is used to control for two sources of **variation** that may be identified with rows and columns. The design is also useful for investigating simultaneous **effects** of three **factors**: rows, columns, and Latin letters in a single **experiment.** The following is an example of a 5×5 Latin square. See also *Graeco–Latin square, hyper-Graeco–Latin square, hyper square.*

Layout of a 5×5 Latin square design

A	B	C	D	E
B	A	E	C	D
C	D	A	E	B
D	E	B	A	C
E	C	D	B	A

lattice design– A type of **incomplete block design** used in agricultural experimentation in order to increase the precision of treatment comparisons. It is also sometimes called a quasi-factorial design because of its analogy to **confounding** in a **factorial experiment.**

law of error– An **empirical rule** that states that **frequencies** with which **errors** of **measurement** and differences between actual values and **estimates** occur tend to form a **symmetrical distribution** approaching a **normal curve.**

law of large numbers– The law that states that the **probability** of a **deviation** of an **empirical probability** value from a theoretical one tends to zero as the number of repetitions of the **random experiment** in question increases to infinity.

LC50– Acronym for *lethal concentration 50.*

LD50– Acronym for *lethal dose 50.*

least absolute deviation estimation– In **regression analysis,** a method of fitting a **regression line** to **data values** so that the sum of the **absolute values** of the vertical **deviations** between the line and the individual data points is minimized. The method is more robust to usual violations of **assumptions** than the ordinary **least squares estimation.** See also *weighted least squares estimation.*

least significant difference test– In **analysis of variance,** a procedure for comparing a set of **means** that controls the overall **error rate** at some predetermined value, say α. The procedure consists of making an overall F **test** of the **hypothesis** of the equality of means at the α **level of significance.** If this test is significant, then the **pairwise comparisons** among

the **treatments** are performed by using an α-level **two-sample t test**; otherwise, the procedure is terminated without making any further **inferences** on pairwise differences. See also
multiple comparison.

least squares– Same as *least squares estimation.*

least squares estimation– In **regression analysis,** a method of fitting a **regression line** to
data values in a **scatter diagram** in such a way that the sum of the squares of the vertical
deviations between the line and the individual data plots is minimized. The method of least
squares is a very general method of curve fitting that selects as the best-fitting curve the one
that minimizes the sum of squares of the data points from the fitted curve. The least squares
method is used extensively in many economic applications, for example, in estimating **secular trend** and for calculating the relationship between two or more **variables** for comparison purposes. It is also referred to as ordinary least squares to distinguish it from the
method of **weighted least squares.** See also *least absolute deviation estimation.*

least squares estimate/estimator– An **estimate/estimator** of a **parameter** using the
method of least squares. A least squares estimator has a smaller **variance** than any other
linear estimator and is unbiased. See also **Gauss–Markov theorem.**

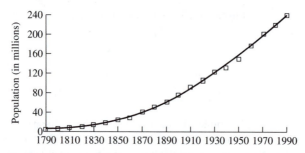

Least squares curve fitting of the population of the United
States, 1790–1990, showing a quadratic trend

least squares method– Same as *least squares estimation.*

least squares regression– See *least squares estimation.*

least squares theory– See *least squares estimation.*

left-skewed distribution– Same as *negatively skewed distribution.*

left-tailed test– Same as *lower-tailed test.*

leptokurtic– A **distribution** is said to be leptokurtic when data points tend to accumulate
more around the **mean** and in the tails than they do in a **normal curve.** Thus, a leptokurtic
distribution is more sharply peaked and has larger tail areas than the **normal distribution.**
Compare *mesokurtic, platykurtic.*

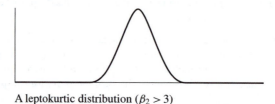

A leptokurtic distribution ($\beta_2 > 3$)

leptokurtic curve– See *leptokurtic.*

leptokurtic distribution– See *leptokurtic.*

lethal concentration 50– Same as *median lethal dose.*

lethal dose 50– Same as *median lethal dose.*

level– In an **experiment** or **study,** a general term referring to the characteristic or amount that defines or designates a particular level, category or classification of a **factor** or **variable.**

level of measurement– Same as *scale of measurement.*

level of significance– Same as *significance level.*

leverage point– In **regression diagnostics,** a leverage point is used to refer to an **observation** that has an extreme value on one or more **explanatory variables,** and therefore a potentially large **effect** on the **regression equation.** See also *Cook's distance, influence statistics, influential observation.*

liberal test– An approximate **statistical test** with the **level of significance** greater than or equal to the nominal value. If it is known that the actual level of significance of a liberal test is not much greater than α (the nominal value), the liberal test can be recommended. See also *approximate test, conservative test, exact test.*

life expectancy– The expected life at a given age, that is, the **average** length of subsequent life remained to be lived. In other words, the number of years a person of a particular age group can hope to live.

life table– A table showing **life expectancy** at various periods of time and/or for different age/sex groups. It shows the number of persons who, out of a given number of persons born and living during a given age group, live to reach successive higher age groups, as well as the number of persons who die in those groups. The life table provides useful indices of **mortality** experience which are unaffected by the age structure of the population concerned. The important elements of a life tables are:

1. $_nq_x$: The **probability** of dying between any two ages x and $x + n$. This is obtained by the **ratio** of total deaths between two ages to the number alive at the beginning of the first age.
2. $_np_x$: The probability of surviving between any two ages x and $x + n$. This is obtained by the ratio of those who are alive between two ages to the number alive at the beginning of the first age. Note that $_np_x + {_nq_x} = 1$.
3. ℓ_x: The number alive at age x out of those starting at age 0.
4. $_nd_x$: The number of deaths between ages x and $x + n$.
5. $_nL_x$: The number alive in the age interval x to $x + n$.
6. T_x: The number alive in this and the subsequent age interval.
7. e_x^0: The expectation of life at age x, that is, the average length of subsequent life lived by those who have reached age x.

The table on the next page gives an abridged life table of the United States for the year 1980.

life table analysis– A technique for analyzing **survival data** containing **censored observations** that have been grouped into intervals. The technique can be applied to the study of not only death, but also any endpoint of interest such as the onset or remission of a

Abridged life table of the United States, 1980

| Age interval | Proportion dying | Of 100,000 born alive | | Stationary population | | Average remaining lifetime |
Period of life between two exact ages stated (in years) (1) x to $x + n$	Proportion of persons alive at beginning of age interval (dying during interval) (2) $_nq_x$	Number living at beginning of age interval (3) ℓ_x	Number dying during age interval (4) $_nd_x$	The number alive in the age interval (5) $_nL_x$	The number alive in this and subsequent age interval (6) T_x	Average number of years of life remaining at beginning of age interval (7) e_x
All races						
0–1	0.0127	100,000	1,266	98,901	7,371,986	73.7
1–5	0.0025	98,734	250	394,355	7,273,085	73.7
5–10	0.0015	98,484	150	492,017	6,878,730	69.8
10–15	0.0015	98,334	152	491,349	6,386,713	64.9
15–20	0.0049	98,182	482	489,817	5,895,364	60.0
20–25	0.0066	97,700	648	486,901	5,405,547	55.3
25–30	0.0066	97,052	638	483,665	4,918,646	50.7
30–35	0.0070	96,414	672	480,463	4,434,981	46.0
35–40	0.0091	95,742	875	476,663	3,954,518	41.3
40–45	0.0139	94,867	1,321	471,250	3,477,855	36.7
45–50	0.0222	93,546	2,079	462,857	3,006,605	32.1
50–55	0.0351	91,467	3,209	449,811	2,543,748	27.8
55–60	0.0530	88,258	4,676	430,230	2,093,937	23.7
60–65	0.0794	83,582	6,638	402,081	1,663,707	19.9
65–70	0.1165	76,944	8,965	363,181	1,261,626	16.4
70–75	0.1694	67,979	11,517	312,015	898,445	13.2
75–80	0.2427	56,462	13,702	248,534	586,430	10.4
80–85	0.3554	42,760	15,197	175,192	337,896	7.9
85 and over	1.0000	27,563	27,563	162,704	162,704	5.9

disease. For example, the technique is often applied in **cohort studies** to examine the **distribution** of **mortality** and/or **morbidity** due to one or more diseases over a fixed period of time.

likelihood function– A mathematical function that gives the **probability** of obtaining observed **data,** given the values of **parameters** of a **probability distribution.** In other words, a likelihood function measures the probability of observing a given set of data, given that certain values are assigned to the parameters. Thus the likelihood function combines data with a given **probability model** and parameters of interest.

likelihood ratio statistic– The **statistic** obtained as the **ratio** of the **likelihood function** calculated under the **null** and the **alternative hypotheses.** In large samples, a function of the likelihood ratio, i.e., $-2 \log_e (L_{H_0}/L_{H_1})$ has approximately a **chi-square distribution** with the **degrees of freedom** equal to the difference in the number of **parameters** in the two hypotheses. See also *chi-square statistic, G^2 statistic, goodness-of-fit statistic, likelihood function, likelihood ratio test.*

likelihood ratio test– A **statistical test** based on the **likelihood ratio statistic.** The test was originally proposed by J. Neyman and E. S. Pearson in 1928.

Likert scale– A widely used scale to measure attitudes and opinions originally developed by Rensis Likert. In developing a Likert scale, **raw scores** are obtained as graded alternative responses to a questionnaire. For example, the respondents are given a series of statements relevant to the construction of scale and are asked to indicate their degree of agreement by stating "strongly agree," "agree," "disagree," "strongly disagree." A number is attached to each possible responses, e.g., 1 for "strongly agree," 2 for "agree," etc. The final scale is constructed as the composite score obtained as the sum of these numbers. Likert scales and Likert-like scales are easy to construct and are widely used in studies of opinions and attitudes in many areas of social and behavioral sciences. A widely used Likert-type scale in medicine is the Apgar scale employed to measure the health status of newly born babies.

linear association– Same as *linear relationship.*

linear combination– A linear combination of a set of k **variables,** $x_1, x_2, \ldots, x_k$, is an expression of the form $\ell_1 x_1 + \ell_2 x_2 + \cdots + \ell_k x_k$ where $\ell_1, \ell_2, \ldots, \ell_k$ are **constants.** An example of a linear combination is a **weighted average** of a set of variables or measures. The **prediction equation** in a **multiple regression analysis** can be considered as a linear combination of the **predictor variables.**

linear contrast– Same as *contrast.*

linear correlation– Same as *linear relationship.*

linear estimator– A **sample statistic** that is a **linear function** of **observations. Sample mean** is an example of a linear estimator.

linear function– Same as *linear combination.*

linear logistic regression– Same as *logistic regression.*

linear model– A **model** in which the equations relating the **random variables** and **parameters** are linear. More precisely, a relationship of the form

$$Y_i = \beta_0 + \beta_1 X_{1i} + \beta_2 X_{2i} + \cdots + \beta_p X_{pi} + e_i \qquad i = 1, 2, \ldots, n$$

where Y is a random variable; $X_1, X_2, \ldots, X_p$ are fixed variables; $\beta_0, \beta_1, \beta_2, \ldots, \beta_p$ are parameters to be estimated; and the **errors** e_i are usually independent normally distributed random variables with **mean** zero and **variance** σ^2. Note that linearity applies to the parameters and not to the variables. Thus, $Y_i = \beta_0 + \beta_1 X_{1i} + \beta_2 X_{2i}^2 + e_i$ is a linear model, but $Y_i = \beta_0 + \beta_1 X_{1i} + \beta_2^2 X_{2i}$ is not a linear model. See also *generalized linear model, linear regression, nonlinear model.*

linear programming– A mathematical technique of optimizing (i.e., maximizing or minimizing) a linear objective function subject to constraints in the form of linear inequalities. It is designed to select from a number of alternative courses of actions the one that is most likely to yield a desired result. The technique provides a decision-making tool for business management and has been employed on a variety of problems ranging from the selection of the ingredients appropriate to producing the most economical cattle feed of a given nutritional value to the determination of the safest site for a nuclear plant.

linear regression– The method of determining a **regression** or **prediction equation** to predict the value of a **dependent variable** from the given value of an **independent variable** by calculating a "best-fitting" straight line on a graph. A linear regression is represented by the model $Y_i = \beta_0 + \beta_1 X_i + e_i$, where Y is a continuous dependent or **response variable,** X is a continuous independent or **explanatory variable,** and e is the **random** or **residual term.** Compare *nonlinear regression.* See also *least squares estimation, linear model, multiple regression.*

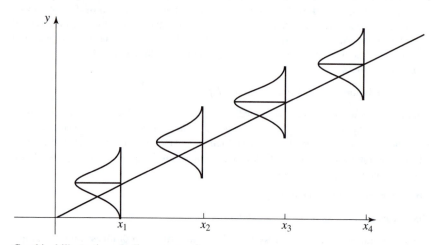

Graphical illustration of a linear regression

linear regression analysis– Same as *linear regression.*

linear relationship– When correlated **data** exhibit only one kind of relationship, either direct or inverse, but not both, the two **variables** involved are said to have a linear or straight-line relationship. When plotted on a graph paper, a linear relationship forms a straight-line.

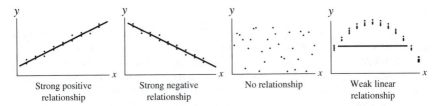

| Strong positive relationship | Strong negative relationship | No relationship | Weak linear relationship |

Graphical illustration of a linear relationship between X and Y

linear transformation– A mathematical **transformation** involving a **linear function** of a set of **variables**. The transformation consists of adding, subtracting, multiplying, or dividing the variables by a **constant.**

linear trend– A relationship between two **variables** such that a unit change in one variable produces a unit change in the other variable. The **trend** is expressed as the **linear function** of the time variable.

line chart– Same as *line graph.*

line diagram– Same as *line graph.*

line graph– A graph constructed by locating the points representing the observed values of the two variable magnitudes, and then connecting these points by either straight lines or smooth lines. It is also called line chart and line diagram.

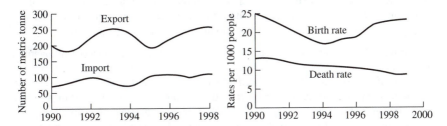

Line graphs for hypothetical data

line of best fit– The line that best fits or averages the **data points** in a **scatter diagram** of a set of **bivariate data**. A plot of a **regression equation** obtained by using the **least squares method** is an example of a line of best fit. The line of best fit may also be drawn freehand by personal judgment as shown in the figure below.

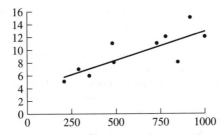

Simple regression line drawn freehand in a scatter diagram

link relative– Same as *trend ratio.*

LISREL– Acronym for LInear Structural RELation, a name given to a **computer program** for fitting **structural equation models** involving **latent variables.** It is a highly versatile program, originally developed by K. Joreskog, to analyze **covariance** structures by the method of **maximum likelihood estimation.** It has gone into numerous versions. It also allows the researcher to perform **exploratory** and **confirmatory factor analyses** as well as **path analyses.** The program has been so popular that it has become synonymous with the methods of analysis as well as the **software** for analyzing the data.

LISREL model– Same as *LISREL.*

local odds ratio– The **odds ratio** computed from a **2 × 2 contingency table** obtained by taking two adjacent rows and columns of an $r \times c$ **contingency table.** It can be shown that $(r - 1)(c - 1)$ local odds ratios determine all $\binom{r}{2}\binom{c}{2}$ odds ratios that can be formed from pairs of rows and pairs of columns. The local odds ratios treat row and column **variables** alike, and their values describe the relative magnitudes of local **associations** in the table. The **independence** of the two variables is equivalent to the condition that the local odds ratios are identically equal to one.

location– See *central tendency.*

location parameter– A **parameter** which describes the central or middle point, or the most typical value of a **distribution,** such as **mean, median,** or **mode.** A location parameter has the property that if a **constant** is added to each value of a **random variable** having the given distribution, then the same constant must be added to the parameter.

logarithmic chart– A graph in which one or more axes are expressed in terms of logarithmic scales. Where only the vertical scale is so designed, the graph is known as a semilogarithmic chart. Where both axes are scaled in terms of logarithms, the graph is known as a double-logarithmic chart. In both cases, the natural numbers are plotted on the logarithmic grids. To construct a logarithmic grid, all one needs to do is measure the required range of logarithms on a normal scale, insert the logarithms of whole numbers at appropriate fractions, at intervals, and the corresponding natural numbers, then erase the logarithms. A geometric series plotted on a semilogarithmic chart would appear a straight line, whereas on a rectilinear graph, it would represent a curve. A double logarithmic chart is used for graphing the series of two **variables** when there is a logarithmic relationship between the two.

logarithmic transformation– A **transformation** of a **variable** to a new variable obtained by using a mathematical operation on a logarithmic scale. A logarithmic transformation is frequently applied in a number of situations in order to achieve **normality** and/or **homogeneity of variances** and to reduce a **nonlinear model** to a **linear model.** For example, large to moderately skewed **data** are sometimes subjected to logarithmic transformation to achieve normality, and methods of **estimation** and **hypothesis testing** are applied to log values, and the results are back-transformed to the original scale. Similarly, logarithmic transformations are employed in **regression analysis** to reduce a **curvilinear relationship** to a **linear relationship.** See also *arc-sine transformation, power transformation, reciprocal transformation, square-root transformation, square transformation.*

logistic model– Same as *logistic regression model.*

logistic regression– A kind of **regression** technique used when the **dependent variable** is a **binary** or **dichotomous measure.** If X is an **independent variable** and Y is a **binary**

response variable with **probability** of success equal to p, then the logistic regression model is given by

$$p = \frac{e^{\alpha+\beta x}}{1 + e^{\alpha+\beta x}} = \frac{1}{1 + e^{-(\alpha+\beta x)}}$$

where e is the (natural) exponential function. The functional form given above is the logistic function, and hence the term logistic model. This model has the desirable range for p, i.e., between 0 and 1, and has many other useful statistical properties. See also *multiple logistic regression*.

logistic regression model– See *logistic regression*.

logit method– A method for constructing **confidence interval** of the **odds ratio** in a **2 × 2 contingency table**. The upper and lower limits of the confidence interval are given by the formula

$$\log_e\left(\frac{ad}{bc}\right) \pm \sqrt{\frac{1}{a} + \frac{1}{b} + \frac{1}{c} + \frac{1}{d}}$$

where a, b, c, and d are four **cell counts**. It is also known as the Taylor series method.

log–likelihood function– The **transformation** of a **likelihood function** using natural logarithms. It is generally employed for mathematical simplicity in performing partial derivatives.

log–linear analysis– A statistical method for analyzing the relationships among three or more **nominal variables**. It may be used similar to a **regression analysis** to predict a dependent nominal outcome from nominal **independent variables**.

log–linear models– **Statistical models** for analyzing **count data**. These models are similar to **analysis of variance** models for **continuous data** except that the interest is now focused on **parameters** representing **interactions** rather than those for **main effects**. Log–linear models are so called because they use equations that are transformed to linear forms by taking their natural logarithms. The analysis of log–linear models is based on **odds** rather than **proportions** as is done in the chi-square analysis. The models can handle count data from several **categorical variables** and can be analyzed either by the **likelihood ratio test** or the usual **chi-square test** for **goodness of fit**.

log–log paper– Same as *double-logarithmic chart*.

lognormal distribution– If $\log_e (X)$ is normally distributed with **mean** μ and **variance** σ^2, then X is said to have a lognormal distribution. The **density function** of the lognormal distribution is given by

$$f(x) = \frac{1}{x\sigma\sqrt{2\pi}} \exp\left[-\frac{1}{2\sigma^2}(\log_e x - \mu)^2\right] \qquad x > 0, \sigma > 0$$

The lognormal distribution is especially useful in modeling **data** from a **positively skewed distribution**. For example, in clinical studies, triglycerides data may sometimes be approximated by a lognormal distribution. See also *logarithmic transformation*.

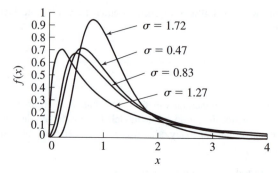

Probability density curves for lognormal distribution for
various values of σ

log paper– See *logarithmic chart.*

logrank test– A **nonparametric method** for comparing two **survival curves** when there
are **censored observations.** The principle of the logrank test is to divide the survival time
scale into intervals according to the distinct observed survival times, ignoring censored
survival times. It then uses the relative **death rate** in intervals to form a test for comparing
the overall survival curves for different **treatment groups.** The **test statistic** essentially involves a comparison of the observed number of deaths occurring at each time period with
the expected number of deaths if the two survival curves were the same. It is a special application of the **Mantel–Haenszel chi-square test,** where an overall comparison of the
groups is performed by summarizing the significance of the differences in survival rates in
each one of the time intervals which constitute the **follow-up period.** See also **stratified
logrank test.**

LOGXACT– See *STATXACT.*

longitudinal data– **Data** arising from a **longitudinal study.** A characteristic of this type of
data is a **correlation** between pairs of **measurements** on the same subject, the magnitude
of which usually depends on the time lag between the measurements. Typically the correlation becomes weaker as the time lag increases. This correlation needs to be properly accounted for if appropriate **inferences** are to be made. Special methods of analysis are often
needed to take into account the correlation structure.

longitudinal study– A study involving a group of subjects that takes place over an
extended period of time. A cohort of individuals is identified and followed through with
observations made at several points in time. A longitudinal study can be carried out
prospectively, and is known as **prospective study,** or retrospectively, and is then known as
retrospective study. See also *cohort study.*

long-term forecast– A business **forecast** extending at least 5 years ahead of the current period, although such forecasts are often made for a period that may extend as far ahead as 15
or 20 years.

Lorenz curve– A curve used to display the nature of any **distribution,** particularly, the
income distribution of a country. The curve is obtained by plotting the cumulative **proportion** of people against the cumulative share of total income that they receive. If there were
a perfect equality in the distribution of income, with every one receiving the same amount

of money, the Lorenz curve would be a 45° straight line. On the other hand, for the hypothetical situation of absolute inequality, with only one person receiving all the money, the curve would form the bottom right side of the square. In any practical situation, income distribution lies between these two hypothetical extremes and is thus represented by a sagging line. It is commonly used in many economic studies to display the extent of equality or inequality in the distribution of money income in an economy.

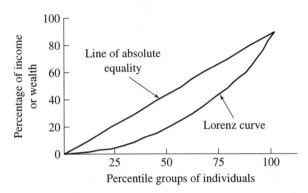

A diagram depicting the Lorenz curve

loss function– In **decision theory,** a mathematical function that assumes numerical values representing a gain or penalty for making correct or incorrect decision. Two popular loss functions are quadratic and absolute deviation.

loss to follow-up– In a **longitudinal study,** the term is applied to subjects who for a variety of reasons cannot be contacted to determine **outcome** measures or other characteristics of interest. Loss to follow-up often leads to censoring since the outcomes remain unknown. See also *censored observations.*

lower confidence limit– See *confidence limits.*

lower hinge– See *five-number summary.*

lower *p*th percentile– Same as *pth percentile.*

lower real limit– See *real limits.*

lower-tailed test– A **one-tailed hypothesis** test in which the entire **rejection region** is located in the lower tail of the **sampling distribution** of the **test statistic.** See also *one-tailed test, two-tailed test, upper-tailed test.*

LSD– Acronym for *least significant difference.*

M

MAD– Acronym for *mean, median or mode absolute deviation.*

Mahalanobis D^2– A measure of distance involving **multivariate data** useful in discriminating between two **populations.** It was proposed by P. C. Mahalanobis to assess the divergence between two populations based on **observations** on p characters or **variates.** The square of the distance (D^2) can be expressed as the **Euclidean distance** squared. It is related to **Fisher's discriminat function** and Hotelling's T^2. It has found extensive applications in many fields including **cluster analysis, profile analysis,** and **discriminant analysis.**

Mahalanobis generalized distance– Same as *Mahalanobis D^2.*

main effect– In an **analysis of variance** or **regression** involving two or more **factors,** where each factor may have a separate **effect,** the main effect is an **estimate** of the effect of an experimental **variable** or **treatment** on the **dependent variable** that is separable from the other factors' effect and from the **interaction effect.** In a **factorial experiment,** the main effect of a factor is the **average** change in response produced by changing the **levels** of the factor.

mainframe– A high-speed digital computer with very large capacity. Originally, the term was employed to refer to the main framework of a central processing unit (CPU) on which the arithmetic unit and associated logic circuits were mounted.

Mallow's C_p statistic– A diagnostic index used in **regression analysis** in the selection of the "best" set of **predictor variables.** The index is defined as

$$C_p = \sum_{i=1}^{n} \left(y_i - \hat{y}_{i(p)} \right)^2 \bigg/ s_e^2 - n + 2p$$

where y_i is the ith observed value of the **dependent variable,** $\hat{y}_{i(p)}$ is the predicted value based on a particular subset of p **explanatory variables,** s_p^2 is the full regression **residual mean square,** and n is the number of **observations.** A **model** with the samllest value of the C_p statistic is considered to provide the best fit.

Malthusian theory– The theory that the population tends to increase faster than the natural resources needed to sustain it. More specifically, the theory states that the population grows at a **geometric progression** while the food supply increases only in **arithmetic progression.**

manifest variable– A term used to describe an **observed variable** that can be measured in contrast to a **latent variable,** which cannot be measured directly. For example, intelligence is a latent variable that cannot be measured directly. But it can be measured in terms of a manifest variable such as an IQ test score. A manifest variable is also called an indicator variable.

Mann–Whitney U test– A **nonparametric test** for detecting differences between two **location parameters** based on the analysis of two **independent samples.** The **test statistic** is formed by counting all the bivariate pairs from the two **samples** in which one sample value is smaller than the other. It is equivalent to the **Wilcoxon rank-sum test.** The procedure is used for comparing two independent samples of **scores** that cannot be compared by means of a **two-sample t test** either because the scores are ordinal in nature or the **normality** or **homogeneity of variance** assumptions cannot be satisfied. See also **normal scores test.**

Mann–Whitney–Wilcoxon test– Same as *Mann–Whitney U test* or *Wilcoxon rank-sum test.*

MANOVA– Acronym for *multivariate analysis of variance.*

Mantel–Haenszel chi-square test– A summary **chi-square test** involving two or more **two-by-two contingency tables.** It is used for stratified **data** involving several 2×2 **tables** with a view to adjust or control for **confounding.** After stratifying the data by the categories of the **confounding variable,** such as age, sex, occupation, etc., the results are pooled together to produce a single summary test based on **chi-square distribution** with one **degree of freedom.**

Mantel-Haenszel estimator– In a **stratified analysis** involving a series of 2×2 **tables,** an **estimator** of the common **odds ratio** that may be derived from matched and unmatched **data sets.** The estimator is a type of **weighted average** of the odds ratio estimators from each individual table where the weights are inversely proportional to the **variances** of the individual **estimates.** Thus, estimates with smaller variance (higher precision) are given more weight, whereas those with larger variance (lower precision) are given less weight. It is calculated by the formula

$$\sum_{i=1}^{k} a_i d_i \bigg/ \sum_{i=1}^{k} b_i c_i$$

where a_i, b_i, c_i, and d_i are the four **cell counts** in the ith table and k is the number of 2×2 tables. It produces an adjusted estimate of the overall odds ratio and provides a method of controlling **confounding** by stratifying a **sample** into a series of strata that are homogenous with respect to the **confounding variable.** Two common applications of the Mantel–Haenszel estimate are the analysis of **case-control studies** and **meta-analysis.** See also *Peto's method.*

Mardia's test– A statistical procedure for testing the **normality** of a **multivariate data set.**

marginal density function– **The probability density function** of one of the (continuous) **random variables** of a set of jointly distributed (continuous) random variables. It is obtained by integrating the **joint density function** with respect to other random variables.

marginal distribution– **The probability distribution** of one of the **random variables** of a set of jointly distributed random variables obtained from a **joint distribution** by summing out, or integrating out, all the other variables.

marginal frequencies (probabilities)– The sum of the **frequencies (probabilities)** in one of the rows or in one of the columns of a two-way table. The marginal frequencies (probabilities) are usually shown at the margins of the table.

marginal frequency (probability) distribution– See *marginal distribution.*

marginally significant– A term used to refer to **statistical significance** of research results that barely reach the **critical value** needed to be **statistically significant.**

marginal probability function– **Probability function** of one of the (discrete) **random variables** of a set of jointly distributed (discrete) random variables. It is obtained by summing the **joint probability function** with respect to other random variables.

marginals– A clipped form for **marginal frequencies** or totals.

marginal totals– Same as *marginal frequencies.*

Markov chain– Same as *Markov process.*

Markov inequality– If a **random variable** X with **mean** μ and finite **variance** can take only positive values, then the Markov inequality states that $P(X \leq x) \leq 1 - \mu/x$.

Markov process– A **discrete stochastic process** in which, in a series of **trials,** the **probability** of an **event** depends upon the results of the event immediately preceding it. Thus, the state of the process is unaffected by the past, except the immediate past.

masking – Same as *blinding.*

matched case-control study– A **case-control study** in which **cases** and **controls** are matched on certain characteristics known to be associated to both disease and the **risk factor.** Some examples of commonly used **matching** variables are age, sex, occupation, and socioeconomic status.

matched groups– Same as *matched samples.*

matched-groups *t* **test–** Same as *paired t test.*

matched pairs– See *matched-pair samples.*

matched-pair samples– Two **samples** taken such that each **experimental unit** in one group has been matched with a unit from another group. In matched-pair samples any **sample observation** about a unit in one group automatically yields an associated **observation** about a unit in another group.

matched-pairs *t* **test–** Same as *paired t test.*

matched samples– **Samples** where two or more groups of subjects are matched or paired according to one or more relevant **variables** such as age, sex, or sociodemographics. See also *matched-pair samples.*

matched-samples *t* test– Same as *paired t test.*

matched set– In a **case-control study,** a form of **matching** in which a number of **controls,** known as a matched set, are matched to each **case.** This form of matching is normally used to increase the **sensitivity** of the design, especially when controls are more economical.

matched-subjects designs– These are **experimental designs** that test two or more groups of subjects, matched according to one or more relevant **variables.** Studies involving identical twins are the ideal examples of such designs. The **scores** for each pair or set of subjects are treated as correlated measures. See also *matched-pair samples, matched samples.*

matching– The process of making two groups of subjects or **experimental units** homogeneous on possible **confounding factors** by matching them according to relevant factors causing **confounding.** Matching can be individual matching, in which study and comparison subjects are paired on the basis of matching variables, or frequency matching, in which the **frequency distribution** of matched variables is similar in study and comparison groups. It is usually done prior to **randomization in clinical trials.** See also *matched-pair samples, matched samples, matched-subjects designs.*

maternal death rate– A measure of **risk** of dying from causes associated with child birth. It is obtained as the number of deaths actually observed due to puerperal causes during a calendar year divided by the total number of births (live + still) (expressed per 100 or 1000).

maternal mortality rate– Same as *maternal death rate.*

mathematical expectation– Same as *expected value.*

mathematical model– A mathematical equation used in a **mathematical modeling.**

mathematical modeling– A term used to describe a mathematical formulation that characterizes the behavior of one or more **variables** that may influence some natural phenomenon or causal system.

matrix– A **rectangular array** of numbers (called elements) or mathematical objects arranged into rows and columns. Matrices are denoted by capital Roman letters **A, B, C,** etc. Two examples of matrices are

$$\mathbf{A} = \begin{pmatrix} 3 & 5 & 9 \\ 4 & 6 & 2 \\ 2 & 8 & 3 \end{pmatrix} \qquad \mathbf{B} = \begin{pmatrix} b_{11} & \cdot & \cdot & \cdot & b_{1n} \\ b_{21} & \cdot & \cdot & \cdot & b_{2n} \\ \cdot & \cdot & \cdot & \cdot & \cdot \\ \cdot & \cdot & \cdot & \cdot & \cdot \\ b_{m1} & \cdot & \cdot & \cdot & b_{mn} \end{pmatrix}$$

matrix algebra– A system of algebra in which basic elements and symbols for unknown quantities including arithmetical operations are presented in terms of matrix notation.

matrix of correlation– Same as *correlation matrix.*

maximax criterion– One of several nonprobabilistic criteria for making an optimal decision under **uncertainty.** According to this criterion, a decision maker determines the maximum benefit associated with each possible action, searches for the maximum among these maxima, and then chooses the action associated with this maximum of maxima.

maximin criterion– One of several nonprobabilistic criteria for making an optimal decision under **uncertainty.** According to this criterion, a decision maker determines the minimum benefit associated with each possible action, searches for the maximum among these minima, and chooses the action associated with this maximum of minima.

maximum *F*-ratio test– Same as *Hartley's test.*

maximum likelihood criterion– One of several probabilistic criteria for making an optimal decision under **uncertainty.** The maximum likelihood criterion is based on the assumption that the most likely factor or factors have generated the most probable **sample.** It attaches the greatest **probability** to the observed **event** and the degree of **reliability** of such values. According to this criterion, a decision maker identifies the event most likely to occur and selects the action that produces the maximum benefit associated with this most likely event.

maximum likelihood estimation– A method of **estimation** of one or more **parameters** of a **population** by maximizing the **likelihood** or **log-likelihood function** of the **sample** with respect to the parameter(s). The maximum likelihood estimators are functions of the **sample observations** that make the **likelihood function** greatest. The proceudre consists of computing the **probability** that the particular **sample statistic** would have occcured if it were the true value of the parameter. Then for the **estimate,** we select the particular value for which the probability of the actual observed value is greatest. Maximum likelihood estimates are determined by using methods of calculus for maximization and minimization of a function. These estimates possess many desirable properties such as **consistency, asymptotic normality,** and **asymptotic efficiency.**

maximum likelihood estimate/estimator– See *maximum likelihood estimation.*

maximum likelihood method– See *maximum likelihood estimation.*

maximum likelihood principle– See *maximum likelihood estimation.*

maximum likelihood procedure– See *maximum likelihood estimation.*

maximum tolerance dose– The highest level of dose of a drug that a patient can tolerate with an acceptable level of toxicity. This is especially important in cytotoxic therapy of cancer where the treatment generally produces some serious side effects.

McNemar's chi-square test– Same as *McNemar's test.*

McNemar's test– A **nonparametric test** for comparing two correlated **proportions** arising from two **dependent** or **paired groups.** It is calculated by the formula $X^2 = (b - c)^2/(b + c)$, where b is the number of pairs in which the individual from group A has positive result and the individual from group B does not; and c is the number of pairs for which it is just the reverse. Under the **null hypothesis** that the **probability** of positive response is the same in two groups, X^2 has a **chi-square distribution** with one **degree of freedom.** It is a special case of the **Mantel–Haenszel chi-square test** for a single 2×2 **table.**

mean– A **measure of location** or the **central tendency** of a **data set.** It is the arithmetic **average** computed by summing all the values in the **data set** and dividing the sum by the number of **data values.** Given $x_1, x_2, \ldots, x_n$, a set of n numbers, it is defined by the formula $\bar{x} = \sum_{i=1}^{n} x_i/n$. It is the most stable and useful measure of central tendency. For a data set with values 7, 8, 8, 9, 12, 13, the mean is $\bar{x} = (7 + 8 + 8 + 9 + 12 + 13)/6 = 9.5$. The physical interpretation of the mean is illustrated in the figure below, where it is the value on the **horizontal axis** that serves as a balance point. When used without any qualification, mean refers to **arithmetic mean.** It is the most widely used and best understood data summary in all **statistics.** Two other means used in statistics are **geometric mean** and **harmonic mean.** The mean is a reliable measure of location if the underlying data set has a **symmetrical distribution.** If the **distribution** in question is skewed, mean does not provide a useful measure, since it is greatly influenced by **extreme observations.** See also *population mean, sample mean.*

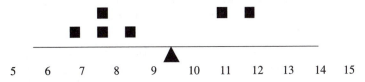

Figure showing the mean as a balance point

mean absolute deviation– See *average absolute deviation.*

mean absolute error– Same as *average absolute deviation.*

mean deviation– See *average absolute deviation.*

mean error– Same as *average absolute deviation.*

mean of squared deviations– Same as *mean square deviation.*

mean square– In an **analysis of variance,** the **sum of squares** divided by its corresponding **degrees of freedom.** This quantity is used in the F ratio to determine if there exist significant differences in **population means.**

mean square between– Same as *mean square between groups.*

mean square between (among) groups– In a **one-way analysis of variance** design, the measure of **variation** between **group means** obtained by dividing the **sum of squares between groups** by its **degrees of freedom.**

mean square contingency coefficient– See *phi coefficient.*

mean square deviation– The square of the **deviation** of a value of a **data set** from the **mean.** The concept is used extensively in many statistical applications, including **correlation, variance,** and **least squares regression.**

mean square error– A measure of **error** of an **estimator** defined as the **expected value** of the squared difference between the estimator and the true value of the **parameter.** For an **unbiased estimator,** mean square error equals the **variance;** for a **biased estimator,** it is equal to the variance plus **bias** square. The square root of the mean square error is referred to as the root mean square error.

mean square for columns– In a **two-way analysis of variance** design, the measure of the differences between columns **means** obtained by dividing the **sum of squares for columns** by its **degrees of freedom.**

mean square for error– In a **one-, two-,** or **multiway analysis of variance** design, the measure of the **variance** due to individual differences between subjects, **measurement**

errors, uncontrolled **variations** in experimental procedures, and so on. It is obtained by dividing the **error sum of squares** by the corresponding **degrees of freedom.**

mean square for interaction– In a **two-** or **multiway analysis of variance** design, the measure of the **interaction** between any two **treatment factors** obtained by dividing the **sum of squares for interaction** by its **degrees of freedom.**

mean square for regression– Same as *regression mean square.*

mean square for rows– In a **two-way analysis of variance** design, the measure of the differences between row **means,** obtained by dividing the **sum of squares for rows** by its **degrees of freedom.**

mean square for treatment– In an **analysis of variance,** an estimate of the **population variance,** based on the observed **variation** among the **treatment groups.** It is obtained by dividing the **treatment sum of squares** by the corresponding **degrees of freedom.**

mean square ratio– In an **analysis of variance,** the **ratio** of two **mean squares.** See also *F statistic.*

mean square within– Same as *mean square within groups.*

mean square within groups– In a **one-way analysis of variance** design, the measure of **variation** obtained by dividing the **within group sum of squares** by its **degrees of freedom.** It is a measure of the **deviations** of the individual **observations** from their respective **group means.**

mean variation– Same as *average absolute deviation.*

mean vector– In a **data set** comprising **multivariate observations,** it is the **vector** containing the **mean** value of each **variable.** It is a multivariate analogue of the mean of a **univariate data set.**

measurement– The process of assigning a label, number, or numerical value to characteristics that are being observed, according to a set of rules.

measurement class– Same as *measurement interval.*

measurement errors– Errors in reading, calculating, or recording a value caused by flaws in the measuring instruments, such as faulty calibration, or the experimenter making the **observations,** as contrasted with other errors, or unknown **variation.**

measurement interval– A range of values assumed by a **variable** into which **observations** can be grouped.

measurement scale– Same as *scale of measurement.*

measure of association– Any numerical measure that shows the degree of relationship between two **variables.** More precisely, it is a numerical index of the strength of the statistical dependence of two or more **qualitative variables.** A measure of association is usually a **statistic** that shows direction and magnitude of the relationship. Examples of measures of association include **coefficient of correlation, lambda, gamma,** and **odds ratio,** among others. See also *asymmetric measure of association, symmetric measure of association.*

measure of risk– Any of various **measures of association,** such as **risk difference, risk ratio,** and **odds ratio,** used to measure **association** between a **risk factor** and the disease or condition of interest.

measures of central tendency– **Summary indices** or **statistics** describing the central or middle point, or the most typical value, of a set of **measurements** around which **observations** tend to cluster. They are also frequently referred to as **average** values. See also *mean, median, mode.*

measures of dispersion– **Summary indices** or **statistics** that describe the **scatter** or **spread** of **observations** about the **central location.** They show the extent to which individual values in a **data set** differ from one another and, hence, differ from their central location. See also *range, standard deviation, variance.*

measures of location– Same as *measures of central tendency.*

measures of shape– Indices or numbers that indicate either the degree of **asymmetry** or the peakedness in a **frequency distribution.** The term is used in contrast to measures of **skewness** and **kurtosis.**

measures of spread– Same as *measures of dispersion.*

measures of variability– Same as *measures of dispersion.*

measures of variation– Same as *measures of dispersion.*

median– A **measure of location** or **central tendency** of a **data set.** It is the value that divides the data set into two equal groups; one with values greater than or equal to the median, and the other with values less than or equal to the median. It is an ordinal measure of central tendency. It is the middle value in a data set which divides a **distribution** exactly in half so that 50 percent of its **scores** are higher than it and 50 percent are lower. Thus, the median is also referred as the 50th **percentile.** In a **frequency distribution,** median is calculated by first ascertaining the **class interval** within which it is located, and then finding its value within this class interval by **interpolation.** For a right-skewed distribution, **mean** is larger than the median; for a left-skewed distribution, mean is smaller than the median; and for a **symmetric distribution,** mean and median are equal. The median is one of several types of **averages** currently in use; and its principal advantage is that it is not unduly influenced by **extreme observations.** It is often used in describing the typical income of a group of individuals. The name "median" was first used by Francis Galton in 1883. See also *population median, sample median.*

median absolute deviation– See *average absolute deviation.*

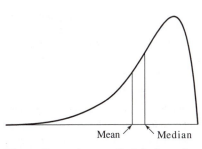

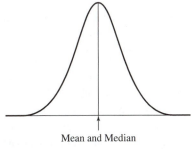

The median and mean of a left-skewed distribution

The median and mean of a symmetric distribution

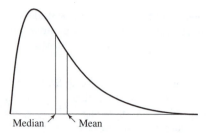

The median and mean of a right-skewed
distribution

median class– In a **grouped frequency distribution,** the **class interval** that contains the **median.**

median deviation– The **median** of the **absolute values** of the **deviations** about some **measure of central tendency.** It is also called median error and sometimes, improperly, **probable error.**

median effective concentration– Same as *median lethal dose.*

median effective dose– Same as *median lethal dose.*

median error– Same as *median deviation.*

median lethal concentration– Same as *median lethal dose.*

median lethal dose– In **biological assay** involving a toxic substance, the amount of stimulus or quantity of a dose that will result in a desired response (say mortality) in 50% of the subjects in the **population** under study during a specified period of time. It is denoted by LD50 for lethal dose, ED50 for effective dose, LC50 for lethal concentration, EC50 for effective concentration, and Tlm 50 for tolerance limit.

median test– A **nonparametric test** performed to test the **hypothesis** that two **populations** have the same **median.**

median tolerance limit– Same as *median lethal dose.*

median unbiased estimator– An **estimator** is said to be median unbiased if its **median** equals the true value of the **parameter** being estimated. See also *unbiased estimator.*

median unbiasedness– The term is used to indicate the property of a **median unbiased estimator.**

medical decision making– The application of **decision analysis** in making diagnostic and/or treatment inferences in clinical medicine. It synthesizes all the accumulated evidence and other relevant information concerning diagnostic and/or treatment alternatives and associated **risks,** consequences of a particular diagnosis or treatment, and **uncertainties** in making decisions about diagnoses or treatments. Its aim is to assist the physician in making the correct diagnosis and choosing the appropriate therapy.

medical record– A file of information containing cumulative narrative history of a patient, the treatment given, final diagnosis, and continuing care following release. The full range of **data** in a medical record includes a variety of other clinical, sociodemographic, economic, administrative and behavioral information.

medical statistics– Statistical methods and techniques applied to the study of medical and health-related problems. In the United States the term is synonymous with **biostatistics.**

mesokurtic– A **frequency distribution** or **curve** is said to be mesokurtic when it exhibits a moderate clustering of **scores** around the **mean** as does the **normal curve,** which by definition, is mesokurtic. See also *leptokurtic, platykurtic.*

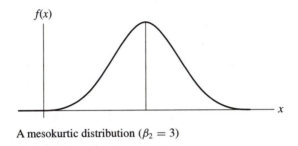

A mesokurtic distribution ($\beta_2 = 3$)

mesokurtic curve– See *mesokurtic.*

mesokurtic distribution– See *mesokurtic.*

meta-analysis– The process of using statistical methods for combining or summarizing the results from several independent studies of the same **outcome** so that an overall **effect size** and *p* **value** may be determined. Meta-analysis is frequently used in pooling results from several smaller studies, none of them large enough to show **statistically significant** differences, but the pooling increases the **power** of the study. The pooling is usually done by taking a **weighted average** of the individual results according to their study size. It uses methods such as the **Mantel–Haenszel estimator** and **Peto's method** to calculate the combined **estimate.** The technique is particularly popular among researchers interested in summarizing results from **randomized controlled trials** of therapies or interventions. However, it is also being used in many epidemiological studies involving **risk factors** or **diagnostic tests.** Meta-analysis suffers from several **biases** and limitations. Some of the controversies surrounding meta-analysis include **publication bias, heterogeneity of effect size,** use of individual or aggregated **data,** and choice of **fixed** or **random effects models.**

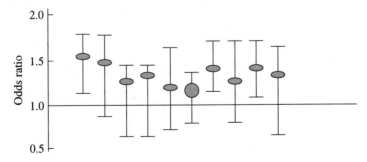

Meta-analysis of 9 hypothetical randomized clinical trials: observed odds ratio and 95% confidence limits. The overall odds ratio is shown by a circle.

method of least squares– Same as *least squares estimation.*

method of maximum likelihood– Same as *maximum likelihood estimation.*

method of moment estimation– Same as *method of moments.*

method of moments– A method of **estimation of parameters** by equating the **sample moments** to their respective population values. It is the oldest general method for estimating unknown parameters, and was proposed by Karl Pearson about 1891. It is generally applicable and provides a fairly simple method for obtaining **estimates** in most cases. The method, however, yields **estimators** that, in certain cases, are less efficient than those obtained by the **method of maximum likelihood.** See also *least squares estimation.*

Michael's test– A test of **normality** based on **order statistics** from **sample data.** See *also Anserson–Darling test, Cramér–von Mises test, D'Agostino test, Shapiro–Francia test, Shapiro–Wilk W test.*

midpoint– The value located halfway between the **lower** and **upper real limits** of an interval. It is obtained as the **mean** of the lower and upper real limits of an interval. In plotting **grouped data,** the **midpoints** are used to represent the **observations** within each interval.

mid-p value– A modification of the conventional p **value** that is used in some analyses involving a **test statistic** based on a **discrete distribution.** Let T denote a test statistic based on a discrete distribution and t be the observed number of **outcomes.** Then, the mid-p value is defined as

$$\text{mid } p = \frac{1}{2}P(T = t) + P(T \geq t + 1)$$

while the conventional p value is determined as $p = P(T \geq t)$. In other words, mid p averages the exact p value for the observed number of outcomes t and $t + 1$.

midrange– The **mean** of the smallest and largest values in a **data set.** Given a set of values $x_1, x_2, \ldots, x_n$ arranged in ascending or descending order of magnitude, the midrange is defined as $(x_1 + x_n)/2$. It provides a crude **estimate** of the center of a **symmetrical distribution.**

midvalue– Same as *midpoint.*

minimax criterion– In **decision** or **game theory,** one of several nonprobabilistic criteria for making an optimal decision under **uncertainty.** According to this criterion, a decision maker determines the maximum cost associated with each possible action, searches the minimum of these maxima, and chooses the action associated with this minimum of maxima.

minimax regret criterion– In **decision** or **game theory,** one of several nonprobabilistic criteria for making an optimal decision under **uncertainty.** According to this criterion, a decision maker finds the maximum regret value associated with each possible action, searches the minimum among these maxima, and chooses the action associated with this minimum of maxima.

minimax strategy– Same as *minimax criterion.*

minimin criterion– In **decision** or **game theory,** one of several nonprobabilistic criteria for making an optimal decision under **uncertainty.** According to this criterion, a decision maker who seeks to minimize some cost or loss determines the minimum cost associated with each possible action, searches the minimum among these minima, and chooses the action associated with this minimum of minima.

minimum chi-square estimation– A method of **estimation** in which an **estimate** of a **parameter** is determined by minimizing a **chi-square statistic.** The procedure involves determining the values of the parameters so as to minimize X^2 calculated from **observed frequencies** and **expected frequencies** expressed in terms of the parameters. The minimum chi-square estimators are asymptotically equivalent to the **maximum likelihood estimators.**

minimum effective dose– The lowest level of dose of a drug that can produce the desired clinical effect in a patient.

MINITAB– A general-purpose **statistical software package** designed to perform interactive **data analysis.** The package is very easy to use and proved to be very popular with both students and instructors. It includes a wide variety of methods for statistical and graphical analysis. It is based on a two-dimensional spreadsheet concept in which columns are **variables** and rows are cases.

Minkowski distance– A generalized measure of the distance between two points as determined by the location of their coordinates. It includes **Euclidean distance** as a special case.

missing data– Same as *missing values.*

missing values– **Observations** missing from a **data set** for a variety of reasons. For example, information may not be available because a subject may drop out of the study or may fail to answer one of the questions in a **survey,** or certain measuring instrument may break down, or animals and plants may die during the course of the **experiment.** The presence of missing values greatly complicates the methods of analysis. Several approaches for analyzing **data** containing missing values have been developed, but none of them seem to be entirely satisfactory. See also *imputation.*

mixed data– **Data** containing a mixture of **continuous** and **discrete data.**

mixed effects model– An **analysis of variance** model in which at least one **treatment level** is fixed and at least one treatment level is **random,** excluding the **residual term** which is always considered random. It is also called Model III. See also *fixed effects model, random effects model.*

mixed model– Same as *mixed effects model.*

mixed time-series model– A **time-series model** that is a mixture of **additive** and **multiplicative time-series models;** for example, $Y = T \times C \times I + S$.

MLE– Acronym for *maximum likelihood estimation.*

modal class– The **class interval** (generally from a **frequency table** or **histogram**) that contains the highest **frequency** of **observations.** See also *mode.*

modal group– Same as *modal class.*

modal interval– Same as *modal class.*

modal range– Same as *modal class.*

mode– A **measure of central tendency** or **location** of a **data set.** It is defined as the **data value** that occurs most frequently. When **grouped data** are involved, the **class interval** having the highest **frequency** is called the **modal class.** Its **midpoint** is often used to represent the mode. More precisely, it can be calculated by first ascertaining the class interval within which it is located, and then finding its value within this interval by **interpolation.** In a **frequency distribution** involving a **categorical variable,** the name of the category of **scores** that has the highest frequency is referred to as mode. It is the most primitive measure of central tendency. A set of **data** can have more than one mode or no mode when all values are different. Like the **median,** the mode is not influenced by unusually high or low values, but it is used less frequently in statistical analysis than either the median or the **mean.**

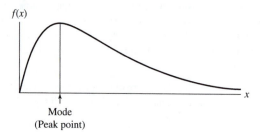

Mode
(Peak point)

Mode of a continuous distribution

mode absolute deviation– See *average absolute deviation.*

model– A construct or formulation that provides a description of the assumed structure of a set of **data.** A model involves a set of **assumptions** about relationships used to describe the data structure in a manner that may aid in understanding the process assumed to have generated the data. See also *deterministic model, mathematical model, mathematical modeling, probability model, stochastic model.*

model building– A procedure for finding the simplest **model** that provides an adequate description of the **data.**

model equation– Mathematical equation used in a **model.**

Model I– Same as *fixed effects model.*

Model II– Same as *random effects model.*

Model III– Same as *mixed effects model.*

model misspecification– The use of an incorrect **model** to fit a given set of **data.**

moment generating function– A function of a **variable** t associated with the **probability distribution** of a **random variable** X, and defined by

$$M_x(t) = E(e^{tX}) \qquad \text{for } -h < t < h$$

If $M_x(t)$ is expanded as a power series in t, the coefficient of $t^k / k!$ gives the kth **moment** of X about the origin. See also *characteristic function, probability generating function.*

moments– Values used to characterize the **probability distribution** of a **random variable** or describe a set of **data.** For a random variable X, its kth moment about the origin is defined as $\mu'_k = E(X^k)$, so that μ'_1 is simply the **mean** of the distribution and is commonly denoted by μ. The kth moment about the mean is defined as $\mu_k = E(X - \mu)^k$, so that μ_2 is the **variance** of the distribution and is commonly denoted by σ^2. For a set of **sample observations** $x_1, x_2, \ldots, x_n$, the kth moment about the origin is defined as $m'_k = \frac{1}{n}\sum_{i=1}^{n} x_i^k$, so that m'_1 is simply the **sample mean** and is commonly denoted by $\bar{x}$. The kth sample moment about the mean is defined as $m_k = \frac{1}{n}\sum_{i=1}^{n}(x_i - \bar{x})^k$, so that m_2 is the **sample variance** and is commonly denoted by s^2. The kth moment about the mean is also known as the kth central moment.

moments about the origin– See *moments.*

monitoring– A term used in a **clinical trial** to describe the **follow-up** and **observation** of the conduct and progress of an ongoing trial according to a set of predefined guidelines contained in the **protocol.**

Monte Carlo method– A term that has most commonly been used in the solution of any mathematical and statistical problem by performing **sampling** experiments involving generation of **random numbers** from a given **probability distribution.** It provides an **empirical** method of finding solutions to many mathematical and statistical problems for which no simple analytical solutions are available. For example, suppose we want to find the area of the closed curve of an irregular shape contained within a unit square as shown below. It is evident that the area in question is rather complicated and there does not seem to be a simple method for determining it. Now, suppose a pair of random numbers (x, y), such that $0 \le x \le 1$, $0 \le y \le 1$, is selected and the point (x, y) is plotted within the unit square. The process is continued a large number of times, say N, and let n be the number of points that have fallen within the closed curve. Then by a famous theorem in **probability theory,** called the **law of large numbers,** it follows that the ratio n/N approaches to the true value of the area, provided the points selected are truly **random.**

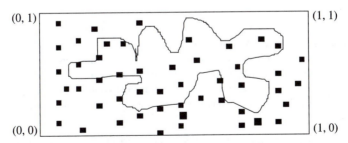

Finding the area of a closed curve by the Monte Carlo method

Monte Carlo simulation– Same as *Monte Carlo method.*

Mood's test– A **nonparametric procedure** for testing the equality of **variances** of two **populations** having a **symmetric distribution** with a common **median.** The procedure is based on the assignment of **ranks** to the original **observations** in the combined **sample**

arranged in ascending order. The **asymptotic relative efficiency** of the Mood's test compared to the classical **F test** is 0.76, which is slightly higher than the Siegel–Tukey **efficiency** measure of 0.61. See also *Ansari–Bradley test, Barton–David test, Conover test, F test for two population variances, Klotz test, Rosenbaum test, Siegel–Tukey test.*

morbidity– A term used to describe sickness, illness, or any other disorder in a human population.

morbidity rate– The number of subjects in a given population who develop sickness, illness, or any other morbid condition over a given period of time divided by the total number of people at **risk** during that period. The term is indiscriminately used to refer to **incidence** or **prevalence rates** of disease and should preferably be avoided.

more-than-fair gamble– A game of chance in which the expected monetary **payoff** of what is being lost is less than the expected monetary gain of what is being received.

mortality– A term used in **vital statistics** to describe deaths in a human population. Mortality data are usually obtained from the information contained in death certificates.

mortality rate– Same as *death rate.*

most powerful test- A test of a **null hypothesis** that provides the maximum **power** against a given **alternative hypothesis.**

moving averages– In the **time-series analysis,** an artificially constructed series obtained by successively averaging overlapping groups of two or more consecutive values in a set of **time-series data** and substituting the **average** value in each group by the group's average. For instance, one begins by selecting a fixed number of successive items in a series, computing the average, then dropping the first item and adding the next succeeding one, computing the average of this second group, dropping the second item and adding the next succeeding one, computing the average of this third group, and so on. It is a method of **smoothing** the curve representing the **data.** The method is used primarily for the smoothing of **time series** and elimination of **seasonal variation,** in which each **observation** is substituted by a **weighted average** of the observations and its neighboring values.

MSE– Acronym for *mean square error.*

multicenter clinical trial– A **clinical trial** conducted at a number of research centers in which all follow a common set of predefined guidelines with independent **randomization** performed within each center. Such a study allows a larger **sample size** and permits generalization of findings to a much greater and diverse group of patients and treatment settings than would normally be possible if the study were to be performed at a single location.

multicollinearity– The presence of high or near-perfect intercorrelations between or among various **independent variables** in a **multiple regression analysis.** The multicollinearity results in imprecise **estimates** of the **regression coefficients,** and this makes it difficult to determine their separate **effects** on the **dependent variable.** Extreme multicollinearity can also cause problems in estimating regression coefficients. The use of **exploratory analysis** prior to the model fitting can usually clarify any problems arising from the high **correlations** between **predictor variables** and between **predictors** and **outcome variables.**

multidimensionality– A term generally used to refer to a phenomenon having more than one aspect or dimension. The term is employed to describe attitudes requiring a multiphasic decision.

multidimensional scaling– A class of **multivariate techniques** involving a **graphical representation** of statistical similarities or differences with a view to trace a map of how individuals' attitudes or characteristics cluster. The procedure consists of plotting pairs of values with highest **correlations** closest together and those with the lowest correlations farther apart.

multilevel modeling– A term used to refer to a class of **statistical models** such as **regression analysis** where observational **data** have a hierarchical or clustered structure. Many kinds of data in social and biological sciences have a natural hierarchy. For example, many animal and human studies deal with hierarchies where offspring are grouped within families. Similarly, studies on school children involve a hierarchy where children are grouped within schools. Many designed **experiments** such as **clinical trials** also have a hierarchy where subjects are grouped into several randomly chosen centers. A hierarchy usually consists of units grouped at different levels. For instance, offspring may be the level 1 units in a two-level structure where the level 2 units are the families; students may be the level 1 units clustered within schools that are the level 2 units. Multilevel models are designed to take into account differences between levels of a hierarchy.

multilevel models– See *multilevel modeling.*

multilevel regression– An extension or generalization of ordinary **multiple regression** to take into account differences between different levels of a hierarchy. In a multilevel regression, when a higher order **interaction** term is included, all the lower order terms are also included. See also *multilevel modeling.*

multimodal distribution– A **frequency** or **probability distribution** in which two or more different values occur with the highest or nearly highest **frequency** indicating **data values** with more than one **mode.** Such a **distribution** probably indicates that several distributions of relatively distinct groups of **observations** are present. See also *bimodal distribution, trimodal distribution, unimodal distribution.*

multimodal frequency (probability) distribution– See *multimodal distribution.*

multinomial coefficient– The number of distinct arrangements in which n distinguishable objects with n_1 of the first kind, n_2 of the second kind, . . . , n_k of the kth kind can be distributed into k compartments. It is given by the formula $n!/(n_1!n_2! \ldots n_k!)$.

multinomial distribution– A generalization of the **binomial distribution** when there are more than two **outcomes** for each **Bernoulli trial.** The **probability function** of a multinomial distribution is given by the formula

$$P(r_1, r_2, \ldots, r_k) = \frac{n!}{r_1!r_2! \ldots r_k!}(p_1)^{r_1}(p_2)^{r_2} \cdots (p_k)^{r_k}$$

where $r_1, r_2, \ldots, r_k$ are the numbers of observations corresponding to k different outcomes with respective **probabilities** of occurrence $p_1, p_2, \ldots, p_k$ ($\sum_{i=1}^{k} r_i = n, \sum_{i=1}^{k} p_i = 1$). It can be shown that the **expected value (mean)** of X_i is np_i, its **variance** is $np_i(1 - p_i)$, and the **covariance** between X_i and X_j is $- np_i p_j$.

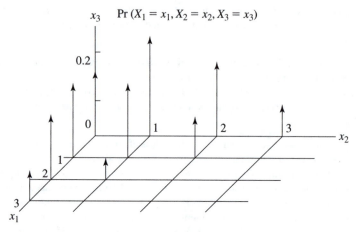

x_3 $\Pr(X_1 = x_1, X_2 = x_2, X_3 = x_3)$

Multinomial distribution for $n = 3$, $p_1 = 0.2$, and $p_2 = 0.3$

multinomial experiment– A sequence of n **independent trials** of a **random experiment** where each trial can result in one of k possible **outcomes.** When $k = 2$, the experiment is known as the **binomial experiment.** When $k = 3$, the experiment is known as **trinomial experiment,** and so forth.

multinomial qualitative variable– Same as *multinomial variable.*

multinomial variable– A nominally scaled or **qualitative variable** in which there are more than two categories or classes of **observations.**

multinormal distribution– Same as *multivariate normal distribution.*

multiphase sampling– An extension of two-phase or **double sampling** to three or more phases.

multiple causation– A term used to describe the view that any "effect" is produced by multiplicity of causes.

multiple coefficient of determination– Same as *coefficient of multiple determination.*

multiple comparison– A statistical procedure that, on the basis of the same **data set,** makes a number (more than one) of tests (comparisons) concerning the various **parameters** of interest controlling for the overall **error rate.** If an overall error rate is fixed at 5 percent, then each test must be performed at a **significance level** less than 5 percent. In an **analysis of variance,** multiple comparison is used to test which **mean** (or a set of means) differs from which other (or a set of means). It is used as a follow-up to significant *F* **tests.** It is also called a **posthoc comparison.** No single test is found to be best in all situations, and a major difference between then lies in the manner in which they control the increase in **type I error** due to multiple testing. Some most commonly used multiple comparison tests are the **Bonferroni procedure, Duncan multiple range test, Dunnett's multiple comparison test, Newman–Keuls test, Scheffe's test,** and **Tukey's test.**

multiple comparison test– Same as *multiple comparison.*

multiple correlation– Same as *multiple correlation coefficient.*

multiple correlation analysis– A method of analysis for determining **correlations** among many **variables** simultaneously.

multiple correlation coefficient– The **product moment correlation** between the actual values of the **dependent variable** and the predicted values as determined by the **multiple regression equation.** It is a measure of the degree of **linear association** between more than two **variables** and is equal to the square root of the **coefficient of multiple determination.** The square of the multiple correlation coefficient provides a measure of the **proportion** of **variation** of the **response variable** that is explained by the **explanatory variables** and is denoted by R^2.

multiple correspondence analysis– See *homogeneity analysis.*

multiple discriminant analysis– See *discriminant analysis.*

multiple logistic regression– The **logistic regression** involving several **independent variables.** If $X_1, X_2, \ldots, X_p$ are p independent variables and Y is a **binary response variable** with **probability** of success equal to p, then the multiple logistic regression model is given by

$$p = \frac{e^{\alpha + \beta_1 x_1 + \cdots + \beta_p x_p}}{1 + e^{\alpha + \beta_1 x_1 + \cdots + \beta_p x_p}} = \frac{1}{1 + e^{-(\alpha + \beta_1 x_1 + \cdots + \beta_p x_p)}}$$

where e is the (natural) exponential function. After applying the log odds **transformation,** the **regression model** is written as:

$$\log\left(\frac{p}{1-p}\right) = \beta_0 + \beta_1 x_1 + \beta_2 x_2 + \cdots + \beta_p x_p$$

Note that the effect of each **explanatory variable** is to multiply the baseline log odds. In epidemiological studies, multiple logistic regression is frequently used for controlling **confounding** or assessing **interactions.** The results from logistic regression are often expressed in terms of an **odds ratio.**

multiple logistic regression model– See *multiple logistic regression.*

multiple R– Same as *multiple correlation coefficient.*

multiple regression– Same as *multiple regression analysis.*

multiple regression analysis– An **analysis of regression** involving two or more **independent variables** as **predictors** to estimate the value of a single **dependent** or **response variable.** The dependent variable is usually continuous, but the independent variables can be continuous or categorical. The **regression model** being fitted is $E(Y) = \beta_0 + \beta_1 X_1 + \beta_2 X_2 + \cdots + \beta_p X_p$, where Y is the dependent or response variable, $X_1, X_2, \ldots, X_p$ are the independent variables, β_0 is the intercept, and $\beta_1, \beta_2, \ldots, \beta_p$ are, the corresponding **regression coefficients.** The **parameters** $\beta_0, \beta_1, \beta_2, \ldots, \beta_p$ are generally estimated by the **method of least squares.** Each regression coefficient is interpreted as the change in the magnitude of the dependent variable corresponding to a unit change in the appropriate independent variable while holding the **effects** of other independent variables as **constants.** See also *regression analysis.*

multiple regression coefficient– See *regression coefficient.*

multiple regression equation– In a **multiple regression analysis,** an algebraic equation relating the **independent variables** to the **expected value** of the **dependent variable.**

multiple regression model– See *multiple regression analysis.*

multiple significance testing– See *multiple comparison.*

multiple-stage sampling– **Sampling** by stages, where the **sampling units** at each stage are subsampled from the larger units chosen at the previous stage. Thus, a municipality may be divided into a certain number of zones and a number of those zones are selected randomly. Within each zone drawn in the **sample,** a number of schools are chosen **at random.** Within each school drawn in the sample, a sample of students can be randomly selected. This is an example of a three-stage sampling where students drawn within schools compose the sample to be analyzed. It is often used in combination with **area sampling** and **cluster sampling.**

multiple testing– See *multiple comparison.*

multiple time series– A multivariate analogue of a univariate **time series** comprising a set of ordered observation vectors measured on several quantitative characteristics taken at different points in time.

multiplication rule for probabilities– A **probability rule** used to determine the **probability** of an intersection of two or more **events.** For any two arbitrary events A and B, it is given by the formula $P(A \cap B) = P(A)P(B|A)$ or $P(A \cap B) = P(B)P(A|B)$. For two **independent events,** it reduces to $P(A \cap B) = P(A)P(B)$. In a series of **independent trials,** the probability that each of a specified series of events takes place is the product of the probabilities of the individual events.

multiplicative model– A **model** in which the combined **effect** of a number of **factors** is taken as the product of effects that can be attributed to the individual factors. See also *additive model.*

multiplicative time-series model– A **classical time-series model** that expresses the actual value of a time series as the product of its components; for example, $Y = T \times C \times S \times I$. See also *additive time-series model, mixed time-series model.*

multistage sampling– Same as *multiple-stage sampling.*

multivariable analysis– A term sometimes used in contradistinction to **multivariate analysis.** When there are several **independent variables,** but only a single **dependent variable,** the term 'multiple' or 'multivariable' is preferable to multivariate.

multivariate analysis– A class of statistical methods and techniques involving multiple **independent** or **dependent variables.** Examples of multivariate analysis include **factor analysis, discriminant analysis, multiple regression** and **correlation analysis,** and many other techniques. Such techniques play an important role in investigating **multivariate data.** See also *bivariate analysis, univariate analysis.*

multivariate analysis of variance– An advanced statistical procedure that provides an overall test when there are multiple measures of **dependent variables** and the **independent variables** are nominal. It is a generalization of the univariate **analysis of variance** with multiple outcome measures for the dependent variable. It is used to test group differences on profiles of **measurements,** in contrast to the use of ANOVA to test group differences on measurements of a single variable. It is widely used in business, psychological, and social science research. Unlike the univariate case where F **tests** are used to test **hypotheses** of interest, in the multivariate case there does not exist a single optimal **test**

procedure. Three most commonly used test criteria are: Wilk's lambda (λ), Roy's largest root criterion, and the Hotelling–Lawley trace. If the dependent variables are not correlated, separate ANOVAs for each dependent variable would suffice.

multivariate contingency table– An extension of a **contingency table** for **bivariate data** to **multivariate data.**

multivariate contingency table analysis– Methods and techniques for analyzing relationships among several **categorical variables** forming a **multivariate contingency table.**

multivariate data– Same as *multivariate data set.*

multivariate data set– A **data set** containing information on two or more **variables.** Such data are usually displayed in the form of a **data matrix.**

multivariate density function– A multivariable continuous function $f(x_1, x_2, \ldots, x_p)$ defined for all possible p-tuples $(x_1, x_2, \ldots, x_p)$ in the range of **continuous random variables** $X_1, X_2, \ldots, X_p$, such that $f(x_1, x_2, \ldots, x_p) \geq 0$ and

$$\int_{-\infty}^{\infty} \int_{-\infty}^{\infty} \cdots \int_{-\infty}^{\infty} f(x_1, x_2, \ldots, x_p) \, dx_1 dx_2 \cdots dx_p = 1$$

See also *bivariate density function, joint density function.*

multivariate distribution– Same as *multivariate probability distribution.*

multivariate methods– See *multivariate analysis.*

multivariate normal distribution– A generalization of a **bivariate normal distribution** to three or more **random variables.** Geometrically, it can be represented as concentric ellipsoids of **constant** density in multidimensional space. The form of its **probability density function,** however, involves the use of complex matrix notations and can be found in any book on **multivariate analysis.** Like its univariate and bivariate counterparts, the distribution has a number of simple properties that make its use as a **probability model** for observed **multivariate data** very popular. See also *normal distribution, trivariate normal distribution.*

multivariate observations– Same as *multivariate data.*

multivariate probability distribution– See *joint probability distribution.*

multivariate probability function– A multivariate discrete function $p(x_1, x_2, \ldots, x_p)$ defined for all possible p-tuples $(x_1, x_2, \ldots, x_p)$ in the range of **discrete random variables** $X_1, X_2, \ldots, X_p$, such that $p(x_1, x_2, \ldots, x_p) \geq 0$ and $\sum_{x_1, x_2, \ldots, x_p} p(x_1, x_2, \ldots, x_p) = 1$. See also *joint probability function.*

multivariate statistical analysis– Same as *multivariate analysis.*

multivariate statistical methods– See *multivariate analysis.*

multivariate statistical procedures– See *multivariate analysis.*

multivariate statistical techniques– See *multivariate analysis.*

multivariate techniques– See *multivariate analysis.*

multivariate time series– Same as *multiple time series.*

multiway analysis of variance– An **analysis of variance** procedure involving the study of several **factors** simultaneously. It is an extension of the analysis of variance methodology for the case of two factors to three or more factors involving a single experiment. Multi-factor ANOVA designs usually provide more information and often can be even more economical than separate one-way or two-way designs. See also *one-way analysis of variance, two-way analysis of variance, three-way analysis of variance.*

multiway classification– A classification of a set of **observations** according to three or more characteristics or **factors.** See also *one-way classification, two-way classification.*

mutual independence– In **probability theory,** when each subset of a set of n **events** defined on the same **sample space,** e.g., $((A_i, A_j; i < j, = 1, 2, \ldots, n), (A_i, A_j, A_k; i < j < k = 1, 2, \ldots, n)$, etc., is independent, the set are said to be mutually independent. For example, three events A_1, A_2, and A_3 defined on the same sample space are mutually independent if

$$P(A_1 \cap A_2) = P(A_1)P(A_2), \; P(A_1 \cap A_3) = P(A_1)P(A_3), \; P(A_2 \cap A_3) = P(A_2)P(A_3)$$

and

$$P(A_1 \cap A_2 \cap A_3) = P(A_1)P(A_2)P(A_3)$$

See also *pairwise independence.*

mutually exclusive events– In **probability theory,** two or more **events** are said to be mutually exclusive if they cannot occur simultaneously or do not have any simple elements in common. A single toss of a coin for example must result in either a head or a tail. These outcomes are mutually exclusive. Compare *nonmutually exclusive events.*

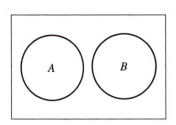

Two mutually exclusive events

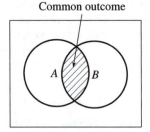

Two nonmutually exclusive events

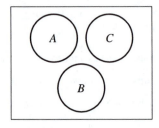

Three mutually exclusive events

negative binomial distribution– For a series of **Bernoulli trials,** the negative binomial distribution gives the **probability** of the total number of **trials** (n) required to obtain k successes. It is given by the formula

$$P(n) = \binom{n-1}{k-1} p^k (1-p)^{n-k} \qquad n = k, k+1, \ldots$$

where p is the probability of success on a single trial. It is also called the Pascal distribution. Note that the **geometric distribution** is a special case of the negative binomial distribution with $k = 1$.

negative correlation– In **correlation analysis,** two **variables** are said to have negative correlation when high values of one variable tend to be associated with low values of the other and vice versa. Some examples of negative correlations are selling price and demand, absenteeism and production output, sales and competitors' expenditure on advertising, among others. The concept applies only to pairs of variables, i.e., to **simple correlation.** It does not apply to **multiple correlation.** See also *coefficient of correlation, inverse relationship, positive correlation.*

negatively skewed distribution– See *skewed distribution.*

negative multinomial distribution– A generalization of the **negative binomial distribution** to the **sampling** involving a **multinomial experiment.**

negative predictive value– Same as *predictive value negative.*

negative relation– Same as *negative correlation.*

negative relationship– Same as *negative correlation.*

negative skewness– See *skewed distribution.*

negative study– A study that fails to establish the viability of the **research hypothesis.** A negative study does not result in the rejection of the **null hypothesis** and the results are **statistically nonsignificant.**

negative synergism– See *synergism.*

neonatal death rate– See *infant death rate.*

neonatal mortality rate– Same as *neonatal death rate.*

nested case-control study– A type of **case-control study** in which a **cohort** is followed through a period of time to select **cases** of interest, and for each case the **controls** are selected from within the cohort.

nested design– An **experimental design** in which **levels** of one or more **factors** are nested within one or more other factors. More specifically, given two factors *A* and *B*, the levels of *B* are said to be nested within the levels of *A* if each level of *B* appears with only a single level of *A* in the **observations.** For example, an **experiment** may be designed where water samples are taken from different sources of water supply. Here, water samples are nested within sources of water supplies. Similarly, in a simple **parallel group design,** patients receive only one **treatment,** i.e., patients are nested within treatments. Such designs are common in many fields of study and are particularly popular in **surveys** and industrial experiments. Compare *factorial design.*

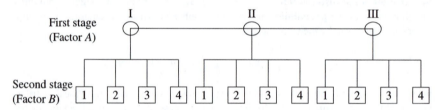

A layout for the two-way nested design

nested model– An **analysis of variance** model involving a **nested design.** See also *crossed model, crossed-nested model.*

nesting– A term sometimes used to describe the characteristic or propensity of a **nested design.**

net reproduction rate– A measure of the rate of replacement of females in the population per generation, with the current values of **fertility** and **mortality.** In a **cohort** subject to a given set of **age-specific fertility rates, age-specific mortality rates,** and given sex **ratio** at birth, it is the **average** number of female children born per woman. See also *gross reproduction rate.*

Newman–Keuls test– A type of **multiple comparison** procedure for comparing pairwise **means** following a significant *F* test in an **analysis of variance.** The procedure involves a step-by-step approach where the **sample ranges** are tested against the **Studentized range** of the subsets rather than the range of the mean values. See also *Bonferroni procedure, Duncan multiple range test, Dunnett's multiple comparison test, Scheffe's test, Tukey's test.*

Newton–Raphson method– A numerical **algorithm** normally employed for optimization of a mathematical function. The procedure involves solving equations iteratively, in which each successive approximation is determined by using the first derivative of its numerical estimates.

nominal category– A category or group defined by a **nominal** or **categorical variable.**

nominal data– **Data** obtained by using nominal **scales of measurement.** See also *categorical data, nominal scale, numerical data, qualitative data.*

nominal level of measurement– Same as *nominal scale.*

nominal measure– Same as *nominal variable.*

nominal scale– **Measurement scales** representing qualitative differences among categories or groups. Numbers may be assigned for purposes of identification, but the measure assigned to an item is simply a label used for identification. A nominal scale has only one property, class inclusion/exclusion for each one of the categories or classes; no quantitative relationships between classes are referred to or implied. Nominal scales produce **nominal** or **categorical data.**

nominal significance level– A term used to denote the actual **level of significance** of a **statistical test** when all its **assumptions** are satisfied.

nominal variable– Same as *categorical variable.*

nomogram– A **graphical representation** for the **variables** involved in a formula on a plane surface. It shows scales for the variables, their relative magnitudes, and their positions in manners such that the corresponding values of the variables are found at the points on the scales that are intersected by the same straight line. It is also called nomograph and alignment chart.

nomograph– Same as *nomogram.*

nomographic– Pertaining to the **graphical device** used in a **nomograph.**

nonadditive model– A **statistical model** in which the **explanatory variables** do not have an additive effect on the **response measure** of interest. In a **factorial experiment,** the term is used to refer to the tendency for the combination of **factors** to yield a result that is different from the sum of their individual contributions. Compare *additive model.* See also *interaction.*

nonadditivity– See *Tukey's test for nonadditivity.*

nonbalanced data– Same as *nonorthogonal data.*

noncentral chi-square distribution– See *noncentral distributions.*

noncentral distributions– The term is applied to a number of **probability distributions** that are closely linked to some commonly used **sampling distributions,** such as t, χ^2, and F distributions, and that arise in the form of the distributions of the **test statistics** derived under some specified **alternative hypotheses.** Some of the well-known distributions are noncentral t, χ^2, and F distributions. These distributions are useful in calculating the power of the tests on the basis of the corresponding central distributions. Some further details on noncentral t, χ^2, and F distributions are given in App. E.

noncentral F distribution– See *noncentral distributions.*

noncentral t distribution– See *noncentral distributions.*

noncompliance– A term used to describe the behavior of patients who do not follow one or more of the guidelines laid in the study **protocol.**

nondirectional hypothesis– An **alternative hypothesis** that does not indicate the direction of the possible differences from the value specified by the **null hypothesis.** See also *directional hypothesis, one-sided hypothesis.*

nondirectional test– Same as *two-tailed test.*

nonindependent events– In **probability theory,** when the occurrence of one **event** influences the **probability** of occurrence of another event, such events are said to be nonindependent. See also *dependent events, independent events.*

nonindependent samples– Same as *dependent samples.*

noninformative prior– A term used in **Bayesian statistics** to describe a prior whose **probability distribution** does not contain any empirical or theoretical information regarding the unknown **parameters.** An example of a noninformative prior is a **uniform distribution.** It is alternatively known as **diffuse** or **vague prior.**

nonlinear model– A **statistical model** in which the **parameters** are nonlinear. For example, the model $y = \alpha e^{-\beta x} + \varepsilon$ represents a nonlinear model. Some of the nonlinear models can be converted into **linear models** by making appropriate mathematical **transformations.** See also *nonlinear regression.*

nonlinear regression– The method of determining a **regression** in which a curve other than a straight line best describes the relationship between two **variables.** This is also called curvilinear regression. A nonlinear regression is based on a **nonlinear model.** Compare *linear regression.*

nonlinear regression model– A **regression model** that is nonlinear in the **parameters.** See also *nonlinear model, nonlinear regression.*

nonmutually exclusive events– In **probability theory,** two or more **events** are said to be nonmutually exclusive if the occurrence of one event does not preclude the occurrence of the other events. Compare *mutually exclusive events.*

non-normal distribution– A **probability distribution** other than a **normal distribution.**

non-normality– A term used to denote the property of a **random variable** having a **non-normal distribution.**

non-normal probability distribution– Same as *non-normal distribution.*

nonorthogonal data– **Experimental data** obtained by using a **nonorthogonal design.** Compare *orthogonal data.*

nonorthogonal design– A term used to denote an **analysis of variance** design with two or more **factors** having unequal numbers of **observations** in each **cell.** Compare *orthogonal design.*

nonparametric analysis– See *nonparametric methods.*

nonparametric methods– Methods of testing a **hypothesis** or obtaining a **confidence interval** that do not require knowledge of the form of the underlying **parent population.** These are statistical methods or tests that do not involve the **estimation** or **hypothesis testing** of **population parameters.** They are also called **distribution-free methods,** since they supposedly do not require that the underlying distributions be either normal in **shape** or homogeneous in terms of **variance.** The **data** that exhibit **positive** or **negative skewness**

can be analyzed by nonparametric methods. These methods can be applied when only **rank order** or preference data are available. In many cases, these methods are only slightly less powerful than their parametric analogues that assume a specific form of the population distribution (usually a **normal distribution**), even when that assumption is true. The non-parametric methods include the **Mann–Whitney U test; Wilcoxon signed-rank** and **rank-sum tests; Kruskal–Wallis** and **Freidman tests; Pearson chi-square test;** and the **Spearman rank correlation, point biserial, phi,** and **Cramér's V coefficients,** among others.

nonparametric procedure– Same as *nonparametric method.*

nonparametric regression– A **regression model** that does not assume any parametric form. There are currently a number of techniques for performing a nonparametric regression.

nonparametric statistical methods– Same as *nonparametric methods.*

nonparametric statistical test– See *nonparametric methods.*

nonparametric techniques– Same as *nonparametric methods.*

nonparametric test– Same as *nonparametric statistical test.*

nonprobability sample– A **sample** selected in such a manner that the **probability** of each element being selected in the sample is unknown. **Convenience** and **judgment samples** are examples of nonprobability samples. See also *probability sample, random sample.*

nonprobability sampling– Any **sampling** procedure in which the **probability** of an element being included in the **sample** is not known.

nonrandomized clinical trial– A **clinical trial** in which patients are assigned to **treatment** and **control groups** by some subjective criteria or a mechanism other than a randomized procedure. Such a trial is subject to several sources of **biases.** For example, patients who respond to a treatment may be healthier than those who do not respond, giving a false impression that the treatment is beneficial.

nonrandom sampling– Same as *nonprobability sampling.*

nonrecursive model– A **causal model** in which there is two-way causal flow in the system. Compare *recursive model.* See also *path analysis, structural equation model.*

nonresponse– A term used to denote the lack of response on the part of the respondent or the failure to obtain the relevant information being collected in a **survey.** The general problem of nonresponse arises because the characteristics of nonrespondents usually differ to some degree from those of respondents. A nonresponse can occur for a number of reasons (such as absence, death, or refusal to reply) and a high **nonresponse rate** can introduce **bias** into the results. See also *nonresponse bias.*

nonresponse bias– A systematic tendency for selected **elementary units** with particular characteristics not to respond in a **survey,** while other such units in the **sample,** with different characteristics, do. The units or individuals that do not respond are usually not representative of those that do. See also *nonresponse, nonresponse rate.*

nonresponse rate– The **proportion** of individuals in a **sample survey** that fail to provide the relevant information being sought by the investigator. Compare *response rate.* See also *nonresponse, nonresponse bias.*

nonsampling error– An **error** in a **sample estimate** that is not related to **sampling error.** Such errors may arise from many different sources such as flaws in the **sampling frame,** errors in the collection of **data,** mistakes in the processing of data, and so forth.

nonsense correlation– Same as *spurious correlation.*

normal approximation– A term used to denote the act of approximating a **non-normal probability distribution** by a **normal distribution;** for example, a **binomial distribution** with number of **trials** n and **probability** of a success p can be approximated by a normal distribution with **mean** np and **variance** $np(1 - p)$.

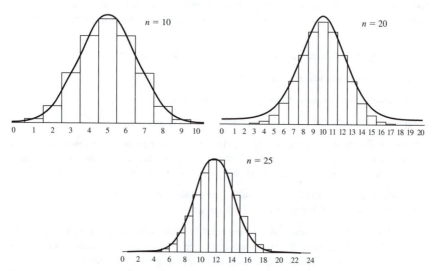

Normal approximations to binomial distribution, $n = 10, 20, 25$

normal curve– The normal curve, or more accurately the family of normal curves, is represented by the **normal distribution.** Normal curves are **mesokurtic,** symmetrical, bell-shaped curves with tails extending indefinitely in both directions from the center, approaching but never touching the **horizontal axis.** Theoretically speaking, the curve extends from $-\infty$ to ∞ with the horizontal axis as an asymptote. The normal curve has many interesting mathematical properties and can be used to approximate the **distributions** of many other **variables.** See also *standard normal curve.*

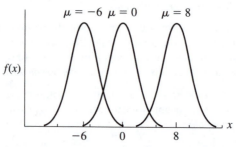

Normal curves with $\mu = -6, 0, 8$ and $\sigma = 2$

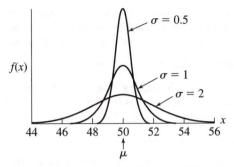

Normal curves with $\mu = 50$ and $\sigma = 0.5, 1, 2$

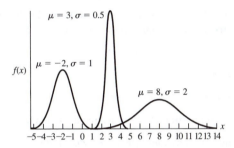

Normal curves with $\mu = -2, \sigma = 1$;
$\mu = 3, \sigma = 0.5$; $\mu = 8, \sigma = 2$

normal curve ordinate– The height of the **normal curve** at any point along its **abscissa** is the **ordinate** of the curve at that point.

normal deviate– The value of a **deviate** of the **normal distribution.**

normal distribution– A **probability distribution** of a **continuous random variable** X represented by the **probability density function**

$$f(x) = \frac{1}{\sigma\sqrt{2\pi}} \exp\left\{-(x - \mu)^2/2\sigma^2\right\} \qquad -\infty < x < \infty$$

where μ and σ are, respectively, the **mean** and **standard deviation** of the **distribution.** It is also called the **gaussian distribution.** In any normal distribution: (1) 68% of the observations fall within σ of the mean μ, (2) 95% of the observations fall within 2σ of μ, and (3) 99.7% of the observations fall within 3σ of μ. This is known as 68–95–99.7 rule and is graphically illustrated in the figure below.

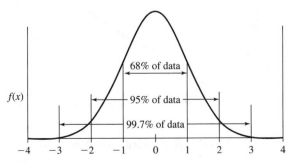

The 68–95–99.7 rule for normal distribution

normal equations– The set of simultaneous equations obtained as in the **estimation** of the **regression coefficients** by the **method of least squares.** The solution of the normal equations yields the least squares estimates of the regression coefficients.

normal equivalent deviate– See *probit transformation.*

normal form analysis– In **decision theory,** a tabular form of **preposterior analysis** that systematically calculates an expected **payoff** value for every possible strategy and then selects the strategy with the largest payoff as the optimum one.

normal interval– Same as *normal range.*

normality– A term used to denote the property of a **random variable** having a **normal distribution.**

normality assumption– Many of the parametric **tests of significance** require that the **distribution** of the **parent population**(s) involved be normal or nearly normal in **shape.**

normal law of error– Same as *law of error.*

normal limits– See *normal values.*

normal plot– Same as *normal probability plot.*

normal population– A **population** of values having a **normal distribution.**

normal probability density function– See *normal distribution.*

normal probability distribution– Same as *normal distribution.*

normal probability paper– Same as *arithmetic probability paper.*

normal probability plot– A **graphical method** of assessing the assumption of **normality** of a **sample.** The ordered sample values $x_{(1)}, x_{(2)}, \ldots, x_{(n)}$ are plotted against the values $\Phi^{-1}(p_i)$ where $p_i = i - 0.5/n$ and

$$\Phi(x) = \int_{-\infty}^{x} \frac{1}{\sqrt{2\pi}} \exp\left(-\frac{t^2}{2}\right) dt.$$

For a sample from a **normal distribution** the plot appears as a straight line and any departure from normality in the plot is indicative of the lack of normality of the **data.**

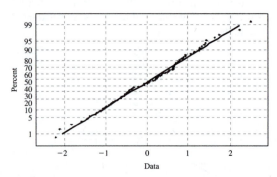

Normal probability plot: normally distributed data

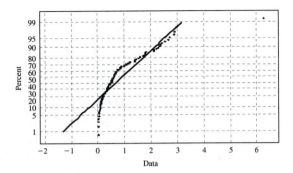

Normal probability plot: negatively skewed data

normal probability tables– Tables that give **probabilities** of a **normal distribution** for various possible combinations of values of μ (**mean**) and σ (**standard deviation**). A short version of normal probability tables for the **standard normal distribution** is given on page 180.

normal random variable– A **random variable** having a **normal distribution.**

normal range– See *normal values.*

normal scores– The **expected values** of the **order statistics** $x_{(1)}, x_{(2)}, \ldots, x_{(n)}$ drawn from the **standard normal distribution.** Normal scores are used in plots to assess **normality.**

normal scores test– A **nonparametric procedure** for comparing **locations** of two **populations.** The procedure consists of first transforming the **observations** to **rank order** in the combined **sample** and then converting the **ranks** by a **transformation,** which involves **standard normal distribution.** See also *Mann–Whitney–Wilcoxon test, Wilcoxon rank-sum test.*

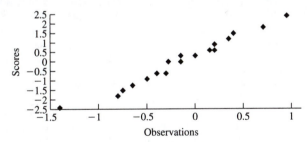

Normal score plot: normally distributed data

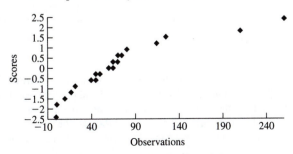

Normal score plot: exponentially distributed data

Pocket Dictionary of Statistics

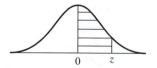

Standard normal table

z	.00	.01	.02	.03	.04	.05	.06	.07	.08	.09
0.0	.0000	.0040	.0080	.0120	.0160	.0199	.0239	.0279	.0319	.0359
0.1	.0398	.0438	.0478	.0517	.0557	.0596	.0636	.0675	.0714	.0753
0.2	.0793	.0832	.0871	.0910	.0948	.0987	.1026	.1064	.1103	.1141
0.3	.1179	.1217	.1255	.1293	.1331	.1368	.1406	.1443	.1480	.1517
0.4	.1554	.1591	.1628	.1664	.1700	.1736	.1772	.1808	.1844	.1879
0.5	.1915	.1950	.1985	.2019	.2054	.2088	.2123	.2157	.2190	.2224
0.6	.2257	.2291	.2324	.2357	.2389	.2422	.2454	.2486	.2518	.2549
0.7	.2580	.2612	.2642	.2673	.2704	.2734	.2764	.2794	.2823	.2852
0.8	.2881	.2910	.2939	.2967	.2995	.3023	.3051	.3078	.3106	.3133
0.9	.3159	.3186	.3212	.3238	.3264	.3289	.3315	.3340	.3365	.3389
1.0	.3413	.3438	.3461	.3485	.3508	.3531	.3554	.3577	.3599	.3621
1.1	.3643	.3665	.3686	.3708	.3729	.3749	.3770	.3790	.3810	.3830
1.2	.3849	.3869	.3888	.3907	.3925	.3944	.3962	.3980	.3997	.4015
1.3	.4032	.4049	.4066	.4082	.4099	.4115	.4131	.4147	.4162	.4177
1.4	.4192	.4207	.4222	.4236	.4251	.4265	.4279	.4292	.4306	.4319
1.5	.4332	.4345	.4357	.4370	.4382	.4394	.4406	.4418	.4429	.4441
1.6	.4452	.4463	.4474	.4484	.4495	.4505	.4515	.4525	.4535	.4545
1.7	.4554	.4564	.4573	.4582	.4591	.4599	.4608	.4616	.4625	.4633
1.8	.4641	.4649	.4656	.4664	.4671	.4678	.4686	.4693	.4699	.4706
1.9	.4713	.4719	.4726	.4732	.4738	.4744	.4750	.4756	.4761	.4767
2.0	.4772	.4778	.4783	.4788	.4793	.4798	.4803	.4808	.4812	.4817
2.1	.4821	.4826	.4830	.4834	.4838	.4842	.4846	.4850	.4854	.4857
2.2	.4861	.4864	.4868	.4871	.4875	.4878	.4881	.4884	.4887	.4890
2.3	.4893	.4896	.4898	.4901	.4904	.4906	.4909	.4911	.4913	.4916
2.4	.4918	.4920	.4922	.4925	.4927	.4929	.4931	.4932	.4934	.4936
2.5	.4938	.4940	.4941	.4943	.4945	.4946	.4948	.4949	.4951	.4952
2.6	.4953	.4955	.4956	.4957	.4959	.4960	.4961	.4962	.4963	.4964
2.7	.4965	.4966	.4967	.4968	.4969	.4970	.4971	.4972	.4973	.4974
2.8	.4974	.4975	.4976	.4977	.4977	.4978	.4979	.4979	.4980	.4981
2.9	.4981	.4982	.4982	.4983	.4984	.4984	.4985	.4985	.4986	.4986
3.0	.4986	.4987	.4987	.4988	.4988	.4989	.4989	.4989	.4990	.4990

The entries in this table are the probabilities that a random variable having the standard normal distribution assume a value between 0 and z

Source: Computed by using software.

normal values– Values regarded as being within the usual range of **variation** in a given **population** or population subgroup. The range of such values is called the normal range. The limits of the normal range are called normal limits. Normal values provide useful descriptive tools and, for normally distributed **data,** can be calculated by using the **sample mean** and the **standard deviation.** The normal values are often used as the basis for evaluating the results of a diagnostic test in classifying individuals as normal or abnormal.

not statistically significant– In **hypothesis testing,** any **sample data** that do not lead to the rejection of the **null hypothesis** because it has a high **probability** of occurring when the null hypothesis is true. Compare *statistically significant.*

nuisance parameter– In **statistical estimation** and **hypothesis testing,** the term is used to designate a **parameter** that is needed to specify the **sampling distribution** of interest, but is not of direct interest for making the **inference.** The presence of a nuisance parameter makes the problem of inference more difficult and it is often necessary to find a statistical procedure that does not depend on it. For example, in testing or setting a **confidence interval** for the **mean** of a **normal population,** the unknown parent **variance** is a nuisance parameter and the problem is solved by use of the **Student's *t* distribution,** which does not depend on the parent variance.

null distribution– The **probability distribution** of a **test statistic** evaluated under the **null hypothesis.**

null hypothesis– In statistical testing, the general procedure is to assume a **hypothesis** tentatively for the purpose of rejecting or refuting it. Such a statement is called a null hypothesis. It is always a statement of some exact value or values for one or more **population parameters** usually expressed as a negative statement. This hypothesis is assumed to be true until such time as **observations** indicate that it is unlikely to be, that is, the **sample observations** show whether or not the null hypothesis should be rejected. An example is the hypothesis that a particular **treatment** has the same effect as a **placebo.** In general, the term refers to a particular hypothesis being tested, as distinct from the **alternative hypotheses** that are under consideration. The null hypothesis can be considered the hypothesis of "no difference" or, more correctly, the hypothesis that the observed difference is entirely due to **sampling error,** i.e., that it occurred purely by **chance.** In a **test of significance,** the null hypothesis is postulated to form the basis for calculating the **probability** that the difference occurred entirely by chance. When the difference is not significant, the null hypothesis is not rejected; when the difference is significant, the null hypothesis is rejected in favor of other hypotheses about the causes of the difference. Note that the null hypothesis is never proven right or wrong, or true or false, but is only rejected or not rejected at the arbitrarily chosen **level of significance,** i.e., 0.05, 0.01, 0.1, etc. It is usually denoted by H_0.

number of cases– Same as *size of a sample.*

numerical data– **Data** obtained by using numerical **scales of measurement.** These are data in numerical quantities involving continuous measurements or counts. See also *numerical scale.*

numerical distribution– A **frequency distribution** in which **data** are grouped according to numerical values. It is also called a quantitative distribution.

numerical observations– Same as *numerical data.*

numerical scale– It is used for characteristics that can be given numerical values and the differences between numbers have meaning. Some examples of such characteristics are height, weight, and blood pressure level. It is also called an **interval** or **ratio scale** and is the highest **level of measurement.**

numerical taxanomy– Methods and techniques used in the numerical evaluation of the affinity or similarity between species or subspecies in biological material and the ordering and grouping of these units into taxa on the basis of their affinities. More generally, the term is used as a synonym for **cluster analysis.**

numerical variable– Same as *quantitative variable.*

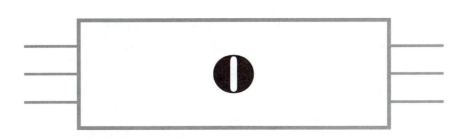

objective probability– In contrast to **subjective probability,** an **estimate** of **probability** based on **empirical** evidence from observable **events** or phenomena interpreted in the **frequency** sense. See also *classical probability, empirical probability.*

oblique rotation– See *factor rotation.*

observation– Process of a study or investigation; a **measurement, score,** or **datum** obtained from an **experiment.**

observational study– An epidemiologic study that does not involve an intervention or manipulation on the part of the investigator. In an observational study, the nature is allowed to take its course and differences in one characteristic are investigated in relation to differences in other characteristics without any human intervention. **Sample surveys** and most of the epidemiologic studies belong to this class. It is called a **case-control, cross-sectional,** or **cohort study,** according to the choice of the **study design.** See also *experimental study, prospective study, retrospective study.*

observational unit– The unit in an **experiment** on which an **observation** is made or recorded. An observational unit, however, may differ from an **experimental unit.** For example, in a **household survey,** a household may be an experimental unit but an individual within the household could be an observational unit.

observed frequency– In a **contingency table** the number of actual **observations** counted in each **cell** or category. In general, the number of times a particular **event** or phenomenon occurs. Compare *expected frequency.*

observed significance level– Same as *p value.*

observed variable– A synonym for **manifest variable.**

occupational death rate– The **death rate** calculated for a specific occupational or professional group or category. See also *age-specific death rate, cause-specific death rate.*

occupational mortality rate– Same as *occupational death rate.*

odds– The **ratio** of the **probability** that an **event** will occur to the probability that the event will not occur. It is calculated by the formula odds $= p/(1 - p)$, where p is the probability of the event. The odds are used to convey the idea of probability, although for rare events the two are nearly the same. For a common event, such as getting a head or tail when a coin is tossed, the probability is 0.5 or 50%, but the odds are 1 (50:50). See also *odds ratio*.

odds ratio– A measure of the **relative risk** estimated in a **case-control study.** It is the **ratio** of the **odds** that a **case** was exposed to a given **risk factor** to the odds that a **control** was exposed to the risk factor. In general, the odds ratio represents the ratio of the odds favoring the occurrence of an **event** to that of another event. It is a measure of **association** between two **variables.** An odds ratio of 1 indicates that there is no relationship between the variables. An odds ratio less than 1 indicates an inverse or **negative relation** and an odds ratio greater than 1 indicates a direct or **positive relation.** In a **2 × 2 contingency table** it is calculated by the formula $(ad)/(bc)$, where a, b, c, and d are the appropriate **cell counts.** The odds ratio is related to the **risk ratio** or relative risk in that, when the **probability** of the occurrence of the event is small (i.e., $a \ll b$ and $c \ll d$), the odds ratio equals the risk ratio. However, the odds ratio is a useful measure of difference in **risks** between two groups, irrespective of whether it approximates the relative risk or not, and arises in many important **statistical models** such as **logistic regression.** It is also called cross-product ratio.

ogive– A graph of the **cumulative frequency distribution** or **cumulative relative frequency distribution.** The cumulative frequency distribution may be plotted so that each **ordinate** of the ogive expresses either the number or **proportion** of **observations** "less than" or "greater than" the corresponding **abscissa.**

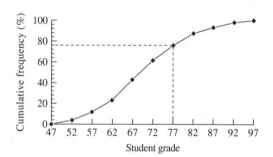

Ogive based on the cumulative frequency (percentage)
column in the table under frequency distribution

ogive curve– Same as *ogive*.

OLS– Acronym for *ordinary least squares*.

one-factor analysis of variance– Same as *one-way analysis of variance*.

one-sample *t* test– A **test procedure** used to compare the **mean** of a single **sample** with a hypothetical **population mean,** when the **population variance** is unknown and estimated by the **sample variance.** See also *two-sample t test*.

one-sided alternative– An **alternative hypothesis** that allows or holds for the **deviation** from the **null hypothesis** to be in only one particular direction. For example, if the null hypothesis asserts that the **parameter** of interest μ is equal to some specified value μ_0, the alternative $\mu > \mu_0$ is a one-sided alternative. A **test of significance** based on a one-sided alternative is called **one-sided test.**

one-sided hypothesis– See *directional hypothesis.*

one-sided test– Same as *one-tailed test.*

one-tailed hypothesis– Same as *one-sided hypothesis.*

one-tailed hypothesis test– A **test of hypothesis** in which rejection of the **null hypothesis** occurs in only one tail of the **sampling distribution** of the **test statistic.** The **critical region** of a one-tailed test is located completely at one end of the distribution of the test statistic. A one-tailed test takes into account deviations in only one direction from the value stated under the null hypothesis, either those that are greater than it or those that are less than it. The one-tail is the area of the sampling distribution that serves as basis for the rejection or nonrejection of the null hypothesis. See also *lower-tailed test, two-tailed test, upper-tailed test.*

one-tailed test– Same as *one-tailed hypothesis test.*

one-way analysis of variance– An **analysis of variance** procedure involving only one **factor** or **independent variable.** The analysis of a **completely randomized design** is an example of a one-way analysis of variance. See also *multiway analysis of variance, two-way analysis of variance, three-way analysis of variance.*

One-way ANOVA table for equal group sizes

Source of variation	Degrees of freedom	Sum of squares	Mean square	Variance ratio
Between groups	$k-1$	$SS_B = n \sum_{i=1}^{k} (\bar{Y}_{i.} - \bar{Y}_{..})^2$	$MS_B = \dfrac{SS_B}{k-1}$	$\dfrac{MS_B}{MS_W}$
Within groups	$k(n-1)$	$SS_W = \sum_{i=1}^{k} \sum_{j=1}^{n} (Y_{ij} - \bar{Y}_{i.})^2$	$MS_W = \dfrac{SS_W}{k(n-1)}$	
Total	$nk-1$	$\sum_{i=1}^{k} \sum_{j=1}^{n} (Y_{ij} - \bar{Y}_{..})^2$		

One-way ANOVA table for unequal group sizes

Source of variation	Degrees of freedom	Sum of squares	Mean square	Variance ratio
Between groups	$k-1$	$SS_B = \sum_{i=1}^{k} n_i (\bar{Y}_{i.} - \bar{Y}_{..})^2$	$MS_B = \dfrac{SS_B}{k-1}$	$\dfrac{MS_B}{MS_W}$
Within groups	$\sum_{i=1}^{k} (n_i - 1)$	$SS_W = \sum_{i=1}^{k} \sum_{j=1}^{n_i} (Y_{ij} - \bar{Y}_{i.})^2$	$MS_W = \dfrac{SS_W}{\sum_{i=1}^{k} (n_i - 1)}$	
Total	$\sum_{i=1}^{k} n_i - 1$	$\sum_{i=1}^{k} \sum_{j=1}^{n_i} (Y_{ij} - \bar{Y}_{..})^2$		

one-way classification– A **classification** of a set of **observations** according to a single characteristic. See also *one-way analysis of variance, single factor experiment.*

one-way design– Same as *one-way classification.*

one-way layout– Same as *one-way classification.*

open-ended class intervals– Class intervals that have only one stated end point, the upper or lower limit.

open-ended interval– In a **grouped frequency distribution,** the highest (or lowest) interval that includes all values above (or below) a particular value.

operational research– Same as *operations research.*

operations research– A collection of quantitative methods and techniques involving optimization and **stochastic models** applicable to problems and activities of a complex system, such as those arising in a large business, industrial, or governmental organization, with a view to making optimal decisions and increase efficiency.

opinion poll– Same as *opinion survey.*

opinion survey– A **survey** designed to measure opinions possessed by members of a community concerning certain social, political, or other topics of interest. Field workers are employed for this purpose where each interviews a quota of people in the streets or other public places. See also *sample survey.*

opportunity loss– In **decision theory,** when a decision maker maximizes benefit, the opportunity loss is the difference between (1) the optimal **payoff** for a given **event** and (2) the actual payoff achieved as a result of taking a specified course of action and the subsequent occurrence of that event. When a decision maker minimizes cost, it is the difference between (1) the actual cost incurred as a consequence of taking a specified course of action and the subsequent occurrence of an event and (2) the minimum cost achievable for that event.

optimal strategy– In **decision theory,** a complete plan specifying the course of actions to be taken at each possible **action point,** if the expected monetary or utility **payoff** is to be the best one available.

optimization methods– A loosely defined term often used to designate procedures and techniques useful in finding optimal solutions of a given problem, which generally involve finding the maxima or minima of functions of several variables.

optimum allocation– In a **stratified random sampling,** the method of allocation of total **sample size** to various **strata** so as to maximize **precision** for a fixed cost. See also *proportional allocation.*

ordered alternative– An **alternative hypothesis** that specifies an order for a set of **parameters** being tested. For example, in a **one-way analysis of variance** problem with means $\mu_1, \mu_2, \ldots, \mu_k$, the null and ordered alternative hypotheses are: $H_0 : \mu_1 = \mu_2 = \cdots = \mu_k$ versus $H_1 : \mu_1 \leq \mu_2 \leq \cdots \leq \mu_k$.

ordered alternative hypothesis– Same as *ordered alternative.*

ordered array– Same as *array.*

ordered logistic regression– A **logistic regression** method involving an **ordinal variable** as the **dependent variable.** See also *polytomous logistic regression.*

order statistics– A **sample** of **variate** values arranged in ascending order of magnitude are known as order statistics. For a sample of n **measurements** with values $x_1, x_2, \ldots, x_n$ the order statistics are denoted by $x_{(1)}, x_{(2)}, \ldots, x_{(n)}$. The ith largest value is called the ith order statistic and is denoted by $x_{(i)}$.

ordinal contingency table– A **contingency table** in which either row or column, or both, follow an ordinal **ranking.** If both row and column follow an ordinal ranking, the table is known as a doubly ordinal contingency table.

ordinal data– Data obtained by using an **ordinal level of measurement.**

ordinal kappa statistic– See *kappa statistic.*

ordinal level of measurement– Same as *ordinal scale.*

ordinal scale– Ordered scales in which the categories are defined in relationship to one another by the algebra of inequalities (less than and greater than). It is the process of rank ordering objects or persons with respect to some attribute from the "smallest" to the "largest." The measure assigned allows the items to be rank ordered with respect to a criterion. An ordinal scale has two properties: It classifies **observations** into classes in terms of the relationship of greater than or less than. There is no provision made for specifying the degree to which the observations differ from one another. Ordinal scaling produces ordinal or rank-ordered data. Some examples of an ordinal scale are social class and the Apgar score used to appraise the status of newborn infants.

ordinal variable– A **variable** measured on an **ordinal scale.** See also *categorical variable, continuous variable, discrete variable.*

ordinary least squares– Same as *least squares estimation.*

ordinate– The **vertical axis** or y **axis** on a graph using the **cartesian coordinate** system. Compare *abscissa.*

orthogonal contrasts– See *contrast.*

orthogonal data– Experimental data obtained by using an **orthogonal design.** Compare *nonorthogonal data.*

orthogonal design– A term used to denote an **analysis of variance** design with two or more **factors** having an equal number of **observations** in each **cell** or **level** of a factor, and where each **treatment** occurs the same number of times at all the levels. Compare *nonorthogonal design.*

orthogonal matrix– A **square matrix A** is said to be an orthogonal matrix if $\mathbf{AA'} = \mathbf{I}$ where $\mathbf{A'}$ is the transpose of $\mathbf{A}$ and $\mathbf{I}$ is the **identity matrix.** Thus, for an orthogonal matrix, its transpose is equal to its inverse.

orthogonal rotation– See *factor rotation.*

orthogonal variables– Variables that do not have any relationship to each other. More specifically, two variables are said to be orthogonal if they are statistically independent of each other.

outcome– A general term for the result of any **experiment** or **trial** measured as a **response value** of a **variable.** The term is also used as a synonym for **elementary event.**

outcome space– Same as *sample space.*

outcome variable– Same as *criterion variable.*

outlier– An **observation** that is so extreme that it stands apart from the rest of the observations; that is, it differs so greatly from the remaining observations that it give rises to the question whether it is from the same **population** or involves **measurement error. Statistical tests** are normally used to determine whether such an observation is indeed an outlier. The presence of outliers violates the assumption of **normality** and it may be necessary to transform the **data** or use **nonparametric methods.**

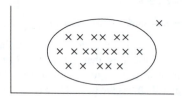

Example of an outlier

overfitted model– A term used for a **model** in which the number of **parameters** being fitted is larger than can be accommodated by the **data.** See also *overparametrized model.*

overmatching– A term used in the context of **matching** in **case-control studies** when the **cases** and **controls** are matched for **variables** that are not **confounding factors.** The use of overmatching results in a loss of **efficiency** of the design.

overparametrized model– A term used for a **model** in which the number of **parameters** being fitted is larger than the number of **observations** available for **estimation.** See also *overfitted model.*

overviews– An alternative term for **meta-analysis.**

Paasche's index number– A form of weighted aggregate price index based on combination of several items, proposed by German economist Hermann Paasche in 1874, with quantities in the given period taken as weights. If p_0^i $(i = 1, 2, \ldots, n)$ denote the prices of a set of n commodities in a base period and p_1^i, q_1^i $(i = 1, 2, \ldots, n)$ denote the corresponding prices and quantities sold in a given period, then the Paasche's index is defined as

$$P_{01} = \frac{\sum\limits_{i=1}^{n} p_1^i q_1^i}{\sum\limits_{i=1}^{n} p_0^i q_1^i}$$

Thus, in the Paasche index, the prices are given weights equal to the corresponding quantities consumed in the current year. It is one of the two basic **index numbers** of the Laspeyres–Paasche group. It is similar in form to **Laspeyres' index number,** but is weighted instead with current-year quantities. Although Paasche's index is generally considered to be as good as Laspeyres, it is rarely used in constructing official index numbers.

package– Same as *computer package.*

paired comparison– Same as *pairwise comparison.*

paired data– Sample data obtained using **paired samples.**

paired-difference test– A **statistical test** for the comparison of two **population means** that is based on **paired observations,** one from each of the two **populations.**

paired-difference *t* test– Same as *paired t test.*

paired groups– Same as *paired samples.*

paired observations– Observations that are correlated, for example, when obtained from the same individuals tested under two conditions, or from two groups of subjects matched on one or more relevant **variables.** See also *correlated samples, paired t-test, sign test.*

paired samples– Two or more **samples** having the characteristic that each **observation** in one sample has one and only one **matching** observation in the other samples. Paired samples can arise in a number of different ways. For example, in a **clinical trial,** an individual may serve as his own **control** resulting in before and after **treatment groups.** In many studies involving **matching** of twins or chicks from the same litter, we have examples of what are known as natural pairing. In **case-control studies,** paired samples arise as a consequence of matching each **case** to a control in terms of certain characteristics known to be related to both the disease and the **risk factor.**

paired-sample *t* test– Same as *paired t-test.*

paired *t* test– The **statistical test** based on **Student's *t* statistic** for comparing the differences between **paired observations.** It is used when there are two **paired** or **matched groups** or in **crossover designs** involving pre- and postmeasurements made on the same group of subjects. The test is based on the differences between the **observations** of the matched pairs. The number of **degrees of freedom** for the paired *t* test is $n - 1$ where n is the number of pairs. The use of the paired *t* test requires the assumption of **normality.** Some nonparametric alternatives to the paired *t* test are the **sign test** and the **Wilcoxon signed-rank test.**

pairwise comparison– A comparison of the difference between two **treatment group** means taken in pairs. See also *analysis of variance, multiple comparison, two-sample t test.*

pairwise independence– In **probability theory,** when each pair of a set of **events** is independent, they are said to be pairwise independent. For example, three events A_1, A_2, A_3 defined on the same **sample space** are pairwise independent if

$$P(A_1 \cap A_2) = P(A_1)\, P(A_2), \qquad P(A_1 \cap A_3) = P(A_1)P(A_3) \qquad P(A_2 \cap A_3) = P(A_2)P(A_3)$$

Pairwise independence does not imply **mutual independence.**

panel study– A type of **longitudinal study** in which a group of subjects (called a "panel") are surveyed on more than one occasion and their responses on some topic under investigation are solicited. For example, a group of high school seniors may be followed for several years and **data** collected about their future education, family life, and career and educational opportunities.

parallel design– Same as *parallel-group design.*

parallel-group design– An **experimental design** involving two or more separate groups of subjects, each receiving just one of the **treatments** being compared.

parameter– The numerical characteristic or descriptive measure of a **population** resulting from the combination of population **measurements** according to certain mathematical operations. Some examples of a parameter are the **population mean,** designated as μ, and the **population standard deviation,** designated as σ. Parameters are usually denoted by Greek letters to distinguish them from corresponding characteristics of **samples** called **statistics,** which are denoted by Roman letters. In a **statistical** or **probability model** a parameter is a **constant** that wholly or partially characterizes a function or a **probability distribution.** The values of a parameter are usually restricted by the particular problem under study.

parameter space– The set of all possible values of one or more **parameters** of a **probability distribution.**

parameter value– The particular numerical value assumed by a **parameter.**

parametric hypothesis– A **hypothesis** concerning the **parameter**(s) of a **population.** The hypothesis that the **mean** of a population is equal to some given value is an example of a parametric hypothesis.

parametric methods– These are statistical procedures that are based on **estimates** of one or more **population parameters** obtained from the **sample data,** such as the *t* **test,** *F* **test,** and **Pearson's correlation coefficient,** to mention just a few. Parametric methods are used for estimating parameters or testing **hypotheses** about population parameters. They generally involve the assumption that the **parent populations** are normally distributed. See also *distribution-free methods, nonparametric methods.*

parent population– The **population** or **universe** from which a **sample** is derived. See also *sampled population, target population.*

Pareto diagram– A **graphical device** that is used to illustrate the predominance of varying causes or sources of poor quality by graphing the causes in decreasing order of **frequency** or magnitude from left to right. A Pareto diagram can be thought of as an extension of a **cause-and-effect diagram.** It is named after the Italian economist Vilfredo Pareto, but its use to industrial problems was popularized by the American statistician J. M. Juran.

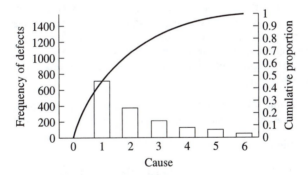

Pareto diagram for six underlying causes of poor quality

Pareto distribution– A **probability distribution,** having **parameter** α, defined by the mathematical equation

$$f(x) = \alpha k^{\alpha}/x^{\sigma+1} \qquad x \geq k \text{ (the minimum value of } x) > 0, \alpha > 0$$

The distribution was originally introduced by Vilfredo Pareto in 1897 to describe an empirical relationship between the number of persons whose income is x. Nowadays, it is used to denote any distribution of the form given above, whether related to income or not. In the economic literature, a great deal of attention has been devoted to the determination of an appropriate value of α. It is found to oscillate around 1.5 with a range of 1.6 to 1.8. More recent **data** indicate that the values of α have increased to between 1.9 and 2.1 in the developed countries at the present time.

part correlation– The **correlation** between the **dependent variable** and one of the **independent variables** in a **multiple correlation analysis** after the **effect** on the dependent variable of the other independent variables has been parceled out. The **coefficient of correlation** thus calculated is called the coefficient of part correlation.

partial autocorrelation– An **autocorrelation** between the two **observations** of a **time series** after controlling for the **effects** of intermediate observations.

partial correlation– The **correlation** between two **variables** after the **effects** of one or more other variables have been taken into account. The partial correlation coefficient is obtained as the correlation between the **deviations** of the values of a variable from their **least squares estimates** by a **linear regression** function in terms of a set of variables, with the corresponding deviations of another variable from its own **linear regression** on the same set of variables.

partial correlation coefficient– See *partial correlation.*

partially nested model– Same as *crossed-nested model.*

partial multiple correlation coefficient– The **product moment correlation coefficient** between the actual values of the **dependent variable** and the predicted values as determined by the **multiple regression equation** for a group of **explanatory variables** after controlling for a number of other explanatory variables.

partial regression coefficient– In a **multiple regression analysis,** the **coefficient** of an **independent variable** in the **regression equation** involving all the independent variables under consideration. It is interpreted as the measure of the net change in the **dependent variable** for a unit change in the independent variable when the values of other independent variables are kept **constant.** See also *estimated partial regression coefficient, standard partial regression coefficient.*

partitioning of sum of squares– The process of decomposing the **total sum of squares** and **degrees of freedom** into various component sums of squares and degrees of freedom.

Pascal distribution– Same as *negative binomial distribution.*

Pascal's triangle– In a Pascal's triangle, each row begins and ends with a 1, and each other number not equal to 1 is formed from the sum of the two integers immediately above it in the preceding row. Pascal's triangle gives a representation of **binomial coefficients** in the form of a "Christmas tree." The binomial coefficient $\left(\frac{n}{k}\right)$ is obtained by the $(k + 1)$th number in the $(n + 1)$th row.

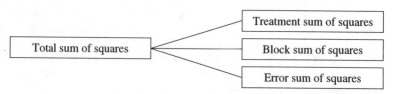

Partitioning of the total sum of squares for a randomized block design

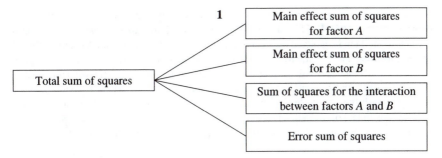

Partitioning of the total sum of squares for a complete two-factor factorial experiment

$$\binom{0}{0}$$
$$\binom{1}{0}\binom{1}{1}$$
$$\binom{2}{0}\binom{2}{1}\binom{2}{2}$$
$$\binom{3}{0}\binom{3}{1}\binom{3}{2}\binom{3}{3}$$
$$\binom{4}{0}\binom{4}{1}\binom{4}{2}\binom{4}{3}\binom{4}{4}$$
$$\binom{5}{0}\binom{5}{1}\binom{5}{2}\binom{5}{3}\binom{5}{4}\binom{5}{5}$$
$$\bullet \quad \bullet$$
$$\bullet \quad \bullet$$

Pascal's triangle in combinatorial notation

path analysis– A method of analyzing **causal models** by examining the direct and indirect **effects** of **variables** hypothesized as causes of variables hypothesized as effects. The purpose of the path analysis is to assess the adequacy of the causal model. The path analysis does not discover a causal model; the model is advanced by the researcher on the basis of substantive or theoretical considerations. See also *causal diagram, causal modeling, causal variable.*

path coefficient– In a **path analysis,** a path coefficient is a measure of the direct **effect** of a **causal variable** on the **variable** taken as effect when all other variables are held **constant.** Path coefficients are calculated in the same way as the **standardized regression coefficients** in a **multiple regression analysis.** Unstandardized path coefficients are also known as path regression coefficients.

path diagram– A **graphical representation** of **path analysis** in which single-headed arrows are used to indicate the direct **effect** of one **variable** on another and two-headed arrows are used to represent correlated variables. The figure below shows a simple path diagram for four variables, 1, 2, 3 and 4. Variables 1 and 2 are **exogeneous** and the **correlation** between them is depicted by a curved line with two-headed arrows. Variables 3 and 4 are **endogenous.** Paths in the form of single-headed arrows are drawn from variables taken as causes (independent) to the variables taken as effects (dependent). The two paths leading from variables 1 and 2 to variable 3 indicate that the variable 3 is dependent on variables 1 and 2. Similarly, three paths leading from variables 1, 2, and 3 to variable 4 indicate that variable 4 is dependent on variables 1, 2, and 3. Note that variable 3 is taken as dependent in relation to variables 1 and 2, but is one of the **independent variables** in relation to variable 4.

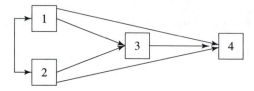

Schematic illustration of a path diagram

path model– A hypothesized **causal model** being postulated in a **path analysis.**

path regression coefficient– See *path coefficient.*

patient case– Same as *case.*

payoff– In **game theory,** the positive or negative net benefit that is associated with each possible action/event combination. It is the amount of money that passes from one player to the other in a two-person game.

payoff matrix– In **game theory,** a two-way table representing the choices of alternate strategies, the states of nature, and the **payoffs** associated with all possible combinations of **actions** and **events.**

payoff table– Same as *payoff matrix.*

***p* chart–** A **graphical device** used to control a process by inspecting the **proportion** of defectives (*p*) taken from various batches or subgroups. The values of *p* taken from each batch are plotted on the **vertical axis** and can then be used to control quality of the batch. The **center line** of the *p* chart is the **average** proportion defectives ($\bar{p}$) taken from a pilot set (about 20 subgroups). **Control lines** are set at three **standard deviations** from the center line (based on the **normal approximation** to the **binomial distribution;** i.e., $\bar{p} \pm 3\sqrt{\bar{p}(1 - \bar{p})/n}$. See also *c chart, control chart, run chart, s chart, x-bar chart.*

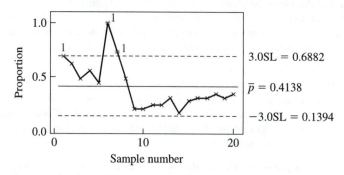

An example of a *p* chart

PDF– Acronym for *probability density function.*

Pearson chi-square statistic/test– See *chi-square statistic/test.*

Pearson coefficient of skewness– Same as *coefficient of skewness.*

Pearson correlation coefficient– Same as *correlation coefficient.*

Pearson measure of skewness– Same as *coefficient of skewness.*

Pearson product moment correlation coefficient– Same as *correlation coefficient.*

Pearson's distributions– The systems of **distributions** first described by Karl Pearson to represent a variety of distributions in mathematical terms. These distributions have been classified into families of distributions known as Pearson's Type I, Type II, Type III, etc. distributions.

percentage frequency distribution– A **frequency distribution** given in terms of percentages. It is obtained from the **distribution** of **relative frequencies** or **proportions** in which every entry has been multiplied by 100.

percentile charts– These are graphs designed to compare an individual value with a set of norms. They are used widely to develop and interpret measures of physical growth and **measurements** of ability and intelligence. The figure below presents a percentile chart of heights and weights for girls from birth to 36 months of age. Note that for girls of 21 months of age the 95th **percentile** of weight is 13.4 kg, as indicated by the arrow in the chart. Similarly, for 21-month-old girls, the **median** or 50th percentile of weight is approximately 11.4 kg.

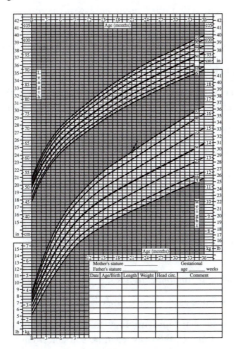

Percentile chart for standard physical growth of
girls: birth to 36 months NCHS percentiles

percentile–percentile plot– Same as *q–q plot.*

percentile point– See *percentiles.*

percentile range– Same as *percentile point.*

percentile rank– Same as *percentile point.*

percentiles– The percentiles divide a **data set** into 100 equal parts, each of which contains 1% of total **observations.** More precisely, a 100*p*th percentile is a value such that 100*p*% of the items in the data set are less than or equal to its value and $100(1 - p)\%$ of the items are greater than or equal to it. The **median** is the 50th percentile, the **first quartile** is the 25th percentile, and the **third quartile** is the 75th percentile. Percentiles were first defined by Francis Galton in 1885, who also introduced **quartiles** a little earlier. See also *centiles, deciles.*

The data arranged in increasing order of magnitude

Schematic representation of percentiles of a data set

per-comparison error rate– Same as *comparisonwise error rate.*

per-experiment error rate– Same as *experimentwise error rate.*

perfect correlation– The **correlation** between two **variables** is said to be perfect if the knowledge of the value of one variable completely determines the value of the other.

perinatal mortality rate– See *stillbirth rate.*

period effect– In a **crossover trial,** a patient's response may vary from one period to the next, and the period effect refers to the effect of time on disease response.

periodic survey– Same as *panel study.*

period of a time series– See *cycle.*

period prevalence rate– See *prevalence rate.*

permutation– A permutation is an arrangement of a set of distinct elements having a particular order among themselves. For example, the permutations of three items *a*, *b*, and *c* are *abc, acb, bac, bca, cab, cba.* The number of possible permutations that can be formed from a set of *n* elements taken *r* at a time is denoted by ^nP_r and is given by the formula $^nP_r = \frac{n!}{(n-r)!}$

permutation test– Same as *randomization test.*

personal probability– Same as *subjective probability.*

person–time– A term used in **epidemiology** to refer to a **measurement** obtained by combining persons and time. In this way, each person contributes to as many time units (usually years) of **observation** to the **population at risk** as she is actually being followed. It is obtained as the sum of individual units of time that the subjects in the **study population** have been exposed to certain **risk.** It can also be obtained as the number of persons at risk of the event of interest multiplied by the **average** length of the study period.

person–time incidence rate– A measure of **incidence rate** of an **event** of interest obtained by using **person–time** at **risk** in the denominator.

Petersen estimator– See *capture–recapture sampling.*

Peto's method– A method of combining **odds ratio** in a **meta-analysis**. It is similar to the **Mantel-Haenszel estimator** and is based on the **ratio** of **observed** to **expected frequencies.** It can, however, lead to substantial **bias** if the odds ratio differs greatly from the null value. See also *stratified analysis.*

phase I trial– A **clinical trial** designed to assess the distribution, metabolism, excretion, and toxicity of a new drug.

phase II trial– A **clinical trial** designed to test the feasibility and efficacy of a drug including the level of activity or optimum dose.

phase III trial– A **clinical trial** designed to assess the relative efficacy of a **treatment** against the standard treatment or **placebo.**

phase IV trial– A surveillance trial designed to assess the safety, side effects, interactions, and usage profile after a drug is marketed.

phi (Φ) coefficient– A **measure of association** or relationship between two **nominal variables** whose **data** are cross classified in a **2 $\times$ 2 contingency table.** It is a symmetric measure and is equivalent to the **Pearson correlation coefficient** for **variables** involving **binary** outcomes. It is denoted by the Greek letter Φ. It is calculated by the formula

$$\Phi = \sqrt{\chi^2 / n}$$

where χ^2 is the usual **chi-square statistic** for testing the **independence** and n is the **sample size.** The coefficient has a maximum value of 1, and the closer its value to 1, the stronger the **association.** The square of the Φ coefficient is known as the mean square contingency coefficient. It is related to the **Cramer's V coefficient** by the formula, $\Phi = V\sqrt{\min(r-1, c-1)}$.

pictogram– A chart that uses pictures of the objects being compared to show relative differences in magnitudes and the nature of the items by repeating the pictures a number of times. It is a visual presentation to dramatize differences in **statistical data.**

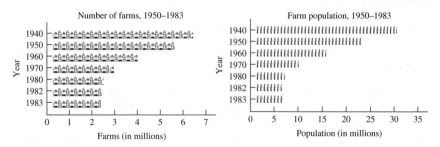

Pictograms showing changes in number of farms and farm population, 1950–1983
(Source: *U.S. Statistical Abstracts,* 1983.)

pie chart– A pictorial device or **graphical display** for presenting **qualitative** or **nominal data** by subdividing a circle into sectors with areas proportional to the quantities (**relative frequency**) for each class. It allocates each slice in the pie (a category) its proportionate share of the 360°. Pie charts are very popular in the media but are not very useful in serious scientific work. It is sometimes referred to as a cake diagram.

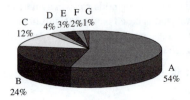

A = Social Security   B = Medicare   C = Pension/retirement

D = Others   E = Medicade   F = Subsidized public housing

G = Supplementary security income

Pie chart showing breakdown of U.S. federal outlays benefiting elderly Americans during 1990

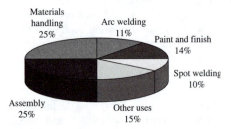

Pie chart showing robot applications in the United States during 1990

(Source: *U.S. Statistical Abstracts*, 1990.)

pie diagram– Same as *pie chart*.

pie graph– Same as *pie chart*.

pilot study– A small-scale research study generally carried out prior to undertaking a large-scale investigation with a view to exploring the feasibility of the research methodology and to obtain some preliminary information concerning certain characteristics of the **study population.**

pilot survey– A small-scale **survey** generally carried out before the main survey in order to obtain some preliminary information about the **study population** to be used later in the main survey. See also *sample survey*.

placebo– A sham **treatment** or procedure given to patients for its psychological effect rather than for its physiological benefits. It is usually an inert or dummy pharmacological or surgical treatment or intervention such as a sugar pill. In clinical studies or experimental research, it is administered to a **control group** in order to reduce **bias** in a comparison where assessment of **outcome** could be affected by patient or investigator knowledge that no treatment was given to one group. In order that a placebo has the desired effect, it is necessary that it be similar to active treatment in every other respect such as appearance, color, taste, mode of administration, among others. It is used in comparison with the treatment that is being tested. See also *placebo effect, placebo reaction.*

placebo effect– The subjective element or psychological effect introduced by the application of any **treatment.** The placebo effect is attributable to the power of suggestion in which patients in a **control group** often show clinical improvements. See also *placebo, placebo reaction.*

placebo reaction– A phenomenon where patients receiving **placebo** report side effects associated with the active **treatment.** See also *placebo effect.*

planned comparison– A comparison of **means** usually suggested before performing the study and collecting **data.** See also *multiple comparison, post-hoc comparison.*

planning of experiments– Same as *experimental planning.*

platykurtic– A **distribution** is said to be platykurtic when **observations** tend to fill out the entire range of distribution, shortening its tails and making it flatter and less peaked than a **normal curve.** Thus, a platykurtic distribution is flatter-topped, with smaller tail areas than the **normal distribution.** See also *leptokurtic, mesokurtic.*

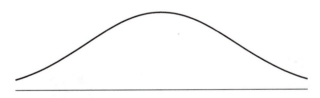

A platykurtic distribution

platykurtic curve– See *platykurtic.*

platykurtic distribution– See *platykurtic.*

platykurtosis– A term used to refer to the properties of a **platykurtic distribution.**

plot– A term used in agriculture field experiments to designate an area of land to be used as an **experimental unit.** In an **experimental design, treatments** are applied to plots in accordance with a certain randomized scheme. In general, the term is used to refer to an experimental unit in any field of scientific research.

point biserial coefficient of correlation– The **correlation coefficient** between a **continuous variable** and a **binary variable** having a natural **dichotomy.** Compare *biserial coefficient of correlation.*

point biserial correlation– A measure of relationship between two **variables** one of which is continuous and the other binary having a natural **dichotomy.** Compare *biserial correlation.*

point estimate– A single numerical value that describes **sample data** used as an **estimate** of the value of a **population parameter.** For example, the value of the **sample mean** $\bar{x}$ provides a point estimate of the **population mean** μ. A point estimate provides a single estimated value of a parameter as compared to an **interval estimate,** which specifies a range of values. See also *interval estimation, point estimation.*

point estimation– The process of **estimation** of a **parameter** in terms of a single numerical value called a **point estimate.** The method of calculating a point estimate from the **sample data** is known as a point estimator.

point estimator– See *point estimation.*

point prevalence rate– See *prevalence rate.*

Poisson distribution– A **probability distribution** used to model the occurrence of a rare event. The **probability function** of a Poisson distribution is given by

$$p(x) = \frac{e^{-\lambda}\lambda^x}{x!} \qquad x = 0, 1, 2, \ldots$$

where e is the base of natural or Napierian logarithm and λ is the **mean** value of the Poisson distribution. Poisson distribution arises as the limiting form of the **binomial distribution** when $n \to \infty$ and $p \to 0$ such that $np \to \lambda$. The Poisson distribution has been widely used in describing **probability models** for such diverse phenomena as radioactive counts per unit of time, the number of bacterial colonies, or the number of birth defects.

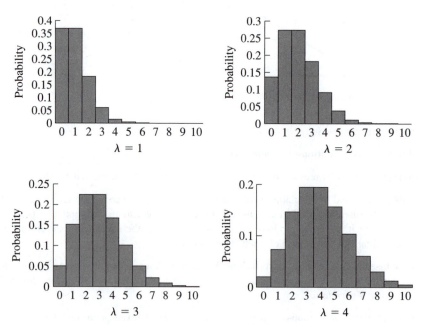

Histograms for the Poisson distribution for $\lambda = 1, 2, 3$ and 4

Poisson probability tables– Tables that give **probabilities** of a **Poisson distribution** for various values of the **parameter** λ. A portion of the Poisson probability tables appears below.

Poisson probability table

x	0.1	0.2	0.3	0.4	0.5	0.6	0.7	0.8	0.9	1.0
					λ					
0	0.9048	0.8187	0.7408	0.6703	0.6065	0.5488	0.4966	0.4493	0.4066	0.3679
1	0.0905	0.1637	0.2222	0.2681	0.3033	0.3293	0.3476	0.3595	0.3659	0.3679
2	0.0045	0.0164	0.0333	0.0536	0.0758	0.0988	0.1217	0.1438	0.1647	0.1839
3	0.0002	0.0011	0.0033	0.0072	0.0126	0.0198	0.0284	0.0383	0.0494	0.0613
4	0.0000	0.0001	0.0002	0.0007	0.0016	0.0030	0.0050	0.0077	0.0111	0.0153
5	0.0000	0.0000	0.0000	0.0001	0.0002	0.0004	0.0007	0.0012	0.0020	0.0031
6	0.0000	0.0000	0.0000	0.0000	0.0000	0.0000	0.0001	0.0002	0.0003	0.0005
7	0.0000	0.0000	0.0000	0.0000	0.0000	0.0000	0.0000	0.0000	0.0000	0.0001

x	1.1	1.2	1.3	1.4	1.5	1.6	1.7	1.8	1.9	2.0
					λ					
0	0.3329	0.3012	0.2725	0.2466	0.2231	0.2019	0.1827	0.1653	0.1496	0.1353
1	0.3662	0.3614	0.3543	0.3452	0.3347	0.3230	0.3106	0.2975	0.2842	0.2707
2	0.2014	0.2169	0.2303	0.2417	0.2510	0.2584	0.2640	0.2678	0.2700	0.2707
3	0.0738	0.0867	0.0998	0.1128	0.1255	0.1378	0.1496	0.1607	0.1710	0.1804
4	0.0203	0.0260	0.0324	0.0395	0.0471	0.0551	0.0636	0.0723	0.0812	0.0902
5	0.0045	0.0062	0.0084	0.0111	0.0141	0.0176	0.0216	0.0260	0.0309	0.0361
6	0.0008	0.0012	0.0018	0.0026	0.0035	0.0047	0.0061	0.0078	0.0098	0.0120
7	0.0001	0.0002	0.0003	0.0005	0.0008	0.0011	0.0015	0.0020	0.0027	0.0034
8	0.0000	0.0000	0.0001	0.0001	0.0001	0.0002	0.0003	0.0005	0.0006	0.0009
9	0.0000	0.0000	0.0000	0.0000	0.0000	0.0000	0.0001	0.0001	0.0001	0.0002

x	2.1	2.2	2.3	2.4	2.5	2.6	2.7	2.8	2.9	3.0
					λ					
0	0.1225	0.1108	0.1003	0.0907	0.0821	0.0743	0.0672	0.0608	0.0550	0.0498
1	0.2572	0.2438	0.2306	0.2177	0.2052	0.1931	0.1815	0.1703	0.1596	0.1494
2	0.2700	0.2681	0.2652	0.2613	0.2565	0.2510	0.2450	0.2384	0.2314	0.2240
3	0.1890	0.1966	0.2033	0.2090	0.2138	0.2176	0.2205	0.2225	0.2237	0.2240
4	0.0992	0.1082	0.1169	0.1254	0.1336	0.1414	0.1488	0.1557	0.1622	0.1680
5	0.0417	0.0476	0.0538	0.0602	0.0668	0.0735	0.0804	0.0872	0.0940	0.1008
6	0.0146	0.0174	0.0206	0.0241	0.0278	0.0319	0.0362	0.0407	0.0455	0.0504
7	0.0044	0.0055	0.0068	0.0083	0.0099	0.0118	0.0139	0.0163	0.0188	0.0216
8	0.0011	0.0015	0.0019	0.0025	0.0031	0.0038	0.0047	0.0057	0.0068	0.0081
9	0.0003	0.0004	0.0005	0.0007	0.0009	0.0011	0.0014	0.0018	0.0022	0.0027
10	0.0001	0.0001	0.0001	0.0002	0.0002	0.0003	0.0004	0.0005	0.0006	0.0008
11	0.0000	0.0000	0.0000	0.0000	0.0000	0.0001	0.0001	0.0001	0.0002	0.0002
12	0.0000	0.0000	0.0000	0.0000	0.0000	0.0000	0.0000	0.0000	0.0000	0.0001

Source: Computed by using software.

Poisson homogeneity test– See *Poisson index of dispersion.*

Poisson index of dispersion– An index or **statistic** used to test the **hypothesis** of equality of several Poisson **parameters.** Given k **samples** of the same size with Poisson counts $x_1, x_2, \ldots, x_k$, it is calculated by the formula

$$\sum_{i=1}^{k} (x_i - \bar{x})^2 / \bar{x} \qquad \text{where } \bar{x} = \sum_{i=1}^{k} x_i / k$$

The significance of the index is tested from the result that, under the **null hypothesis** of the homogeneity of Poisson parameters, the index has approximately a **chi-square distribution** with $k - 1$ **degrees of freedom.** See also *binomial index of dispersion.*

Poisson regression– In Poisson regression, the underlying **distribution** of the **dependent variable** is assumed to follow a Poisson **probability law** and $E(y)$ is modeled as the exponential of the characteristics of the individuals. It is normally used for the analysis of **count data** of a rare **event.** The method of **estimation** of the **regression coefficients** in a Poisson regression is generally based on the **maximum likelihood principle.** Poisson regression is widely used in many medical and epidemiologic studies. It should be noted that the only real conceptual difference between the Poisson regression and standard **multiple regression** is that the former entails the assumption of the **Poisson distribution** in place of the **normal distribution.** The analytic goal in both cases is the same, i.e., to fit a **regression equation** with a **mean** as a function of a set of **independent variables.**

poll– Same as *opinion poll.*

polychotomous variable– A **qualitative variable** or **nominal measure** that can take more than two possible **outcomes.** Compare *dichotomous variable.*

polygon– Same as *frequency polygon.*

polynomial regression– A **curvilinear regression** which includes powers and possibly cross-product terms of **explanatory variables.**

polynomial trend– A **trend** in **time-series data** represented by a **polynomial regression.** It is represented by an equation of the form

$$y = \beta_0 + \beta_1 t + \beta_2 t^2 + \cdots + \beta_n t^n$$

where the β_i ($i = 0, 1, 2, \ldots, n$) are **constants** and t is time. The **coefficients** β_i are usually estimated by the **method of least squares.**

polytomous logistic regression– A **logistic regression** method involving a **categorical variable** with more than two unordered categories as the **dependent variable.** See also *ordered logistic regression.*

polytomous variable– Same as *polychotomous variable.*

pooled estimate– An **estimate** of a **parameter** obtained by combining or pooling two or more estimates.

pooled standard deviation– See *pooled variance.*

pooled variance– An **estimate** of the **variance of the population** based on the combination of two (or more) **sample estimates.** It is the **weighted average** of two or more **sample variances** (the weights being the **degrees of freedom** associated with each **variance**) used to estimate the variance (known to be equal) in each of the **populations** from which the **samples** were taken. For example, if two samples are drawn from the same population or from different populations having equal variances, σ^2, then the sample variances can be pooled or averaged to obtain a better estimate of σ^2. If the two **sample sizes** are n_1 and n_2, with corresponding sample variances S_1^2 and S_2^2, the formula for the pooled estimate is

$$S_p^2 = \frac{(n_1 - 1)S_1^2 + (n_2 - 1)S_2^2}{n_1 + n_2 - 2}$$

The square root of the pooled variance is known as the pooled standard deviation. The pooled variance or standard deviation is appropriate whenever the variances of two (or more) populations are assumed equal.

population– A complete set of objects, **measurements,** or individuals sharing some common observable characteristic of interest. In **statistics,** a population usually refers to **scores** or **observations** and not necessarily to people or other organisms or objects. A population of scores is the collection of all the possible measurements specified by a particular definition. The term is more or less synonymous with **universe.**

population at risk– People who have a chance of contracting a specific disease or health condition (e.g., during outbreak of an epidemic).

population census– See *census.*

population coefficient of correlation– A measure of the degree of **linear relationship** between two **variables** in a **population.** It is usually denoted by the Greek letter ρ. See also *coefficient of correlation, sample coefficient of correlation.*

population coefficient of determination– Same as *population coefficient of multiple determination.*

population coefficient of multiple determination– A measure of how well a true **regression plane** (or hyperplane) fits the **population data** on which it is based. See also *coefficient of multiple determination, sample coefficient of multiple determination.*

population correlation– Same as *population coefficient of correlation.*

population correlation coefficient– Same as *population coefficient of correlation.*

population covariance matrix– A **covariance matrix** where **variances** and **covariances** are **parameters** of a **multivariate probability distribution.** See also *sample covariance matrix.*

population dynamics– The study of changes in population size and structure over a period of time.

population forecasts– The projection of future population growth or decline. The **forecasts** are based on assumed **death rates** and **birth rates** derived from the figures collected at the **census** and are usually prepared by the government's actuarial department.

population mean– The most commonly used **measure of location** of the **population.** For a **finite population** with **measurement** values $X_1, X_2, \ldots, X_N$, it is defined as $\mu = (X_1 + X_2 + \cdots + X_N)/N$. For a continuous population, the mean can be interpreted as the balance point of a **density curve.** See also *mean, sample mean.*

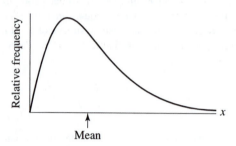

Mean of a continuous population

population median– That value that divides the total **population** into two equal parts. For a **continuous variable** X, it is defined by the equation $P(X > M) = P(X < M) = 0.5$, M being the **median** value. For a **finite population,** an ambiguity may arise, which can be resolved by some convention. For a population of $2N + 1$ objects, the median is the value of the $(N + 1)$th ordered object. For a population of $2N$ objects, it is defined to be the **average** of the values of Nth and $(N + 1)$th ordered objects. See also *sample median.*

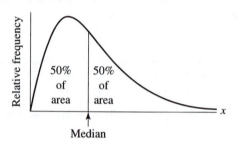

Median of a continuous population

population moments– See *moments.*

population parameter– Same as *parameter.*

population proportion– Same as *binomial proportion.*

population pyramid– A **graphical representation** designed to show the age and sex composition of a human population. It consists of a pair of **histograms,** one for the male and the other for the female, placed on their sides with a common base. It reflects changing composition of the population, associated with age-specific fertility and mortality, and is designed to provide a quick overall picture of the age and sex structure of the population. The figure below shows population pyramids comparing the age–sex structure of India with that of Japan. India's pyramid-like profile has the familiar lower-age bulk of a developing country; Japan's constricted profile represents the aging population typical of a developed economy and society.

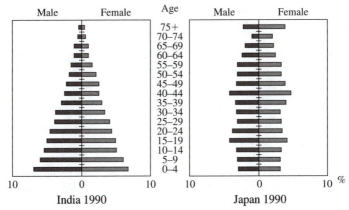

Examples of population pyramids for India and Japan

(Source: *United Nations Statistical Abstracts, 1990*.)

population regression coefficients– Same as *true regression coefficients*.

population regression equation– Same as *regression equation*.

population regression line– Same as *true regression line*.

population size– The total number of elements or items that constitute a certain **population**. For a population with finite size it is usually denoted by the letter N.

population standard deviation– The most commonly used **measure of variability** or **dispersion** of a **population**. For a **finite population** with **measurement** values $X_1, X_2, \ldots, X_N$, it is defined as

$$\sigma = \sqrt{\left\{ \left[\sum_{i=1}^{N} (X_i - \mu)^2 \right] \Big/ N \right\}}$$

where μ is the **population mean**. See also *sample standard deviation, standard deviation*.

population variance– A **parameter** that measures the **variability** or **dispersion** of the characteristics of a **population**. It is equal to the square of the **population standard deviation**. See also *sample standard deviation, sample variance, variance*.

positive correlation– In **correlation analysis,** two **variables** are said to have positive correlation when high values of one variable tend to be associated with high values of the other, and similarly low values of one variable tend to be associated with low values of the other. Some examples of positive correlations are sales and advertising expenditure, production cost and turnover, and productivity and expenditure on labor-saving devices. It is sometimes misleading because of the intervention of a third variable. See also *coefficient of correlation, direct relationship, negative correlation*.

positively skewed distribution– See *skewed distribution*.

positive predictive value– Same as *predictive value positive*.

positive relation– Same as *positive relationship*.

positive relationship– Same as *positive correlation.*

positive skewness– See *skewed distribution.*

positive study– A study that demonstrates the viability of the **research hypothesis.** A positive study results in the rejection of the **null hypothesis** and the results are declared to be **statistically significant.**

positive synergism– See *synergism.*

postal survey– The use of postal services to send **questionnaires** to a selected **sample** of people or organizations who are requested to provide answers and return the questionnaires. A major problem with these types of **surveys** is the very low **response rate.** Usually responders and nonresponders, as groups, each have their own peculiarities, which in many cases may be relevant to the objectives of the survey. It is simply not enough to increase the size of the sample to make up for the **nonresponse bias.**

posterior analysis– A form of **decision making** under **uncertainty** that begins with a set of **prior probabilities,** proceeds to obtain additional information about event probabilities, and then uses this new information to transform the initial prior probabilities, by use of **Bayes' theorem,** into a new set of **posterior probabilities** that are employed in making the final decision.

posterior distribution– In **bayesian statistics,** a posterior distribution for an unknown **parameter** is obtained by combining a **prior distribution** with the **sample data** through the use of **Bayes' theorem.** Compare *prior distribution.* See also *posterior analysis, posterior probabilities.*

posterior probabilities– The revised **probabilities** for **events** obtained by the application of **Bayes' theorem.** Posterior probabilities take into account observed **sample data** and are used in contradistinction to **prior probabilities,** which are probabilities before any **observations** are made. They are also referred to as inverse probabilities. Compare *prior probabilities.* See also *posterior analysis, posterior distribution.*

posterior probability distribution– Same as *posterior distribution.*

post-hoc comparison– A method of conducting statistical comparison of differences between group means after performing **analysis of variance.** A post-hoc comparison is usually not planned at the beginning of the study but is suggested by an examination of the **data.** See also *multiple comparison, planned comparison.*

poststratification– A **classification** of a **sample** into various **strata** after its selection.

post-test odds– In **diagnostic testing** or **screening,** the **odds** that a person has certain disease or condition after a **diagnostic procedure** has been performed and results are known. The notion of post-test odds is similar to that of the **predictive values** of the test. See also *pretest odds, post-test probability.*

post-test probability– In **diagnostic testing** or **screening,** it is an individual's **probability** of actually having a given condition after knowing the results of a **diagnostic procedure.** It is related to **post-test odds** by the following formula

$$\text{Post-test probability} = \frac{\text{post-test odds}}{1 + \text{post-test odds}}$$

power– The power of a **hypothesis test** is defined as the **probability** of rejecting a **null hypothesis,** when it is false, against a specified alternative, that is, the probability of rejecting the null hypothesis when in fact the alternative is true. It depends on a number of factors, including the nature of the **test statistic,** the **sample size,** the **significance level,** the determination of whether the test is directional or nondirectional, and the value of the "true" **population parameter.** Power provides a method of discriminating between different competing tests of the same **hypothesis.** It also provides a basis for estimating the sample size needed to detect an effect of certain magnitude. It is equal to $1 - \beta$ where β is the probability of **type II error.** The power of a test is increased by increasing the sample size, but is decreased with the increasing **variability** of the individual **measurements.**

power efficiency– The power efficiency of test A with respect to test B is defined as n_B/n_A where n_A is the number of **observations** required by the test A to have the same **power** as the test B has on n_B observations; both tests correspond to the same **alternative hypothesis** at the same **significance level.**

power function– The function or curve that represents the **probability** of rejecting the **null hypothesis** for various values of the **alternatives hypothesis.** Thus, for all values of the **parameter,** except those under the null hypothesis, the power function gives the probability of not committing a **type II error.**

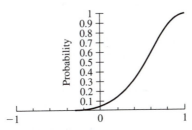

Example of a power function

power of a test– Same as *power.*

power of the hypothesis test– Same as *power.*

power transformation– A class of **transformations** proposed by G. E. P. Box and D. R. Cox to achieve **normality** or **homogeneity** in a **data set.** The general form of the transformation is given by

$$y = \begin{cases} x^\lambda, & \lambda \neq 0 \\ \log_e (x), & \lambda = 0 \end{cases}$$

where λ is a **parameter** to be determined from the **data.** The transformation includes the following ones as special cases:

$$y = 1/x, \lambda = -1 \,; y = 1/\sqrt{x}, \lambda = -\tfrac{1}{2}; y = \log_e (x), \lambda = 0;$$
$$y = \sqrt{x}, \lambda = \tfrac{1}{2}; y = x^2, \lambda = 2$$

See also *arc-sine transformation, logarithmic transformation, reciprocal transformation, square-root transformation, square transformation.*

practical significance– A term used in contrast to **statistical significance** to emphasize the fact that the observed difference is something meaningful in the context of the subject matter under investigation and not simply that it is unlikely to be due to **chance** alone. For example, with a large **sample** very small differences with no practical importance whatsoever may turn out to be **statistically significant.** The practical significance implies importance of research finding for theory, policy, or explanation. The use of **confidence intervals** can often help to assess the practical significance of study results.

precision– In theory of measurement, precision refers to a quality associated with a set of **measurements** by which repeated **observations** approximate to the true value. A precise measurement may not be accurate because of unrecognized **bias** or other errors in methodology. In **statistical estimation,** precision refers to the **spread** of an **estimate** of a **parameter** and is measured by the **standard error** of the **estimator.** See also *accuracy.*

predicted variable– In **regression analysis,** the **variable** that is being regressed is called the **dependent** or **predicted variable.** It is always plotted as the *y* variable in a **scatter diagram.** Compare *predictor variable.*

prediction– Forecast of the values of a **dependent variable** as a function of **explanatory variable(s)** and a **model** that relates the former to the latter.

prediction equation– A **regression equation** representing an **estimated regression model** that is used to predict the value of the **dependent variable** from the given value(s) of the **independent variable(s).**

prediction interval– In a **regression analysis,** a **confidence interval** within which a future **observation** of the **dependent variable,** for a given value of the **independent variable,** lies with a given **probability.** Compare *confidence band.*

predictive value negative– In a **screening** or **diagnostic test** for a disease, the **probability** that a person with a negative diagnostic test result does not have the disease.

predictive value positive– In a **screening** or **diagnostic test** for a disease, the **probability** that a person with a positive diagnostic test result does in fact have the disease.

predictive values– See *predictive value negative, predictive value positive.*

predictor– Same as *predictor variable.*

predictor variable– In a **regression analysis,** the **variable** that serves as the basis for prediction is called the predictor variable. It is also called the **independent** or **explanatory variable.** It is always plotted as the *x* variable in a **scatter diagram.** Compare *predicted variable.*

preposterior analysis– A form of **decision making** under **uncertainty** that entails obtaining additional **experimental** or **sample data** before proceeding to **prior** or **posterior analysis.**

PRESS statistic– A measure of the goodness of a fitted **model** used in a **regression analysis.** It is an acronym for "predicted residual error sum of squares" and is designed as a measure of how well a given **regression model** predicts **data** other than those used to fit it. Models with small PRESS values are deemed to provide an adequate fit in the sense of having small prediction errors.

pretest odds– In **diagnostic testing** or **screening,** the **odds** that a person has a certain disease or condition before a **diagnostic procedure** has been performed and results are known. The notion of pretest odds is similar to that of **prior probabilities.** Compare *post-test odds.* See also *pretest probability.*

pretest probability– In **diagnostic testing** or **screening,** the **probability** that a person has certain disease or condition before relevant **diagnostic procedures** are performed. It is related to **pretest odds** by the formula

$$\text{Pretest probability} = \frac{\text{pretest odds}}{1 + \text{pretest odds}}$$

prevalence– The total number of existing cases of a disease or condition in a population at a specific moment of time or over a time period. The term prevalence is sometimes used to denote **prevalence rate.** See also *incidence.*

prevalence rate– The **proportion** of people in the population who have a disease or condition in question at a specific moment of time or over a period of time. The prevalence rate is calculated from the formula:

$$\frac{\text{Total number of cases of a disease at a specific moment or a given period of time}}{\text{Total number of individuals exposed to the risk at a specific moment or at midpoint of given period of time}} \times 100$$

The prevalence rate measures all the **cases** or the current status of the disease. When measured at a specific point of time it is called point prevalence rate, and when measured over a period of time it is called period prevalence rate. See also *incidence rate.*

prevention trial– A **clinical trial** designed to assess the efficacy of a **treatment** in terms of preventing a disease.

price index number– The **ratio** of the **average** of prices in one period or place (referred to as the given period or place) to the average in another period or place (referred to as the based period).

price relative– The **ratio** of the price of a commodity or service in one period or place to the price in another period or place.

primary data– These are the **data** published by the same organization that originally collected them. For example, the data published by the **U. S. Bureau of the Census** would be considered primary data. These types of data are invaluable to decision makers in both the government and private sectors. Compare *secondary data.*

principal components analysis– A **multivariate statistical procedure** for analyzing **data** that transforms the original **variables** into a new set of **orthogonal variables** known as principal components. The principal components are defined as **linear functions** of the original variables and account for decreasing **proportions** of the **variance** in the data. The technique provides a tool for reducing the dimensionality of the data. For example, if the first few principal components account for a large proportion of the variance of the **observations,** they can be used to display and summarize the data and perform any subsequent **data analysis.**

prior analysis– **Decision making** under **uncertainty** that employs only **probabilities** calculated prior to the collection of new **experimental** or **sample data** about the likelihood of alternative future **outcomes.**

prior distribution– In **Bayesian statistics,** a prior distribution is a description of the prior knowledge of the investigator expressed in the form of a **probability distribution** to characterize a **population parameter.** In a given situation, there usually are great varieties of such distributions available that can be used as a prior. The prior distribution is usually supposed to be known exactly and not to depend on any unknown parameters of its own. Compare *posterior distribution.* See also *Bayes' theorem, prior analysis, prior probabilities.*

prior probabilities– **Probabilities** for a set of **mutually exclusive events** prior to being transformed by the application of **Bayes' theorem.** They are a person's initial subjective **estimates** of the likelihood of the **events,** prior to any **empirical** evidence obtained from observed **sample data.** Prior probabilities are also referred to as antecedent probabilities. Compare *posterior probabilities.* See also *prior analysis, prior distribution.*

probabilistic model– Same as *probability model.*

probability– A numerical measure of the likelihood that an **event** will occur. It expresses the concept of the degree of **uncertainty** in the occurrence of an event. When the **experiment** is performed only once, the probability can be considered as a measure of one's belief that the event will occur. See also *classical probability, empirical probability, objective probability, subjective probability.*

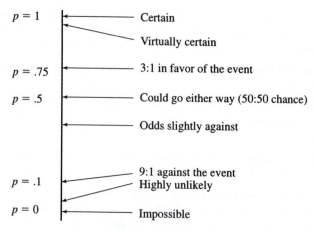

Schematic representation of quantitative versus qualitative descriptions of the likelihood of an event

probability density– Same as *probability density function.*

probability density curve– A curve describing a **continuous probability distribution.** The curve must be nonnegative and include a finite area between itself and the **horizontal axis.** The **probability** that a randomly selected value from the **population** will be between the points a and b is given by

$$P(a \leq X \leq b) = \frac{\text{area under the curve between } a \text{ and } b}{\text{total area under the curve}}$$

It is usually convenient to scale the curve so that the total area under the curve is 1. Then $P(a \leq X \leq b)$ reduces to the area under the curve between a and b.

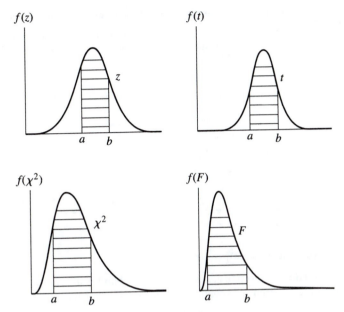

Examples of some probability density curves

probability density function– A **frequency function** that describes the **probability distribution** of a **continuous random variable.** A probability density function may be represented by a smooth continuous curve and **probabilities** are represented by areas under the curve. The area under the curve over an interval is proportional to the probability that the **random variable** will assume a value in the interval.

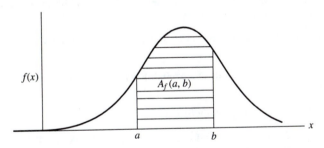

Graphical representation of a probability density function

probability distribution– A **relative frequency distribution** of a **random variable,** giving the **probability** of occurrence of observations of various possible values of the random variable. A probability distribution may be **empirical** or theoretical. The empirical frequency distribution can be generated by using **simulation.**

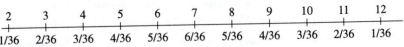

Probability distribution for the outcomes of rolling a pair of dice

Results of a computer simulation of 15,000 rolls of a pair of dice

Sum of the face value	Frequency	Simulated probability	Theoretical probability
2	420	0.0280	.0278 (1/36)
3	815	0.0543	.0556 (2/36)
4	1255	0.0837	.0833 (3/36)
5	1687	0.1125	.1111 (4/36)
6	2060	0.1373	.1389 (5/36)
7	2518	0.1679	.1667 (6/36)
8	2082	0.1388	.1389 (5/36)
9	1673	0.1115	.1111 (4/36)
10	1224	0.0816	.0833 (3/36)
11	841	0.0561	.0556 (2/36)
12	425	0.0283	.0278 (1/36)

Probability distribution for the outcomes of rolling a pair of dice

probability experiment– See *experiment.*

probability function– A function that describes the **probability distribution** of a **discrete random variable.** It assigns a **probability** to each value within range of the discrete random variable.

probability generating function– A function of a **variable** t associated with **probability distribution** of a **discrete random variable** X with **probability function** $p(x)$, and defined by

$$\phi_X(t) = E(t^X) = \sum_x t^x p(x)$$

A probability generating function often provides a useful summarization of the probability distribution of a discrete random variable.

probability law– A principle governing the assignment of **probabilities** to different **events.**

probability mass– The magnitude of a **probability** located at a particular value of a **random variable.**

probability model– Same as *probability law.*

probability of survival– The **probability** that a subject alive at a particular time period will also be alive at a given time in the future.

probability paper– Same as *arithmetic probability paper.*

probability rule– Same as *probability law.*

probability sample– A **sample** obtained in such a manner that every member of the **population** has a known **probability** (but not necessarily equal) of being selected. There are a large number of methods currently available for selecting a probability sample. See also *convenience sample, judgment sample, nonprobability sample, random sample.*

probability sampling– Any **sampling** procedure wherein each element in the **population** has a known **probability** of being included in the **sample. Simple random sampling,**

stratified random sampling, cluster sampling, and **systematic sampling** are examples of probability sampling. Sometimes the word **random sampling** is used to designate a probability sampling.

probability theory– The study of laws of **chance** governing the occurrence of **random phenomena.**

probability value– Same as *p value.*

probable error– A measure of **sampling variability** of a **mean** of a large **sample** (more than 30 **observations**) equal to 0.6745 of the **standard error.** It is an older term now rarely used.

probit analysis– In **bioassay,** the analysis of **quantal response** data where the **probit transformation** of a **proportion** is modeled as a **linear function** of the dose or its logarithm.

probit transformation– A **transformation** z of a **probability** p given by the **distribution function** of the **standard normal distribution,** i.e.,

$$p = \frac{1}{\sqrt{2\pi}} \int_{-\infty}^{z} e^{-(1/2)t^2} dt$$

where z represents dose or logarithm of dose. The value of z is also known as the normal equivalent deviate. The transformation is often used in the analysis of dose–response studies.

product limit estimator– Same as *Kaplan–Meier estimator.*

product moment correlation– Same as *correlation coefficient.*

product moment correlation coefficient– Same as *correlation coefficient.*

profile analysis– The use of methods and techniques in describing the characteristics of **clusters** in order to explain how they may differ on relevant dimensions. The analyst utilizes **data** not previously included in the cluster procedure to profile the characteristics of each cluster. These data typically are demographic characteristics, psychographic profiles, and consumption patterns, among others. Using **discriminant analysis,** the analyst compares **average** score profiles for the clusters. In essence, the profile analysis focuses on describing not what directly determines the clusters but the characteristics of the clusters after they are identified.

prognostic factor– Same as *prognostic variable.*

prognostic variable– In medical investigations, the term is used to refer to an **explanatory variable** that carries information about the future clinical outcomes. Baseline prognostic variables are usually fixed at the time of the commencement of the study. Time-dependent prognostic variables vary over time and generally require more complex methods of modeling.

program– Same as *computer program.*

proportion– The number of **observations** with certain characteristics divided by the total number of observations. It is a fraction employed to show the magnitude of one quantity in comparison to the magnitude of another. It is generally used to summarize **count data.**

proportional allocation– In a **stratified random sampling,** the method for allocating the total **sample** into different **strata** so that the numbers allocated to the strata are proportional to the sizes of the corresponding strata. See also *optimum allocation.*

proportional attributable risk– See *attributable risk.*

proportional hazards– A mathematical assumption in which the **hazard ratio** between the two groups is assumed to be **constant** over time, although the baseline **hazard** can vary.

proportional hazards regression– A **regression analysis** used with **survival data** to relate survival to a set of **risk factors** or **covariates.** The analysis is based on the concept of **hazard function,** which is assumed to be an unknown function of time multiplied by a factor involving the covariates. Thus, the proportional hazards model assumes that the **ratio** of the **risks** of the **event** at any particular time, between any two groups of individuals being compared, is **constant.** The **outcome variable** is whether or not the event of interest has occurred; and if so, the period of its occurrence. The **model** predicts the risk of the occurrence of the event in question when the **predictor variables** are **prognostic factors** or covariates. The model can be considered to be semiparametric, since it does not assume any type of distributional assumptions for survival times. The **estimates** of the **parameters** in the model are obtained by the **maximum likelihood procedure** and depend only on the order in which events can occur, not on the exact time of their occurrence. The technique was proposed by D. R. Cox and is frequently referred to as Cox's regression. It is now widely used to report the results of **longitudinal studies** on survival data in the epidemiologic literature. See also *life table analysis, survival analysis.*

proportional mortality rate– Same as *cause-specific mortality rate.*

proposition– A formal statement about the value of a **population parameter** or about the relationship between certain characteristics.

prospective study– A general name for a **research design** in which **observations** are made on the life changes of subjects over a specified future period in their lives. It is often referred to as **cohort analysis** by epidemiologists. Thus, a prospective study starts with persons not affected by the condition of interest and follows them successfully over a period of time to observe the future **incidence** of the condition in relation to certain characteristics. The most common prospective study is the **cohort study.** A prospective study allows the researcher to investigate the temporal relationship between an **outcome measure** and one or more characteristics of interest. See also *historical cohort study, longitudinal study, retrospective study.*

protected *t* test procedure– Same as least *significant difference test.*

protocol– A formal document delineating the logical plans and the proposed procedures for conducting a clinical study or trial. A protocol usually contains information on such topics as study objectives, patient selection criteria, competing treatments or intervention therapies, evaluation of clinical outcomes, study design, noncompliance, and methods of statistical analysis.

protocol violations– A term used to refer to the lack of **compliance** of one or more guidelines laid down in the **protocol.** For example, patients may not have taken their prescribed **treatments** or switched to other treatments because of undesirable side effects. The exclusion of such cases in analysis can lead to serious **bias.**

pseudorandom numbers– Numbers, generated by computers, that satisfy all-important tests of **randomness,** but are based on deterministic **algorithms.** Pseudorandom numbers are widely used in **simulation** work, but care should be exercised because of the possibility of unsuspected periodicities.

*p***th percentile–** A value such that $100p\%$ of the elements in the **population** have **measurements** less than this value and $100(1 - p)\%$ of the measurements are greater than this value. See also *percentiles.*

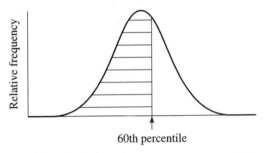

60th percentile

Schematic illustration of the 60th percentile of a distribution

publication bias– The possible **bias** in scientific literature due to the tendency of journals to favor articles that report **statistically significant** results over those which report non-significant results. This practice can usually lead to the publication of many studies of poor quality and misleading results, albeit statistically significant, while excluding the publication of good studies that have conclusively shown lack of any important treatment effect. This issue is especially important in the performance of **meta-analyses** and could greatly affect the validity of their results.

public opinion poll– Same as *opinion poll.*

public opinion survey– Same as *opinion survey.*

p **value–** The **probability** of obtaining a difference between the value of the **test statistic** and the hypothesized value of the **parameter** that is greater than or equal to the difference actually observed. It is the probability of observing a result as extreme as or more extreme than those actually observed from **chance** alone, assuming, of course, that the **null hypothesis** is true. If the *p* value is less than the **level of significance** for the test, the null hypothesis should be rejected. For a given set of **data** and test statistic, the *p* value is the smallest value of the level of significance that we can use and still reject the null hypothesis. A *p* value is often misinterpreted as the probability of the null hypothesis being true or the probability that the observed result is due to chance alone. It is important to recognize that the *p* value assumes that the null hypothesis is true and then accounts for the probability of the observed data or data showing a more extreme departure. In many fields of scientific research, it is conventional to consider a difference as **statistically significant** if $p \le 0.05$. However, it is preferable to report an exact *p* value rather the usual label as "significant" ($p \le 0.05$) or "not significant" ($p > 0.05$). Further, it should be noted that a *p* value is influenced by several factors, making universal criteria of significance almost impossible. This value is also referred to as significance probability or observed significance level. See also *alternative hypothesis.*

q–q plot– A **scatter diagram** in which **quantiles** of two series of **observations** are plotted. It is used as an informal method for checking the assumption of **normality** of a **statistical model.**

qualitative data– **Data** obtained on measures of a **qualitative variable,** i.e., using nominal and ordinal **scales of measurement.** See also *categorical data, nominal data, numerical data.*

qualitative observations– Same as *qualitative data.*

qualitative variable– A **variable** that is normally not expressed numerically because it differs in kind rather than degree among **elementary units.** The term is more or less synonymous with **categorical variable.** Some examples are hair color, religion, political affiliation, nationality, and social class. See also *quantitative variable.*

quality assurance– The use of statistical procedures and techniques designed to ensure the **reliability** or **validity** of a process.

quality control– The use of statistical procedures and techniques for the purpose of maintaining the quality of a manufactured product or a laboratory test within acceptable limits. Central to the use of **statistics** in quality control is the concept of **variance.** If one were to summarize the entire field of statistical quality control, also called statistical process control (SPC), in one word, it would have to be variance. The procedure is aimed at identifying the sources and magnitude of **variability** and reducing them to an acceptable level. The simplest such procedure involves the use of a **control chart.** See also *quality assurance.*

quality control chart– Same as *control chart.*

quantal assay– An **experiment** in which groups of subjects usually animals are exposed to a certain amount of stimulus (e.g., concentration of drugs) and the objective is to estimate the **proportion** of individuals responding to the drug at a particular dose level. For example, groups of mice may be injected with different doses of insulin and the proportion of mice showing convulsion at each does level is recorded.

quantal response– Same as *binary response.*

quantal response assay– Same as *quantal assay.*

quantal variable– Same as *binary variable.*

quantile–quantile plot– Same as *q–q plot.*

quantiles– A general term for the $n - 1$ partitions that divide a **frequency** or **probability distribution** into n equal parts. In a probability distribution, the term is also used to indicate the value of the **random variable** that yields a particular **probability**. The term is essentially synonymous with **fractiles.** See also *deciles, octiles, percentiles, quartiles, quintiles.*

quantitative data– Same as *numerical data.*

quantitative distribution– Same as *numerical distribution.*

quantitative factor– Same as *quantitative variable.*

quantitative observations– Same as *quantitative data.*

quantitative variable– A **variable** that is normally expressed numerically because it differs in degree rather than kind among **elementary units.** See also *qualitative variable.*

quartile deviation– Same as *semi-interquartile range.*

quartiles– Values in a **data set** that divide the **observations** into four quarters, each of which contains 25% of the observed values. The 25th **percentile,** 50th percentile, and 75th percentile are the same as the first, second, and third quartiles, respectively. The first, second, and third quartiles are denoted by Q_1, Q_2, and Q_3 respectively. The first and third quartiles are often called the lower and the upper quartiles and the second quartile is known as **median.** See also *centiles, deciles, octiles, quintiles.*

The data arranged in an increasing order of magnitude

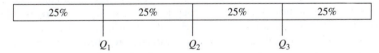

Schematic representation of quartiles of a data set

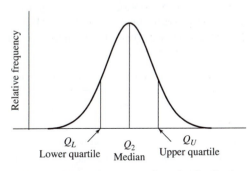

Schematic illustration of quartiles of a distribution

quasi-experiment– A kind of **research design** where the experimenter may be able to manipulate certain **independent variables** but subjects cannot be randomly assigned to **experimental** and **control groups.** Such designs often resemble **experiments** but are weak on some of the characteristics, particularly **randomization.** See also *clinical trial, experimental study, prospective study.*

quasi-factorial design– Same as *lattice design.*

quasi-independence– A term used in the analysis of a **contingency table** to describe the **independence** of rows and columns conditional on only a part of the table.

questionnaire– A document containing a list of questions to be administered to a group of people or organizations under the provisions of strict confidentiality.

Quetlet's index– A measure of obesity calculated by dividing the weight of an individual by the square of the height. It is one of the anthropometric measures of body mass and has the highest **correlation** with skinfold thickness or body density.

queuing theory– A mathematical theory of **probability** concerned with the study of the problem of queues, e.g., the **distribution** of arrival time, the length of the queue at a given time, the **average** waiting time and so forth. It is used in many practical settings to study waiting times. The overall objective in queuing theory is to find means of solving problems of congestion and, in particular, of reducing congestion, which is supposed to be taking place in the form of a queue. The problem of queues arises in a number of situations other than people waiting in line. For example, machines awaiting repair in a factory and the orders report on hold as a result of those machines being out of service are regarded as queues. There are three basic statistical elements in most queuing problems: (1) the average number in the system, (2) the average rate of arrival, and (3) the average rate of departure, which is equal to the average rate of service. There are two broad approaches to the problems: The analytic, which involves the use of mathematical methods, and the computer or **Monte Carlo simulation.**

quick and dirty methods– A term used earlier to describe **nonparametric methods** that were easily performed, but were thought to be inferior to the corresponding **parametric methods.** However, it turns out that many nonparametric procedures require much more computation and in some cases are more efficient than their normal theory counterparts. For example, in the case of **data** with a **normal distribution,** where the *t* test is optimal, Wilcoxon's procedure loses very little efficiency whereas in other nonnormal situations, it is superior to the *t* test.

quintiles– The quintiles divide a **data set** into five equal parts, each of which contains 20% of the total **observations.** The **percentile points** at the 20th, 40th, 60th, and 80th intervals are the same as the first quintile, second quintile, third quintile, and fourth quintile respectively. See also *deciles, octiles, percentiles, quartiles.*

The data arranged in an increasing order of magnitude

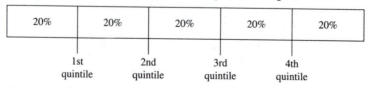

Schematic representation of quintiles of a data set

quota sample– A **nonprobability sample** that is selected by dividing a population into categories and selecting a certain number of subjects (a quota) from each category. For example, the **sample** may consist of individuals with a certain quota for different age, sex, and racial/ethnic groups. The quota assigned to each group is generally proportionate to its share of the population being surveyed. This type of selection procedure can produce biased results, since interviewers are much more likely to choose respondents who are easily accessible and willing to be interviewed. Since **random sampling** procedures are not employed for drawing a quota sample, the **reliability** or **precision** of **sample estimates** cannot be determined.

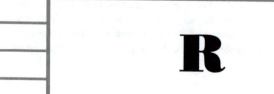

R

random– A term used to denote the quality of something that is unpredictable, nondeterministic, or occurring simply by chance.

random allocation– Same as *random assignment.*

random assignment– The use of a **random** device to assign different **treatments** to subjects or vice versa. The random assignment should not be confused with haphazard assignment. Random assignment increases **internal validity** of a study. See also *block randomization, randomization.*

random-digit dialing– A method of **sampling** households through the selection of telephone numbers by a **random** choice of digits in the telephone numbers. If the households being surveyed have high levels of telephone coverage, the technique can provide a **representative sample** of the households. Random-digit dialing provides the advantage of low cost of conducting a **survey** and it is now considered a useful procedure in many social and health sciences investigation. See also *telephone sampling.*

random effects– A term used to denote effects attributable to a large collection of **levels** of a **factor** or **treatment** (usually infinite) of which only a small **sample** are included in a given study. Random effects are frequently used in the context of **linear models** and **meta-analysis.** Compare *fixed effects.*

random effects analysis of variance– See *random effects model.*

random effects model– An **analysis of variance** or **regression model** in which the **treatment levels** associated with a **factor** are randomly selected and are considered to have **random effects.** Random effects are usually assumed to follow a **normal distribution.** This model is also referred to as model II. In the context of **meta-analysis,** the term is used to describe a model that assumes that the studies being summarized constitute a **random sample** from a larger population of similar studies. See also *fixed effects model, mixed effects model.*

random error– The **variation** in **measurements** that can be expected to occur entirely by chance. Random errors represent **deviations** of an observed value from a true value that are due to chance rather than to one of the other factors being studied. Random errors on the **average** tend to cancel out in the sense of having a **mean** that tends to zero. See also *systematic error.*

random event– An **event** or phenomenon that is unpredictable and whose occurrence is governed purely by chance. A random event may or may not occur at a given **trial** or moment of time, but does possess some degree of statistical regularity, with a **probability** of occurrence determined by some **prability distribution.**

random experiment– Any activity or **trial** that will result in one and only one of several possible **outcomes,** but it cannot be predicted in advance which of these will occur in any particular trial.

random factors– Factors in an **analysis of variance** or **regression model** thought to have a **random effect.** Some examples of factors that are usually considered random are days, subjects, and plots. Compare *fixed factors.* See also *fixed effects.*

randomization– The process of assigning subjects or other **experimental units** to different **treatments** (or vice versa) by using **random numbers** or any other **random** device. The purpose of randomization is to produce comparable **treatment groups** in terms of important **prognostic factors.** The randomization ensures that, within the limits of **chance** variation, the **experimental** and **control groups** are similar at the beginning of the investigation. The randomization eliminates **bias** in the assignment of treatments and provides the sound basis for statistical analysis. The **random assignment,** however, frequently gives rise treatment groups with unequal **sample sizes.** This problem can be overcome by using **block randomization.** See also *cluster randomization.*

randomization test– A **nonparametric test** for **quantitative variables** in which certain aspects of a **sample** are studied by enumerating all possible arrangements of its elements. In a randomization test, the **test statistic** is derived directly from the **data** and does not require the use of a **sampling distribution.**

randomized block design– An **experimental design** employing **blocking** to control for individual differences among **experimental units.** This is a **two-factor analysis of variance** design in which each **block** consists of a set of fairly homogenous experimental units, and **treatments** are allocated to the various units within the blocks in a **random** manner. See also *block design, completely randomized design, randomized group design.*

Block

1	2	3	...	b
T_1	T_1	T_1	...	T_1
T_2	T_2	T_2	...	T_2
T_3	T_3	T_3	...	T_3
$\vdots$	$\vdots$	$\vdots$	...	$\vdots$
T_t	T_t	T_t	...	T_t

Layout of a randomized block design with *b* blocks and *t* treatments

randomized clinical trial– A **clinical trial** where the patients are randomly assigned to different **treatment groups.** See also *randomized controlled clinical trial.*

randomized controlled clinical trial– A **clinical trial** in which subjects are allocated **at random** to the **experimental** and a **concurrent control group.** After the completion of the trial, the results are assessed and compared in terms of the **outcome measure** of interest between the experimental and the control group. Randomized controlled clinical trials are considered as the most scientifically valid method of evaluating the efficacy of a **treatment.**

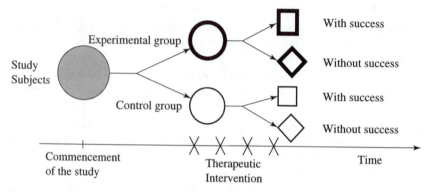

Schematic diagram of a randomized controlled clinical trial

randomized controlled trial– Same as *randomized controlled clinical trial.*

randomized group design– An **experimental design** that creates one **treatment group** for each **treatment** and assigns each **experimental unit** to one of these groups by a **random** device. See also *randomized block design.*

randomized response model– A technique used in **sample surveys** of human populations to eliminate **response bias** in answering personal and sensitive questions. The procedure introduces an element of chance as to what question a respondent has to answer.

randomized response technique– Same as *randomized response model.*

random model– The term is essentially equivalent to **stochastic model,** and sometimes it is used as a short form for **random effects model.**

randomness– A term used to describe an intuitive concept referring to a condition or property of a phenomenon governed purely by **chance.** See also *random, random event, random experiment.*

random normal deviates– **Random numbers** generated from a **standard normal distribution.**

random numbers– Random numbers are a collection of digits 0, 1, 2, . . . , 9 arranged as if they had been generated by a **random** device which gives each digit the same **probability** of occurrence. Random numbers are widely used in the selection of a **random sample.** See also *pseudorandom numbers.*

random-numbers table– A listing of numbers generated by a **random** process such that each possible digit is equally likely to precede or follow any other one. Published tables of **random numbers** generated by a computer **algorithm** are widely available to facilitate the selection of **random samples.** L. H. C. Tippett in 1927, M. G. Kendall and B. Smith in

1940, Rand Corporation in 1955, and C. E. Clark in 1966 published the best-known random number tables. Nowadays, computer algorithms for random number generators have largely superseded random-number tables. A short table of random numbers is given below.

Table of random numbers

Row	|Column| 1	2	3	4	5	6	7	8	9	10	Row
1	80083	77093	00960	49851	44218	64603	50045	73159	55805	50067	1
2	22763	43086	98315	90948	77066	47912	58164	50293	32803	55015	2
3	22125	31789	33826	64132	55537	11451	92836	79580	14996	51984	3
4	56241	99012	29886	92789	78115	72669	34419	06357	96818	16337	4
5	49378	85557	71172	30749	54432	92144	22681	49548	18077	30401	5
6	95083	38793	20028	98540	07752	78539	31495	94052	37987	38911	6
7	02803	26490	81174	27904	84943	57181	52137	68864	94549	77710	7
8	42546	61510	57266	84416	54355	74818	65673	98941	24333	45425	8
9	60198	00328	02233	48032	14609	63395	13759	21971	64000	20404	9
10	55536	89600	43238	11102	90620	31173	22357	15252	14569	98341	10
11	16485	41619	57814	18747	28312	93687	03021	20668	45974	63771	11
12	81634	47135	92210	31022	50800	26336	85622	74093	34899	71644	12
13	75281	85184	67672	49786	20730	43161	95372	28160	82440	02757	13
14	45316	21084	13743	48517	01075	42091	93025	92262	42328	51621	14
15	99985	81537	80566	69397	53509	02336	85126	49640	25196	21145	15
16	23050	34065	33474	94498	91298	03595	58587	96149	47680	30561	16
17	71804	028355	46763	86988	19204	27278	16287	85017	68168	61348	17
18	56461	27640	18455	50462	91258	55424	36463	49124	06467	13484	18
19	26409	04456	47172	16686	98951	77734	93342	50827	60020	02820	19
20	34579	53161	29401	14076	19037	83061	46912	16074	68014	71779	20
21	53326	52317	41398	61470	57492	44730	34602	40589	12409	00818	21
22	64454	15627	14444	26788	41024	31498	47423	43207	63501	21043	22
23	12615	35357	85483	83015	79536	5654	94742	38941	36832	70550	23
24	23172	22867	87620	41610	64224	71306	37504	97015	82065	40710	24
25	96310	86555	87851	03749	40471	20834	98170	87168	23027	67084	25
26	07223	92200	83095	54485	68338	48062	22870	11053	93573	83185	26
27	70736	36539	64310	23948	46399	45513	45821	93469	95533	91941	27
28	53140	75281	42302	26586	18095	97262	69518	23908	63082	15251	28
29	33520	99286	75440	29318	80495	92646	03921	60534	06946	75750	29
30	55041	29226	29602	80254	11099	05099	51359	28084	66690	72343	30

Source: Generated by using software.

random outcome– Same as *random event.*

random phenomenon– See *random event.*

random process– See *random event.*

random sample– A **sample** selected in such a manner that every member of the **population** has a fixed and known **probability** of being included in the sample. For a random sample without replacement selected from a **finite population,** every possible sample has equal probability of selection; for a random sample with replacement each item is selected independently of the other item with equal probability. See also *convenience sample, judgment sample, nonprobability sample, probability sample.*

random sampling– A **sampling** scheme wherein each individual or unit is selected entirely by **chance**. Random sampling is one of the best ways of obtaining a **representative sample.** See also *random sample, simple random sampling.*

random selection– A method of selecting a **sample** of individuals that uses a truly **random** device. In random selection each individual element in the **population** has an equal chance of being selected. It should not be confused with **haphazard selection.**

random variable– A numerical description of the **outcome** of a **random experiment.** The value of a random variable is determined by a random experiment and thus depends on **chance** and cannot be predicted with certainty. It is also called a **chance variable** or **stochastic variable.**

random variation– Same as *random error.*

random walk– A term used in **stochastic process** to describe the movement of a particle from one point to the other in discrete steps with certain known **probabilities.** Random walks have important applications in many real-life situations such as migration of insects, **sequential sampling,** and diffusion processes. See also *Markov process.*

range– A **measure of variability** or **dispersion** for a **data set** obtained by subtracting the smallest value in a data set from the largest value for **ungrouped data** or between the upper limit of the largest class and the lower limit of the smallest class for **grouped data.** Often used in **quality control** and other works as a quick way to calculate a measure of the dispersion, but is generally not recommended for this purpose because of its sensitivity to **outliers** and the fact that its value increases with **sample size.**

rank– A number indicating the relative position of any one **observation** with respect to the others in a **data set** when the observations are arranged according to their size, from the lowest to the highest. The lowest observation will receive a rank of 1, the second lowest a rank 2; and so forth.

rank correlation– A **nonparametric method** for assessing **association** between two **quantitative variables.** A rank correlation is interpreted the same way as the **Pearson product moment correlation coefficient.** However, a rank correlation measures the association between the ranks rather than the original values. Two of the most commonly used methods of rank correlation are **Kendall's tau** and **Spearman's rho.**

rank correlation coefficient– Same as *rank correlation.*

ranking– The process of assigning **ranks** to a given set of **observations.**

rank of a matrix– The number of rows or columns of a **matrix** that are linearly independent.

rank order– A set of **observations** arranged in order of their rank.

rank-order scale– A scale for **observations** arranged according to their size or magnitude, from the lowest to the highest value or vice versa, in which **ranks** are assigned according to relative position in the scale. The rank-order scale gives the relative position of an observation in a series of measurements. Compare *ordinal scale.*

rank-order statistic– A **statistic** based on the **ranks** of the **sample data.**

Rao–Blackwell–Lehman–Scheffé Theorem– A theorem in mathematical statistics that states that an **unbiased estimator** of a **parameter** based on a complete **sufficient statistic** is the unique minimum variance unbiased estimator of the parameter.

Rao–Cramér inequality– Same as *Cramér–Rao inequality.*

rate– A rate is a measure of the **frequency** of occurrence of a phenomenon. In **vital statistics,** a rate represents the frequency with which a vital event such as birth, death, or disease occurs in a defined population. Although there are some exceptions, the rate is usually calculated by an expression of the form $a/(a + b)$ in which the numerator is also a component of the denominator. It is usually multiplied by a power of 10 to convert the rate from a fraction or decimal to a whole number.

rate of natural increase– Relative change in population size brought about only by the balance between births and deaths; it is obtained as the difference between the crude birth and death rates.

rate of population growth– Relative change in population size brought about as a result of births, deaths, and net migration.

ratio– A ratio is the value obtained by dividing one quantity by another. It is used to show the magnitude of one quantity relative to the magnitude of another. It is calculated by an expression of the form a/b in which the numerator is not a component of the denominator. Thus, in a ratio, the numerator and the denominator usually are separate and distinct quantities. The dimensions of the numerator and denominator may be different so that the ratio has dimensions.

ratio data– **Data** obtained using ratio **scale of measurement.**

ratio level of measurement– Same as *ratio scale.*

ratio scale– The process of assigning **measurements** with an **interval scale** that has a true zero point. The ratio scale has four properties: it sorts **observations** into classes, orders them in terms of differences in magnitude, specifies the amount of difference between the observations, and permits the expression of ratios between measurements. Ratio scale yields truly **quantitative data** that can be subjected to all types of mathematical operations. The examples are scales used for measuring height, weight, and cholesterol level. See also *scale of measurement.*

ratio variable– A **continuous** **variable** measured on a **ratio scale.**

raw data– Same as *raw score.*

raw score– A **score** or **measurement** as originally collected or observed, and has not been modified or transformed in any way.

RBD– Acronym for *randomized block design.*

R chart– A **graphical device** used to control the **variance** of a process by inspecting the **range** of a set of **measurements** taken from various batches or subgroups. The values of the range taken from each subgroup are plotted along the **vertical axis** and can then be used to control within subgroup **spread.** The center line of the R chart is the **average** of ranges ($\overline{R}$) from a pilot set (about 20 subgroups). The **control lines** are based on an **estimate** of within-group **standard deviation** obtained from **variance components** analysis. In practice, the engineer sets the limits at $(D_3 \overline{R}, D_4 \overline{R})$ where D_3 and D_4 are obtained from some specially prepared tables.

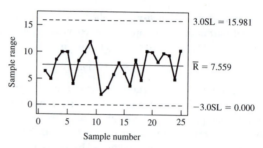

An example of an *R* chart

RCT– Acronym for *randomized control trial.*

real limits– The lower and upper limits based on the actual values observed before round-ing. The real limits of a **class interval** are the boundaries above and below it that include all the values scored as that number. For example, the number 2 has a lower real limit of 1.5 and an upper real limit of 2.5; all values between these two boundaries are scored as 2.

recall bias– A type of **bias** that can occur in a **study design,** particularly in a **retrospective study,** because of different memories of past **exposures** between **cases** and **controls.** See also *information bias.*

receiver operating characteristic curve– In a **diagnostic testing** or **screening test,** a graph showing **sensitivity** or **true positives** on the **y** axis versus the **false positives** on the **x axis.** It is used to assess the property of a **diagnostic test** to discriminate between healthy and diseased individuals. It allows the comparison of performance of different cut points to be made.

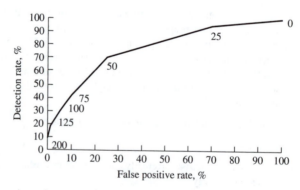

A receiver operating characteristic curve

reciprocal transformation– A **transformation** of the form $y = 1/x$ that is particularly useful to stabilize the **variance** of a **data set** when the **standard deviation** of the data set is proportional to the square of the **mean.** If x represents counts, then $y = 1/(x + 1)$ may be used to avoid the possibility of division by zero. The transformation is generally used when $y = 1/x$ has a definite physical meaning and where the possibility of the **random variable** being less than or equal to zero is negligible. For example, **data** on the failures of a machine may be collected as either the interval between failures or the number of failures per unit time. In some cases the transformation can lead to a **linear relationship** between a pair of **variables.** See also *arc-sine transformation, logarithmic transformation, power transformation, square-root transformation, square transformation.*

rectangular array– An **array** of p rows and n columns representing a collection of $p \times n$ data elements comprising n **measurements** on a set of p **variables.**

$$\begin{bmatrix} x_{11} & x_{12} & \cdots & x_{1j} & \cdots & x_{1n} \\ x_{21} & x_{22} & \cdots & x_{2j} & \cdots & x_{2n} \\ \vdots & \vdots & & \vdots & & \vdots \\ x_{i1} & x_{i2} & \cdots & x_{ij} & \cdots & x_{in} \\ \vdots & \vdots & & \vdots & & \vdots \\ x_{p1} & x_{p2} & \cdots & x_{pj} & \cdots & x_{pn} \end{bmatrix}$$

Schematic representation of a rectangular array

rectangular distribution– Same as *uniform distribution.*

recursive model– A **causal model** in which there is only one-way causal flow in the system. Thus, in a recursive model, reciprocal causation between **variables** is not permitted. Compare *nonrecursive model.* See also *path analysis, structural equation model.*

reference interval– Same as *normal range.*

reference population– The population being chosen as standard for computation of **standardized rates.** In a **sample survey,** the population designated for a particular **sampling design.**

reference range– Same as *normal range.*

region of acceptance– In **hypothesis testing,** the range of possible values of the area in the **sampling distribution** of a **test statistic** that does not lead to rejection of the **null hypothesis.** In other words, it is the region comprising the set of values of a test statistic for which the null hypothesis is accepted. Compare *critical region.*

region of rejection– Same as *critical region.*

regressand– Same as *predicted variable.*

regression– Same as *regression analysis.*

regression analysis– A statistical procedure used to develop a mathematical equation showing how two or more **variables** are related and/or to determine the extent to which one variable changes with changes in another variable or a number of other variables. The procedure allows the unknown value of one variable to be estimated from the known value of one or more other variables. There are a great variety of methods of regression analysis currently being used. See also *multiple regression analysis, simple regression analysis.*

regression artifact– Same as *regression fallacy.*

regression coefficient– The **coefficient** β in the simple **regression equation** $E(Y) = \alpha + \beta X$. It is sometimes called the slope of the **regression line** and is interpreted as the **average** number of units change (increase or decrease) in the **dependent variable** occurring with a unit change in the **independent variable.** In a **multiple regression analysis,** the coefficients are weights applied to the independent variables and are interpreted as measures of the **effect** of that variable while holding the effects of the other independent variables as **constants.** When the **predictor** is a **categorical variable,** the regression coefficient represents the average of difference between any given level of the variable and the value taken as the baseline or standard. See also *estimated regression coefficient.*

regression constants– The values that determine a **regression line** and locate it in a **cartesian space** are called the regression constants. They are the **slope of the regression line** and its **y** or **x intercept,** depending on whether the prediction is made on the basis of X or Y, respectively.

regression curve– A curve that represents the **regression equation** in a **cartesian space.** For a particular point on the curve, the **abscissa** is the value X and the **ordinate** is $\mu_{Y|X}$, the **mean** of the **distribution** of Y for that specified fixed value X. The word curve is used in contrast to straight line to mean a regression equation of a degree higher than the first. Some examples of regression curves are shown below.

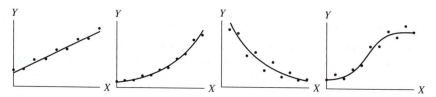

Some examples of regression curves

regression diagnostics– A term used to denote statistical procedures designed to investigate the **assumptions** underlying a **regression analysis.** Regression diagnostics are used to check the assumptions for **normality, homoscedasticity,** and/or examine the influence of particular **observations** on the **estimates** of **regression coefficients.** See also *Cook's distance, DFBETA, DFFITS, influence statistics, residual analysis.*

regression effect– A term originally used to describe the tendency of certain members of any **population** who, with respect to a given characteristic, are in extreme position (below or above the **average** value) at one time to be in a less extreme position at a later time (either personally or by means of their offspring). Thus, an **observation** that is low or high at the time of first observation will tend to be closer to the **mean** at a later time period. The phenomenon was first noted by Sir Francis Galton who discovered that tall parents do not on the average have as tall offspring and short parents do not on the average have as short offspring.

regression equation– An algebraic equation relating the **independent variable(s)** to the **expected value** of the **dependent variable.** A regression equation summarizes the relationship between a **response variable** and one or more **predictor variables.** For a single predictor variable, the regression equation representing a **linear relationship** is written as $E(Y) = \alpha + \beta X$, where Y is a response variable, α is the **intercept,** and β is the **regression coefficient.** It can be used to predict the values of the dependent variable from values of the independent variable(s).

regression fallacy– The incorrect ascription of the **regression effect** to the operation of some important unseen **factor.**

regression forecasting– The use of **regression analysis** for **forecasting** a **time series.**

regression hyperplane– A **graphical display** of a **regression equation** involving three or more **independent variables.** It is a higher-dimensional equivalent of a **regression line** or **plane.**

regression line– A **graphical representation** of a **regression equation.** It is the line drawn on a **scatter diagram** that best describes the relationship between the **dependent variable** and the **independent variable.** The regression line is usually fitted by using the **method of least squares.**

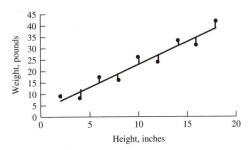

Regression line of weight on height

regression mean square– In **linear regression analysis,** a quantity obtained by dividing the **regression sum of squares** by its **degrees of freedom.**

regression method– See *regression analysis.*

regression model– See *regression equation.*

regression modeling– The term is essentially synonymous with **regression analysis.** It is also sometimes used to refer to a number of methods for selecting the "best" possible set of **predictors** when using regression analysis. The three most commonly used procedures for this purpose are **backward elimination, forward selection,** and **stepwise regression.** See also *all subsets regression.*

regression plane– The three-dimensional equivalent of a **regression line** that minimizes the sum of the squares of vertical **deviations** between the sample points lying in y versus (x_1, x_2) **cartesian space** and their associated **multiple regression equation** estimates, which all lie on the regression plane. See also *regression hyperplane.*

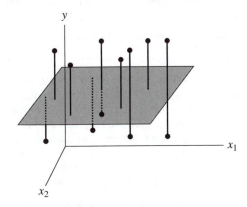

A best-fitted regression plane

regression sum of squares– See *explained variation.*

regression surface– Same as *regression hyperplane.*

regression through the origin– A term used to denote a **regression analysis** in which the **regression line** passes through the origin. It is used when the true **mean** of the **dependent variable** is known to be zero when the value of the **independent variable** is zero.

regression toward the mean– A term used to describe **regression** when the predicted values on the **dependent variable** show less **dispersion** about the **mean** than the observed values do. This occurs because measures of a **dependent variable** are unreliable and there is a less than perfect relationship between the two **variables.**

regression weight– Same as *regression coefficient.*

regressor– See *independent variable.*

regressor variable– Same as *predictor variable.*

regret– Same as *opportunity loss.*

regret table– In **decision theory,** a table showing the **opportunity-loss** values associated with each possible action/**event** or combination of actions and events.

rejection region– Same as *critical region.*

relative class frequency– The **class frequency** expressed as a **proportion** of the total **frequency.** It is calculated by dividing the class frequency by the total number of **observations.**

relative efficiency– Same as *efficiency.*

relative frequency– Same as *relative class frequency.* The term is also used as a synonym for **empirical probability.**

relative frequency curve– Any curve that represents a **relative frequency distribution.** See also *frequency curve.*

relative frequency distribution– A **frequency distribution** expressed in terms of the **relative frequency,** that is, the fraction or **proportion** of the total number of items in each of several nonoverlapping classes or categories.

relative frequency of an event– **Ratio** of the number of ways an **event** can occur to the total number of possible occurrences. See also *empirical probability.*

relative frequency probability– Same as *empirical probability.*

relative power efficiency– Same as *power efficiency.*

relative risk– The **ratio** of two **risks.** It is also called a **risk ratio.** It is designed to measure the degree of **association** in a **2 × 2 table.** If there is no difference between risks among the two groups, the relative risk will be equal to 1. If the exposed group has higher risk than the unexposed group, the risk ratio will be greater than 1. For example, a relative risk of 3 means that the exposed group is 3 times more likely to have the disease than the unexposed group. In **epidemiology,** the term is used mainly to denote the ratio of risk of disease or death among individuals exposed to a certain health hazard (for example, smokers) to the risk among unexposed (for example, nonsmokers).

relative-value index number– An **index number** constructed by (1) assigning the index number 100 to each item in a list of figures representing a period of time chosen as the base period; (2) finding for each item in each of the other periods under consideration an individual index number or a figure that bears the same relation to 100 that the item in question bears to its corresponding items in the base period; (3) finally, calculating a **geometric mean** of the individual index numbers for each period.

reliability– The consistency or stability of a measure or test from one occasion to the next. Thus, it is a measure of the reproducibility of a **measurement.** It is measured by the **kappa statistic** for **nominal measures** and by the **correlation coefficient** for numerical measures. In engineering, the reliability of a product is the **probability** that it will perform within specified limits for a specified length of time. See also *Cronbach's alpha.*

REMLE– Acronym for *restricted maximum likelihood estimation.*

repeatability– Same as *reproducibility.*

repeated measurements– A term used to describe **observations** in which the **response variable** for each **experimental unit** is measured on several occasions and possibly under different experimental conditions. Repeated measurements occur frequently in **observational studies** that are longitudinal in nature, and in **experimental studies** involving **repeated measures design.** The repeated measurements are commonly used in a variety of disciplines including health and life sciences, education, psychology, and social sciences. See also *longitudinal study, repeated measures analysis.*

repeated measures analysis– Analysis of **repeated measures data** taken on one or more groups of subjects. The main problem with this type of analysis is the lack of **independence** of **observations** taken on a single subject. Repeated measures data are frequently analyzed incorrectly by ignoring the lack of independence of observations. Special statistical methods are often needed for the analysis of this type of **data** that take into account the intercorrelations between the set of **measurements** on the same subject. Analysis as a **split-plot design** is appropriate if the **residuals** from different time periods have equal **correlations.** If the correlation structure is more complex, the appropriate analysis is either a **multivariate analysis of variance,** or one that assures a defined **time-series model.** See also *repeated measures design.*

repeated measures data– Same as *repeated measurements.*

repeated measures design– An **experimental design** that measures the same subjects under two or more experimental conditions or on different occasions on the same **dependent variable.** For example, blood pressure may be measured at successive time periods, say once a week, for a group of patients attending a clinic; or animals are injected with different drugs and **measurements** are made after each injection. The **scores** for each subject are treated as correlated **observations.** In repeated measures design, each subject acts as its own **control.** This helps to control for **variability** between subjects, since the same subject is measured repeatedly. See also *repeated measurements, repeated measures analysis.*

replicate– Same as *replication.*

replication– The number of times each **treatment** is repeated in an **experiment.** It is the **sample size** associated with each treatment. The purpose of replication is to obtain more **degrees of freedom** for estimating the **experimental error** and to increase **precision** of **estimates** of **effects.**

representativeness– A term used to describe the extent to which different characteristics of a **sample** accurately represent the characteristics of the **population** from which sample was selected.

representative sample– A **sample** that is similar in terms of characteristics of the **population** to which the findings of a study are being generalized. A representative sample is not biased and therefore does not display any patterns or trends that are different from those displayed by the population from which it is drawn. It is rather difficult and often impossible to obtain a representative sample. **Nonrandom samples** usually tend to have a some kind of **bias.** The use of a **random sample** usually leads to a representative sample.

reproducibility– A term used to refer to the property of **measurements** to reproduce approximately similar results taken under different conditions such as instruments, laboratories, and operations.

resampling– The technique of selecting a **sample** many times and computing the **statistic** of interest with reweighted **sample obsersvations.** Although resampling techniques have been used in **statistical estimation** and **hypothesis testing** for a long time, the computational complexity limited their use to all but the smallest samples. The speed and computing power of modern computers has allowed the statistics with no closed distributional forms or **variance** expressions to be analyzed by resampling techniques. Some commonly used resampling techniques include **bootstrap, jackknife,** and their variants.

research design– Same as *study design.*

research hypothesis– Same as *alternative hypothesis.*

residual– In **regression analysis,** the difference between the actual observed value of the **dependent variable** and the value predicted by the **estimated regression model.** It is the portion of the **score** on the dependent variable not explained by independent variables.

residual analysis– The term is used to refer to statistical methods and techniques for checking the **assumptions** of the **regression models** through examination of **residuals.** See also *Cook's distance, influence statistics, jackknife residuals, regression diagnostics.*

residual autocorrelation– The **autocorrelation** calculated from **residuals.** They are useful for checking the **assumptions** of the **regression models.**

residual effect– Same as *residual.*

residual error– Same as *error term.*

residual error term– Same as *residual.*

residual maximum likelihood estimation– Same as *restricted maximum likelihood estimation.*

residual mean square– Same as *mean square for error.*

residual plot– The plot of **residuals** against the values of the **independent variable.**

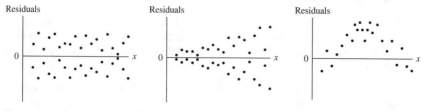

Some examples of residual plots

residual sum of squares– Same as *error sum of squares.*

residual variable– In **path analysis,** an unmeasured **variable** that is posited to cause the **variance** in the **dependent variable** not explained by the **path model.**

residual variation– Same as *unexplained variation.*

response bias– A tendency for individual responses to survey questions to be affected or distorted in some systematic manner.

response measure– Same as *response variable.*

response rate– In a **survey,** the **proportion** of individuals who respond to a particular question or item. Compare *nonresponse rate.*

response surface– A response surface is the geometric representation obtained when a **response variable** is plotted as a function of one or more **quantitative factors** or **variables.**

response value– The particular numerical value assumed by a **response variable.**

response variable– Same as *dependent variable.*

response variate– Same as *dependent variable.*

restricted maximum likelihood estimation– A modification of **maximum likelihood procedure** where **estimators** of **scale parameters** are derived by maximizing the joint likelihood of that part of the **likelihood function** that does not contain any **location parameters.** The term is most commonly used in the context of estimating **variance components** in a **linear model.**

restricted randomization– Same as *block randomization.*

reticulation– The determination of boundaries of census areas, units, and other subdivisions in the country or delineated territory.

retrospective case-control study– Same as *case-control study.*

retrospective cohort study– Same as *historical cohort study.*

retrospective study– A general name for a **research design** in which **data** are collected on life changes of subjects over a specified past period in their lives. Thus, a retrospective study starts with persons already affected by certain condition and looks backward to discover what may have caused the appearance of that effect. Information about possible **exposure factors** is generally obtained by examining past records or interviewing each person and/or the person's relatives. The most common retrospective study is the **case-control study.** See also *cohort study, prospective study.*

ridge regression– A type of **regression analysis** designed to address the problem of **multicollinearity** among the **independent variables.**

ridit analysis– A chi-square analysis applied to a $2 \times k$ table to investigate the **independence** or **homogeneity.** For a dose–response analysis, the column variable must be an ordered sequence of numerical values. The analysis is also applicable to situations where the column variable represents an ordinal measure not necessarily numerical.

right-skewed distribution– Same as *positively skewed distribution.*

right-tailed test– Same as *upper-tailed test.*

risk– The **probability** that a person will develop an illness or any other condition over a specified period of time.

risk aversion– In **decision theory,** an attitude according to which a person considers the **utility** of a certain monetary gain to be higher than the **expected utility** of an uncertain prospect of equal **expected monetary gain.**

risk condition– The particular amount or condition of a **risk factor** to which a group or individual was exposed.

risk difference– Same as *absolute risk difference.*

risk factor– In **epidemiology,** a term used to designate a characteristic, such as inheritance, personal behavior, life style, or environmental condition, that is considered to be associated with a given disease or condition not necessarily a casual factor.

risk measure– Same as *measure of risk.*

risk neutrality– In **decision theory,** an attitude according to which a person considers the **utility** of a certain prospect of money to be equal to the **expected utility** of an uncertain prospect of equal **expected monetary gain.**

risk ratio– Same as *relative risk.*

risk seeking– In **decision theory,** an attitude according to which a person considers the **utility** of a certain prospect of money to be lower than the **expected utility** of an uncertain prospect of **equal expected monetary gain.**

robust estimation– A method of **statistical estimation** which is relatively insensitive to failures in the **assumptions** underlying the use of a **statistical model.**

robust estimator– See *robust estimation.*

robustness– A term used to describe the property of a statistical procedure if it is relatively insensitive to violation of certain **assumptions** on which it depends. Such a method remains useful even when one (or more) of its assumptions is (are) violated.

robust procedure– A statistical procedure that is relatively insensitive to violation of **assumptions** underlying its use. For example, **Student's *t* test** is a robust procedure against departures from **normality.** Similarly, **statistical tests** and **confidence intervals** based on **ranks** are robust against the influence of outlying **observations.**

robust regression– A type of **regression** that is relatively insensitive to failures in the **assumptions** of the **regression model.**

robust statistics– See *robust procedure.*

ROC curve– Same as *receiver operating characteristic curve.*

root mean square error– See *mean square error.*

Rosenbaum test– A **nonparametric procedure** for testing the equality of two **scale parameters** having a common **median.** The **test statistic** is based on the total number of **observations** in one **sample** that are either smaller than the smallest value or larger than the largest value in the second sample. The test was proposed by S. Rosenbaum in 1953, who also gave tables of **critical values** of the test statistic. See also *Ansari–Bradley test, Barton–David test, Conover test, F test for two population variances, Klotz test, Mood test, Siegel–Tukey test.*

rounding– The reporting of numerical information to fewer decimal places by discarding extra digits after a certain number of places and increasing the last of the remaining digits to the next higher digit if the nearest digit being discarded is greater than or equal to 5.

rounding errors– Computing errors caused by rounding values of a quantity to fewer decimal places. Rounding errors can usually be reduced by calculating quantities to more significant figures.

row marginals– In a **cross-tabulation,** the **frequencies** of the **variable** appearing across the rows. Compare *column marginals.*

row sum of squares– Same as *sum of squares for rows.*

Roy's largest root criterion– See *multivariate analysis of variance.*

run– A succession of identical letters or symbols that is followed and preceded by a different letter or no letter at all. The theory of runs allows us to test for **randomness.**

run chart– A simple **graphical device** used to record and display **trends** in **data** over time. In a run chart, the observed values are plotted on the **vertical axis** and the time they were observed on the **horizontal axis.** The main purpose of the run chart is to monitor a system or a process in order to detect any meaningful changes in the process that may take place over time. The figure below is a run chart that shows the observed weights plotted over time. The graph clearly shows an upward drift in the weights of the product, and it indicates the need for a corrective action on the process.

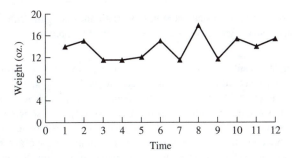

A run chart

run test– A statistical procedure used to test **randomness** of a sequence of **observations.** The procedure consists of counting the number of **runs** and comparing it with the expected number of runs under the **null hypothesis** of **independence.**

saddle point– In a **zero-sum game,** the pure strategies of two players constitute a saddle point if the corresponding entry of the **payoff matrix** is simultaneously a maximum of row minima and a minimum of column maxima.

Sakoda coefficient– A **measure of association** or relationship between two **categorical** or **qualitative variables** whose **data** are cross-classified in an $r \times c$ **contingency table.** It is calculated by the formula

$$S = \sqrt{\frac{p\chi^2}{(p-1)(n+\chi^2)}}$$

where $p = \min(r, c)$, χ^2 is the usual **chi-square statistic** for testing the **independence,** and n is the **sample size.** See also *contingency coefficient, phi coefficient, Tschuprov coefficient.*

sample– A sample is a subset or a portion of the entire aggregate of a **population.** A sample is usually selected according to some specified criteria. In many statistical applications, samples are used to draw **inferences** about the population characteristics, that is, to generalize results from sample to population. To be useful, a sample must be representative of the population from which it is drawn; that is, it must have characteristics similar to those of the population. **Random** or **probability samples** often produce a **representative sample.** There are various methods and techniques available for selecting a sample and drawing inferences from it. See also *judgment sample, nonprobability sample.*

sample autocorrelation– Same as *autocorrelation.*

sample coefficient of correlation– A standardized measure of the **linear relationship** between two **variables** using **sample data.** See also *correlation coefficient, population coefficient of correlation.*

sample coefficient of determination– Same as *sample coefficient of multiple determination.*

sample coefficient of multiple correlation– An **estimate** of the degree of **linear relationship** between more than two **variables** obtained by using **sample data.** See also *coefficient of multiple correlation, coefficient of multiple determination.*

sample coefficient of multiple determination– An **estimate** of the **goodness of fit** of the estimated **regression plane** (or **hyperplane**) obtained by using the **sample data.** See also *coefficient of multiple determination, population coefficient of multiple determination.*

sample coefficient of partial correlation– The square root of the **sample coefficient of partial determination.** See also *coefficient of partial determination.*

sample coefficient of partial determination– An **estimate** of the **coefficient of partial determination** obtained by using the **sample data.**

sample correlation– Same as *sample coefficient of correlation.*

sample correlation coefficient– Same as *sample coefficient of correlation.*

sample covariance– An unstandardized measure of **linear relationship** between the two **variables** X and Y using **sample data.** If a **sample** of n **observations** is (x_1, y_1), $(x_2, y_2), \ldots, (x_n, y_n)$, then the sample covariance, denoted by S_{xy}, is defined as

$$S_{xy} = \frac{\sum\limits_{i=1}^{n} (x_i - \bar{x})(y_i - \bar{y})}{n - 1}$$

A positive **covariance** will result if the factors $(x_i - \bar{x})$ and $(y_i - \bar{y})$ tend to be either both positive or both negative. This happens if there is a tendency for both variables to increase or decrease at the same time. On the other hand, a negative covariance will result if the both factors $(x_i - \bar{x})$ and $(y_i - \bar{y})$ tend to be of opposite sign. This happens if there is a tendency for y to decrease as x increases.

Examples of positive and negative covariance

sample covariance matrix– A **covariance matrix** where **variances** and **covariances** are **sample estimates** of the corresponding **population parameters.** See also *population covariance matrix.*

sample data– Data obtained from a **sample** rather than from the entire **population.**

sampled population– The **population** from which the **sample** is actually selected. See also *parent population, target population.*

sample estimate– Same as *estimate.*

sample estimator– Same as *estimator.*

sample frame– Same as *frame.*

sample mean– The most commonly used **estimate** of the **population mean.** For a **sample** of size n, with **measurement** values $x_1, x_2, \ldots, x_n$, the sample mean is defined as $\bar{x} = (x_1 + x_2 + \cdots + x_n)/n$. See also *mean, population mean.*

sample median– The value that divides the **sample data** into two equal groups. For an odd **sample size,** say a sample of $2n + 1$ **observations,** denote the ordered values by $x_{(1)} \leq x_{(2)} \leq \cdots \leq x_{(2n+1)}$. Then the sample median is $x_{(n+1)}$, the observation that occupies position $(n + 1)$ in the list. For an even sample size, say a sample of $2n$ observations, listed in order as $x_{(1)} \leq x_{(2)} \leq \cdots \leq x_{(2n)}$, it is customary to make the sample median unique by defining it as the **mean** of $x_{(n)}$ and $x_{(n+1)}$, that is, $(x_{(n)} + x_{(n+1)})/2$. The sample median provides a **measure of central tendency** that is more appropriate for **skewed distributions.** It is also relatively insensitive to presence of **outliers.** See also *population median.*

The data arranged in an increasing order of magnitude

50% of the data	50% of the data

Median

Schematic representation of a sample median

sample moments– See *moments.*

sample observations– Same as *sample data.*

sample point– The individual **outcome** of a **random experiment** is called a sample point.

sample proportion– The **estimate** of a **binomial proportion** based on **sample data.** It is calculated by the formula x/n where x is the number of successes in n **independent trials.**

sample range– The **range** calculated from a **sample data** rather than from the entire **population.**

sample regression line– Same as *estimated regression line.*

sample size– Same as *size of a sample.*

sample space– In **probability theory,** the collection of all possible **outcomes** of an **experiment** is called sample space.

Sample space for five tossed coins

HHHHH	HTHHH	THHHH	TTHHH	HHHHT	HTHHT	THHHT	TTHHT
HHHTH	HTHTH	THHTH	TTHTH	HHHTT	HTHTT	THHTT	TTHTT
HHTHH	HTTHH	THTHH	TTTHH	HHTHT	HTTHT	THTHT	TTTHT
HHTTH	HTTTH	THTTH	TTTTH	HHTTT	HTTTT	THHTT	TTTTT

Sample space for two tossed dice

sample standard deviation– The most commonly used **estimate** of the **population standard deviation.** For a **sample** of size n, with **measurement** values $x_1, x_2, \ldots, x_n$, the sample standard deviation is defined as

$$s = \sqrt{\frac{\sum\limits_{i=1}^{n} (x_i - \bar{x})^2}{n - 1}}$$

where $\bar{x}$ is the **sample mean.** See also *standard deviation.*

sample statistic– Same as *statistic.*

sample survey– A **survey** in which **observations** are made about one or more characteristics of interest for only a **sample** of human populations, business, industry, or other institutions. The **sample observations** are used to estimate particular population characteristics of interest.

sample unit– Same as *sampling unit.*

sample values– Same as *sample data.*

sample variance– The most commonly used **estimate** of the **population variance.** It is equal to the square of the **sample standard deviation.** See also *variance.*

sampling– The process of selecting a **sample** from a **population,** in order to use the sample information to draw conclusions of the source population. The aim of sampling is to provide the required information with minimum investment of time, effort, and money. In some cases samples may provide more accurate results than a **census** or complete enumeration. Two types of sampling procedures commonly used are: (1) **probability sampling,** in which each unit is chosen with a given **chance** of being selected, and (2) **nonprobability sampling,** in which the selection of the sample is based on convenience or judgment. See also *cluster sampling, random sampling, simple random sampling, stratified random sampling, systematic sampling.*

sampling design– A procedure for drawing a **sample** from a given **population.** The term "sampling design" is often understood to mean all the necessary steps and procedures in the selection of a sample and subsequent analysis, including choice of a **sample frame,** recruiting and training of interviewers, data collection procedures, and methods of **estimation** and **hypothesis testing.**

sampling distribution– A theoretical **probability distribution** of any **statistic** that results from drawing all possible **samples** of a given size from a **population** and can be calculated on the basis of a sample of a given size. Some useful examples are the sampling distribution of **means** or **proportions** and the sampling distribution of the difference between two means or proportions. It is described by showing all possible values of a **sample statistic** and its corresponding **probabilities.** Sampling distribution is useful in drawing **inferences** about the population based on the statistic in question.

sampling distribution of mean– See *sampling distribution.*

sampling distribution of proportion– See *sampling distribution.*

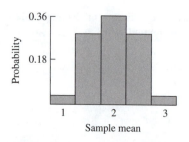

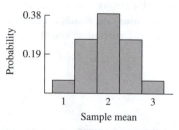

Distribution of the sample mean of samples of size 2 drawn (without replacement) from the population {1, 1, 2, 2, 2, 2, 3, 3}

Distribution of the sample mean of samples of size 2 drawn (with replacement) from the population {1, 1, 2, 2, 2, 2, 3, 3}

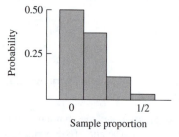

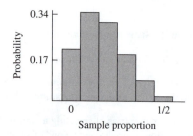

Distribution of the sample proportion for samples of size 6 with $p = 0.1$

Distribution of the sample proportion for samples of size 16 with $p = 0.1$

sampling error– The difference between a **point estimate** and the value of the **population parameter** being estimated. It is a measure of inaccuracies in estimating a parameter because a **sample** rather than the entire **population** has been taken. Although the sampling error is usually unknown, with an appropriate **sampling design** it can usually be kept small within a desired level of **precision.**

sampling fraction– The **proportion** of **sampling units** to be drawn from a specified **population** for selection in the **sample.** It is obtained as the **ratio** of **sample size** to **population size.** A 5% sample has a sampling fraction of $\frac{1}{20}$.

sampling frame– Same as *frame.*

sampling procedure– Same as *sampling design.*

sampling scheme– Same as *sampling design.*

sampling unit– The unit of selection in the sampling process, e.g., a person, a household, a district, etc. It is not necessarily the unit of **observation** or study.

sampling variability– Same as *sampling variation.*

sampling variance– The **variance** of the **sampling distribution** of a **statistic** or the square of its **standard error.**

sampling variation– The unaccounted fluctuations (**random error**) in results as exhibited from one **sample** to the other. See also *sampling distribution.*

sampling without replacement– A method of **sampling** such that once a **sampling unit** from a **population** has been selected, it is removed from the population and cannot be selected in a second or subsequent draw.

sampling with replacement– A method of **sampling** such that, as each **sampling unit** from a **population** is selected, it is returned to the population being sampled. It is possible that a previously selected item may be selected again and, therefore, appear in the **sample** more than once.

SAS– A widely used **statistical computing package** for data management, report writing, and statistical analysis. It is an acronym for Statistical Analysis System. SAS is a powerful **statistical software package,** and is currently available on thousands of computing facilities throughout the world. The package includes a great variety of elementary and advanced statistical procedures suitable for myriads of business and scientific applications. It is an extremely flexible package containing a complete range of statistical procedures with powerful graphical capabilities, and all can be accessed with a single run.

Satterthwaite's approximation– Same as *Satterthwaite's procedure.*

Satterthwaite's procedure– A general procedure for approximating the **probability distribution** of a **linear combination** of independent **random variables** where each variable has a scaled **chi-square distribution** with known **degrees of freedom.** The procedure is frequently employed for constructing **confidence intervals** for the **mean** and the **variance components** in a **random** or **mixed effects analysis of variance.**

saturated model– A **model** that contains as many **parameters** as there are **cells** or **means** and consequently results in a perfect fit for a given set of **data.**

Savage's test– A **nonparametric procedure** for testing the difference between two **cumulative distribution functions.** See also *goodness-of-fit test, Kolmogorov–Smirnov test.*

scalar– A single number in contrast to a **vector** in a matrix context.

scale– A term used to describe the property of a **distribution** that is related to the scale of the **variable,** e.g., the **standard deviation** of a **normal distribution.**

scale of measurement– A term used to describe the degree of **precision** with which an **attribute** or characteristic can be measured. It is generally classified into **nominal, ordinal, interval,** and **ratio scales.** These four scales are arranged in order of strength, from the lowest to the highest. The **data** obtained at a higher scale of measurement can usually be described with a lower scale of measurement, but the converse is not true.

scale parameter– A term generally used to refer to a **parameter** of a **distribution** that determines its scale.

scatter– The extent to which the **data points** in a **scatter diagram** fail to fall into alignment. The term is often used as a synonym for **variability.**

scatter diagram– A two-dimensional graph displaying the relationship between two characteristics or **variables** of a set of **bivariate data** in which one variable appears on the

horizontal axis and the other appears on the **vertical axis.** It is drawn on a **cartesian plane** where one set of **score** values is displayed on the horizontal *x* axis, called the **abscissa;** the other is displayed on the vertical *y* axis, called the **ordinate.** Each **data point** represents a pair of scores, an *x* value and a *y* value. For example, *x* and *y* may represent height and weight, and each dot represents the associated height and weight. The **independent variable** usually appears on the horizontal axis and the **dependent variable** appears on the vertical axis. A set of *n* (*x*, *y*) **observations** thus provides *n* points on the plot and the **scatter** or clustering of the points exhibits the relationship between *x* and *y*. In using a **regression model** in order to assess the **association** between the two variables, it is always useful to draw a scatter diagram. The diagram provides an important visual aid in assessing the type of relationship between the two variables. See also *bivariate plot, correlation coefficient, measure of association.*

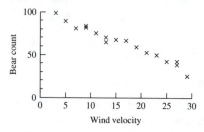 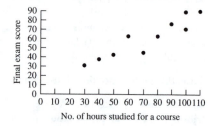

Scatter diagrams of two bivariate data sets

scattergram– Same as *scatter diagram.*

scatter plot– Same as *scatter diagram.*

***s* chart–** A **graphical device** used to control the **variance** of a process by inspecting the **standard deviation** of a set of **measurements** taken from various batches or subgroups. The values of standard deviation taken from each subgroup are plotted along the **vertical axis** and can then be used to control within subgroup **spread.** The **center line** of the *s* chart is the **average** of standard deviations ($\bar{s}$) from a pilot set (about 20 rational subgroups). The **control lines** are set at $\bar{s} \pm 3(0.389/0.9123)\bar{s}$. In practice, the engineer sets the limits at $B_3\bar{s}$ and $B_4\bar{s}$, where B_3 and B_4 are obtained from some specially prepared tables. See also *c chart, control chart, p chart, run chart, x-bar chart.*

Scheffé's test– A **multiple comparison** procedure for comparing **means** following a significant *F* test in an **analysis of variance.** It can be used to make any comparisons among means, not simply pairwise. It is one of the most conservative of all multiple comparison procedures. The method is equally applicable with both equal and unequal **sample sizes.** See also *Bonferroni procedure, Duncan multiple range test, Dunnett multiple comparison test, Newman–Keuls test, Tukey's test.*

scientific sample– Another term for a **probability sample** commonly used in popular media and scientific publications.

score– A numerical value assigned to a **measurement** or **observation.**

score data– **Numerical data** that have some of the characteristics or properties of **data** measured on an **interval scale** but are inherently ordinal in nature.

score interval– Same as *class interval.*

scoring method– A numerical **algorithm** normally employed for optimization of a mathematical function. It is an **iterative procedure** that is useful for solving nonlinear maximum likelihood equations.

scree diagram– A plot used in the **principal components analysis** to provide a visual aid for determining the number of **factors** that explain most of the **variability** in the **data set.**

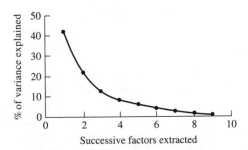

Schematic illustration of a scree diagram
showing the percentage of total variance
accounted for by each of nine successively
extracted factors

screening– Screening is an initial attempt to identify the presence or absence of a disease or disorder by means of test procedures that can be administered rather quickly and economically. In general, the term is used to refer to clinical, laboratory, radiological, or any other procedure performed for the purpose of identifying **risk factors** for a disease.

screening test– Same as *screening.*

SD– Acronym for *standard deviation.*

SE– Acronym for *standard error.*

seasonal chart– A graph showing a plot of a **time series** month by month or quarter by quarter for each of a number of years. Seasonal charts are used as a preliminary to estimating regular **seasonal components.**

seasonal component– In **time-series analysis,** narrow up and down swings of the series of interest around the **trend** and **cyclical components,** with the swings generally repeating each other within periods of 1 year or less. The seasonal components repeat each other regularly with more or less the same intensity as a result of **seasonality.** Although the term is used to denote yearly **cycles,** it is sometimes used to indicate other periodic movements. There are various statistical methods currently available for estimating seasonal components. They are used for making seasoal corrections to **data** such as those in calculating business ratios and budgeting. See also *time series.*

seasonal fluctuation– Same as *seasonal variation.*

seasonality– A term sometimes used to refer to **seasonal variation** of a **time-series data.**

seasonally adjusted– In **time-series analysis,** a term used to refer to series from which periodic fluctuations with a period of 1 year have been eliminated.

seasonal variation– A term used to indicate regular **variation** in **seasonal components** such as variations in sales turnover or current costs, due to regularly recurring seasonal factors.

secondary data– This refers to the **data** that are published by an organization different from the one that originally collected and published them. The *Statistical Abstract of the United States,* which compiles data from several primary government sources and is updated annually, is a popular source of secondary data. Compare *primary data.*

second quartile– The 0.50 **fractile** or 50th **percentile point** in a **data set,** below which half of all **observations** lie. See also *first quartile, median, quartiles, third quartile.*

secular trend– Same as *trend.*

selection bias– A systematic tendency to favor the inclusion in a **sample** of certain selected **elementary units** with particular characteristics, while excluding those with other characteristics. A selection bias leads to a systematic difference between the characteristics of a sample and its source **population.** Conclusions drawn from a sample with selection bias are not generalizable to the entire population. Many medical and epidemiological studies are prone to selection bias. For example, in **case-control studies, cases** with higher levels of **exposure** are more likely to be diagnosed and therefore to be included in the studies. In **clinical trials,** a selection bias can occur because of methods of allocation, which may lead to imbalance between **treatment groups** with respect to important **prognostic factors.** Thus, a selection bias causes a sample to be unrepresentative of the population from which it is drawn.

self-controlled study– An investigation in which the **study subjects** serve as their own **controls.** This is usually achieved by measuring the **response measure** of interest before and after administering the **treatment.**

semi-interquartile range– A **measure of variability** or **dispersion** obtained by dividing the **interquartile range** by 2. Thus, semi-interquartile range is one half of the distance between two **quartiles** of a **sample** or a **distribution.** It is also called **quartile deviation.**

semilogarithmic chart– See *logarithmic chart.*

semilog paper– See *semilogarithmic chart.*

sensitivity– In a **screening** or **diagnostic test,** the **probability** that the test will yield a positive result when administered to a person who has the disease or condition of interest. It is the measure of the goodness of a diagnostic test in detecting individuals who have the disease or condition in question. In **hypothesis testing,** it refers to the **power** of a **statistical test** to detect **deviations** from some specified hypothetical value. Compare *specificity.* See also *Bayes' theorem, receiver operating characteristic curve.*

sensitivity analysis– A term used to describe a method for determining how the final outcome of an analysis changes as a function of varying one or more input parameters. A sensitivity analysis quantifies how changes in the values of the input parameters affect the values of the **outcome variable.** Sensitivity analysis is frequently carried out to assess the impact of different assumptions or scenarios on the results of a study. For example, it can be used to calculate the **sample size** requirements for different values of **significance level, power,** expected differences between groups, and **variability** of **measurements,** among others. In **meta-analysis,** sensitivity analysis can be used to assess the impact of removing some studies, which may be of poorer quality, from the overviews. See also *uncertainty analysis.*

separate variance *t* test– Same as *unequal variance t test.*

sequential analysis– See *sequential sampling.*

sequential sampling– A method of **sampling** in which the **sample size** is not fixed in advance, but in which a decision is made, after the selection of each unit, as to whether to continue the sampling. In sequential sampling, the **sample units** are drawn one by one or in groups of a given size, and the decision is made after each **observation** whether to continue or terminate the sampling. The sample size is thus not fixed in advance and depends on the actual observations and varies from one **sample** to another. This kind of sampling often results in much fewer observations than would be required if the sample size were fixed in order to provide the same control over **type I** and **type II errors.** This is often used in **quality control** procedures where testing is expensive, i.e., where it involves destruction in testing for estimating length of life.

serial correlation– In a **longitudinal study,** the term is used to describe the **correlation** between pairs of **measurements** on the same subject. The magnitude of such correlation usually depends on the time lag between the measurements; as the time lag increases, the correlation usually becomes weaker. In a **time-series analysis,** the term is used to refer to the correlation between **observations** that either lead or lag by a specified time interval. A **statistical test,** based on the **ratio** of the mean square successive difference to the **variance,** can be used to test the significance of serial correlation.

serial measurements– In a **longitudinal study,** the **observations** made on the same subject at different points in time.

set– In **set theory,** a collection, class, or aggregate of objects or things. The objects of a set are called elements.

set theory– A branch of mathematics that is concerned with the study of the characteristics and relations among sets.

shape– A term used to describe the degree of **asymmetry** or the peakedness in a **frequency distribution.** It is that aspect of the form of a **distribution** that is distinct from the property of **skewness** and **kurtosis.**

shape parameter– A term generally used to refer to a **parameter** of a **distribution** that determines its **shape,** in contrast to **location** and **scale** of the distribution. The term was earlier thought to be associated with **skewness** and **kurtosis,** but the usual measures of skewness and kurtosis are not good representations of shape.

Shapiro–Francia test– A test of **normality** based on **order statistics** from **sample data.** It is a modification of the **Shapiro–Wilk *W* test,** and the **null distribution** of the **test statistic** can be approximated by the **standard normal distribution.** See also *Anderson–Darling test, Cramér–von Mises test, D'Agostino's test, Michael's test.*

Shapiro–Wilk *W* test– A test of **normality** based on **order statistics** from **sample data.** The **test statistic** is calculated as the **ratio** of the square of a **linear combination** of sample **order statistics** to the usual **sample variance.** A **statistic** commonly reported in addition to the test statistic *W* is *V*, which is equal to 1 if the **data** are normally distributed, or greater than 1 if not. It is one of most powerful omnibus tests for normality. The test has been found to be good against short- or very long-tailed **distributions** even for **samples** as small as 10. See also *Anderson–Darling test, Cramér–von Mises test, D'Agostino's test, Michael's test, Shapiro–Francia test.*

Sheppard's corrections– The corrections used in the computation of **moments** due to the approximation introduced by considering the values of a **grouped frequency distribution** as if they were concentrated at the **midpoints** of **class intervals.** For example, if the **distribution** is continuous and tails off smoothly, the second moment about the origin calculated from grouped frequencies should be corrected by subtracting from it $h^2/12$, where h is the length of the interval.

short-term forecast– A business **forecast** which usually extends as much as six quarters ahead of the current period. Forecasts for the short term are usually more popular than those involving medium or long time intervals.

Siegel–Tukey test– A **nonparametric procedure** for testing the equality of **variances** of two **populations** having the common **median.** It is a modification of the **Wilcoxon rank-sum test;** the **test statistics** of both tests have the same **null distribution.** For this test, one assigns a **rank** of 1 to the smallest **observation,** a rank of 2 to the largest, a rank of 3 to the second largest, a rank of 4 to the second smallest, a rank of 5 to the third smallest, a rank of 6 to the third largest, and so on. If the **null hypothesis** of no difference in **spread** is true, then the **means** of rank values in two **samples** should be nearly equal. If the populations also differ in **locations,** the Siegel–Tukey test may not be useful, since the rejection of the null hypothesis of equal variances may result from differences in locations. If it is known that the populations differ in location, the **data** should be adjusted by subtracting the appropriate means or medians from each observation. The test procedure should then be performed on the adjusted data. The **asymptotic relative efficiency** of this test compared to the classical **F test** for **normal populations** is only 0.61. However, for the **double exponential distribution,** the efficiency increases to 0.94. See also *Ansari–Bradley test, Barton–David test, Conover test, F test for two population variances, Klotz test, Mood test, Rosenbaum test.*

signed-rank test– Same as *Wilcoxon signed-rank test.*

significance level– The significance level of a **statistical test** refers to the **probability** level at which the investigator is prepared to reject the **null hypothesis** as being very unlikely and to favor the **alternative hypothesis** instead. It is the **probability** of selecting a value of the **test statistic** that is as extreme or more extreme than the value observed. It is interpreted as the probability level of a difference arising largely by **chance,** below which it is considered sufficiently unlikely for the difference to be **statistically significant.** In many scientific investigations, it is usually set by the researcher and is conventionally taken as 0.05. It is the probability of committing **type I error** and is denoted by the Greek letter α. See also *p value.*

significance probability– Same as *p value.* See also *significance level.*

significance test– Same as *statistical test.*

significant– Same as *statistically significant.*

sign test– A **nonparametric procedure** for detecting differences between the **locations** of two **populations** by the analysis of two **matched** or **paired samples.** It is based on the number of plus or minus signs of pairwise differences, which is then considered a **sample**

from a **binomial population.** The test is also applicable for testing a **hypothesis** about the **median.** The sign test is one of simplest and oldest of all **nonparametric statistical tests** available.

simple correlation– Same as *correlation.*

simple correlation analysis– **Correlation analysis** that measures the **association** or **correlation** between two **variables** only.

simple event– Same as *elementary event.*

simple hypothesis– A **hypothesis** that completely specifies the **distribution** of a **random variable.**

simple linear regression analysis– Same as *simple regression analysis.*

simple random sample– A **sample** selected from a **population** of size N in such a manner that each possible sample of a given size n has the same **probability** of being selected. Thus, in a simple random sample, all the $\binom{N}{n}$ samples have the same probability of being selected. For an infinite population, it is a sample selected such that each item comes from the same population and each item is selected independently of the other. See also *simple random sampling.*

simple random sampling– The method of **sampling** that gives all **sampling units** in a specified **sampling frame** an equal **chance** of being selected for inclusion in the **sample,** and an equal chance for selection for each of all possible samples of the same size. Thus, a simple random sampling of n objects from a **population** of N objects is any procedure that assures that each possible sample of size n has an equal chance or **probability** of being selected. The procedure also assures that each possible sample has the probability $1/\binom{N}{n}$ of being selected. Simple random sampling is not very simple to use in field work, particularly when the population is large and the individuals are not numbered. See also *simple random sample.*

simple randomized design– Another term for the basic **one-way analysis of variance** design, the so-called **completely randomized design.**

simple regression analysis– **Regression analysis** that uses a single **variable** as the **predictor** of a **dependent variable.** It is used in contrast to **multiple regression analysis** in which two or more predictors are used to explain one dependent variable. The **regression model** for a simple linear regression analysis is $E(Y) = \alpha + \beta X$ where Y is the dependent or response variable, X is the **independent variable,** α is the **intercept,** and β is the **regression coefficient.** The **parameters** α and β are generally estimated by the **method of least squares.** The regression coefficient β measures the change in the magnitude of Y corresponding to a unit change in the magnitude of X.

simple regression model– See *simple regression analysis.*

simplex algorithm– An optimization **algorithm** for minimizing and maximizing a function of several variables.

Simpson's paradox– A phenomenon that occurs when either the magnitude or direction of the **association** between two **variables** is influenced by a third variable which may act as a **confounder.** By failing to control for its effect, the value of the observed association may appear to be greater than the reality.

simulation– Same as *Monte Carlo method.*

simultaneous confidence intervals– Confidence intervals for several **parameters** being determined simultaneously. In an ordinary confidence interval, we make a **probability** statement about a single parameter while in simultaneous confidence intervals, the probability statement is valid for intervals for more than one parameters simultaneously.

single-blind study– Same as *single-blind trial.*

single-blind trial– A **clinical trial** in which the patient has no knowledge of the **treatment** he is receiving. See also *blind study, double-blind trial, triple-blind trial.*

single-factor experiment– Experiment or design that entails only one **factor.** It is also called **one-way classification.**

single-masked study– Same as *single-blind trial.*

single-masked trial– Same as *single-blind trial.*

single-sample *t* test– Same as *one-sample t test.*

size of a sample– The number of cases or **observations** included in a specific **sample.** It is usually denoted by the letter n. It is generally determined to estimate a **parameter** with a given bound of error or to detect an effect of a particular size for given values of **type I** and **type II errors.** In complex surveys involving **multistage sampling,** it refers to the number of units at the final stage in the **sampling.**

size of the test– Same as *significance level.*

skewed distribution– An **asymmetrical distribution** of values of a **variable** that is characterized by extreme values at one end of the **distribution** or the other. In a **skewed distribution,** the **scores** accumulate at one end and spread out markedly toward the other. If the skew, or thin end, points to the right, the distribution is positively skewed. If the skew points to the left, the distribution is negatively skewed. See also *symmetrical distribution.*

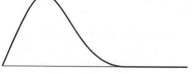   

A positively or right-skewed distribution   A negatively or left-skewed distribution

skewness– The lack of **symmetry** in a **distribution.** It is the property of a distribution that refers to the extent of its **asymmetry.** See also *coefficient of skewness, skewed distribution.*

slope of the regression line– The slope of the **regression line** $E(Y) = \alpha + \beta X$ is equal to the **coefficient** β and specifies the amount of increase in the **ordinate** or **y axis** for each unit increase in the **abscissa** or **x axis.** It is analogous to the concept of grade or angle of inclination in surveying or road building.

smoothing– In **time-series analysis,** a statistical technique such as the construction of a **moving averages** series, that reduces or averages out fluctuations in a series.

smoothing constant– In **time-series analysis** and **forecasting,** a **parameter** employed in the **exponential smoothing** formula.

SMR– Acronym for *standardized mortality ratio.*

Snedecor's *F* distribution– Same as *F distribution.*

snowball sampling– A method of selecting a **sample** from a human population in which individuals selected in the sample are asked to provide information about other potential individuals to be included in the sample.

software– Same as *computer package.*

software package– Same as *computer package.*

Somer's *D*– An **asymmetric measure of association** in a **contingency table** where row and column **variables** are measured on an **ordinal scale.** The measure is appropriate when one variable is considered dependent and the other independent. See also *measure of association, symmetric measure of association.*

Spearman's rank correlation– Same as *Spearman's rho.*

Spearman's rank correlation coefficient– Same as *Spearman's rho.*

Spearman's rho (ρ)– A **correlation coefficient** between two **random variables** whose paired values have been replaced by their **ranks** within their respective **samples** or which are based on **rank order** measured on an **ordinal scale.** It provides a measure of the **linear relationship** between two **variables.** This measure is usually used for correlating variable(s) measured with rank-order **scores.** It is calculated by the formula

$$\rho = 1 - \frac{6 \sum_{i=1}^{n} d_i^2}{n(n^2 - 1)}$$

where d_i is the difference between the ranks of the ith pair. This correlation is equal to the coefficient of correlation when there are no ties. See also *Kendall's rank correlation.*

specific death rate– **Mortality rate** calculated for a specific subgroup of a population. See also *death rate.*

specificity– In a **screening** or **diagnostic test,** the **probability** that the test will yield a negative result when given to a person who does not have the disease or condition of interest. It is a measure of the goodness of a diagnostic test in detecting individuals who do not have the disease or condition in question. Compare *sensitivity.* See also *Bayes' theorem, receiver operating characteristic curve.*

specific mortality rate– Same as *specific death rate.*

specific rate– A **rate** calculated for a special group or segment of the population. Some examples are **age-specific fertility rate** and **cause-specific death rate.**

split-half method– A method of estimating the **reliability** of a test by dividing it into two comparable halves (usually the odd- versus even-numbered items), and then calculating the **correlation** between the **scores** of the two halves. In order to estimate the reliability of a test twice as long as each half, split-half correlations are increased by a factor to correspond to the length of the original test.

split-plot design– An **experimental design** that introduces an additional **factor** into the **experiment** by dividing an **experimental unit** known as a whole plot into smaller units called split plots or subplots. Any one of the experimental designs can be used for this purpose in which each unit can be divided into smaller units. For example, in industrial experimentation, **levels** of one factor may require a rather large bulk of experimental materials, such as types of furnaces for the preparation of alloys, but the levels of the other factor can be compared through use of small materials, such as the molds into which alloy is poured. Such an experiment can be run through the use of a split-plot design where large materials are applied to whole plots and small materials are applied to split plots. A split-plot design provides more precise information about one factor (whose levels are applied to split plots) and the **interaction** between the two, but less precise information about the other factor (whose levels are applied to the whole plots). The design given below shows a split-plot arrangement obtained by using a **randomized block design** in which whole plots within a block are used to allocate three levels of factor A and the split plots are used to allocate four levels of the factor B.

Layout of a split-plot design

Block I			Block II			Block III		
A_2	A_1	A_3	A_1	A_3	A_2	A_3	A_1	A_2
B_3	B_4	B_1	B_3	B_2	B_4	B_2	B_4	B_1
B_2	B_3	B_3	B_2	B_4	B_3	B_1	B_1	B_3
B_1	B_1	B_2	B_1	B_3	B_2	B_3	B_3	B_4
B_4	B_2	B_4	B_4	B_1	B_1	B_4	B_2	B_2

split–split-plot deign– In a **split-plot design,** each one of the subplots may be further subdivided into a number of sub-subplots to which a third set of treatments may be applied. Such a design is known as split–split-plot design, where three sets of treatments are assigned to various levels of **experimental units** using three distinct stages of **randomization.** The details of statistical analysis follow the some general pattern as that of the split-plot design.

S-PLUS– A general-purpose, command-driven, highly interactive **software package.** It includes hundreds of functions that operate on **scalars, vectors, matrices,** and more complex objects. Statistical procedures available in S-PLUS are extremely versatile and offer powerful tools for comprehensive **data analysis.**

spot sample– A small **sample** taken on the spot without regard to its **randomness** or **representativeness.**

spread– Same as *variability.*

SPSS– A popular **statistical computing package** for data management and statistical analysis. This is an integrated system of **computer programs** initially developed for the analysis of social science data. It is an acronym for Statistical Package for the Social Sciences.

spurious correlation– High **positive** or **negative correlation** observed between two **variables** in spite of the original **observations** being made on uncorrelated **variates.** It is usually caused by a third variable and there is no causal link between the two variables. When the effects of the third variable are removed, the observed correlation usually disappears.

SQC– Acronym for *statistical quality control.*

square matrix– A **matrix** having the same number of rows and columns.

square-root transformation– A **transformation** of the form $y = \sqrt{x}$ often used to stabilize **variance** of the **data** suspected to follow a **Poisson distribution.** If some of the **observations** are very small (particularly zero), the **homogeneity of variance** is more likely to be achieved by the transformations of the form $y = \sqrt{x + 0.5}$ or $y = \sqrt{\left(x + \frac{3}{8}\right)}$. See also *arc-sine transformation, logarithmic transformation, power transformation, reciprocal transformation, square transformation.*

square transformation– A **transformation** of the form $y = x^2$ that is often useful to stabilize the **variance** of a **data set** when the **distribution** is skewed to the left. See also *arc-sine transformation, logarithmic transformation, power transformation, reciprocal transformation, square-root transformation.*

stable population– A population that has been growing at a constant rate over a number of years.

standard deviation– A **measure of variability** or **dispersion** of a **data set** calculated by taking the positive square root of the **variance.** It can be interpreted as the average distance of the individual **observations** from the **mean.** The standard deviation is expressed in the same units as the **measurements** in question. It is usually employed in conjunction with the mean to summarize a data set. It is the most widely used measure of the dispersion and plays a central role in statistical theory and methods. It is commonly used to express the **spread** of the individual observations around the mean. See also *population standard deviation, sample standard deviation.*

standard deviation of the population– Same as *population standard deviation.*

standard error– The **standard deviation** of the **sampling distribution** of a **statistic** or the positive square root of the **sampling variance.** The standard error can be interpreted as a **measure of variation** that might be expected to occur merely by **chance** in the various characteristics of **samples** drawn equally randomly from one and the same **population.** Its magnitude depends on the **sample size** and **variability** of **measurements.** It indicates the degree of **uncertainty** in calculating an **estimate** from a **data set.** The smaller the standard error, the better the **sample statistic** is as an **estimate** of the **population parameter.**

standard error of the difference between sample means– The name given to the **standard deviation** of the **sampling distribution** of the difference between two **sample means.** The estimated standard error of the difference between sample means is used as the denominator in the *t* **test for independent samples.**

standard error of the mean difference– The standard error of the mean difference is the **standard deviation** of the **sampling distribution** of mean differences based on **paired**

data. The estimated standard error of the mean difference is used as the denominator in the *t* **test for correlated samples.**

standard error of the sample mean– The **standard deviation** of the **sampling distribution** of the **sample mean** is called the standard error of the mean. It is calculated by the formula $\sigma/\sqrt{n}$ where σ is the **standard deviation of the population** and *n* is the **sample size.** Since all possible sample means are usually not available, one rarely works with the actual standard error of the means and generally uses an estimate based on **sample data.**

standard error of the sample proportion– The **standard deviation** of the **sampling distribution** of the **sample proportion** ($\bar{p}$) is called the standard error of the proportion. It is calculated by the formula $\sqrt{pq/n}$ where *p* is the **proportion** in the **population** having the characteristic, $q = 1 - p$ and *n* is the **sample size.**

standardization– The process of adjusting a crude **mortality** or **morbidity rate** in order to remove as for as possible the effects of differences in age, sex, ethnicity/race, or other **confounding variables** when comparing two or more populations. The rationale for standardization is the potential for **confounding** that exists in many **observational studies** and may lead to biased or erroneous results. The usual procedure involves computing **weighted averages** of **rates** applicable to different confounding variables according to specific **distribution** of these variables. There are two commonly used procedures for standardization, known as direct standardization and indirect standardization. In direct standardization, the **specific rates** of the **study population** are averaged by using weights as the distribution of a specified **reference** or **standard population.** In indirect standardization, the specific rates of the reference population are averaged by using weights as the distribution of the study population. This rate shows what the mortality or morbidity would be in the study population if it had the same distribution as the reference population with respect to the **variable** for which the adjustments are being made. For example, to compare cancer mortality rates between two populations, one younger and the other older, **age-specific mortality rates** from each of the two populations would be applied to the age distribution of a reference population to yield mortality rates that could be directly compared. In indirect standardization, the specific rates of the reference population are averaged by using weight as the distribution of the study population. This rate shows what the mortality in the reference population would be if it had the same distribution as the study population. In the example above, age-specific cancer mortality rates in the reference population would be applied separately to the age distribution of the two populations to determine the expected number of deaths in each. These would then be combined with the observed number of deaths in the two populations to determine comparable mortality rates. This method is normally used when the specific rates of the study population are unreliable or unknown. The term is also sometimes used in the context of standardizing a variable by dividing by its standard deviation so that the new variable has unit **variance.**

standardized coefficient– Same as *standardized regression coefficient.*

standardized death rate– A measure of **mortality** of a population that takes into account the age and sex composition of the population involved. Compare *crude death rate.* See also *standardization.*

standardized deviate– The value of a **deviate** that is reduced to standardized form (zero **mean** and unit **variance**) by subtracting the mean and then dividing it by the **standard deviation.** See also *standard normal deviate, standard score.*

standardized event rate– A **mortality** or **morbidity rate** commonly adjusted for age and sex distribution of the population. See also *standardization.*

standardized mortality rate– Same as *standardized death rate.*

standardized mortality ratio– It is the **ratio** of the observed to the expected number of deaths in the **study population** if it had the same age and sex-specific rate structure as the **standard population** (expressed per 1000).

standardized rate– See *standardization.*

standardized regression coefficient– A **regression coefficient** that removes the effect of the **measurement scale** so that the relative size of the **coefficients** can be compared. A standardized regression coefficient measures the change in the **dependent variable** for an increase of one **standard deviation** in the **independent variable.** It can be compared directly with another and with the beta coefficients of other **regression models.** It is calculated by using **standard scores** for all the variables. It can also be obtained from the corresponding (raw) regression coefficient by multiplying it by the standard deviation of the independent variable.

standardized score– Same as *standard score.*

standard normal curve– It is a curve represented by the **probability density function** of the **normal distribution** with a **mean** of zero and a **standard deviation** of one. Some important properties of the standard normal curve are:

- The total area under the standard normal curve is equal to 1.
- The standard normal curve extends indefinitely in both directions, approaching but never touching the **horizontal axis.**
- The standard normal curve is symmetric about 0. That is, the part of the curve to the left of the vertical line through 0 is identical to the part of the curve to the right of it.
- Almost all the area under the standard normal curve lies between -3 and 3.

See also *normal curve, standard normal distribution.*

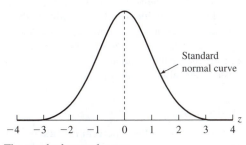

The standard normal curve

standard normal deviate– The values of the **deviation** from the **mean** of any normally distributed **random variable** measured in units of **standard deviations.**

standard normal distribution– A **normal distribution** with a **mean** of zero and a **standard deviation** of one is called the standard normal distribution. A general normal distribution with mean μ and standard deviation σ can be converted to the standard normal distribution by the **linear transformation** $z = (x - \mu)/\sigma$.

General normal distribution

$$f(x) = \frac{1}{\sigma\sqrt{2\pi}} e^{-(1/2)[(x-\mu)/\sigma]^2}$$

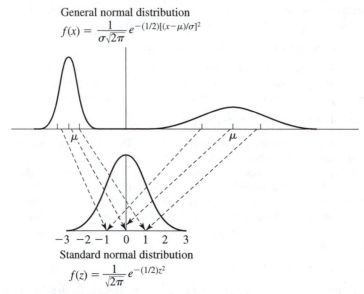

−3 −2 −1 0 1 2 3
Standard normal distribution

$$f(z) = \frac{1}{\sqrt{2\pi}} e^{-(1/2)z^2}$$

Schematic diagram illustrating a linear transformation of a general normal distribution to a standard normal distribution

standard normal probability density function– The **probability density function** of a **standard normal distribution.** It is represented by the mathematical equation

$$f(x) = \frac{1}{\sqrt{2\pi}} e^{-(1/2)x^2} \qquad -\infty < x < \infty$$

standard normal variable– A **random variable** having the **standard normal distribution.**

standard partial regression coefficient– In a **multiple regression analysis,** the standardized regression coefficient of an **independent variable** in the **regression equation** involving all the independent variables under consideration. A standard partial regression coefficient measures the change in the **dependent variable** for an increase of one **standard deviation** in the independent variable when the values of other independent variables are kept constant. See also *estimated partial regression coefficient, partial regression coefficient.*

standard population– See *reference population.*

standard score– A standard or z score, like a **percentile rank,** is used to express the relative standing of a **score** with respect to the **distribution** to which it belongs. The **mean** of any standard score is always 0 and the **standard deviation** is always 1. The standard score for a particular **raw score** expresses its distance from the mean, expressed in units of standard deviation. It is calculated by subtracting the mean from each score and dividing by the standard deviation.

STATA– A general-purpose, command-oriented interactive statistical and graphical **software package.** It is one of the most complete and comprehensive software packages for routine **data analysis.** It is especially useful for longitudinal and epidemiological data analysis. Graphical capabilities of STATA include numerous charts, graphs, and plots for **quantitative** and **qualitative data.**

stationary population– A population with no migration and for which the **crude birth rate** is equal to the **crude death rate.**

statistic– A numerical value used as a **summary measure** for a **sample** calculated according to certain rules or procedures. Some examples are the **sample mean** and the **sample standard deviation.** A statistic when derived to estimate some **parameter** is called an **estimator.**

STATISTICA– A general-purpose, menu-driven **statistical software package.** The package contains well-integrated modules for data management, statistical analysis, and high-quality graphics for **numerical** and **qualitative data.** It supports a wide variety of statistical procedures for routine as well as specialized **data analysis.**

statistical algorithms– The term is employed to refer to the **algorithms** having useful applications to problems encountered in **statistics.**

statistical computing package– Same as *computer package.*

statistical data– Same as *data.*

statistical description– A term used to refer to the use of **descriptive statistics** in describing a **data set.**

statistical estmation– Same as *estimation.*

statistical hypothesis– A proposition or statement about one or more **population.** A statistical hypothesis stems from questions, such as, "Does cigarette smoking cause lung cancer?," "Is treatment A better than treatment B in treating a disease?" See also *alternative hypothesis, hypothesis, null hypothesis.*

statistical inference– Same as *inferential statistics.*

statistically nonsignificant– In **hypothesis testing** any **sample** result that does not lead to the rejection of the **null hypothesis.** A nonsignificant result should not be interpreted as the "null hypothesis is true" but rather as "the data have not shown that the null hypothesis is false." See also *p value, statistically significant, statistical significance.*

statistically significant– In **hypothesis testing,** any **sample** result that leads to the rejection of the **null hypothesis** because it has a low **probability** of occurring when that **hypothesis** is true is called statistically significant. Thus, when a sample result is declared statistically significant, it means that the result deviates from some hypothetical value by more than can be reasonably attributed to the **chance** errors of **sampling.** See also *p value, statistically nonsignificant, statistical significance.*

statistical map– A **graphical representation** of **data** for area units by such devices as differentiated cross-hatching or shading of these units on a geographic map.

statistical measure– Same as *statistical description.*

statistical model– Same as *stochastic model.*

statistical package– Same as *computer package.*

statistical population– Same as *population.*

statistical power– Same as *power.*

statistical process control– Same as *quality control.*

statistical quality control– Same as *quality control.*

statistical significance– Said of a result of **hypothesis testing** if the value of the **test statistic** used to test it is smaller or larger than the value that would be expected to occur by **chance** alone, assuming that the **null hypothesis** is true. It is generally interpreted as a result that would occur by chance less than 1 time in 20, with a **p value** less than or equal to 0.05. It is said to occur when the investigator rejects the null hypothesis. When this happens, conclusions based on a **sample** of **observations** also hold true for the **population** from which the sample is selected. See also *statistically nonsignificant, statistically significant.*

statistical software– Same as *computer package.*

statistical software package– Same as *computer package.*

statistical table– A presentation of numerical facts usually arranged in the form of columns and rows. A statistical table either summarizes or displays the results of a statistical analysis.

statistical test– A statistical procedure or any of several tests of **statistical significance** used to test a **null hypothesis.** The test assesses the compatibility of the **experimental data** with the null hypothesis. The procedure rejects the null hypothesis if an observed difference (or a more extreme one) would have a small **probability** if the null hypothesis were true. Some examples of statistical tests are t, χ^2, and F **tests.**

statistical tolerance intervals– A statistical tolerance interval establishes limits that include a specified **proportion** of the response in a **population** or a processes with a prescribed degree of confidence.

statistician– A person trained in statistical methods and **data analysis.** Statisticians are found in a variety of fields, ranging from business and engineering to psychology and medicine.

statistics– A field of study that is concerned with making decision in the face of **uncertainty.** In particular, it is the study of inferential process, especially the planning and analysis of **experiments** and **surveys.** It develops and utilizes techniques for the collection, presentation, analysis, and interpretation of **numerical data** relating to aggregates of individuals. The term is also applied to the numerical data themselves. See also *descriptive statistics, inferential statistics.*

STATXACT– A powerful **statistical package** for personal computers that supports exact inference for the analysis of **binary, categorical,** and **continuous data.** The programs in STATXACT produce exact **p values** and **confidence intervals** for small **sample data.** It includes over 80 **test procedures** covering all the important problems of interest to a data analyst. A related package is LOGXACT, which provides exact inference for **logistic regression models,** including conditional and unconditional inferences. It produces p values and confidence intervals that remain valid for small **samples.**

steepest descent– An optimization **algorithm** for finding the maximum or minimum value of a function of several variables by looking in the direction of positive (negative) gradient of the function with respect to the **parameters.** See also *Newton–Raphson method, simplex method.*

stem-and-leaf diagram– Same as *stem-and-leaf plot.*

stem-and-leaf plot– An **exploratory data analysis** technique pioneered by John W. Tukey that simultaneously rank-orders the **data** and provides representation of the shape of the underlying **frequency distribution.** It presents **raw data** in a **histogram**-like display and combines features of both a **frequency table** and a histogram. For example, consider the following data on cholesterol levels of 20 patients in an hypothetical study:

Cholesterol levels of 20 patients (in mg/100 mL) in a hypothetical study

211	210	213	209	218	208	211	204	209	211
211	200	216	222	214	219	203	219	201	215

To construct a stem-and-leaf plot, since these data are three-digit numbers, we use the first two digits as the stems and the third digit as the leaves. A stem-and-leaf plot for the cholesterol levels is then given as follows:

Stem-and-leaf plot for cholesterol level data

20	9	8	4	9	0	3	1				
21	1	0	3	8	1	1	1	6	4	9	9	5
22	2										

The stem-and-leaf plot displayed above is not very useful because there are very few stems. We can construct a better stem-and-leaf plot by using two lines for each stem, with the first line for the leaf digits 0 to 4 and the second line for the leaf digits 5 to 9. This stem-and-leaf plot is shown below.

**Stem-and-leaf plot for cholesterol level data
using two lines per stem**

20	4	0	3	1			
20	9	8	9				
21	1	0	3	1	1	1	4
21	8	6	9	9	5		
22	2						
22							

See also *back-to-back stem-and-leaf plot.*

stepwise procedure– Same as *stepwise regression.*

stepwise regression– In a **multiple regression analysis,** a technique for selecting the "best" set of **independent variables** to be included in the final **regression model** by entering or deleting **regressor variables** sequentially in various combinations and orders. The technique begins by including the **variables** one at a time (forward) or by starting with the entire set of variables and deleting them one at a time (backward). Thus, the stepwise regression combines **forward selection** and **backward elimination procedures.** Variables are selected and eliminated until there are no more that meet the criterion. The criterion for entering or deleting a variable depends on the extent to which it alters the **multiple correlation coefficient** or, equivalently, the **error variance.** The rationale behind the stepwise regression is the need to develop a parsimonious prediction model that excludes highly correlated and redundant **predictor variables.** A researcher usually collects information on a number of potential **explanatory variables** and wishes to find which of them provides a stable and optimum predictive model.

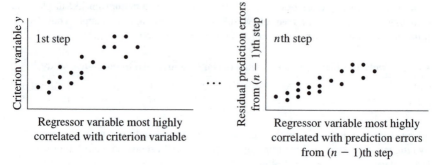

Schematic illustration of the stepwise regression procedure

stillbirth– A late fetal death; i.e., a fetal death that occurred after 28 completed weeks of gestation.

stillbirth rate– The number of **stillbirths** actually observed during a given calendar year divided by the total births occurring during the calendar year (expressed per 1000). Perinatal mortality rate is based on stillbirths plus deaths in the first year of life.

Stirling's formula– A highly accurate mathematical formula for evaluation of the values of $n!$ (factorial). It is given by $n! = \sqrt{2\pi}\, n^{n+0.5} e^{-n}$. It gives an asymptotic approximation of $n!$ in the sense that $n!/\sqrt{2\pi}\, n^{n+0.5} e^{-n} \approx 1$. For $n = 5$, the percentage error in using the formula is roughly 2%. For $n = 10$, it is 0.8%, and for $n = 100$ it is just 0.08%. Stirling's formula is used in calculating **probabilities** of a **binomial distribution** for large values of n.

stochastic independence– In **probability theory,** this term is synonymous with **mutual independence.** See also *independent events, independent random variables, pairwise independence.*

stochastic model– A **mathematical model** containing **random** or probabilistic elements. It is based on a **stochastic relationship** between two or more **variables** where specific statistical **assumptions** are made to allow for **error.** Compare *deterministic model.*

stochastic process– A physical process that is governed at least in part by some **random** mechanism. In a stochastic process, the **probabilities** of the occurrence of an **event** change over time and one is especially concerned with interdependence and limiting behavior of **empirical probabilities.** A stochastic process can be discrete or continuous in time, and its value at any given time can be a value of a **discrete** or a **continuous variable.** An example of a stochastic process is provided by the growth of populations such as bacterial colonies.

stochastic relationship– A relationship between any two **variables,** X and Y, such that any possible values of Y can be associated with any one value of X.

stochastic variable– Same as *random variable.*

stopping rule– A procedure for performing **interim analysis** at certain specified periods of time.

strata– **Levels** of a **categorical variable** such as age, sex, or age–sex groups, where each **stratum** corresponds to a single level or combination of levels of one or more **factors.** See also *stratification.*

stratification– The division of a **population** into a number of subpopulations commonly known as **strata.** Stratification is normally used for the purpose of drawing a **stratified sample.** The term is also used to describe the process of performing a statistical procedure separately in groups (strata) in order to reduce the effects of the **stratifying variable.** Thus, separate **estimates** and **significance tests** for each **stratum** of a **confounding variable** are performed in order to produce a single estimate or **test statistic** across all strata. In **clinical trials** or other **experimental studies,** the term is used for the creation of strata for the purpose of implementing a **stratified randomization.**

stratified analysis– A term commonly used in epidemiologic **data analysis** to refer to a statistical procedure for evaluating and removing **confounding** by stratifying a **sample** into a series of **strata** that are homogenous with respect to the **confounding variable.** See also *Mantel–Haenszel chi-square test, Mantel–Haenszel estimator.*

stratified logrank test– A **nonparametric statistical procedure** for comparing two **survival curves** when the subjects are stratified by age, sex, or some other **prognostic variable.** See also *logrank test.*

stratified randomization– A method of **randomization** in which subjects are classified by sex and age, usually 5- or 10-year age groups. Then the subjects in each sex and age **stratum** are randomly assigned to one of the two **treatment groups** from that stratum. Sometimes, patients are also stratified by severity of disease, inasmuch as severity generally has an effect on the outcome of the disease. Participants are then assigned to a **treatment** or **control group** within each category of severity. The goal of stratified randomization is to achieve approximate balance of important **prognostic factors** while retaining the advantages of randomization. Stratified randomization in conjunction with **block randomization** reduces the **variability** due to the stratifying variables.

stratified (random) sample– A **sample** consisting of **random samples** selected from each **stratum** or subpopulation of a **population.** It is used to ensure that each subpopulation of a large heterogeneous population is appropriately represented in the sample. A stratified random sample usually leads to better **precision** than the **simple random sample.**

stratified (random) sampling– A **sampling** procedure in which the **population** is first divided into parts, known as **strata,** and a **simple random sample** is selected from each one of the strata. The procedure gives every individual in a **stratum** an equal and independent chance of appearing in the **sample.** The strata are formed such that they are internally homogenous, but differ from one another with respect to some characteristics of interest. For example, in the sample used for the **Current Population Survey,** which is conducted monthly by the **U.S. Bureau of the Census,** all the 31,000 counties in the United States are classified into 333 strata and sample counties or groups of counties are chosen from each stratum. In the construction of strata, such characteristics as geographic area, **population size,** income, occupation, and race/ethnicity are taken into account, so that the counties in any given stratum are similar. The goal of a stratified random sampling is to select a sample that is representative of all strata in a given population and to minimize the size of the whole sample for a given level of representativeness. Usually, the same **proportion** of individuals is selected from each stratum, so that the composition in the population is reflected in the sample. See also *stratified random sample.*

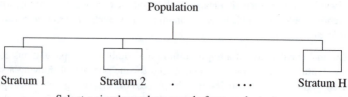

Schematic diagram for stratified random sampling

stratifying variable– A **variable** used to create **strata** for the purpose of drawing a **stratified random sample** or to control for **confounding** in an epidemiological study. Some examples of a stratifying variable are age, sex, income, or geographical boundary.

stratum– A single subpopulation formed by a single **level** or combination of levels of one or more **factors**; a singular form of **strata**.

structural equation model– The structural equation model refers to a method of analyzing relations between the sets of **endogenous** and **exogenous variables**. The procedure consists of the combined application of **multiple regression** and **factor analysis** to investigate the relationships between the **variables**. Equations describing **causal relations** among the variables are formulated and estimated by the **method of maximum likelihood** or **least squares theory.** Most often the endogenous and exogenous variables used in a structural equation model are theoretical constructs or **latent variables.** The purpose of the analysis is to assess the adequacy of the **causal model** proposed by the researcher. See also *LISEREL, path analysis.*

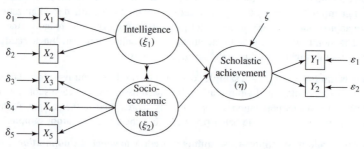

The observed variables are the indicators of intelligence, X_1 = Wechsler IQ score and X_2 = Stanford–Binet IQ score; the indicators of socioeconomic status, X_3 = father's education, X_4 = mother's education, and X_5 = parent's total income; and the indicators of scholastic achievement. Y_1 = verbal score and Y_2 = quantitative score on a scholastic achievement test

Schematic illustration of a structural equation model for scholastic achievement as endogenous and intelligence and socioeconomic status as exogenous latent variables

Studentized range– Same as *studentized range statistic.*

Studentized range statistic– A statistic defined by the formula

$$q = \frac{\bar{x}_{max} - \bar{x}_{min}}{\sqrt{MSE/n}}$$

where $\bar{x}_{max}$ and $\bar{x}_{min}$ are the maximum and minimum values among a set of **group means** and **MSE** is the **error mean square** from an **analysis of variance** of the groups. It is widely used in **multiple comparison** tests.

Studentized residuals– Same as *jackknife residuals.*

Student's *t* distribution– Same as *t distribution.*

Student's *t* statistic– Same as *t statistic.*

Student's *t* test– Same as *t test.*

study design– A logical plan for selecting a **sample** and collecting **data** necessary to answer a research question by estimating **parameters** or **testing hypotheses.** Some examples of a study design are **clinical trial, cohort study,** and **case-control study.**

study group– Same as *study sample.*

study population– A **population** used to select the **study sample.** Sometimes the term is used to refer to the group of people from whom data are collected. See also *sampled population, target population.*

study sample– A **sample** of subjects selected to undertake a study.

study subjects– Same as *study sample.*

sturdy statistics– Same as *robust statistics.*

Sturges' rule– A general rule for determining the number of **class intervals** in a **grouped frequency distribution.** It is given by the formula $k = 1 + 3.322 \log_{10} n$ where k denotes the number of class intervals and n is the number of values in the **data set.** For example, with $n = 29$, the rule gives $k = 1 + 3.322 \log_{10} 29 \approx 5$ groups.

subgroup analysis– Statistical analysis performed on a subgroup of cases with certain common characteristics, such as males, females, elderly, and urban/rural. The purpose of a subgroup analysis is to know whether the results of an analysis differ from one group of cases to the other.

subjective probability– The definition of **probability** based on an individual's subjective judgment or belief in the occurrence or nonoccurrence of an **event** or phenomenon. It expresses a purely personal degree of belief in the likelihood of specific occurrence of an event or phenomenon. A subjective probability may differ from one individual to the other who may assign different probabilities to the same event. Subjective probabilities are useful in **bayesian inference** to develop **prior distributions** for the **parameters** of interest. See also *empirical probability, objective probability, posterior probabilities, prior probabilities.*

substantive significance– Same as *practical significance.*

sufficient statistic– A **statistic** that in certain sense contains all the information obtainable from a **sample** of **observations** about a particular **parameter** it is used to estimate.

summary indices– Numerical values summarizing a set of **observations.**

summary measures– Descriptive statistics, such as, **mean, median, proportion, standard deviation,** etc.

summary statistics– Same as *summary measures.*

sum of squares– In an **analysis of variance,** the sum of squared deviations around a particular mean, i.e., either the **grand mean** or the individual **group mean.** See also *sum of* *squares between groups, sum of squares for columns, sum of squares for error, sum of squares for interaction, sum of squares for rows, sum of squares for total, sum of squares within groups.*

sum of squares between groups– In a **one-way analysis of variance,** the sum of the squared deviations of the **group means** from the **grand mean.** It is calculated by subtracting each group mean from the grand mean, squaring these differences for all items and then summing them.

sum of squares due to regression– Same as *regression sum of squares.*

sum of squares due to residuals– Same as *residual sum of squares.*

sum of squares for columns– In a **two-way analysis of variance,** the **variability** between **treatments,** which are represented in the columns, calculated as the sum of the squared deviations of the column means from the **grand mean,** weighted by the number of cases in the column.

sum of squares for error– In a **two-way analysis of variance,** the **variability** due to individual differences between subjects, **measurement errors,** uncontrolled variations in experimental procedures, and so on, calculated by subtracting the **sum of squares for rows, columns,** and **interaction** from the **total sum of squares.**

sum of squares for interaction– In a **two-way analysis of variance,** the **variability** due to the **interaction** between the two experimental **factors.**

sum of squares for rows– In a **two-way analysis of variance,** the **variability** between blocks of subjects, which are represented in the rows, calculated as the sum of the squared deviations of the row means from the **grand mean,** weighted by the number of cases in the row.

sum of squares for total– In an **analysis of variance,** the overall sum of squared deviations within all the groups. It is obtained by subtracting each individual **observation** from the **mean** of all observations, squaring, and summing these values.

sum of squares for treatment– In an **analysis of variance,** the sum of the squared deviations between each **treatment mean** and the **grand mean.** It is the component of the **total sum of squares** that can be attributed to possible differences among the **treatments.**

sum of squares within groups– In a **one-way analysis of variance,** the overall sum of squared deviations within all the groups. It is obtained by subtracting each **observation** from its **group mean,** squaring these differences, and then summing them.

suppression of zero– A term used for choice of scales in a misleading graph that does not use a break or a jagged line in the *y* **axis** to show that part of the scale which has been omitted.

surrogate outcome– A term used in **clinical trial** to refer to an **outcome measure** that can be used as a substitute for a definitive clinical **outcome** or disease. In order to be useful, a surrogate outcome should be highly correlated with the outcome of interest. Some examples include prostatic specific antigen (PSA) as a surrogate for prostate cancer and blood pressure as a surrogate for cardiovascular disease.

survey– A research or study of a **population,** usually human subjects, to collect **data** regarding social, economic, or political issues of the day without any particular control over other factors that may affect the characteristics of interest being observed. The information collected is usually of quantitative nature or a type that can be summarized in quantitative terms. Surveys are **observational studies** usually conducted by studying a cross section of the **target population.** In order to ensure **reliability** of the results, it is important that surveys are conducted by using a **probability sample.** See also *opinion survey, sample survey*

survey data– **Data** obtained from a **sample survey** rather than from the enumeration of the entire population.

survey design– Same as *sampling design.*

survey research– Same as *survey.*

survey sampling design– Same as *sampling design.*

survival analysis– The statistical methods for analyzing survival data when there are **censored observations.** Survival analysis focuses on how long subjects persist (survive) in a given state. It has been used in demography to study life expectancy and in medical research to study the duration of illnesses and making inferences about the effects on it of **treatments, prognostic factors, exposures** and other **covariates.** The main aim of survival analysis is to make **inference** about the distribution of survival time. Survival data usually involve **censoring** in which the **outcome** for some individuals is not known at the end of the study period. In addition, the **follow-up period** may also vary from one subject to the other. The usual **summary statistics** such as **proportion** (people cured or died) and **mean** (survival time) are not appropriate in analyzing survival data. The appropriate methods of analyzing survival data include **life table analysis, Kaplan-Meier estimator, Cox regression,** and **logrank test** among others.

survival curve– See *survival function.*

survival data– See *survival analysis.*

survival function– In **survival analysis,** if X denotes the period of time for a specified event (such as death or relapse) to occur, then the survival function gives an **estimate** of $S(t) = \Pr\{X > t\}$ for each time period t. A plot of this **probability** against time is called a **survival curve.** See also *hazard function.*

survival probability– Same as *probability of survival.*

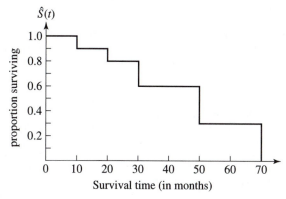

Example of a survival curve

survivor function– Same as *survival function.*

syllogism– A kind of **deductive reasoning** involving a formal argument that consists of two premises, followed by a conclusion. For example, all men are mortal, all kings are men; therefore all kings are mortal.

symmetrical distribution– A **distribution** is said to be symmetrical if a vertical line drawn from the center divides it into two equal halves. In a symmetrical distribution, the values having equal distance from the **mean** have the same **frequencies, probabilities,** and **probability densities.** Thus, a symmetrical distribution has the same **shape** on both sides of the mean. Compare *asymmetrical distribution.* See also *skewed distribution.*

symmetrical population– A **population** or theoretical **distribution** that is symmetrical.

symmetric matrix– A **square matrix** that is symmetrical about its leading diagonal. Thus, a matrix **A** is symmetric if $\mathbf{A}' = \mathbf{A}$, that is $a_{ij} = a_{ji}$ for all pairs i and j. **Correlation matrix** and **covariance matrix** are examples of a symmetric matrix.

symmetric measure of association– A **measure of association** that does not depend on the choice of **independent** and **dependent variables.** Compare *asymmetric measure of association.*

symmetry– The property of the **shape** of a **frequency** or **probability distribution** that exhibits similarity of form or arrangement on either side of a dividing line or plane. Compare *asymmetry.* See also *symmetrical distribution.*

synergism– A term often used in medical and epidemiological studies when the combined **effect** of two **treatments** is greater or less than the sum of their separate individual effects. When the combined effect is greater than the sum of their effects, it is called positive synergism; when it is less than the sum of their effects, it is called negative synergism or antagonism.

synergistic effect– See *interaction.*

synthetic birth cohort– An artificial **birth cohort,** composed of a cross-sectional **sample** of the **population.** A real birth cohort is a group of births occurring at the same time.

SYSTAT– A general-purpose **statistical software package** for personal computers. It offers an extremely flexible language and contains an extensive list of statistical procedures with powerful graphical capabilities.

systematic allocation– A procedure for assigning **treatments** to subjects by using some systematic scheme such as assigning the **active treatment** to those with even birth dates and **control treatment** to those with odd dates. A systematic allocation is not the same as **random allocation.**

systematic error– A nonrandom **error** that introduces a **bias** into all the **observations.** As opposed to a **random error,** a systematic error is the same (or **constant**) over all the observations. It is usually caused by faulty or poorly adjusted measuring instruments.

systematic review– A review of individual research studies in terms of design, data collection, and results, performed to answer a particular research question. The term is also commonly used as a synonym for **meta-analysis.**

systematic sample– A **sample** obtained by using a systematic method of **sampling.**

systematic sampling– A **sampling** procedure in which a **sample** is obtained by selecting from a list of sampling units every kth subject or object at equally spaced intervals. The size of k, called the sampling interval, is obtained by dividing the **population size** N by the desired **sample size** n; i.e., $k = N/n$. A systematic sampling from an area is carried out by determining a pattern of points on a map and then selecting the desired sample of points in a systematic manner. For example, suppose one wants to select a **systematic sample** of 100 cases from a list of 10,000 items. One would first divide 10,000 by 100 to get 100, and then randomly select a number between 1 and 100, say 27. Finally, one would select the 27th item from the list and every 100th item thereafter, i.e., the 127th, the 227th, the 327th, and so on. Systematic sampling provides a useful alternative to **simple random sampling** because it is easier to perform in the field and can provide greater information per unit cost than **simple random sampling.** It is commonly used in a wide variety of contexts, e.g., sampling of dwellings from a list of city blocks, sampling of manufactured items moving along an assembly line, sampling from a list of accounts to check compliance with accounting procedures, sampling customers at checkout counters for their opinion on food products, and so forth. If the elements of a population are distributed in a **random** order, then systematic sampling gives results that are equivalent to simple random sampling. If the elemens of a population are ordered in magnitude according to some scheme, then systematic sampling provides more information per unit cost than does a simple random sampling. Finally, if the elements of the population have **cyclical variation,** then systematic sampling provides less information per unit cost than does simple random sampling.

T

tabular representation– The term is more or less synonymous with **statistical table.**

tabulation– Same as *tabular representation.*

tally– A **frequency count** of a **cell,** category, or **outcomes** observed for a **variable.**

tally sheet– The recording of tallies on a sheet of paper or an electronic device.

target population– The **population** about which the researcher wishes to draw **inferences** or to which she wishes to generalize findings on the basis of the research **data.** Often the target population differs from the population being sampled, and this may result in some misleading conclusions. See also *parent population, sampled population.*

Tarone–Ware test– A modification of the **logrank test** for comparing two **survival curves** with **censored data.**

Taylor series method– Same as *logit method.*

Tchebycheff inequality– Same as *Chebyshev's theorem.*

t **distribution–** A family of **probability distributions** that can be used to make inferences about a **population mean** whenever the **parent population** is normal and the **sample standard deviation** is used as an **estimate** of the **population standard deviation.** The *t* distribution is characterized by its **degree of freedom** which is one less than the number of **observations.** Like the **standard normal distribution,** it has **mean** at zero but its **standard deviation** depends on the degrees of freedom. The *t* distribution is also characterized by a symmetric **bell-shaped curve** but it is more spread than the standard normal distribution. This distribution, among the other things, is the distribution of the **statistic** $t = \sqrt{n}\,(\overline{X} - \mu)/S$, where $\overline{X}$ is the **sample mean** of a **random sample** of size n from a **normal population** with unknown mean μ and S is the sample standard deviation. In this case, the distribution has $n - 1$ degrees of freedom. This distribution is also referred to as the Student's *t* distribution, after William Salley Gosset, who used the pen name Student. The accompanying *t* distribution table gives the **critical values** of a *t* **statistic,** which denotes the value for which the area to its right under the *t* distribution with ν degrees of freedom is equal to α.

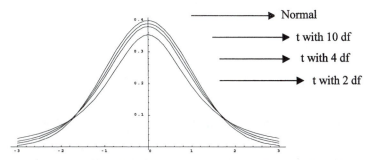

A *t* distribution with 2, 4, and 10 degrees of freedom; the figure shows how the *t* distribution approaches the standard normal distribution as the degrees of freedom become large

telephone sampling– The use of telephones for identifying **sampling units,** selecting a **sample,** and collecting information by interviewing. The use of telephone sampling involves several unique features and may vary from country to country as telephone system characteristics vary. The telephone sampling methods have largely been developed in the context of household surveys, but can be adapted to other **populations** such as institutions and other establishments. See also *random digit dialing.*

testing hypothesis– Same as *hypothesis testing.*

test of hypothesis– See *hypothesis testing.*

test of significance– Same as *statistical test.*

test procedure– Same as *statistical test.*

test size– Same as *significance level.*

test statistic– A function of **sample observations** that provides a basis for testing a **statistical hypothesis.** In order to be useful, a test statistic must have a known **distribution** when the **null hypothesis** is true. A comparison of the calculated value of the test statistic to the theoretical or **critical value** provides the basis for decision whether to accept or reject a given **hypothesis.** The *t,* **chi-square,** and *F* **statistics** are examples of some test statistics.

Theil's test– A **nonparametric procedure** for testing the **hypothesis** that the slope in a **simple regression model** is equal to a given value.

theory of games– Same as *game theory.*

therapeutic ratio– A term used in a **clinical trial** to refer to the **ratio** of the measure of efficacy response to that of toxicity response. A high value of the ratio indicates that the **treatment** is beneficial without causing much toxicity. A low value indicates that the **chance** of benefit is low compared to the **risk** of toxicity. In a pharmaceutical trial, the value of therapeutic ratio generally depends on the dose level and the objective is to select a dose level that yields the best chance of benefit with the least chance of toxicity.

t distribution table

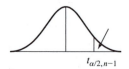

$$t_{\alpha/2,\,n-1}$$

$\to \alpha$ $v\downarrow$	0.400	0.250	0.10	0.05	0.025	0.01	0.005	0.001	0.0005
1	0.325	1.000	3.078	6.314	12.706	31.821	63.657	318.309	636.62
2	0.289	0.816	1.886	2.920	4.303	6.965	9.925	22.327	31.598
3	0.277	0.765	1.638	2.353	3.182	4.541	5.841	10.215	12.924
4	0.271	0.741	1.533	2.132	2.776	3.747	4.604	7.173	8.610
5	0.267	0.727	1.476	2.015	2.571	3.365	4.032	5.893	6.869
6	0.265	0.718	1.440	1.943	2.447	3.143	3.707	5.208	5.959
7	0.263	0.711	1.415	1.895	2.365	2.998	3.499	4.785	5.408
8	0.262	0.706	1.397	1.860	2.306	2.896	3.355	4.501	5.041
9	0.261	0.703	1.383	1.833	2.262	2.821	3.250	4.297	4.781
10	0.260	0.700	1.372	1.812	2.228	2.764	3.169	4.144	4.587
11	0.260	0.697	1.363	1.796	2.201	2.718	3.106	4.025	4.437
12	0.259	0.695	1.356	1.782	2.179	2.681	3.055	3.930	4.318
13	0.259	0.694	1.350	1.771	2.160	2.650	3.012	3.852	4.221
14	0.258	0.692	1.345	1.761	2.145	2.624	2.977	3.787	4.140
15	0.258	0.691	1.341	1.753	2.131	2.602	2.947	3.733	4.073
16	0.258	0.690	1.337	1.746	2.120	2.583	2.921	3.686	4.015
17	0.257	0.689	1.333	1.740	2.110	2.567	2.898	3.646	3.965
18	0.257	0.688	1.330	1.734	2.101	2.552	2.878	3.610	3.922
19	0.257	0.688	1.328	1.729	2.093	2.539	2.861	3.579	3.883
20	0.257	0.687	1.325	1.725	2.086	2.528	2.845	3.552	3.850
21	0.257	0.686	1.323	1.721	2.080	2.518	2.831	3.527	3.819
22	0.256	0.686	1.321	1.717	2.074	2.508	2.819	3.505	3.792
23	0.256	0.685	1.319	1.714	2.069	2.500	2.807	3.485	3.767
24	0.256	0.685	1.318	1.711	2.064	2.492	2.797	3.467	3.745
25	0.256	0.684	1.316	1.708	2.060	2.485	2.787	3.450	3.725
26	0.256	0.684	1.315	1.706	2.056	2.479	2.779	3.435	3.707
27	0.256	0.684	1.314	1.703	2.052	2.473	2.771	3.421	3.690
28	0.256	0.683	1.313	1.701	2.048	2.467	2.763	3.408	3.674
29	0.256	0.683	1.311	1.699	2.045	2.462	2.756	3.396	3.659
30	0.256	0.683	1.310	1.697	2.042	2.457	2.750	3.385	3.646
40	0.255	0.681	1.303	1.684	2.021	2.423	2.704	3.307	3.551
60	0.254	0.679	1.296	1.671	2.000	2.390	2.660	3.232	3.460
120	0.254	0.677	1.289	1.658	1.980	2.358	2.617	3.160	3.373
240	0.254	0.676	1.285	1.651	1.970	2.342	2.596	3.125	3.332
∞	0.253	0.675	1.282	1.645	1.960	2.326	2.576	3.090	3.291

The entries in this table are values of $t_{v,\alpha}$, such that area to their right under the t distribution with v degrees of freedom is equal to α. For $\alpha > 0.50$, use the relationship $t_{v,\alpha} = -t_{v,1-\alpha}$.
Source: Computed by usinsg software.

therapeutic trial– Same as *clinical trial.*

third quartile– The 0.75 **fractile** or 75th **percentile point** in a **data set** below which three-quarters of all **observations** lie. See also *first quartile, median, quartiles, second quartile.*

three-stage sampling– See *multiple-stage sampling.*

three-way analysis of variance– An **analysis of variance** procedure involving three independent **factors.** See also *multiway analysis of variance, one-way analysis of variance, two-way analysis of variance.*

tie– Two **observations** are said to have a "tie" when they take the same value for a given **variable.** For many **continuous data,** tied observations occur because of **rounding errors.**

tied observations– See *tie.*

tied ranks– When **tied observations** are ranked, they are placed under the same rank category. To complete the **ranking,** equal **rank** values are assigned to each observation, which are then said to be tied. Generally, one assigns to each observation the **mean** of the ranks that the tied observations would have if they were ordered. See also *average rank.*

time chart– A **diagram** showing the points of a **time series** on the vertical scale and the time on the horizontal scale. A **seasonal chart** is a type of time chart. Its presentation is also useful for estimating time lags in a series.

time-dependent covariates– **Covariates** that change over time, in contrast to covariates that remain **constant** and are called time-independent covariates. Time-dependent covariates present some special problems and require more complex methods of modeling. An important class of time-dependent covariates is biochemical variables such as blood pressure, serum creatine or latate dehydrogenase, adenosine deaminase in leukemia cells, and urea.

time-independent covariates– See *time-dependent covariates.*

time reversal test– A method for determining mathematical validity of an **index number.** The procedure consists of changing the **base period** originally designated to some subsequent period for which an index number has been calculated. Then a new index number is calculated for the former base period and multiplied by the original index number. If the product is unity, the original index is considered to be mathematically valid. **Aggregate index number** and **Fisher's ideal index number** satisfy the criterion of the test. **Relative-value index number** meets this criterion only if calculated by the **geometric mean.**

time series– A series consisting of a set of ordered **observations** on a quantitative characteristic pertaining to units of a given **population** that have been observed repeatedly at different points in time or during different periods of time. Time-series data exhibit up-and-down movement and are composed of four different components called **secular trend, seasonal variation, cyclical components,** and **irregular fluctuations. Data** in the form of a time series frequently occur in business, engineering, economics, physical sciences, meterology, and many other fields.

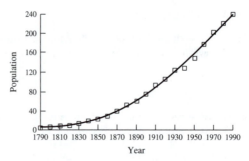

A time series of population (millions) of the United
States at 10-year intervals, 1790–1990

A time series of strikes (thousands) in the United States,
1950–1980

time-series analysis– A statistical technique that employs **time-series data,** usually for the
purpose of explaining past behavior or predicting future **outcomes.** It involves the separation or decomposition of a **time series** into its individual components by some **model.** It is
not a distinct single technique, but a collection of procedures, the choice of which depends
on the periodicity of the series, the number of **observations,** and the purpose of the analysis. The procedures include analysis by **moving averages,** by statistical progression, by
seasonal variations, and by fitting a **trend** line.

time-series data– See *time series.*

time-series line graph– A **graphical representation,** by a continuous line, of **data** that are
linked with time.

time-series model– Same as *classical time-series model.*

time trend– The **trend** of a **time series.**

time-varying covariates– Same as *time-dependent covariates.*

Tlm 50– Acronym for *tolerance limit 50.*

tolerance limit 50– Same as *median lethal dose.*

total fertility rate– Sum of all the **age-specific fertility rates** for each year of age from
15 to 49 years. It is the **average** number of children a synthetic cohort of women would

have at the end of its childbearing years, if there were no deaths among the women. It is obtained by summing the age-specific fertility rates for all ages and multiplying by the interval into which the ages are grouped.

total sum of squares– Same as *sum of squares for total.*

trace of a matrix– The sum of all the elements on the principal diagonal of a **square matrix.**

transformation– A change in the **scale** for the values of a **variable** obtained by using some mathematical operations. Sometimes transformations are performed to simplify calculations. Frequently, transformations are made so that transformed **data** can satisfy the **assumptions** underlying a given statistical procedure. Some examples of transformations are: **arc-sine transformation, logarithmic transformation, reciprocal transformation, square-root transformation, square transformation,** and z **transformation.**

transpose of a matrix– Let $\mathbf{A} = (a_{ij})$ be an $m \times n$ **matrix,** then the transpose of $\mathbf{A}$, written $\mathbf{A}'$ is the $n \times m$ matrix obtained by interchanging the rows and columns of $\mathbf{A}$. For a matrix

$$B = \begin{bmatrix} 2 & 3 & 1 \\ -1 & 4 & 6 \end{bmatrix},$$

the transpose will be

$$B' = \begin{bmatrix} 2 & -1 \\ 3 & 4 \\ 1 & 6 \end{bmatrix}$$

treatment– In scientific experimentation, a stimulus or **intervention** applied to **experimental units** to observe the effect on the experimental condition. A treatment may be a procedure, a substance, or any type of intervention capable of controlled application. In statistical analysis, treatment is considered an **independent variable.**

treatment effect– In an **analysis of variance,** the contribution to the **variance** that results from receiving different **levels** of a **treatment variable.** It represents the change in response produced by a given **treatment.**

treatment factor– In **experimental design,** a **variable** used to represent the **treatment levels** being studied.

treatment group– The subjects in an **experiment** that receive an active **treatment** or **intervention** in contrast to those assigned to the **placebo** or **control condition.**

treatment level– In **experimental design,** a term used to denote a **treatment group** being studied.

treatment mean– The **mean** of all the **observations** in a particular **treatment group** used in an **experimental design.**

treatment mean square– Same as *mean square for treatment.*

treatment period interaction– In a **crossover trial,** the presence of **interaction** between the **treatments** and the order of administration of the treatment. This usually occurs as a result of the effect of the treatment given the first period being carried over into the second period. See also *carryover effect.*

treatment sum of squares– Same as *sum of squares for treatment.*

treatments variation– In an **analysis of variance, variation** among **sample means** from different **treatment groups** that is attributable to inherent differences among treatment populations. See also *treatment mean square, treatment sum of squares.*

treatment trial– Same as *clinical trial.*

treatment variable– Same as *treatment factor.*

tree diagram– A **graphical representation** useful in enumerating **sample points** of an ex- **periment** involving multiple steps that are represented as branches of a tree. It is used in **decision theory** and also in making **probability** calculations.

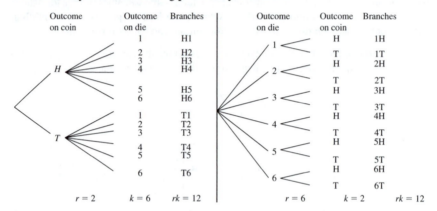

Tree diagram showing sample points when a coin and a die are tossed

trend– In **time-series analysis,** the component of a series giving its general long-term movement. It is a relatively smooth, consistently upward or downward movement of the series of interest over a number of years. In general, movement in the values of a **variable** in any particular direction, i.e., the tendency of values to increase or decrease over a period of time. There are currently various methods of estimating trend in a **time series.**

Time series with a clear trend

trend coefficient– An arbitrary measure of the **trend** in a **time series** designed to discern the direction of the trend where it is not perceived by visual inspection. It is computed by taking the **ratio** of the **average** of the series weighted by reference to an **arithmetic progression,** i.e., 0, 1, 2, . . . , n to the **weighted average.** When the ratio is less than 1, the trend is downward; when it is greater than 1, it is upward; and when it is equal to 1, there is no trend.

trend ratio– A method of analyzing the **trend** in a series by calculating the **ratio** of the figure for period n to that for a period $n-1$ throughout the series. It is sometimes called "link relatives." It is generally used in **forecasting** and **time-series analysis.**

trial– In **probability theory,** each performance, or run, of a simple **experiment** is called a trial; e.g., the tossing of a coin is a trial, the **outcome** being one of two possible **events,** a head or tail. In general, the term is used to designate one of a series of repeated experiments, where one is interested in a particular outcome of the experiment. In **medical statistics,** a trial is a clipped form of a **clinical trial.**

triangular distribution– A **continuous probability distribution** defined by the **probability density function** of the from

$$f(x) = \begin{cases} \dfrac{2x}{h} & 0 \le x \le h \\[2ex] \dfrac{2(1-x)}{1-h} & h \le x \le 1 \end{cases}$$

The **distribution** derives its name from the triangular shape of its graph. If $h = \frac{1}{2}$, the distribution is symmetrical with probability density function given by

$$f(x) = \begin{cases} 4x & 0 \le x \le \frac{1}{2} \\[1ex] 4(1-x) & \frac{1}{2} \le x \le 1 \end{cases}$$

In general, a triangular distribution with base located at points $(a, 0)$ and $(b, 0)$ has the probability density function given by

$$f(x) = \begin{cases} 0, & x \le a \\[1ex] \dfrac{4(x-a)}{(b-a)^2} & a < x \le \dfrac{a+b}{2} \\[2ex] \dfrac{4(b-x)}{(b-a)^2} & \dfrac{a+b}{2} < x < b \\[2ex] 0 & x \ge b \end{cases}$$

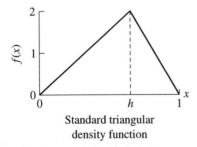
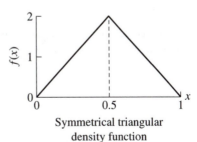

Standard triangular density function   Symmetrical triangular density function

Examples of triangular density functions

trimodal distribution– A **distribution** that has three distinct peaks separated by two definite troughs is said to be trimodal. Such a distribution indicates that three different **populations** or groups of **measurements** are present. See also *bimodal distribution, multimodal distribution, unimodal distribution.*

trinomial distribution– A generalization of the **binomial distribution** when there are three **outcomes** for each **Bernoulli trial.** See also *multinomial distribution.*

trinomial experiment– A generalization of the **binomial experiment** when there are three **outcomes** for each **Bernoulli trial.** See also *multinomial experiment.*

triple-blind study– Same as *triple-blind trial.*

triple-blind trial– A **clinical trial** in which neither the physician nor the patient nor the person analyzing the **data** have any knowledge of the particular **treatment** being assigned to patients in the study. See also *blind study, double-blind trial, single-blind trial.*

triple-masked study– Same as *triple-blind trial.*

triple-masked trial– Same as *triple-blind trial.*

triserial correlation– A measure of the strength of the relationship between two **variables,** one continuous and the other recorded as trichotomous, but having underlying continuity and **normality.**

trivariate normal distribution– A generalization of a **bivariate normal distribution** to three **variables.** Geometrically, it can be represented by concentric ellipsoids of constant density in three-dimensional space. See also *multivariate normal distribution.*

trohoc study– A term used for **retrospective study;** it is derived from *cohort* by spelling it in reverse order. See also *cohort study, prospective study.*

true negative– A test result of a **diagnostic procedure** that gives a disease-free indication to a person who does not have the disease. Compare *false negative, true positive.*

true positive– A test result of a **diagnostic procedure** that gives a disease indication to a person who has the disease. Compare *false positive, true negative.*

true regression coefficients– The values of the **parameters** $\beta_1, \beta_2, \ldots, \beta_k$ determined in the equation of the true **regression plane,** i.e., $E(Y) = \alpha + \beta_1 X_1 + \beta_2 X_2 + \cdots + \beta_k X_k$.

true regression line– The **regression line** $E(Y) = \alpha + \beta X$, determined from **population data** by the **method of least squares** or any other procedure.

truncated data– **Sample data** for which values larger or smaller than certain fixed values are not recorded.

Tschuprov coefficient– A **measure of association** or relationship between two **categorical variables** whose **data** are classified in an $r \times c$ **contingency table.** It is calculated by the formula

$$T = \sqrt{\frac{\chi^2}{n\sqrt{(r-1)(c-1)}}}$$

where χ^2 is the usual **chi-square statistic** for testing the **independence** and n is the **sample size.** See also *contingency coefficient, phi coefficient, Sakoda coefficient.*

***t* scores–** In education and psychology, **scores** that are used in constructing norms for standardized tests. They are linearly transformed **standardized** scores whose **distribution** has a **mean** of 50 and a **standard deviation** of 10. See also *z scores.*

***t* statistic–** In general, any **statistic** that has a *t* **distribution.** There are many statistical applications of the *t* statistic. One of the most common situations involves making inferences about the unknown **population mean** μ. In this case the t statistic is defined as $t = \sqrt{n}(\overline{X} - \mu)/S$, where $\overline{X}$ is the **sample mean** of a **random sample** of size n from a **normal population** with unknown mean μ, and S is the **sample standard deviation.**

t **test–** The **statistical test** for comparing a **mean** with a standard mean when the **population standard deviation** is unknown or for comparing two means with equal but unknown **standard deviations.** It is also used for testing whether a true **correlation coefficient** or a **regression coefficient** is zero. These tests are based on **statistics** having the t **distribution.** The higher the calculated value of a t **statistic,** the lower the **probability** that it arises from **chance** alone and therefore the more **significant** the mean, the correlation coefficient, or the regression coefficient. An assumption of the t test is that the **variable** of interest has a **normal distribution** although the test is robust against mild departures from **normality.** See also *one-sample t test, paired t test, two-sample t test.*

t **test for correlated samples–** Same as *paired t test.*

t **test for independent samples–** Same as *two-sample t test.*

Tukey's test– A type of **multiple comparison** procedure for making **pairwise comparison** between **means** following a significant F **test** in an **analysis of variance.** It is also called the honestly significant difference (HSD) test. See also *Bonferroni procedure, Duncan multiple range test, Dunnett's multiple comparison test, Newman–Keuls test, Scheffé's test.*

Tukey's test for nonadditivity– A procedure for testing **interaction** in a **randomized block design** with one **observation** per cell. The test has one **degree of freedom** and is obtained by isolating a **sum of squares** from the error for the purpose of testing nonadditivity. The procedure has also been generalized for the **Latin square** and other higher order **designs.**

two-by-two contingency table– A fourfold table obtained by classifying a **bivariate data set** according to two **dichotomous attributes.** A typical 2×2 table is shown below.

Schematic diagram for a 2×2 table

		First attribute		
		Yes	No	Total
Second attribute	Yes	a	b	$a + b$
	No	c	d	$c + d$
	Total	$a + c$	$b + d$	N

The testing of the difference between the two **proportions** of an **attribute** or the **bivariate association** between the two attributes is carried out by using a **chi-square statistic** calculated as

$$X^2 = \frac{N(ad - bc)^2}{(a + c)(b + d)(a + b)(c + d)}$$

The **statistic** X^2 has an approximate **chi-square distribution** with 1 **degree of freedom,** provided sufficient **observations** are taken to ensure that the tested proportions are normally distributed. We can improve the approximation for testing the difference between two proportions by a method due to Frank Yates known as **Yates' correction for continuity.** He has shown that if each observed value in the 2×2 table is altered by $\frac{1}{2}$ to make the observed difference less extreme, the chi-square approximation has greater validity. However, if the **sample size** is too small to use the **chi-square test,** an "exact" conditional test known as **Fisher's exact test** may be more appropriate.

two-by-two table– Same as *two-by-two contingency table.*

two-factor analysis of variance– Same as *two-way analysis of variance.*

two-means problem– Same as *Behrens–Fisher problem.*

two-phase sampling– Same as *double sampling.*

two-sample *t* test– The two-sample *t* test is used to compare the **means** of two groups of subjects sampled independently. It is used to test the **null hypothesis** that the two groups have equal means.

two-sided alternative– Same as *two-tailed alternative.*

two-sided hypothesis– See *two-tailed alternative.*

two-sided test– Same as *two-tailed test.*

two-stage least squares– A method of estimating **regression coefficients** in an econometric model where some of the **predictor variables** are correlated with the **error term.**

two-stage sampling– See *multiple-stage sampling.*

two-tailed alternative– An **alternative hypothesis** that states only that the **parameter** is different from the one specified under the **null hypothesis.** Thus, the two-tailed alternative permits the **deviations** from the null hypothesis to be in either direction. For example, if the null hypothesis states that the parameter of interest μ is equal to some specified value μ_0, the alternative $\mu > \mu_0$ or $\mu < \mu_0$ is a two-tailed alternative. See also *two-tailed test.*

two-tailed test– A two-tailed test takes into account **deviations** in both directions from the value stated in the **null hypothesis,** those that are greater than it and those that are less than it. In a two-tailed test, the rejection of the null hypothesis occurs in either tail of the **sampling distribution,** and thus the **critical region** consists of both extremes of the sampling distribution of the **test statistic.** It is customary, but not essential, to assign one-half of the **probability** of rejection to each extreme tail, giving a symmetrical test. See also *two-tailed alternative.*

two-way analysis of variance– An **analysis of variance** procedure involving two independent **factors.** In a two-way analysis of variance, the **total sum of squares** is partitioned between the two independent factors (called **main effects**) and the **error** or **residual effect.** When the **measurements** are replicated for each combination of the **levels** of the two factors, it is possible to calculate the **sum of squares for interaction** and thereby test for the **interaction effect** between two factors. The analysis of a **randomized block design** is an example of a two-way analysis of variance. See also *multiway analysis of variance, one-way analysis of variance, three-way analysis of variance.*

Two-way ANOVA table without interaction

Source of variation	Degrees of freedom	Sum of squares	Mean square	Variance ratio
Factor A	$t - 1$	$SS_A = b \sum_{i=1}^{t} (\bar{Y}_{i\cdot} - \bar{Y}_{\cdot\cdot})^2$	$MS_A = \dfrac{SS_A}{t - 1}$	$\dfrac{MS_A}{MS_E}$
Factor B	$b - 1$	$SS_B = t \sum_{j=1}^{b} (\bar{Y}_{\cdot j} - \bar{Y}_{\cdot\cdot})^2$	$MS_B = \dfrac{SS_B}{t - 1}$	$\dfrac{MS_B}{MS_E}$
Error	$(t-1)(b-1)$	$SS_E = \sum_{i=1}^{t} \sum_{j=1}^{b} (Y_{ij} - \bar{Y}_{i\cdot} - \bar{Y}_{\cdot j} + \bar{Y}_{\cdot\cdot})^2$	$MS_E = \dfrac{SS_E}{(t-1)(b-1)}$	
Total	$tb - 1$	$\sum_{i=1}^{t} \sum_{j=1}^{b} (Y_{ij} - \bar{Y}_{\cdot\cdot})^2$		

Two-way ANOVA table with interaction

Source of variation	Degrees of freedom	Sum of squares	Mean square	Variance ratio
Factor A	$t - 1$	$SS_A = bn \sum_{i=1}^{t} (\bar{Y}_{i\cdot\cdot} - \bar{Y}_{\cdots})^2$	$MS_A = \dfrac{SS_A}{t - 1}$	$\dfrac{MS_A}{MS_E}$
Factor B	$b - 1$	$SS_B = tn \sum_{j=1}^{b} (\bar{Y}_{\cdot j \cdot} - \bar{Y}_{\cdots})^2$	$MS_B = \dfrac{SS_B}{b - 1}$	$\dfrac{MS_B}{MS_E}$
Interaction	$(t-1)(b-1)$	$SS_{AB} = n \sum_{i=1}^{t} \sum_{j=1}^{b} (\bar{Y}_{ij\cdot} \bar{Y}_{i\cdot\cdot} - \bar{Y}_{\cdot j\cdot} + \bar{Y}_{\cdots})^2$	$MS_{AB} = \dfrac{SS_{AB}}{(b-1)(t-1)}$	$\dfrac{MS_{AB}}{MS_E}$
Error	$tb(n-1)$	$SS_E = \sum_{i=1}^{t} \sum_{j=1}^{b} \sum_{k=1}^{n} (Y_{ijk} - \bar{Y}_{ij\cdot})^2$	$MS_E = \dfrac{SS_E}{tb(n-1)}$	
Total	$tbn - 1$	$\sum_{i=1}^{t} \sum_{j=1}^{b} \sum_{k=1}^{n} (Y_{ijk} - \bar{Y}_{\cdots})^2$		

two-way classification– A classification of a set of **observations** according to two characteristics or **factors.** The **randomized block design** is an example of a two-way classification when the data are grouped according to **treatment** as well as **blocks.** See also *multiway classification, one-way classification.*

type I error– An **error** in **decision making** or **hypothesis testing** that results from rejecting a **null hypothesis** when in fact it is true. It occurs when there is really no difference between **the population parameters** being tested, but the investigator is misled by **chance** differences in the **sample data.** The **probability** of making a type I error is usually predetermined by the **significance level** α chosen for the test.

type II error– An **error** in **decision making** or **hypothesis testing** that results from not rejecting a **null hypothesis** when in fact it is false. It occurs when there really is a difference between the **population parameters** being tested, but the investigator misses the difference. A type II error can result from either too much **sampling variability** or the insensitivity of the test employed, or both, and depends on the number of **observations** included in the study.

Schematic diagram for type I and type II errors

	H_0 is correct	H_1 is correct
Reject H_0	Type I error Probability $= \alpha$	Correct decision Probability $= 1 - \beta$
Do not reject H_0	Correct decision Probability $= 1 - \alpha$	Type II error Probability $= \beta$

unbalanced data– Same as *nonorthogonal data.*

unbalanced design– Same as *nonorthogonal design.*

unbiased confidence interval– A **confidence interval** is said to be unbiased if the **probability** of containing any value not equal to the true **parameter** value is less than or equal to $1 - \alpha$. See also *uniformly most accurate interval, uniformly most accurate unbiased interval.*

unbiased estimator– An **estimator** whose **expected value** or **mean** equals the true value of the **parameter** being estimated. Thus, an unbiased estimator on the **average** assumes a value equal to the true **population parameter.** An unbiased estimator neither systematically overestimates or underestimates the value of the parameter in question. Compare *biased estimator.*

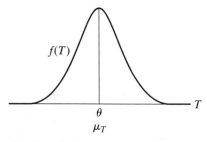

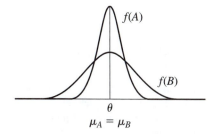

Sampling distribution of an unbiased estimator of θ

Sampling distribution of two unbiased estimators of θ with different variances

unbiased linear estimator– An **unbiased estimator** that is a **linear function** of **observations.**

unbiasedness– A term used to describe the property of an **unbiased estimator.** Compare *biasedness.* See also *biased estimator.*

uncertainty– A term denoting the lack of certainty inherent in a **random phenomenon.** When a coin is tossed it is uncertain whether it will turn up a head or tail. There is 0.5 **probability** that it will show up a head or tail. It is probability that is measurable, but not the uncertainty.

uncertainty analysis– A method of analysis carried out to determine the **variability** in the final **outcome** of a **variable** that is due to **uncertainty** inherent in the values of one or more input **parameters.** See also *sensitivity analysis.*

unconditional probability– A measure of the likelihood that a particular **event** occurs, irrespective of whether another event occurs or not. Compare *conditional probability.*

uncontrolled clinical trial– Same as *uncontrolled trial.*

uncontrolled trial– A clinical trial that has no **control group.** Compare *controlled trial.*

unequal probability sampling– A **sampling design** in which each **sampling unit** in a **population** has a different **probability** of being included in the **sample.** Unequal probability sampling can often reduce the **variance** of an **estimator** by sampling each unit with probability proportional to a measure of the size of the unit. **Cluster sampling** provides an ideal situation in which the unequal probability sampling, with probability proportional to the number of elements in the **cluster,** results in reducing the bound on the **error of estimation.**

unequal variance t test– When the **sample variances** (S_1^2 and S_2^2) suggest that there may be a problem in assuming that the two **population variances** are equal, we can modify the usual t **statistic** to obtain an approximate t test or t **confidence interval.** B. L. Welch in 1938 showed that the distribution of the **statistic**

$$t' = \frac{\bar{y}_1 - \bar{y}_2}{\sqrt{\dfrac{S_1^2}{n_1} + \dfrac{S_2^2}{n_2}}}$$

can be approximated by a t **distribution** with **degrees of freedom** (df) given by

$$\mathrm{df} = \frac{(n_1 - 1)(n_2 - 1)}{(n_2 - 1)c^2 + (1 - c)^2(n_1 - 1)} \qquad \text{where } c = \frac{S_1^2/n_1}{S_1^2/n_1 + S_2^2/n_2}$$

unexplained variation– In an **analysis of variance,** the **variation** of the **sample data** within each of the **samples** about the respective **sample means;** it is attributed to **chance** and equals the **total sum of squares** minus **explained variation.** In a **regression analysis,** it is the **sum of the squares** of all the unexplained **deviations.** It is also referred to as **error** or **residual sum of squares.**

unfair gamble– In the **theory of games,** a game of chance in which the **expected monetary gain** of what is being lost exceeds the expected monetary gain of what is being received. Compare *fair gamble.*

ungrouped data– **Data values** in their original form that have not been grouped into **class intervals** in order to reduce the number of scoring categories. Compare *grouped data.* See also *ungrouped frequency distribution.*

ungrouped frequency distribution– A **frequency distribution** that lists **frequencies** for individual **scores** that have not been grouped into **class intervals.** Compare *grouped frequency distribution.*

uniform distribution– A **distribution** that, in the continuous case, has a constant **density** over a given interval and, in the discrete case, assigns the same **probability** to each value within its domain. The **probability density function** of a **continuous random variable** is

$$f(x) = \frac{1}{\beta - \alpha} \qquad \alpha < x < \beta$$

The **probability function** of a **discrete random variable** is

$$p(x) = \frac{1}{k} \qquad x = x_1, x_2, \ldots, x_k$$

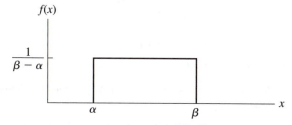

Probability distribution of a continuous random variable having a uniform distribution

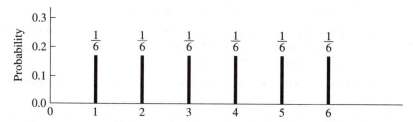

Probability distribution of a discrete random variable having a uniform distribution

uniformly most accurate interval– A **confidence interval** is said to be uniformly most accurate if the interval has a smaller **probability** of containing a value not equal to the true **parameter** value than any other interval with the same **confidence coefficient.**

uniformly most accurate unbiased interval– A **confidence interval** is said to be uniformly most accurate unbiased if it is uniformly most accurate within the class of all **unbiased confidence intervals.**

uniformly most powerful one-sided test– Same as *uniformly most powerful test.*

uniformly most powerful test– A test of a **hypothesis** against a composite alternative that is at least as powerful as any other test for all the values of the alternative and more powerful against one of the alternatives. In most situations, uniformly most powerful tests exist when the **alternative hypothesis** is constrained in some way; for example in testing $H_0: \theta = \theta_0$ against $H_1: \theta < \theta_0$ or $\theta > \theta_0$, but not both. If the test is uniformly most powerful for either one of the two sets of alternatives, it is called a uniformly most powerful one-sided test.

uniformly shortest length interval– A **confidence interval** is said to be uniformly short-est length if it has a shorter expected length than, or the shortest expected length of, any other interval with the same **confidence coefficient.**

unimodal distribution– A **distribution** having only one **mode.** See also *bimodal distribution, multimodal distribution, trimodal distribution.*

union of two events– The union of two **events** A and B, denoted by $A \cup B$, is the event that consists of all **outcomes** that belong to A, to B, or to both.

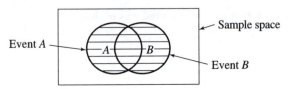

The shaded region depicits $A \cup B$

Figure showing union of two events A and B

unit normal (random) variable– A term used to denote a **normal random variable** with unit **standard deviation.**

unit of analysis– The level of aggregates that is being studied or investigated. The unit of analysis may be individuals, schools, hospitals, countries, and so forth.

univariable analysis– A term sometimes used in contradistinction to **univarite analysis** to refer to an analysis that contains one **independent variable** at a time.

univariate analysis– Statistical analysis involving **measurements** on only one **variable.** The term is used in contrast to **bivariate** and **multivariate analysis** involving measure-ments on two or more variables simultaneously.

univariate data set– A **data set** containing **measurement** values on one **variable** only.

univariate distribution– The **distribution** of a set of **scores** that measures only one **vari-able** at a time. This is the usual type of distribution that displays the score values for a single **random variable.**

univariate k statistic– See k *statistics.*

univariate normal distribution– Same as *normal distribution.*

universal set– In **set theory,** the set consisting of all elements.

universe– The aggregate values, of which the values observed in the **sample** constitute **a representative sample,** and to which the findings of the sample can be generalized. The universe may be a hypothetical or a real population of values, and it may be finite or infi-nite, depending on the type of sample and the nature of the information under study. In any statistical practice, the universe under study or investigation needs to be carefully circum-scribed. The term is more or less synonmous with **population.**

unreplicated factorial design– A term sometimes used for a 2^k **factorial design** contain-ing a single **replicate.**

unstandardized score– A **score** in the original unit that has not been transformed into a z **score** or any other **standard score.**

unweighted mean– An **arithmetic mean** of a set of **observations** in which no weights are assigned to them. Compare *weighted mean.*

unweighted means analysis– A method of analysis in two-way and higher-order **factorial designs** containing unequal numbers of **observations** in each **cell.** The procedure consists of calculating the **cell means** and then carrying out a **balanced data** analysis by assuming that the cell means constitute a single observation in each cell.

upper confidence limit– See *confidence limits.*

upper hinge– See *five-number summary.*

upper pth percentile– A value such that $100p\%$ of the **observations** in the **population** have **measurements** greater than this value and $100(1 - p)\%$ of the observations are less than its value.

upper real limit– See *real limits.*

upper-tailed test– A **one-tailed hypothesis test** in which the entire **rejection region** is located in the upper tail of the **sampling distribution** of the **test statistic.** See also *lower-tailed test, one-tailed test, two-tailed test.*

U. S. Bureau of the Census– Same as *Bureau of the Census.*

U-shaped distribution– An asymmetrical **frequency distribution** having general resemblance to the shape of the letter U. The **distribution** has maximum **frequencies** at both ends of the distribution, which decline rapidly at first and then more slowly, reaching a minimum between them.

utility– In **decision analysis,** the term used to denote the monetary value of an **outcome.** It is the gain often expressed in terms of money derived from the decision outcome.

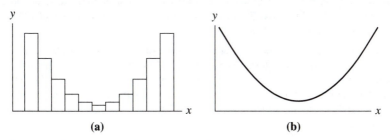

(a)   (b)

U-shaped distribution: **(a)** histogram and **(b)** continuous curve

utility analysis– In **decision analysis,** a method for making decisions under **uncertainty** that is based on certain axioms of rational behavior.

utility-of-money function– The relationship between alternative amounts of money a player might possess and the different utility values associated with these amounts.

utility theory– A branch of **decision theory,** in which **utilities** of different **outcomes** are assigned numerical values in order of preference, made by referring to the **expected monetary return** and the risks involved. The values range from 0 to 1, 0 being alloted to the least preferred and 1 to the most preferred outcome.

vague prior– A term used in **Bayesian statistics** to refer to a prior when the analyst lacks any information about the value of the unknown **parameter.** See also *informative prior, noninformative prior.*

validity– The property of a measuring instrument or test that measures the characteristic it is supposed to measure, i.e., the extent to which a **measurement** is free of any **systematic error.** It provides a measure of the **accuracy** of the concept it is intended to measure. The term is also used for a measurement or assessment that is not biased. See also *external validity, internal validity.*

validity checks– Routine checks in **data editing** to ensure that all the **data values** are correct within the allowable range. For example, an age of 193 years or a height of 123 inches clearly is not permissible a value.

variability– Variability refers to the characteristic of a set of **data points** to spread out and vary among themselves. It is the complementary quality to the **central tendency** of a **distribution.** The variability of a distribution is also referred to as its **dispersion, spread,** or **scatter.** Various **data sets** may have the same center but different amount of spreads. The **standard deviation** and **variance** are two of the most commonly used **measures of variability.**

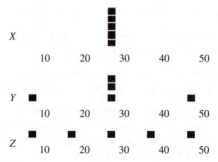

Three data sets with the same mean and
sample size but different amounts of spread

variable– Any quantity that varies; that is, an aspect or characteristic of a person, object, or situation that can assume different values. Examples of a variable are the height of men and the price on the New York Stock Exchange. The opposite of a variable is a **constant.** The term is often used as a clipped form of **random variable.**

variable sampling– A **sampling procedure** in which the characteristic of interest is measured on a numerical scale rather then merely classified by its quality or **attribute.** Compare *attribute sampling.*

variable selection– The problem of selecting the "best" possible set of **predictors** in using a **regression model.** See also *all subsets regression, backward elimination procedure, forward selection procedure, stepwise regression.*

variance– A **measure of variability** or **dispersion** of the values of a **data set** found by averaging the squared **deviations** about the **mean.** It is calculated by summing the squared deviations of the **data values** about the mean and then dividing the total by N if the data set is a **population** or by $n - 1$ if the data set is from a **sample.** See also *population variance, sample variance.*

variance analysis– Same as *analysis of variance.*

variance components– A term used to denote **variances** of **random effects** terms in an **analysis of variance** or **regression model.** Variance components are widely used in a variety of fields requiring the measurement of variance.

variance components model– In an **analysis of variance** or **regression model,** a term used to designate a **random** or a **mixed effects model.**

variance–covariance martix– Same as *covariance matrix.*

variance efficiency– See *efficiency.*

variance of the population– Same as *population variance.*

variance ratio– The **ratio** of two independent **estimates** of the **population variance.** The term is also used as an alternative name for the **F statistic.**

variance ratio distribution– Same as *F distribution.*

variance ratio test– Same as *F test.*

variance stabilizing transformation– The use of algebraic **transformation** on **data values** to make the **variances** constant for different groups of **data sets.** See also *data transformation.*

variate– A synonym for **variable.**

variate difference method– A technique for the analysis of **time-series data** whose **variations** stem from a systematic and a random component. It is based on the assumption that, if the systematic part of the series can be represented by a polynomial, then the successive differences will eliminate this component and thus help to estimate the **random variation.**

variation– The **scatter** or **variability** in **measurements** or **observations** of the same object or subject; that is, the extent to which observations are spread out. It may occur naturally or may represent an **error** in measurement. The term is often used as a synonym for **variability.**

vector– A one-dimensional **array** of numbers or mathematical objects. A row or column of a **matrix** constitutes a vector.

Venn diagram– A **graphical device** for symbolically representing the **sample space, events,** and operations of union, intersection, and complements involving events. Usually a rectangle is drawn to represent the sample space and various events are represented by circles contained within the rectangle. It is useful to demonstrate relationship or covariation among a set of events or **variables.**

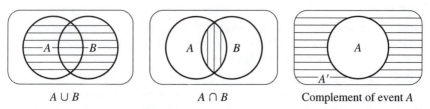

$A \cup B$ $A \cap B$ Complement of event A

Some examples of Venn diagrams

vertical axis– The **ordinate** or vertical dimension of a two-dimensional **cartesian graph.** It is also called the **y axis.**

vital index– Same as *birth–death ratio.*

vital statistics– The **statistics** on **mortality** and **morbidity** such as birth, death, marriage, and divorce; so called because they have to do with life (la vita). More loosely any information about health and sickness is referred to as vital statistics.

volunteer bias– A possible source of **bias** that occurs when the subjects in a study are volunteers rather than a **representative sample** of the **study population.** Studies have shown that volunteers in a study tend to be different from nonvolunteers in terms of demographic characteristics and other psychosocial profiles.

Wald–Wolfowitz run test– A **nonparametric test** for testing the **null hypothesis** that **the distribution functions** of two continuous **populations** are the same. The **observations** from two **independent samples** taken from respective populations are arranged in increasing order of magnitude, irrespective of the population from which they came. Each value is then replaced by 1 or 2, depending on the sample to which it originally belonged. The total number of **runs,** say U, of like elements, i.e., 1s or 2s, is then counted and used as the **test statistic.** If the two populations differ among themselves, elements of one type (1s or 2s) would be expected to cluster together, tending to make U small, whereas if the populations are identical, the arrangement of 1s or 2s should be **random,** tending to make U large. Thus, small values of U do not support the **hypothesis** and the appropriate *p* **value** is a left-tailed **probability.** The test has a very low **power;** its **asymptotic relative efficiency** compared to the traditional *t* **test** for equal **variances** is zero. Furthermore, it has the least power compared to other nonparametric tests applied to the same **data.** See also *Kolmogorov–Smirnov two-sample test.*

washout period– In a **crossover study,** the time interval allowed between the two consecutive **treatments** in order to control for the effect of the treatments given in one period to be carried over to the next period. It helps to reduce the **treatment period interactions** so that the effect of the second period can be assessed without being contaminated by the effect of the first period.

Weibull distribution– A **distribution** having the general **probability density function** given by

$$
f(x) = \begin{cases} \dfrac{\alpha}{\beta} \left(\dfrac{x-\gamma}{\beta} \right)^{\alpha-1} \exp\left[-\left(\dfrac{x-\gamma}{\beta} \right)^{\alpha} \right] & x > \gamma, \alpha > 0, \beta > 0 \\ 0 & \text{elsewhere} \end{cases}
$$

is known as a Weibull distribution. The **parameters** γ, α, and β determine the **location, shape,** and **scale,** respectively, of the distribution. The above distribution is the so-called three-parameter Weibull distribution. The two-parameter Weibull distribution has location at the origin, i.e., $\gamma = 0$, and its probability density function is given by

$$
f(x) = \begin{cases} \dfrac{\alpha}{\beta^{\alpha}} x^{\alpha-1} \exp\left[-(x/\beta)^{\alpha}\right] & x > 0, \alpha > 0, \ \beta > 0 \\ 0 & \text{elsewhere} \end{cases}
$$

The distribution was originally proposed to describe **data** from life testing. It can be used to model data involving a wide variety of shapes including both left- and right-skewed data sets.

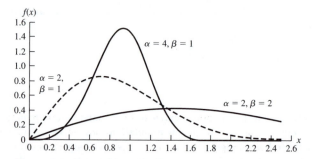

Probability density curves for Weibull distributions for various values of α and β

weighted average– An **average** formed by multiplying each number in a set of numbers by a value called a weight and then adding the resulting products and dividing it by the sum of the weights. In a **grouped frequency distribution,** the individual values are very often weighted by their respective **frequencies.** Weighted averages are frequently used for combining the **means** of two or more groups of different sizes to take into account the sizes of the groups in computing the overall or grouped mean. In many economic applications, weighted averages are frequently employed in the construction of **index numbers.** Price and quantity index numbers are examples of weighted averages.

weighted kappa statistic– A modified version of the **kappa statistic** that allows for the assignment of weight to the difference in the degrees of disagreement between the raters. The main difficulty in applying the weighted kappa lies in the determination of, and the justification for, a set of weights.

weighted least squares estimation– A general method of estimation in which **estimates** are obtained by minimizing a weighted sum of squares of the differences between the observed value and its predicted value in terms of the **statistical model** of interest. The weights employed are generally taken as the reciprocals of the **variances.** See also *least absolute deviation estimation, least squares estimation.*

weighted mean– Compare *unweighted mean.* Same as *weighted average.*

Welch's analysis of variance test– Same as *Welch's test.*

Welch's test– The **test procedure** used for testing the equality of a set of **treatment means** having unequal **population variances.** The **test statistic** is a generalization of the **two-sample** t **statistic** with unequal population variances. The test has been found to perform rather well, although it is little less robust to the **ANOVA *F* test** to departures from **normality.** A number of parametric alternatives to Welch's test have also been proposed. However, if the underlying **assumptions** of **ANOVA** are seriously violated, one should consider the possibility of a **nonparametric analysis** instead of either Welch or other parametric procedures.

Wilcoxon matched-pair signed rank test– Same as *Wilcoxon signed rank test.*

Wilcoxon rank-sum test– A **nonparametric test** used for detecting differences between two **location parameters** based on the analysis of two **independent samples.** The **test statistic** is formed by combining the two **samples, ranking** the **observations** in the combined sample, and summing the **ranks** of the observations belonging to one of the samples. It is used in place of the **two-sample *t* test** either because **scores** are ordinal in nature or because the **normality** or **homogeneity** assumptions cannot be satisfied. The test is equivalent to the **Mann–Whitney *U* test.** See also *normal scores test.*

Wilcoxon signed-rank test– A **nonparametric test** for detecting differences between two **location parameters** based on the analysis of two **matched** or **paired samples.** This procedure is used to compare two **correlated samples** of **scores** that cannot be compared by means of a **paired *t* test** either because the scores are ordinal in nature or because the **normality** and **homogeneity** assumptions cannot be met. The **test statistic** is formed by **ranking** the **absolute values** of the pairwise differences of two **samples** and summing the **ranks** with either the positive sign or negative sign (whichever sum is smaller).

Wilk's lambda– See *multivariate analysis of variance.*

Wishart distribution– A **multivariate distribution** of **variances** and **covariances** in a **sample** of given size from a **multivariate normal distribution.** For a **univariate distribution,** Wishart distribution reduces to that of a **chi-square distribution.** It also follows many of the properties of **chi-square variables.**

within-group mean square– Same as *mean square within groups.*

within-group sum of squares– Same as *sum of squares within groups.*

within-patient trial– Same as *crossover trial.*

within-sample sum of squares– Same as *sum of squares within groups.*

Woolfs' estimator– In a **stratified analysis** involving a series of **2×2 tables,** an **estimator** of the common **odds ratio** obtained as the **weighted average** of the odds ratio estimators from each individual table where the weights are inversely proportional to the **variances** of the individual estimators. It is calculated by the formula

$$\frac{\sum_{i=1}^{k} w_i \mathrm{OR}_i}{\sum_{i=1}^{k} w_i}$$

where $\mathrm{OR}_i = a_i d_i / b_i c_i$, $w_i = (1/a_i + 1/b_i + 1/c_i + 1/d_i)$; a_i, b_i, c_i, d_i are four **cell counts** in the ith table; and k is the number of 2×2 tables.

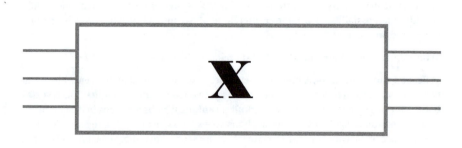

x axis– Same as *horizontal axis* or *abscissa*.

x-bar– An upper-or lower-case letter *x* with a line over the top of it ($\bar{x}$). It is often used to denote the **mean** of a **sample.**

x-bar chart– A **graphical device** used to control a process **average** by inspecting the **mean** of a set of **measurements** taken from various batches or subgroups (from a pilot set of about 20 rational subgroups). The values of mean taken from each subgroup are plotted along the **vertical axis** and can then be used to control within subgroup **variation.** The **center line** of the $\bar{x}$ chart is the average of all subgroup means ($\bar{\bar{x}}$). **Control lines** are fixed at three **standard deviations** from the center line, where the standard deviation is generally estimated from the **range.** In practice, the engineer sets the limits at $\bar{\bar{x}} \pm A_2 \bar{R}$ where $\bar{R}$ is the average of all the subgroup ranges and A_2 is a multiplier determined from some specially prepared tables. See also *c chart, control chart, p chart, run chart, s chart.*

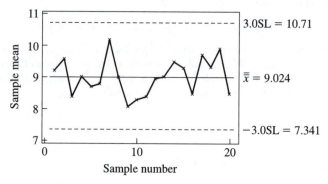

An example of an $\bar{x}$-chart

x coordinate– The distance measured parallel to the **x axis,** from the **y axis** to a point.

x distance– Same as *x coordinate.*

x **intercept–** The point where the **regression line** for *x* predicted on the basis of *y* crosses the **abscissa** is called the *x* intercept. This point marks the location of the regression line.

x^2 **statistic–** The term is commonly used to denote a **chi-square statistic** for testing the **independence** in a **contingency table** or testing the **goodness of fit** of a hypothesized **probability distribution** describing the characteristics of a **population.**

x **variable–** In a **simple regression analysis,** the term is used to refer the **independent** or **explanatory variable.** In a **scatter diagram,** it is plotted on the *x* **axis.**

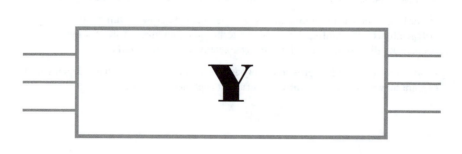

Yates' algorithm– An **algorithm** proposed by Frank Yates in 1937 for calculating **sums of squares** of all the **contrasts** simultaneously from a 2^k **factorial design.** The algorithm is fairly simple and can be easily carried out on a hand-held calculator.

Yates' correction for continuity– This is a procedure for correcting the **chi-square statistic** in a 2×2 **contingency table.** For each **cell,** the difference between the **observed** and **expected frequencies** is reduced by one-half (subtracting 0.5 from the positive difference and adding 0.5 to the negative difference). The general aim is to bring the **distribution** based on discontinuous **frequencies** nearer to the continuous **chi-square distribution.** However, the corrected chi-square distribution approximates more closely the **hypergeometric distribution** obtained by using **Fisher's exact test.** The procedure leads to a **conservative test** and has been the subject of a longstanding controversy among **statisticians.** See also *correction for continuity.*

y **axis–** Same as *vertical axis* or *ordinate.*

y **intercept–** The point where the **regression line** for *y* predicted on the basis of *x* crosses the **ordinate.** This point marks the location of the regression line.

Youden's index– An index designed to combine the **sensitivity** and **specificity** of a **diagnostic test** into a single number. For a 2×2 **table,** it is calculated by the formula $a/(a + c) + d/(b + d) - 1$, where a, b, c, and d are appropriate **cell counts.**

Youden square– A design constructed by rearranging a **balanced incomplete block design.** It has the property of "two-way control" of a **Latin square.** It is a special type of Latin square in which the number of rows, columns, and treatments are not all equal. If a column or row is deleted from a Latin square, the remaining layout is a Youden square.

Yule's *Q***–** A **measure of association** between two **nominal variables** measured on a dichotomous scale. It is a **symmetric measure of association** calculated for the **data** cross-classified in the form of a 2×2 **table.** Calculated by $(ad - bc)/(ad + bc)$.

y **variable–** In a **simple regression analysis,** the term is used to refer the **dependent** or **response variable.** In a **scatter diagram,** it is plotted on the *y* **axis.**

Z

z approximation– An approximation of a **test statistic** to the **standard normal distribution.**

z distribution– Same as *standard normal distribution.*

zero-order table– A **cross-tabulation** involving two **variables** without controlling for any other variable.

zero population growth– Absence of any growth in the population.

zero-sum game– In **theory of games,** any game in which one player can gain only at the expense of another and in which one player gains exactly the amount the other player loses.

z ratio– The **test statistic** used in the z **test.** It is calculated by subtracting the hypothesized **mean** from the observed mean and dividing the difference by the **standard error** of the mean.

z score– Same as *standard score.*

z statistic– Same as *z-ratio.*

z test– The **statistical test** for comparing a **mean** with a standard or hypothesized mean, comparing two means, or any other **test procedure** that is based on the z **statistic.** See also *z ratio.*

z transformation– A mathematical **transformation** that converts a normally distributed **variable** with **mean** μ and **standard deviation** σ to the **standard normal distribution** with mean 0 and standard deviation 1. The term is also used to denote a transformation of the **sample correlation coefficient** r by means of the formula

$$Z = \frac{1}{2} \log_e \left(\frac{1+r}{1-r} \right)$$

The latter transformation is also referred to as **Fisher's z transformation.**

Appendix A

The greek alphabet

Greek name	Capital letter	Small letter	Greek name	Capital letter	Small letter
alpha	A	α	nu	N	ν
beta	B	β	xi	Ξ	ξ
gamma	Γ	γ	omicron	O	o
delta	Δ	δ	pi	Π	π
epsilon	E	ε	rho	P	ρ
zeta	Z	ζ	sigma	Σ	σ
eta	H	η	tau	T	τ
theta	Θ	θ	upsilon	Υ	υ
iota	I	ι	phi	Φ	ϕ
kappa	K	κ	chi	X	χ
lambda	Λ	λ	psi	Ψ	ψ
mu	M	μ	omega	Ω	ω

Appendix B

Metric measures and their conversion: metric to British and British to metric

Metric measures

Length		Weight	
1000 micrometers	= 1 millimeter (mm)	1000 micrograms	= 1 milligram (mg)
10 millimeters	= 1 centimeter (cm)	10 milligrams	= 1 centigram (cg)
10 centimeters	= 1 decimeter (dm)	10 centigrams	= 1 decigram (dg)
10 decimeters	= 1 meter (m)	10 decigrams	= 1 gram (g)
10 meters	= 1 decameter (dam)	10 grams	= 1 decagram (dag)
10 decameters	= 1 hectometer (hm)	10 decagrams	= 1 hectogram (hg)
10 hectometers	= 1 kilometer (km)	10 hectograms	= 1 kilogram (kg)
		1000 kilograms	= 1 tonne

Volume and capacity		Area	
10 millimeters (mL)	= 1 cintiliter (cL)	1 are	= 100 square meters (m^2)
10 centiliters	= 1 deciliter (dL)	1 decare	= 10 ares
10 deciliters	= 1 liter (L)	1 hectare	= 100 ares
10 liters	= 1 decaliter (daL)	1 deciare	= 1/10 of an are
10 decaliters	= 1 hectoliter (hL)	1 centiare	= 1/100 of an are
10 hectoliters	= 1 kiloliter (kL)		= 1 square meter (m^2)

Conversion (Metric to British and British to Metric)

Length		Weight		Volume and Capacity	
1 cm	= 0.39370 in	1 g	= 0.03527 oz	1 cm^3	= 0.06102 cubic in (in^3)
1 m	= 39.37011 in	1 kg	= 2.20462 lb	1 m^3	= 1.30795 cubic yd (yd^3)
	= 3.28084 ft	1 tonne	= 0.98421 ton	1 liter	= 1.75980 pints
	= 1.09361 yd				= 0.21998 gallon
1 km	= 0.62137 mi	1 oz	= 28.34953 g	1 cubic in	= 16.38702 cubic cm (cm^3)
1 in	= 2.54000 cm	1 lb	= 0.45359 kg	1 cubic yd	= 0.76455 cubic m (m^3)
1 yd	= 0.91440 m	1 ton	= 1.01605 tonne	1 pint	= 0.56825 liter
1 mi	= 1.60934 km			1 gallon	= 4.54596 liters

Area			
1 cm^2 = 0.15500 in^2	1 hectare (ha) = 2.47106 acres	1 acre = 0.40469 hectare (ha)
1 m^2 = 1.19599 yd^2	1 in^2 = 6.45159 cm^2	1 m^2 = 2.58998 km^2
1 km^2 = 0.38610 m^2	1 yd^2 = 0.83613 m^2	

Appendix C

Some important constants

Number	log	Number	log
$\pi \approx 3.14159265$	0.4971499		
$2\pi \approx 6.28318531$	0.7981799	$\pi^2 \approx 9.86960440$	0.9942997
$4\pi \approx 12.56637061$	1.0992099	$\dfrac{1}{\pi^2} \approx 0.10132118$	$9.0057003 - 10$
$\dfrac{\pi}{2} \approx 1.57079633$	0.1961199	$\sqrt{\pi} \approx 1.77245385$	0.2485749
$\dfrac{\pi}{3} \approx 1.04719755$	0.0200286	$\dfrac{1}{\sqrt{\pi}} \approx 0.56418958$	$9.7514251 - 10$
$\dfrac{4\pi}{3} \approx 4.18879020$	0.6220886	$\sqrt{\dfrac{3}{\pi}} \approx 0.97720502$	$9.9899857 - 10$
$\dfrac{\pi}{4} \approx 0.78539816$	$9.8950899 - 10$	$\sqrt{\dfrac{4}{\pi}} \approx 1.12837917$	0.0524551
$\dfrac{\pi}{6} \approx 0.52359878$	$9.7189986 - 10$	$\sqrt[3]{\pi} \approx 1.46459189$	0.1657166
$\dfrac{1}{\pi} \approx 0.31830989$	$9.5028501 - 10$	$\dfrac{1}{\sqrt[3]{\pi}} \approx 0.68278406$	$9.8342834 - 10$
$\dfrac{1}{2\pi} \approx 0.15915494$	$9.2018201 - 10$	$\sqrt[3]{\pi^2} \approx 2.14502940$	0.3314332
$\dfrac{3}{\pi} \approx 0.95492966$	$9.9799714 - 10$	$\sqrt[3]{\dfrac{3}{4\pi}} \approx 0.62035049$	$9.7926371 - 10$
$\dfrac{4}{\pi} \approx 1.27323954$	0.1049101	$\sqrt[3]{\dfrac{\pi}{6}} \approx 0.80599598$	$9.9063329 - 10$

(Continued)

Some important constants (*Continued*)

e = Euler constant	≈ 2.71828183	0.43429448
$M = \log_{10} e$	≈ 0.43429448	$9.63778431 - 10$
$1/M = \log_e 10$	≈ 2.30258509	0.36221569
$180/\pi$ = grades in radian	≈ 57.2957795	1.75812263
$\pi/180$ = radians in $1°$	≈ 0.01745329	$8.24187737 - 10$
$\pi/10800 =$ radians in $1'$	≈ 0.0002908882	$6.46372612 - 10$
$\pi/648000 =$ radians in $1''$	$\approx 0.000004848136811095$	$4.68557487 - 10$
$\sin 1°$	$\approx 0.000004848136811076$	$4.68557487 - 10$
$\tan 1°$	$\approx 0.000004848136811133$	$4.68557487 - 10$
Centimeters in 1 foot	≈ 30.480	1.4840150
Feet in 1 centimeter	≈ 0.032808	$8.5159850 - 10$
Inches in 1 meter	≈ 39.37	1.5951654
Pounds in 1 kilogram	≈ 2.20462	0.3433340
Kilograms in 1 pound	≈ 0.453593	$9.6566663 - 10$

$$\pi \approx 3.14159\ 26535\ 89793\ 23846\ 26433\ 83280$$
$$e \approx 2.71828\ 18284\ 59045\ 23536\ 02874\ 71353$$
$$M \approx 0.43429\ 44819\ 03251\ 82765\ 11289\ 18917$$
$$1/M \approx 2.30258\ 50929\ 94045\ 68401\ 79914\ 54684$$
$$\log_{10} \pi \approx 0.49714\ 98726\ 94133\ 85435\ 12682\ 88291$$
$$\log_e \pi \approx 1.14472\ 98858\ 49400\ 17414\ 34273\ 51353$$

Appendix D

Some frequently used symbols and notations

Symbol/notation	Explanation
$=$	equal to
$\neq$	not equal to
$<$	less than
$>$	greater than
$\leq$	less than or equal to
$\geq$	greater than or equal to
$\equiv$	identical to
$\approx$	approximately equal to
$\cong$	congruent to
$\sim$	equivalent or similar
$:$	the ratio of, as the ratio of 4:7
$\|\ \|$	absolute value
$*$	over a Greek letter, an estimate (biased)
$\wedge$	over a Greek letter, an estimate (unbiased)
$\sqrt{\ }$	square root
$\cup$	union
$\cap$	intersection
$\subset$	is a subset of
$\supset$	contains as a subset
$\emptyset$	empty set or null set
Ω	universal set
e, exp	Euler's constant, approximately equal to 2.71828
$\log_a$	logarithm to the base a
$\log_e$, ln	natural logarithm or logarithm to the base e
$P(A)$	probability of an event A
$P(A|B)$	probability of A given B
$P(X = x)$	probability that a discrete random variable X assumes the value x
$E(X)$	expected value of a random variable X
$M_x(t)$	moment generating function of a random variable X
$\phi_x(t)$	characteristic function of a random variable X
$\bar{X}$	arithmetic mean of a sample
μ	arithmetic mean of a population
s	standard deviation of a sample

Symbol/notation	Explanation
σ^2	variance of a population (second moment about mean)
μ_r	the rth moment about mean
μ_r'	the rth moment about origin
$\sqrt{\beta_1}$	coefficient of skewness
β_2	coefficient of kurtosis
$A:B$	A divided by B
$\propto$	is proportional to
$[a, b]$	closed interval from a to b
(a, b)	open interval from a to b
$\ni$	such that
$A \cup B, A + B$	union of two sets A and B
$A \cap B, AB$	intersection of two sets A and B
$A - B$	difference of two sets A and B
$A = B$	identity of two sets A and B
$A \neq B$	inequality of two sets A and B
$A \subset B$	A is a proper subset of B
$A \supset B$	A contains B as a proper subset
$A \not\subset B$	A is not conatined in B or A is not a subset of B
$A \subseteq B$	A is a subset of B
$A \supseteq B$	A contains B
$\bar{A}$	complement of the set A
$\bigcup_{i=1}^{m} A_i$	the union of the sets $A_1, A_2, \ldots, A_m$
$\bigcap_{i=1}^{m} A_i$	the intersection of the sets $A_1, A_2, \ldots, A_m$
$x!$	x factorial
$\binom{n}{r}, {}^nC_r$	combination of n things taken r at a time
${}^nP_r$	permutation of n things taken r at a time
$\lim_{x \to a}$	limit as x approaches a
$\int f(x)\, dx$	integral of $f(x)$ with respect to x
$\int_b^a f(x)\, dx$	definite integral from a to b of $f(x)$ with respect to x
$\int f(x, y)\, dx$	integral of $f(x, y)$ with respect to x holding y constant
$\iint f(x, y)\, dx\, dy$	double integral of $f(x, y)$ with respect to x and y
χ^2	chi-square
z	Fisher's z statistic
t	Student's t statistic
F	F ratio
df	degrees of freedom
Q_1	first quartile
Q_2	second quartile
Q_3	third quartile
ANOVA	analysis of variance
ANCOVA	analysis of covariance
r	sample correlation coefficient

(Continued)

Symbol/notation	Explanation
ρ	population correlation coefficient
CV	coefficient of variation
$r_{12.34...n}$	partial correlation coefficient between variables 1 and 2 in a set of n variables
$R_{1.234...n}$	multiple correlation coefficient between variable 1 and the remainder of a set of n variables
H_0	null hypothesis
H_A, H_1	alternative hypothesis
α	population regression intercept (in a regression equation), significance level or probability of Type I error (in hypotesis testing)
β	population regression coefficient or slope (in a regression equation), probability of Type II error (in hypothesis testing)
$1 - \beta$	power

Appendix E

Some continuous probability distributions and their characteristics

Arc-Sine Distribution

Probability density function $f(x) = \dfrac{1}{\pi\sqrt{x(1-x)}}$ $0 < x < 1$

Mean: $\mu = 1/2$	Variance: $\sigma^2 = 1/8$	Skewness: $\sqrt{\beta_1} = 0$
Kurtosis: $\beta_2 = 3/2$		

Beta Distribution

Probability density function $f(x) = \dfrac{\Gamma(\alpha+\beta)}{\Gamma(\alpha)\Gamma(\beta)}x^{\alpha-1}(1-x)^{\beta-1}$ $0 < x < 1, \alpha, \beta > 0$

Mean: $\mu = \dfrac{\alpha}{\alpha+\beta}$	Variance: $\sigma^2 = \dfrac{\alpha\beta}{(\alpha+\beta)^2(\alpha+\beta+1)}$
Skewness: $\sqrt{\beta_1} = \dfrac{2(\beta-\alpha)(\alpha+\beta+1)^{1/2}}{(\alpha+\beta+2)(\alpha\beta)^{1/2}}$	Kurtosis: $\beta_2 = \dfrac{3(A+1)[2A^2+\alpha\beta(A-6)]}{\alpha\beta(A+2)(A+3)}$ where $A = \alpha+\beta$
Moment generating function: $M(\alpha, \alpha+\beta, t)$ where $M(p, q, x)$ denotes a confluent hypergeometric function	

Cauchy Distribution

Probability density function

$$f(x) = \frac{1}{b\pi}\left[1+\left(\frac{x-a}{b}\right)^2\right]^{-1} \qquad -\infty < x < \infty, -\infty < a < \infty, b > 0$$

Mean:	Variance:	Skewness:
Does not exist	Does not exist	Does not exist
Kurtosis:	**Moment generating function:**	**Characteristic function:**
Does not exist	Does not exist	$\phi_X(t) = \exp\left[ait - b\,|t|\right]$

Chi Distribution

Probability density function $f(x) = \dfrac{(x)^{n-1}e^{-x^2/2}}{2^{(n/2)-1}\Gamma(n/2)} \qquad 0 < x < \infty, n = 1, 2, 3, \ldots$

Mean:	Variance:
$\mu = \dfrac{\Gamma\left(\frac{n+1}{2}\right)}{\Gamma\left(\frac{n}{2}\right)}$	$\sigma^2 = \dfrac{\Gamma\left(\frac{n+2}{2}\right)}{\Gamma\left(\frac{n}{2}\right)} - \left[\dfrac{\Gamma\left(\frac{n+1}{2}\right)}{\Gamma\left(\frac{n}{2}\right)}\right]^2$

Chi-Square Distribution

Probability density function $f(x) = \dfrac{(x)^{(v/2)-1}e^{-x/2}}{2^{v/2}\Gamma(v/2)} \qquad 0 < x < \infty, v = 1, 2, 3, \ldots$

Mean:	Variance:	Skewness:
$\mu = v$	$\sigma^2 = 2v$	$\sqrt{\beta_1} = 2\sqrt{2}/\sqrt{v}$
Kurtosis:	**Moment generating function:**	**Characteristic function:**
$\beta_2 = 3 + 12/v$	$M_X(t) = (1-2t)^{-v/2}\, t < \dfrac{1}{2}$	$\phi_X(t) = (1-2it)^{-v/2}$

Erlang Distribution

Probability density function $f(x) = \dfrac{1}{\beta^n\Gamma(n)}x^{n-1}e^{-x/\beta} \qquad x \geq 0, \beta > 0, n = 1, 2, 3, \ldots$

Mean:	Variance:	Skewness:
$\mu = n\beta$	$\sigma^2 = n\beta^2$	$\sqrt{\beta_1} = 2/\sqrt{n}$
Kurtosis:	**Moment generating function:**	**Characteristic function:**
$\beta_2 = 3 + 6/n$	$M_X(t) = (1-\beta t)^{-n}$	$\phi_X(t) = (1-\beta it)^{-n}$

Exponential Distribution

Probability density function $f(x) = \dfrac{1}{\beta}e^{-x/\beta} \qquad x \geq 0, \beta > 0$

Mean:	Variance:	Skewness:
$\mu = \beta$	$\sigma^2 = \beta^2$	$\sqrt{\beta_1} = 2$
Kurtosis:	**Moment generating function:**	**Characteristic function:**
$\beta_2 = 9$	$M_X(t) = (1-\beta t)^{-1}$	$\phi_X(t) = (1-\beta it)^{-1}$

Extreme-Value Distribution

Probability density function

$$f(x) = \exp\left(-e^{-(x-\alpha)/\beta}\right) \qquad -\infty < x < \infty, -\infty < \alpha < \infty, \beta > 0$$

Mean:	Variance:	Skewness:
$\mu = \alpha + \gamma\beta$ $\gamma = 0.5772\ldots$ is Euler's constant	$\sigma^2 = \dfrac{\pi^2\beta^2}{6}$	$\sqrt{\beta_1} = 1.29857$
Kurtosis: $\beta_2 = 5.4$	Moment generating function: $M_X(t) = e^{\alpha t}\Gamma(1 - \beta t) \qquad t < \dfrac{1}{\beta}$	Characteristic function: $\phi_X(t) = e^{\alpha i t}\Gamma(1 - \beta i t)$

F Distribution

Probability density function

$$f(x) = \frac{\Gamma\left(\dfrac{\nu_1 + \nu_2}{2}\right)}{\Gamma\left(\dfrac{\nu_1}{2}\right)\Gamma\left(\dfrac{\nu_2}{2}\right)} \left(\frac{\nu_1}{\nu_2}\right)^{\nu_1/2} x^{(\nu_1/2)-1}\left(1 + \frac{\nu_1}{\nu_2}x\right)^{-(\nu_1+\nu_2)/2}$$

$$0 < x < \infty, \nu_1, \nu_2 = 1, 2, 3, \ldots$$

Mean:	Variance:
$\mu = \dfrac{\nu_2}{\nu_2 - 2} \qquad \nu_2 > 2$	$\sigma^2 = \dfrac{2\nu_2^2(\nu_1 + \nu_2 - 2)}{\nu_1(\nu_2 - 2)^2(\nu_2 - 4)} \qquad \nu_2 >$
Skewness: $\sqrt{\beta_1} = \dfrac{(2\nu_1 + \nu_2 - 2)[8(\nu_2 - 4)]^{1/2}}{(\nu_2 - 6)[\nu_1(\nu_1 + \nu_2 - 2)]^{1/2}} \quad \nu_2 > 6$	Kurtosis: $\beta_2 = 3 + \dfrac{12[a^2 b + \nu_1(\nu_1 + a)(5\nu_2 - 22)]}{\nu_1(\nu_2 - 6)(\nu_2 - 8)(\nu_1 + a)}$ where $a = \nu_2 - 2, b = \nu_2 - 4, \nu_2 > 8$
Moment generating function: Does not exist	Characteristic function: $\phi_X(t) = F\left[\dfrac{1}{2}\nu_1, -\dfrac{1}{2}\nu_2, \dfrac{\nu_2}{\nu_1}it\right]$ Here $F[\alpha, \beta, x]$ is the confluent hypergeometric function defined as $F[\alpha, \beta, x] = 1 + \dfrac{\alpha}{\beta \cdot 1!}x + \dfrac{\alpha(\alpha + 1)}{\beta(\beta + 1)2!}x^2 + \cdots$

Gamma Distribution

Probability density function $\qquad f(x) = \dfrac{1}{\Gamma(\alpha)\beta^\alpha}x^{\alpha-1}e^{-x/\beta} \qquad 0 < x < \infty, \alpha > 0, \beta > 0$

Mean:	Variance:	Skewness:
$\mu = \alpha\beta$	$\sigma^2 = \alpha\beta^2$	$\sqrt{\beta_1} = 2/\sqrt{\alpha}$
Kurtosis: $\beta_2 = 3 + 6/\alpha$	Moment generating function: $M_X(t) = (1 - \beta t)^{-\alpha}$	Characteristic function: $\phi_X(t) = (1 - \beta i t)^{-\alpha}$

Half-Normal Distribution

Probability density function $f(x) = \dfrac{2\theta}{\pi} e^{-\theta^2 x^2/\pi}$ $x \geq 0, \theta > 0$

Mean: $\mu = \dfrac{1}{\theta}$	Variance: $\sigma^2 = \left(\dfrac{\pi - 2}{2}\right)\dfrac{1}{\theta^2}$	Skewness: $\sqrt{\beta_1} = \dfrac{4 - \pi}{\theta^3}$
Kurtosis: $\beta_2 = \dfrac{3\pi^2 - 4\pi - 12}{4\theta^4}$		

LaPlace (Double Exponential) Distribution

Probability density function

$$f(x) = \frac{1}{2\beta} e^{-|x - \eta|/\beta} \qquad -\infty < x < \infty, \beta > 0, -\infty < \eta < \infty$$

Mean: $\mu = \eta$	Variance: $\sigma^2 = 2\beta^2$	Skewness: $\sqrt{\beta_1} = 0$
Kurtosis: $\beta_2 = 6$	Moment generating function: $M_X(t) = \dfrac{e^{\eta t}}{1 - \beta^2 t^2}$	Characteristic function: $\phi_X(t) = \dfrac{e^{\eta i t}}{1 + \beta^2 t^2}$

Logistic Distribution

Probability density function

$$f(x) = \frac{\exp[(x - \alpha)/\beta]}{\beta(1 + \exp[(x - \alpha)/\beta])^2} \qquad -\infty < x < \infty, -\infty < \alpha < \infty, \beta > 0$$

Mean: $\mu = \alpha$	Variance: $\sigma^2 = \dfrac{\beta^2 \pi^2}{3}$	Skewness: $\sqrt{\beta_1} = 0$
Kurtosis: $\beta_2 = 4.2$	Moment generating function: $M_X(t) = e^{\alpha t} \pi \beta t \csc(\pi \beta t)$	Characteristic function: $\phi_X(t) = e^{\alpha i t} \pi \beta i t \csc(\pi \beta i t)$

Lognormal Distribution

Probability density function

$$f(x) = \frac{1}{x\sigma\sqrt{2\pi}} e^{-(1/2)[(\ln x - \mu)/\sigma]^2} \qquad 0 < x < \infty, -\infty < \mu < \infty, \sigma > 0$$

Mean: $\mu = e^{\mu + (\sigma^2/2)}$	Variance: $\sigma^2 = e^{2\mu + \sigma^2}(e^{\sigma^2} - 1)$	Skewness: $\sqrt{\beta_1} = (e^{\sigma^2} + 2)(e^{\sigma^2} - 1)^{1/2}$
Kurtosis: $\beta_2 = e^{4\sigma^2} + 2e^{3\sigma^2} + 3e^{2\sigma^2} - 3$	Moment generating function: Does not exist in closed form	

Noncentral Chi-Square Distribution

Probability density function

$$f(x) = \frac{\exp\left[-\frac{1}{2}(x+\lambda)\right]}{2^{\nu/2}} \sum_{j=0}^{\infty} \frac{x^{(\nu/2)+j-1}\lambda^j}{\Gamma\left(\frac{\nu}{2}+j\right) 2^{2j} j!} \qquad x > 0, \lambda > 0, \nu = 1, 2, 3, \ldots$$

Mean:	Variance:	Skewness:
$\mu = \nu + \lambda$	$\sigma^2 = 2(\nu + 2\lambda)$	$\sqrt{\beta_1} = \dfrac{\sqrt{8}(\nu + 3\lambda)}{(\nu + 2\lambda)^{3/2}}$
Kurtosis:	**Moment generating function:**	**Characteristic function:**
$\beta_2 = 3 + \dfrac{12(\nu + 4\lambda)}{(\nu + 2\lambda)^2}$	$M_X(t) = (1 - 2t)^{-\nu/2}$ $\exp\left(\dfrac{\lambda t}{1 - 2t}\right)$	$\phi_X(t) = (1 - 2it)^{-\nu/2}$ $\exp\left(\dfrac{\lambda it}{1 - 2it}\right)$

Noncentral F Distribution

Probability density function

$$f(x) = \sum_{i=0}^{\infty} \frac{\Gamma\left(\frac{2i+\nu_1+\nu_2}{2}\right)\left(\frac{\nu_1}{\nu_2}\right)^{(2i+\nu_1)/2} x^{(2i+\nu_1-2)/2} e^{-\lambda/2}\left(\frac{\lambda}{2}\right)}{\Gamma\left(\frac{\nu_2}{2}\right)\Gamma\left(\frac{2i+\nu_1}{2}\right)\nu_1!\left(1 + \frac{\nu_1}{\nu_2}x\right)^{(2i+\nu_1+\nu_2)/2}} \qquad \begin{array}{l} x > 0; \lambda > 0; \\ \nu_1, \nu_2 = 1, 2, 3, \ldots \end{array}$$

Mean:		Variance:	
$\mu = \dfrac{(\nu_1 + \lambda)\nu_2}{(\nu_2 - 2)\nu_1}$	$\nu_2 > 2$	$\sigma^2 = \dfrac{(\nu_1 + \lambda)^2 + 2(\nu_1 + \lambda)\nu_2^2}{(\nu_2 - 2)(\nu_2 - 4)\nu_1^2} - \dfrac{(\nu_1 + \lambda)^2\nu_2^2}{(\nu_2 - 2)^2\nu_1^2}$	$\nu_2 > 4$

Noncentral t Distribution

Probability density function

$$f(x) = \frac{\nu^{\nu/2}}{\Gamma\left(\frac{\nu}{2}\right)} \frac{e^{-\delta^2/2}}{\sqrt{\pi}(\nu + x^2)^{(\nu+1)/2}} \sum_{i=0}^{\infty} \Gamma\left(\frac{\nu + i + 1}{2}\right)\left(\frac{\delta^i}{i!}\right)\left(\frac{2x^2}{\nu + x^2}\right)^{i/2}$$
$$-\infty < x < \infty, -\infty < \delta < \infty, \nu = 1, 2, 3, \ldots$$

rth moment about the origin:

$$\mu_r' = c_r \frac{\Gamma\left(\frac{\nu-r}{2}\right)\nu^{r/2}}{2^{r/2}\Gamma\left(\frac{\nu}{2}\right)} \qquad \nu > r$$

where
$$c_{2r-1} = \sum_{i=1}^{r} \frac{(2r-1)!\delta^{2r-1}}{(2i-1)!(r-i)!2^{r-i}}$$

$$c_{2r} = \sum_{r=0}^{r} \frac{(2r)!\delta^{2i}}{(2i)!(r-i)!2^{r-i}} \qquad r = 1, 2, 3, \ldots$$

Normal Distribution

Probability density function

$$f(x) = \frac{1}{\sigma\sqrt{2\pi}} e^{-(x-\mu)^2/2\sigma^2} \qquad -\infty < x < \infty, -\infty < \mu < \infty, \sigma > 0$$

Mean: $\mu = \mu$	Variance: $\sigma^2 = \sigma^2$	Skewness: $\sqrt{\beta_1} = 0$
Kurtosis: $\beta_2 = 3$	Moment generating function: $M_X(t) = \exp\left[\mu t + \dfrac{\sigma^2 t^2}{2}\right]$	Characteristic function: $\phi_X(t) = \exp\left[\mu i t - \dfrac{\sigma^2 t^2}{2}\right]$

Pareto Distribution

Probability density function

$$f(x) = \frac{\alpha \beta^\alpha}{x^{\alpha+1}} \qquad x \geq \beta, \alpha > 0, \beta > 0$$

Mean: $\mu = \dfrac{\alpha\beta}{\alpha - 1} \quad \alpha > 1$	Variance: $\sigma^2 = \dfrac{\alpha\beta^2}{(\alpha-1)^2(\alpha-2)} \quad \alpha > 2$
Skewness: $\sqrt{\beta_1} = \dfrac{2(\alpha+1)}{\alpha-3}\sqrt{\dfrac{\alpha-2}{\alpha}} \quad \alpha > 3$	Kurtosis: $\beta_2 = \dfrac{3(\alpha-2)(3\alpha^2+\alpha+2)}{\alpha(\alpha-3)(\alpha-4)} \quad \alpha > 4$
Moment generating function: Does not exist	

Rayleigh Distribution

Probability density function $\qquad f(x) = \dfrac{x}{\sigma^2} \exp\left(-\dfrac{x^2}{2\sigma^2}\right) \qquad x \geq 0, \sigma > 0$

Mean: $\mu = \sigma\sqrt{\pi/2}$	Variance: $\sigma^2 = 2\sigma^2\left(1 - \dfrac{\pi}{4}\right)$	Skewness: $\sqrt{\beta_1} = \dfrac{\sqrt{\pi}}{4}\dfrac{(\pi-3)}{\left(1-\frac{\pi}{4}\right)^{3/2}}$	Kurtosis: $\beta_2 = \dfrac{2 - \frac{3}{16}\pi^2}{\left(1-\frac{\pi}{4}\right)^2}$

t Distribution

Probability density function

$$f(x) = \frac{1}{\sqrt{\pi\nu}} \frac{\Gamma\left(\dfrac{\nu+1}{2}\right)}{\Gamma\left(\dfrac{\nu}{2}\right)} \left(1 + \frac{x^2}{\nu}\right)^{-(\nu+1)/2} \qquad -\infty < x < \infty, \nu = 1, 2, 3, \ldots$$

Mean:	Variance:	Skewness:
$\mu = 0 \quad \nu > 1$	$\sigma^2 = \dfrac{\nu}{\nu - 2} \quad \nu > 2$	$\sqrt{\beta_1} = 0 \quad \nu > 3$
Kurtosis: $\beta_2 = 3 + \dfrac{6}{\nu - 4} \quad \nu > 4$	Moment generating function: Does not exist	Characteristic function: $\phi_X(t) = \dfrac{\sqrt{\pi}\,\Gamma(\nu/2)}{\Gamma[(\nu + 1)/2]}$ $\displaystyle \int_{-\infty}^{\infty} \dfrac{e^{itz\sqrt{\nu}}}{(1 + z^2)^{(\nu+1)/2}}\, dz$

Triangular Distribution

Probability density function
$$f(x) = \begin{cases} 0 & x \le a \\ 4(x - a)/(b - a)^2 & a < x \le (a + b)/2 \\ 4(b - x)/(b - a)^2 & (a + b)/2 < x < b \\ 0 & x \ge b \end{cases}$$
$$-\infty < a < b < \infty$$

Mean:	Variance:	Skewness:
$\mu = \dfrac{a + b}{2}$	$\sigma^2 = \dfrac{(b - a)^2}{24}$	$\sqrt{\beta_1} = 0$
Kurtosis: $\beta_2 = \dfrac{12}{5}$	Moment generating function: $M_X(t) = \dfrac{4(e^{at/2} - e^{bt/2})^2}{t^2(b - a)^2}$	Characteristic function: $\phi_X(t) = \dfrac{4(e^{ait/2} - e^{bit/2})^2}{t^2(b - a)^2}$

Two-Parameter Exponential Distribution

Probability density function
$$f(x) = \frac{1}{\beta} e^{-(x-\eta)/\beta} \qquad \eta < x < \infty, \beta > 0$$

Mean:	Variance:	Skewness:
$\mu = \beta + \eta$	$\sigma^2 = \beta^2$	$\sqrt{\beta_1} = 2.0$
Kurtosis: $\beta_2 = 9.0$	Moment generating function: $M_X(t) = \dfrac{e^{\eta t}}{1 - \beta t}$	Characteristic function: $\phi_X(t) = \dfrac{e^{\eta it}}{(1 - \beta it)}$

Uniform Distribution

Probability density function
$$f(x) = \frac{1}{\beta - \alpha} \qquad \alpha \le x \le \beta, -\infty < \alpha < \beta < \infty$$

Mean:	Variance:	Skewness:
$\mu = \dfrac{\alpha + \beta}{2}$	$\sigma^2 = \dfrac{(\beta - \alpha)^2}{12}$	$\sqrt{\beta_1} = 0$
Kurtosis: $\beta_2 = \dfrac{9}{5}$	Moment generating function: $M_X(t) = \dfrac{e^{\beta t} - e^{\alpha t}}{(\beta - \alpha)t}$	Characteristic function: $\phi_X(t) = \dfrac{(e^{\beta it} - e^{\alpha it})}{(\beta - \alpha)it}$

Weibull Distribution

Probability density function $f(x) = \dfrac{\alpha}{\beta^\alpha} x^{\alpha-1} \exp[-(x/\beta)^\alpha]$ $0 < x < \infty, \alpha, \beta > 0$

Mean:	Variance:
$\mu = \beta\Gamma\left(\dfrac{\alpha+1}{\alpha}\right)$	$\sigma^2 = \beta^2\left[\Gamma\left(\dfrac{\alpha+2}{\alpha}\right) - \left\{\Gamma\left(\dfrac{\alpha+1}{\alpha}\right)\right\}^2\right]$
Skewness:	**Kurtosis:**
$\sqrt{\beta_1} = \dfrac{c - 3ab + 2a^3}{(b - a^2)^{3/2}}$	$\beta_2 = \dfrac{d - 4ac + 6a^2 b - 3a^4}{(b - a^2)^2}$
	where $a = \Gamma\left(\dfrac{\alpha+1}{\alpha}\right),\quad b = \Gamma\left(\dfrac{\alpha+2}{\alpha}\right)$
	$c = \Gamma\left(\dfrac{\alpha+3}{\alpha}\right),\quad \text{and}\quad d = \Gamma\left(\dfrac{\alpha+4}{\alpha}\right)$
Moment generating function:	**Characteristic function:**
$M_X(t) = \beta^t\Gamma(1 + t/\alpha)$	$\phi_X(t) = \beta^{it}\Gamma(1 + it/\alpha)$

Appendix F

Some discrete probability distributions and their characteristics

Bernoulli Distribution

Probability function $\quad p(x) = p^x q^{n-1} \quad\quad x = 0, 1$, where $q = 1 - p$

Mean: $\mu = p$	Variance: $\sigma^2 = pq$	Skewness: $\sqrt{\beta_1} = \dfrac{1 - 2p}{\sqrt{pq}}$
Kurtosis: $\beta_2 = 3 + \dfrac{1 - 6pq}{\sqrt{pq}}$	Moment generating function: $M_X(t) = q + pe^t$	Characteristic function: $\phi_X(t) = q + pe^{it}$
Probability generating function: $\psi_X(t) = q + pt$		

Beta-Binomial Distribution

Probability function

$$p(x) = \frac{1}{(n+1)} \frac{B(a + x, b + n - x)}{B(x + 1, n - x + 1)B(a, b)} \quad\quad x = 0, 1, 2, \ldots, n; \; a, b > 0; \; B(a, b) \text{ is the}$$

beta function

Mean: $\mu = \dfrac{na}{a + b}$	Variance: $\sigma^2 = \dfrac{nab(a + b + n)}{(a + b)^2(a + b + 1)}$

Beta-Pascal Distribution

Probability function

$$p(x) = \frac{\Gamma(x)\Gamma(v)\Gamma(\rho + v)\Gamma[v + x - (\rho + r)]}{\Gamma(r)\Gamma(x - r + 1)\Gamma(\rho)\Gamma(v - \rho)\Gamma(v + x)} \qquad x = r, r+1, \ldots; v > \rho > 0$$

Mean:	Variance:
$\mu = r\dfrac{v - 1}{\rho - 1} \qquad \rho > 1$	$\sigma^2 = r(r + \rho - 1)\dfrac{(v - 1)(v - \rho)}{(\rho - 1)^2(\rho - 2)} \qquad \rho > 2$

Binomial Distribution

Probability function $\quad p(x) = \binom{n}{x} p^x q^{(n-x)} \qquad x = 0, 1, 2, \ldots, n; 0 < p < 1; q = 1 - p$

Mean:	Variance:	Skewness:
$\mu = np$	$\sigma^2 = npq$	$\sqrt{\beta_1} = \dfrac{1 - 2p}{\sqrt{npq}}$
Kurtosis: $\beta_2 = 3 + \dfrac{1 - 6pq}{npq}$	**Moment generating function:** $M_X(t) = (q + pe^t)^n$	**Characteristic function:** $\phi_X(t) = (q + pe^{it})^n$
Probability generating function: $\psi_X(t) = (q + pt)^n$		

Geometric Distribution

Probability function $\quad p(x) = pq^{x-1} \qquad x = 1, 2, 3, \ldots; 0 < p < 1; q = 1 - p$

Mean:	Variance:	Skewness:
$\mu = \dfrac{1}{p}$	$\sigma^2 = \dfrac{q}{p^2}$	$\sqrt{\beta_1} = \dfrac{2 - p}{\sqrt{q}}$
Kurtosis: $\beta_2 = 3 + \dfrac{p^2 + 6q}{q}$	**Moment generating function:** $M_X(t) = \dfrac{pe^t}{1 - qe^t}$	**Characteristic function:** $\phi_X(t) = \dfrac{pe^t}{1 - qe^{it}}$
Probability generating function: $\psi_X(t) = \dfrac{pt}{1 - qt}$		

Hypergeometric Distribution

Probability function $\quad p(x) = \dfrac{\dbinom{M}{x}\dbinom{N-M}{n-x}}{\dbinom{N}{n}} \quad x = 0, 1, 2, \ldots, n;$

$$x \le M; n - x \le N - M; 1 \le n \le N; 1 \le M \le N; N = 1, 2, \ldots$$

Mean: $\quad \mu = \dfrac{nM}{N}$	**Variance:** $\quad \sigma^2 = \dfrac{nM}{N}\left[\dfrac{N-M}{N}\right]\left[\dfrac{N-n}{N-1}\right]$
Skewness: $\quad \sqrt{\beta_1} = \dfrac{(N-2M)(N-2n)(\sqrt{N-1})}{(N-2)\sqrt{nM(N-M)(N-n)}}$	**Kurtosis:** $\quad \beta_2 = \left[\dfrac{N^2(N-1)}{n(N-2)(N-3)(N-n)}\right](A+B)$ where $A = \dfrac{N(N+1) - 6n(N-n)}{M(N-M)}$ $B = \dfrac{3\left\{N^2(n-2) - Nn^2 + 6n(N-n)\right\}}{N^2}$
Moment generating function: $\quad M_X(t) = \dfrac{(N-M)!(N-n)!}{N!}$ $\times F(-n, -M, N-M-n+1, e^t)$	**Characteristic function:** $\quad \phi_X(t) = \dfrac{(N-M)!(N-n)!}{N}$ $\times F(-n, -M, N-M-n+1, e^{it})$

Probability generating function:

$$\psi_X(t) = \left[\frac{N-M}{N}\right]^n F\left(-n, -M, N-M-n+1, t\right)$$

where $F(\alpha, \beta, \gamma, x)$ is the hypergeometric function defined as

$$F(\alpha, \beta, \gamma, x) = 1 + \frac{\alpha\beta}{\gamma}\frac{x}{1!} + \frac{\alpha(\alpha+1)\beta(\beta+1)}{\gamma(\gamma+1)}\frac{x^2}{2!} + \cdots$$

Multinomial Distribution

Probability function $\quad p(x_1, \ldots, x_k) = \dfrac{n!}{x_1! \cdots x_k!} p_1^{x_1} \cdots p_k^{x_k} \quad x_i = 0, 1, 2, \ldots, n;$

$$\sum_{i=1}^{k} x_i = n; \sum_{i=1}^{k} p_i = 1$$

Mean: $\mu = np_i, i = 1, 2, \ldots, k$	**Variance:** $\sigma^2 = np_i(1 - p_i)$ $i = 1, 2, \ldots, k$	**Moment generating function:** $M_X(t) = (p_1 e^{t_1} + \cdots + p_k e^{t_k})^n$
Characteristic function: $\phi_X(t) =$ $(p_1 e^{it_1} + \cdots + p_k e^{it_k})^n$	**Probability generating function** $\psi_X(t) =$ $(p_1 t_1 + p_2 t_2 + \cdots + p_k t_k)^n$	

Negative Binomial Distribution

Probability function

$$p(x) = \binom{x-1}{r-1} p^r q^{x-r} \qquad x = r, r+1, \ldots; 0 < p < 1; q = 1 - p$$

Mean: $\mu = \dfrac{r}{p}$	Variance: $\sigma^2 = \dfrac{rq}{p^2}$	Skewness: $\sqrt{\beta_1} = \dfrac{2-p}{\sqrt{rq}}$
Kurtosis: $\beta_2 = 3 + \dfrac{p^2 + 6q}{rq}$	Moment generating function: $M_X(t) = \left(\dfrac{pe^t}{1 - qe^t}\right)^r$	Characteristic function: $\phi_X(t) = \left(\dfrac{pe^{it}}{1 - qe^{it}}\right)^r$
Probability generating function: $\psi_X(t) = \left(\dfrac{pt}{1 - qt}\right)^r$		

Poisson Distribution

Probability function $\quad p(x) = \dfrac{e^{-\lambda}\lambda^x}{x!} \qquad x = 0, 1, \ldots; \lambda > 0$

Mean: $\mu = \lambda$	Variance: $\sigma^2 = \lambda$	Skewness: $\sqrt{\beta_1} = \dfrac{1}{\sqrt{\lambda}}$
Kurtosis: $\beta_2 = 3 + \dfrac{1}{\lambda}$	Moment generating function: $M_X(t) = e^{\lambda(e^t - 1)}$	Characteristic function: $\phi_X(t) = e^{\lambda(e^{it} - 1)}$
Probability generating function: $\phi_X(t) = e^{\lambda(t-1)}$		

Uniform Distribution

Probability function $\quad p(x) = \dfrac{1}{n} \qquad x = 1, 2, \ldots, n$

Mean: $\mu = \dfrac{n+1}{2}$	Variance: $\sigma^2 = \dfrac{n^2 - 1}{12}$	Skewness: $\sqrt{\beta_1} = 0$
Kurtosis: $\beta_2 = \dfrac{3}{5}\left(3 - \dfrac{4}{n^2 - 1}\right)$	Moment generating function: $M_X(t) = \dfrac{e^t(1 - e^{nt})}{n(1 - e^t)}$	Characteristic function: $\phi_X(t) = \dfrac{e^{it}(1 - e^{nit})}{n(1 - e^{it})}$
Probability generating function: $\psi_X(t) = \dfrac{t(1 - t^n)}{n(1 - t)}$		

Appendix G

Relationships among distributions

This appendix exhibits relationships among some of the common univariate (discrete and continuous) distributions. The first line in each box gives the name of the distribution and the second line lists the parameters of the distribution. The flowchart, as shown on the next page, represents the three types of relationships: transformations (independent random variables are assumed) and special cases (both indicated with a solid arrow), and limiting distributions (indicated with a dashed arrow).

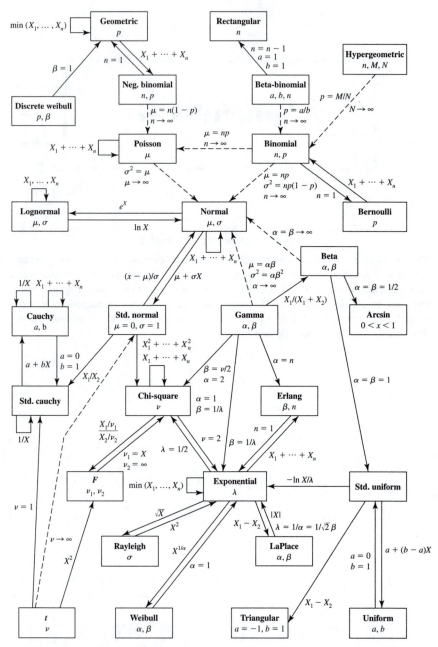

Adapted from Leemis, L. M. (1986), "Relationships among common univariate distributions," *The American Statistician*, Vol. 40, No. 2, pp. 143–146. With permission.

Appendix H

Maximum likelihood (ML) and unbiased estimators for parameters of some common probability distributions

Distribution	Parameter	ML estimator	Unbiased estimator
Uniform	α	$X_{(1)}$	$X_{(1)} - \left(\dfrac{X_{(n)} - X_{(1)}}{n-1} \right)$
	β	$X_{(n)}$	$X_{(n)} + \left(\dfrac{X_{(n)} - X_{(1)}}{n-1} \right)$
Normal	μ	$\overline{X}$	$\overline{X}$
	σ^2	$\displaystyle\sum_{i=1}^{n} \frac{(X_i - \overline{X})^2}{n}$	$\displaystyle\sum_{i=1}^{n} \frac{(X_i - \overline{X})^2}{n-1}$
Exponential	θ	$\dfrac{1}{\overline{X}}$	$\dfrac{n-1}{n\,\overline{X}}$
Poisson	λ	$\overline{X}$	$\overline{X}$
Binomial	p	$\dfrac{Y}{n}$	$\dfrac{Y}{n}$
Negative binomial	p	$\dfrac{k}{\overline{X}}$	$\dfrac{k(n-1)}{n\,\overline{X}}$
Geometric	p	$\dfrac{1}{\overline{X}}$	$\dfrac{n-1}{n\,\overline{X}}$

Note: $X_{(n)} = \max(X_{(1)}, X_{(2)}, \ldots, X_{(n)})$
$X_{(1)} = \min(X_{(1)}, X_{(2)}, \ldots, X_{(n)})$
$\overline{X} = (X_1 + X_2 + \cdots + X_n)/n$
Y = total number of successes
k = number of items in a population labeled "successes"
n = sample size

Appendix I

Some important statistical formulas

Classification of Data

Relative frequency of a class
$$\frac{\text{Frequency of the class}}{\text{Total frequency}}$$

Approximate number of classes
$$\frac{\text{Largest data value} - \text{smallest data value}}{\text{Class width}}$$

Real lower limit (lower class boundary)
$$(\text{Apparent lower limit}) - \frac{1}{2}(\text{unit difference})$$

Real upper limit (upper class boundary)
$$(\text{Apparent upper limit}) - \frac{1}{2}(\text{unit difference})$$

Midpoint of a class
$$\frac{\text{Lower class limit} + \text{upper class limit}}{2}$$

Frequency density of a class
$$\frac{\text{Frequency of the class}}{\text{Class size}}$$

Descriptive Statistics

Finite population mean

    Ungrouped data
$$\mu = \frac{\sum_{i=1}^{N} X_i}{N}$$

    Grouped data
$$\mu = \frac{\sum_{i=1}^{k} f_i X_i}{\sum_{i=1}^{k} f_i}$$

Sample mean

    Ungrouped data
$$\bar{x} = \frac{\sum_{i=1}^{n} x_i}{n}$$

Grouped data

$$\bar{x} = \frac{\sum\limits_{i=1}^{k} f_i x_i}{\sum\limits_{i=1}^{k} f_i}$$

Weighted arithmetic mean

$$\bar{x}_w = \frac{\sum\limits_{i=1}^{n} w_i x_i}{\sum\limits_{i=1}^{n} w_i}$$

Geometric mean
    Ungrouped data

$$GM = \sqrt[n]{x_1 x_2 \ldots x_n}$$

    grouped data

$$GM = \left(\prod_{i=1}^{k} x_i^{f_i} \right)^{1 \Big/ \sum\limits_{i=1}^{k} f_i}$$

Harmonic mean

    Ungrouped data

$$HM = \frac{n}{\sum\limits_{i=1}^{n} \frac{1}{x_i}}$$

    Grouped data

$$HM = \frac{\sum\limits_{i=1}^{k} f_i}{\sum\limits_{i=1}^{k} \left(\frac{f_i}{x_i} \right)}$$

Median
Ungrouped data
        odd number of observations — the $(n+1)/2$ th observation in an ordered set
        even number of observations — mean of $(n/2)$th and $(n/2+1)$th observations in an ordered set

Grouped data

$$\text{Median} = l_1 + \frac{h}{f} \left(\frac{N}{2} - CF \right)$$

where ℓ_1 = lower class boundary of the median class
     h = size of the class interval of the median class
     f = frequency of the median class
     N = total frequency
    CF = cumulative frequency preceding the median class
     Median class is the $(N/2)$th frequency class

Mode
    Ungrouped data — Most frequent data value

    Grouped data

$$\text{Mode} = \ell_1 + \left(\frac{f_m - f_1}{2f_m - f_1 - f_2} \right) \times h$$

where ℓ_1 = lower class boundary of the modal class
     h = size of the class interval of the modal class
    f_m = frequency of the modal class
     f_1 = frequency preceding the modal class
     f_2 = frequency following the modal class
     Modal class is the most frequent data class

Mean deviation about mean

Ungrouped data

$$MD = \frac{\sum\limits_{i=1}^{n} |x_i - \bar{x}|}{n}$$

Grouped data

$$MD = \frac{\sum\limits_{i=1}^{k} f_i |x_i - \bar{x}|}{\sum\limits_{i=1}^{k} f_i}$$

Mean deviation about median

Ungrouped data

$$MD = \frac{\sum\limits_{i=1}^{n} |x_i - \tilde{x}|}{n}$$

Grouped data

$$MD = \frac{\sum\limits_{i=1}^{k} f_i |x_i - \tilde{x}|}{\sum\limits_{i=1}^{k} f_i}$$

Range   Largest data value − Smallest data value
Finite population variance

Ungrouped data

$$\sigma^2 = \frac{\sum\limits_{i=1}^{N} (X_i - \mu)^2}{N}$$

Ungrouped data (computing formula)

$$\sigma^2 = \frac{\sum\limits_{i=1}^{N} X_i^2 - \left(\sum\limits_{i=1}^{N} X_i\right)^2 \Big/ N}{N}$$

Grouped data

$$\sigma^2 = \frac{\sum\limits_{i=1}^{k} f_i (X_i - \mu)^2}{\sum\limits_{i=1}^{k} f_i}$$

Grouped data (computing formula)

$$\sigma^2 = \frac{\sum\limits_{i=1}^{k} f_i X_i^2 - \left(\sum\limits_{i=1}^{k} f_i X_i\right)^2 \Big/ \sum\limits_{i=1}^{k} f_i}{\sum\limits_{i=1}^{k} f_i}$$

Sample variance

Ungrouped data

$$s^2 = \frac{\sum\limits_{i=1}^{n} (x_i - \bar{x})^2}{n - 1}$$

Ungrouped data (computing formula)

$$s^2 = \frac{\sum\limits_{i=1}^{n} x_i^2 - \left(\sum\limits_{i=1}^{n} x_i\right)^2 \Big/ n}{n - 1}$$

Grouped data

$$s^2 = \frac{\sum\limits_{i=1}^{k} f_i (x_i - \bar{x})^2}{\sum\limits_{i=1}^{k} f_i - 1}$$

Grouped data (computing formula)

$$s^2 = \frac{\displaystyle\sum_{i=1}^{k} f_i x_i^2 - \left(\sum_{i=1}^{k} f_i x_i\right)^2 \Big/ \sum_{i=1}^{k} f_i}{\displaystyle\sum_{i=1}^{k} f_i - 1}$$

Standard deviation
Population

$$\sigma = \sqrt{\sigma^2}$$

Sample

$$s = \sqrt{\frac{\displaystyle\sum_{i=1}^{n} (x_i - \bar{x})^2}{n - 1}}$$

Coefficient of variation
Covariance

$$\left(\frac{\text{Standard deviation}}{\text{Mean}}\right) \times 100\%$$

Population

$$\sigma_{xy} = \frac{\displaystyle\sum_{i=1}^{N} (X_i - \mu_x)(Y_i - \mu_y)}{N}$$

Sample

$$s_{xy} = \frac{\displaystyle\sum_{i=1}^{n} (x_i - \bar{x})(y_i - \bar{y})}{n - 1}$$

Probability

Probability of an event

$$P(A) = \frac{\text{number of outcomes in event } A}{\text{number of equally likely and mutually exclusive outcomes in the sample space}}$$

Complement rule

$$P(A) = 1 - P(\bar{A}) \qquad \text{or} \qquad P(\bar{A}) = 1 - P(A)$$

Addition rule
    For two events

$$P(A \cup B) = P(A) + P(B) - P(A \cap B)$$
$$P(A \cup B) = P(A) + P(B) \qquad \text{if } A \text{ and } B \text{ are mutually exclusive}$$
$$P(A \cup B) = P(A) + P(B) - P(A)P(B) \qquad \text{if } A \text{ and } B \text{ are independent}$$

    For three events

$$P(A \cup B \cup C) = P(A) + P(B) + P(C) - P(A \cap B)$$
$$- P(A \cap C) - P(B \cap C) + P(A \cap B \cap C)$$

    For n events

$$P\left(\bigcup_{i=1}^{n} A_i\right) = \sum_{i=1}^{n} P(A_i) - \sum_{i<j} P(A_i \cap A_j) + \sum_{i<j<k} P(A_i \cap A_j \cap A_k)$$
$$- \cdots + (-1)^{n+1} P\left(\bigcap_{i=1}^{n} A_i\right)$$

Conditional probability

$$P(A \mid B) = \frac{P(A \cap B)}{P(B)} \qquad \text{provided } P(B) \neq 0$$

$$P(B \mid A) = \frac{P(A \cap B)}{P(A)} \qquad \text{provided } P(A) \neq 0$$

Multiplication rule
    For two events

$$P(A \cap B) = P(A)P(B \mid A) = P(B)P(A \mid B)$$
$$P(A \cap B) = P(A)P(B) \qquad \text{if A and B are independent}$$

    For three events

$$P(A \cap B \cap C) = P(A)P(B \mid A)P(C \mid A \cap B)$$
$$P(A \cap B \cap C) = P(A)P(B)P(C) \qquad \text{if } A, B, C \text{ are independent}$$

Theorem of total probability

$$P(A) = P(A \mid B_1)P(B_1) + P(A \mid B_2)P(B_2) + \cdots + P(A \mid B_n)P(B_n)$$

Bayes' theorem $$P(B_i \mid A) = \frac{P(A \mid B_i)P(B_i)}{P(A \mid B_1)P(B_1) + P(A \mid B_2)P(B_2) + \cdots + P(A \mid B_n)P(B_n)}$$

Mathematical Expectation

Expected value (mean) of a random variable

     Discrete
$$\mu = E(X) = \sum_x x\,p(x)$$

     Continuous
$$\mu = E(X) = \int_{-\infty}^{\infty} x f(x)\, dx$$

Variance of a random variable

     Discrete
$$\sigma^2 = \mathrm{Var}(X) = \sum_x (x - \mu)^2 p(x)$$

     Continuous
$$\sigma^2 = \mathrm{Var}(X) = \int_{-\infty}^{\infty} (x - \mu)^2 f(x)$$

Variance of a random variable (computational formula)

     Discrete
$$\sigma^2 = \mathrm{Var}(X) = \sum_x x^2 p(x) - \mu^2$$

     Continuous
$$\sigma^2 = \mathrm{Var}(X) = \int_{-\infty}^{\infty} x^2 f(x)\, dx - \mu^2$$

Properties of the mean and variance of a random variable
If X is a random variable and a and b are any arbitrary constants, then

     Mean of $(a + bX)$ $\mu_{(a+bX)} = a + b\mu_X$

     Variance of $(a + bX)$ $\sigma_{(a+bX)}^2 = b^2\sigma_X^2$

Properties of a discrete probability
distribution $p(x)$

     1. $p(x) \geq 0$ for any value of x

     2. $\sum_x p(x) = 1$

Properties of a continuous probability
distribution $f(x)$

     1. $f(x) \geq 0$ for any value of x

     2. $\int_{-\infty}^{\infty} f(x)\, dx = 1$

Moment generating function (about origin)

     Discrete
$$M_X(t) = E(e^{tX}) = \sum_X e^{tx} p(x)$$

     Continuous
$$M_X(t) = E(e^{tX}) = \int_{-\infty}^{\infty} e^{tx} f(x)\, dx$$

Moment generating function (about mean)

     Discrete
$$M_{(X-\mu)}(t) = E\left(e^{t(X-\mu)}\right) = e^{-\mu t} \sum_x e^{tx} p(x)$$

     Continuous
$$M_{(X-\mu)}(t) = E\left(e^{t(X-\mu)}\right) = e^{-\mu t} \int_{-\infty}^{\infty} e^{tx} f(x)\, dx$$

Characteristic function (about origin)

Discrete
$$\phi_X(t) = E(e^{itX}) = \sum_x e^{itx} p(x)$$

Continuous
$$\phi_X(t) = E(e^{itX}) = \int_{-\infty}^{\infty} e^{itx} f(x) dx$$

$\left.\begin{array}{c}\\ \\ \\ \\ \\ \end{array}\right\} i = \sqrt{-1}$

Characteristic function (about mean)

Discrete
$$\phi_{X-\mu}(t) = E\left(e^{it(X-\mu)}\right) = e^{-i\mu t} \sum_x e^{itx} p(x)$$

Continuous
$$\phi_{X-\mu}(t) = E\left(e^{it(X-\mu)}\right) = e^{-i\mu t} \int_{-\infty}^{\infty} e^{itx} f(x) dx$$

$\left.\begin{array}{c}\\ \\ \\ \\ \\ \end{array}\right\} i = \sqrt{-1}$

Combinatorics

Number of permutations

For n distinct objects taken all together

$$n! = n(n-1)(n-2)\cdots 3\cdot 2\cdot 1$$

For n distinct objects taken r at a time

$$P_r^n = \frac{n!}{(n-r)!}$$

For n objects in which n_1 are of first kind, n_2 are of second kind, ..., n_k are of kth kind, such that $n_1 + n_2 + \cdots + n_k = n$

$$\frac{n!}{n_1!n_2!\cdots n_k!}$$

Circular arrangement for n distinct objects

$$(n-1)!$$

Number of combinations

For r objects selected from n distinct objects

$$\binom{n}{r} = {}^nC_r = \frac{n!}{r!(n-r)!}$$

Number of experimental outcomes with r successes in n Bernoulli trials

$$\frac{n!}{r!(n-r)!}$$

Binomial expansion

$$(a+b)^n = \sum_{k=0}^{n} \binom{n}{k} a^k b^{n-k}$$

Multiplicative rule

Total number of possible outcomes for a sequence of k events in which the first one has n_1 possibilities, the second one has n_2 possibilities, the third one has n_3 possibilities, ..., and the kth event has n_k possibilities

$$n_1 \cdot n_2 \cdot n_3 \cdots n_k$$

Total number of possible outcomes for a sequence of k events in which each event has n possibilities

$$n^k$$

Sampling Distributions

Inferences about a population mean μ and variance σ^2

Sample mean

$$\bar{X} = \frac{\sum_{i=1}^{n} X_i}{n}$$

Sample variance

$$S^2 = \frac{\sum_{i=1}^{n} (X_i - \bar{X})^2}{n-1}$$

Sample standard deviation

$$S = \sqrt{S^2}$$

Expected value of $\bar{X}$

$$E(\bar{X}) = \mu$$

Standard deviation of $\bar{X}$
(with correction for finite population)

$$\sigma_{\bar{X}} = \sqrt{\frac{N-n}{N-1}} \frac{\sigma}{\sqrt{n}}$$

Standard deviation of $\bar{X}$
(without correction for finite population, if
the sample size is less than or equal to 5%
of the population size)

$$\sigma_{\bar{X}} = \frac{\sigma}{\sqrt{n}}$$

Sampling distribution of $\bar{X}$
(when parent population is normal
and σ^2 is known)

$$Z = \frac{\bar{X} - \mu}{\sigma/\sqrt{n}}$$

Sampling distribution of $\bar{X}$
(when parent population is not necessarily
normal, σ^2 is unknown, and sample is large)

$$Z = \frac{\bar{X} - \mu}{S/\sqrt{n}}$$

Sampling distribution of $\bar{X}$
(when parent population is normal, σ^2 is
unknown, and sample is small)

$$t_{n-1} = \frac{\bar{X} - \mu}{S/\sqrt{n}}$$

Sampling distribution of S^2
(when parent population is normal and the
mean μ is unknown)

$$\chi^2_{n-1} = \frac{(n-1)S^2}{\sigma^2}$$

Inferences about a population proportion p

Sample proportion $\bar{p}$

$$\bar{p} = \frac{\sum_{i=1}^{n} x_i}{n} \qquad x_i = 0, 1$$

Sample variance

$$S^2 = \frac{\bar{p}(1 - \bar{p})}{n}$$

Sample standard deviation

$$S = \sqrt{\frac{\bar{p}(1 - \bar{p})}{n}}$$

Expected value of $\bar{p}$

$$E(\bar{p}) = p$$

Standard deviation of $\bar{p}$
(with correction for finite population)

$$\sigma_{\bar{p}} = \sqrt{\frac{N-n}{N-1} \frac{p(1-p)}{n}}$$

Standard deviation of $\bar{p}$
(without correction for finite population,
if the sample size is less than or equal to
5% of the population size)

$$\sigma_{\bar{p}} = \sqrt{\frac{p(1-p)}{n}}$$

Sampling distribution of $\bar{p}$
[when p is known and sample is large
$(np(1 - p) \geq 5)$]

$$Z = \frac{\bar{p} - p}{\sqrt{p(1 - p)/n}}$$

Sampling distribution of $\bar{p}$
[when p is unknown and sample is large
$(n\bar{p}(1 - \bar{p}) \geq 5)$]

$$Z = \frac{\bar{p} - p}{\sqrt{\bar{p}(1 - \bar{p})/n}}$$

Inferences about the difference between two population means $(\mu_1 - \mu_2)$

Sample means
$$\bar{X}_1 = \frac{\sum_{i=1}^{n_1} X_{1i}}{n_1} \qquad \bar{X}_2 = \frac{\sum_{i=1}^{n_2} X_{2i}}{n_2}$$

Sample variances
$$S_1^2 = \frac{\sum_{i=1}^{n_1} (X_{1i} - \bar{X}_1)^2}{n_1 - 1} \qquad S_2^2 = \frac{\sum_{i=1}^{n_2} (X_{2i} - \bar{X}_2)^2}{n_2 - 1}$$

Sample standard deviations $\qquad S_1 = \sqrt{S_1^2} \qquad S_2 = \sqrt{S_2^2}$

Expected value of $\bar{X}_1 - \bar{X}_2$ $\qquad E(\bar{X}_1 - \bar{X}_2) = \mu_1 - \mu_2$

Standard deviation of $\bar{X}_1 - \bar{X}_2$
$$\sigma_{\bar{X}_1 - \bar{X}_2} = \sqrt{\frac{\sigma_1^2}{n_1} + \frac{\sigma_2^2}{n_2}}$$

Sampling distribution of $\bar{X}_1 - \bar{X}_2$
(when parent populations are normal
and σ_1^2 and σ_2^2 are known)
$$Z = \frac{(\bar{X}_1 - \bar{X}_2) - (\mu_1 - \mu_2)}{\sqrt{(\sigma_1^2/n_1) + (\sigma_2^2/n_2)}}$$

Sampling distribution of $\bar{X}_1 - \bar{X}_2$
(when parent populations are not necessarily
normal, σ_1^2 and σ_2^2 are unknown, and samples
are large)
$$Z = \frac{(\bar{X}_1 - \bar{X}_2) - (\mu_1 - \mu_2)}{\sqrt{(S_1^2/n_1) + (S_2^2/n_2)}}$$

Sampling distribution of $\bar{X}_1 - \bar{X}_2$
(when parent populations are normal, σ_1^2
and σ_2^2 are unknown, $\sigma_1^2 = \sigma_2^2$, and samples
are small)
$$t_v = \frac{(\bar{X}_1 - \bar{X}_2) - (\mu_1 - \mu_2)}{S_p \sqrt{(1/n_1) + (1/n_2)}}$$

$$\text{where } S_p = \sqrt{\frac{(n_1 - 1)S_1^2 + (n_2 - 1)S_2^2}{n_1 + n_2 - 2}}$$

$$v = n_1 + n_2 - 2$$

Sampling distribution of $\bar{X}_1 - \bar{X}_2$
(when parent populations are normal, σ_1^2
and σ_2^2 are unknown, $\sigma_1^2 \neq \sigma_2^2$, and samples
are small)
$$t_v = \frac{(\bar{X}_1 - \bar{X}_2) - (\mu_1 - \mu_2)}{\sqrt{(S_1^2/n_1) + (S_2^2/n_2)}}$$

$$\text{where } v' = \frac{\left(\frac{s_1^2}{n_1} + \frac{s_2^2}{n_2}\right)^2}{\frac{(s_1^2/n_1)^2}{n_1-1} + \frac{(s_2^2/n_2)^2}{n_2-1}}$$

Inferences about the difference between two population proportions $(p_1 - p_2)$

Sample proportions
$$\bar{p}_1 = \frac{\sum_{i=1}^{n_1} x_{1i}}{n_1} \qquad \bar{p}_2 = \frac{\sum_{i=1}^{n_2} x_{2i}}{n_2}$$

$$x_{1i}, x_{2i} = 0, 1$$

Sample variances
$$S_1^2 = \frac{\bar{p}_1(1 - \bar{p}_1)}{n_1} \qquad S_2^2 = \frac{\bar{p}_2(1 - \bar{p}_2)}{n_2}$$

Sample standard deviations
$$S_1 = \sqrt{\frac{\bar{p}_1(1 - \bar{p}_1)}{n_1}} \qquad S_2 = \sqrt{\frac{\bar{p}_2(1 - \bar{p}_2)}{n_2}}$$

Expected value of $(\bar{p}_1 - \bar{p}_2)$ $\qquad E(\bar{p}_1 - \bar{p}_2) = p_1 - p_2$

Standard deviation of $(\bar{p}_1 - \bar{p}_2)$
$$\sigma_{\bar{p}_1-\bar{p}_2} = \sqrt{\frac{p_1(1-p_1)}{n_1} + \frac{p_2(1-p_2)}{n_2}}$$

Sampling distribution of $(\bar{p}_1 - \bar{p}_2)$
[when p_1 and p_2 are known and
samples are large
$(n_1 p_1(1-p_1) \geq 5, n_2 p_2(1-p_2) \geq 5)$]
$$Z = \frac{(\bar{p}_1 - \bar{p}_2) - (p_1 - p_2)}{\sqrt{\frac{p_1(1-p_1)}{n_1} + \frac{p_2(1-p_2)}{n_2}}}$$

Sampling distribution of $\bar{p}_1 - \bar{p}_2$
[when p_1 and p_2 are unknown and
samples are large
$(n_1 \bar{p}_1(1-\bar{p}_1) \geq 5, n_2 \bar{p}_2(1-\bar{p}_2) \geq 5)$]
$$Z = \frac{(\bar{p}_1 - \bar{p}_2) - (p_1 - p_2)}{\sqrt{\frac{\bar{p}_1(1-\bar{p}_1)}{n_1} + \frac{\bar{p}_2(1-\bar{p}_2)}{n_2}}}$$

Inferences about the ratio of two population variances

Sampling distribution of S_1^2/S_2^2
[when parent populations are normal
and their means (μ_1 and μ_2) are unknown
$$F_{v_1, v_2} = \frac{S_1^2/\sigma_1^2}{S_2^2/\sigma_2^2}$$

where $v_1 = n_1 - 1$, $v_2 = n_2 - 1$

Tests for Goodness of Fit and Independence

Chi-square statistic for goodness of fit
$$\chi^2 = \sum_i \frac{(O_i - E_i)^2}{E_i}$$

**Expected frequencies for contingency table
under the assumption of independence
or homogeneity**
$$E_{ij} = \frac{(i\text{th row total})\,(j\text{th column total})}{\text{grand total}}$$

Chi-square statistic for contingency table
$$\chi^2 = \sum_i \sum_j \frac{(O_{ij} - E_{ij})^2}{E_{ij}}$$

Analysis of Variance

Completely randomized design

Total sum of squares
$$SS_T = \sum_{i=1}^{k} \sum_{j=1}^{n_i} (x_{ij} - \bar{x}_{..})^2 = \sum_{i=1}^{k} \sum_{j=1}^{n_i} x_{ij}^2 - \frac{x_{..}^2}{N}$$

Sum of squares due to treatments
$$SS_{Tr} = \sum_{i=1}^{k} n_i (\bar{x}_{i.} - \bar{x}_{..})^2 = \sum_{i=1}^{k} \frac{x_{i.}^2}{n_i} - \frac{x_{..}^2}{N}$$

Sum of squares due to error
$$SS_E = \sum_{i=1}^{k} \sum_{j=1}^{n_i} (x_{ij} - \bar{x}_{i.})^2 = \sum_{i=1}^{k} \sum_{j=1}^{n_i} x_{ij}^2 - \sum_{i=1}^{k} \frac{x_{i.}^2}{n_i}$$

Randomized block design

Total sum of squares
$$SS_T = \sum_{i=1}^{t} \sum_{j=1}^{b} (x_{ij} - \bar{x}_{..})^2 = \sum_{i=1}^{t} \sum_{j=1}^{b} x_{ij}^2 - \frac{x_{..}^2}{tb}$$

Sum of squares due to treatments
$$SS_{Tr} = b \sum_{i=1}^{t} (\bar{x}_{i.} - \bar{x}_{..})^2 = \sum_{i=1}^{t} \frac{x_{i.}^2}{b} - \frac{x_{..}^2}{tb}$$

Sum of squares due to blocks
$$SS_B = t \sum_{j=1}^{b} (\bar{x}_{.j} - \bar{x}_{..})^2 = \sum_{j=1}^{b} \frac{x_{.j}^2}{t} - \frac{x_{..}^2}{tb}$$

Sum of squares due to error

$$SS_E = \sum_{i=1}^{t}\sum_{j=1}^{b}(x_{ij} - \bar{x}_{i.} - \bar{x}_{.j} + \bar{x}_{..})^2$$

$$= \sum_{i=1}^{t}\sum_{j=1}^{b}x_{ij}^2 - \sum_{i=1}^{t}\frac{x_{i.}^2}{b} - \sum_{j=1}^{b}\frac{x_{.j}^2}{t} + \frac{x_{..}^2}{tb}$$

Randomized block design with replication

Total sum of squares

$$SS_T = \sum_{i=1}^{t}\sum_{j=1}^{b}\sum_{k=1}^{n}(x_{ijk} - \bar{x}_{...})^2 = \sum_{i=1}^{t}\sum_{j=1}^{b}\sum_{k=1}^{n}x_{ijk}^2 - \frac{x_{...}^2}{tbn}$$

Sum of squares due to treatments

$$SS_{Tr} = bn\sum_{i=1}^{t}(\bar{x}_{i..} - \bar{x}_{...})^2 = \sum_{i=1}^{t}\frac{x_{i..}^2}{bn} - \frac{x_{...}^2}{tbn}$$

Sum of squares due to blocks

$$SS_B = tn\sum_{j=1}^{b}(\bar{x}_{.j.} - \bar{x}_{...})^2 = \sum_{j=1}^{b}\frac{x_{.j.}^2}{tn} - \frac{x_{...}^2}{tbn}$$

Sum of squares due to interaction

$$SS_{TB} = n\sum_{i=1}^{t}\sum_{j=1}^{b}(\bar{x}_{ij.} - \bar{x}_{i..} - \bar{x}_{.j.} + \bar{x}_{...})^2$$

$$= \sum_{i=1}^{t}\sum_{j=1}^{b}\frac{x_{ij.}^2}{n} - \sum_{i=1}^{t}\frac{x_{i..}^2}{bn} - \sum_{j=1}^{b}\frac{x_{.j.}^2}{tn} + \frac{x_{...}^2}{tbn}$$

Sum of squares due to error

$$SS_E = \sum_{i=1}^{t}\sum_{j=1}^{b}\sum_{k=1}^{n}(x_{ijk} - \bar{x}_{ij.})^2$$

$$= \sum_{i=1}^{t}\sum_{j=1}^{b}\sum_{k=1}^{n}x_{ijk}^2 - \sum_{i=1}^{t}\sum_{j=1}^{b}\frac{x_{ij.}^2}{n}$$

Latin square design

Total sum of squares

$$SS_T = \sum_{i=1}^{p}\sum_{j=1}^{p}\sum_{h=1}^{p}(x_{ij(h)} - \bar{x}_{...})^2 = \sum_{i=1}^{p}\sum_{j=1}^{p}x_{ij(h)}^2 - \frac{x_{...}^2}{p^2}$$

Sum of squares due to rows

$$SS_R = p\sum_{i=1}^{p}(\bar{x}_{i..} - \bar{x}_{...})^2 = \sum_{i=1}^{p}\frac{x_{i..}^2}{p} - \frac{x_{...}^2}{p^2}$$

Sum of squares due to columns

$$SS_C = p\sum_{j=1}^{p}(\bar{x}_{.j.} - \bar{x}_{...})^2 = \sum_{j=1}^{p}\frac{x_{.j.}^2}{p} - \frac{x_{...}^2}{p^2}$$

Sum of squares due to treatments

$$SS_{Tr} = p\sum_{h=1}^{p}(\bar{x}_{..(h)} - \bar{x}_{...})^2 = \sum_{h=1}^{p}\frac{x_{..(h)}^2}{p} - \frac{x_{...}^2}{p^2}$$

Sum of squares due to error

$$SS_E = \sum_{i=1}^{p}\sum_{j=1}^{p}\sum_{h=1}^{p}(x_{ij(h)} - \bar{x}_{i..} - \bar{x}_{.j.} - \bar{x}_{..(h)} + 2\bar{x}_{...})^2$$

$$= \sum_{i=1}^{p}\sum_{j=1}^{p}\sum_{h=1}^{p}x_{ij(h)}^2 - \sum_{i=1}^{p}\frac{x_{i..}^2}{p} - \sum_{j=1}^{p}\frac{x_{.j.}^2}{p} - \sum_{h=1}^{p}\frac{x_{..(h)}^2}{p} + \frac{2x_{...}^2}{p}$$

Regression and correlation

Pearson product moment correlation coefficient

Population

$$\rho = \frac{\sum\limits_{i=1}^{N} (x_i - \mu_x)(y_i - \mu_y)}{\sqrt{\sum\limits_{i=1}^{N} (x_i - \mu_x)^2} \sqrt{\sum\limits_{i=1}^{N} (y_i - \mu_y)^2}}$$

Sample

$$r = \frac{\sum\limits_{i=1}^{n} (x_i - \bar{x})(y_i - \bar{y})}{\sqrt{\sum\limits_{i=1}^{n} (x_i - \bar{x})^2} \sqrt{\sum\limits_{i=1}^{n} (y_i - \bar{y})^2}}$$

• Computational
  formula

$$r = \frac{\sum\limits_{i=1}^{n} x_i y_i - \left(\sum\limits_{i=1}^{n} x_i \sum\limits_{i=1}^{n} y_i\right)/n}{\left\{\left(\sqrt{\sum\limits_{i=1}^{n} x_i^2 - \left(\sum\limits_{i=1}^{n} x_i\right)^2/n}\right)\left(\sqrt{\sum\limits_{i=1}^{n} y_i^2 - \left(\sum\limits_{i=1}^{n} y_i\right)^2/n}\right)\right\}}$$

Slope and y intercept of a regression line

Slope

$$b = \frac{\sum\limits_{i=1}^{n} (x_i - \bar{x})(y_i - \bar{y})}{\sum\limits_{i=1}^{n} (x_i - \bar{x})^2}$$

• Computational formula

$$b = \frac{\sum\limits_{i=1}^{n} x_i y_i - \left(\sum\limits_{i=1}^{n} x_i \sum\limits_{i=1}^{n} y_i\right)/n}{\sum\limits_{i=1}^{n} x_i^2 - \left(\sum\limits_{i=1}^{n} x_i\right)^2/n}$$

Intercept

$$a = \bar{y} - b\bar{x}$$

Estimated regression line

$$\hat{y} = a + bx$$

Total sum of squares

$$SS_T = \sum\limits_{i=1}^{n} (y_i - \bar{y})^2$$

• Computational formula

$$SS_T = \sum\limits_{i=1}^{n} y_i^2 - \left(\sum\limits_{i=1}^{n} y_i\right)^2/n$$

Sum of squares due to regression

$$SS_R = \sum\limits_{i=1}^{n} (\hat{y}_i - \bar{y})^2$$

• Computational formula

$$SS_R = \frac{\left[\sum\limits_{i=1}^{n} x_i y_i - \left(\sum\limits_{i=1}^{n} x_i \sum\limits_{i=1}^{n} y_i\right)/n\right]^2}{\sum\limits_{i=1}^{n} x_i^2 - \left(\sum\limits_{i=1}^{n} x_i\right)^2/n}$$

Sum of squares due to error

$$SS_E = \sum\limits_{i=1}^{n} (y_i - \hat{y}_i)^2$$

• Computational formula

$$SS_E = SS_T - SS_R$$

Coefficient of determination

$$r^2 = \frac{SS_R}{SS_T} = 1 - \frac{SS_E}{SS_T}$$

Estimate of σ^2

$$MS_E = \frac{SS_E}{n - 2}$$

Estimated variance of b

$$S_b^2 = \frac{MS_E}{\sum_{i=1}^{n}(x_i - \bar{x})^2}$$

Mean square due to regression

$$MS_R = \frac{SS_R}{\text{regression degrees of freedom}}$$

F statistic

$$F = \frac{MS_R}{MS_E}$$

Confidence interval for $E(y_p)$

$$\bar{y}_p \pm t_{(n-2),\,\alpha/2}\sqrt{MS_E\left(\frac{1}{n} + \frac{(x_p - \bar{x})^2}{\sum_{i=1}^{n}(x_i - \bar{x})^2}\right)}$$

Prediction interval for y_p

$$\hat{y}_p \pm t_{(n-2),\,\alpha/2}\sqrt{MS_E\left(1 + \frac{1}{n} + \frac{(x_p - \bar{x})^2}{\sum_{i=1}^{n}(x_i - \bar{x})^2}\right)}$$

Nonparametric Methods

Sign test

Test statistic: $X =$ number of positive or negative signs $\quad E(X) = \frac{1}{2}n$

Null distribution: binomial $b(x; n, 0.5)$ $\qquad \text{Var}(X) = \frac{1}{4}n$

Wilcoxon signed-rank test

Test statistic: $T =$ sum of positive or negative ranks $\quad E(T) = \frac{n(n+1)}{4}$

Null distribution (large sample): Normal $\qquad \text{Var}(T) = \frac{n(n+1)(2n+1)}{24}$

Run test for randomness

Test statistic: $R =$ number of runs $\qquad E(R) = \frac{2n_1 n_2}{n_1 + n_2} + 1$

Null distribution (large sample): Normal $\qquad \text{Var}(R) = \frac{2n_1 n_2(2n_1 n_2 - n_1 - n_2)}{(n_1 + n_2)^2(n_1 + n_2 - 1)}$

where n_1 and n_2 are the number of symbols of type I and type II, respectively

Wilcoxon rank-sum test

Test statistic: $W =$ sum of the ranks of the first sample $\qquad E(W) = \frac{1}{2}n_1(n_1 + n_2 + 1)$

Null distribution (large sample): Normal $\qquad \text{Var}(W) = \frac{1}{12}n_1 n_2(n_1 + n_2 + 1)$

where n_1 and n_2 are sample sizes of the first and second samples, respectively

Mann–Whitney test
Test statistic: $U =$ number of pairs (x_i, y_i) such that $x_i < y_i$ $\qquad E(U) = \frac{1}{2}n_1 n_2$

Null distribution (large sample): Normal $\qquad \text{Var}(U) = \frac{1}{12}n_1 n_2(n_1 + n_2 + 1)$

where n_1 and n_2 are sample sizes of the first and second samples, respectively

Kruskal–Wallis test

Test statistic:

$$H = \frac{12}{N(N+1)} \sum_{i=1}^{k} \frac{R_i^2}{n_i} - 3(N+1)$$

where R_i = sum of the ranks of the observations in the ith treatment group

n_i = number of observations in the ith group

k = number of groups

$N = n_1 + n_2 + \cdots + n_k$

Null distribution (large sample): χ^2_{k-1}

$$E(R_i) = \frac{n_i(N+1)}{2}$$

$$\text{Var}(R_i) = \frac{n_i(N+1)(N-n_i)}{12}$$

Friedman's test

Test statistic:

$$F_r = \frac{12}{bk(k+1)} \sum_{i=1}^{k} \left[R_i - \frac{b(k+1)}{2} \right]^2$$

where R_i = sum of the ranks of the observations in the ith treatment group

b = number of blocks

k = number of treatment groups

Null distribution (large sample): χ^2_{k-1}

$$E(R_i) = \frac{b(k+1)}{2}$$

$$\text{Var}(R_i) = \frac{b(k+1)(k-1)}{12}$$

Spearman's rho test

Test statistic:

$$R_s = 1 - \frac{6 \sum_{i=1}^{n} d_i^2}{n(n^2 - 1)}$$

where d_i is the difference between the ranks of the ith pair

Null distribution (large sample): Normal

$$E(R_s) = 0$$

$$\text{Var}(R_s) = \frac{1}{n-1}$$

Control Charts

Control lines for the $\bar{x}$-chart

$$\text{LCL}_{\bar{x}} = \bar{\bar{x}} - A_2 \bar{R}$$

$$\text{UCL}_{\bar{x}} = \bar{\bar{x}} + A_2 \bar{R}$$

where $\bar{\bar{x}}$ is the average of all the subgroup means $\bar{x}_i$, $\bar{R}$ is the average of all the subgroup ranges (taken from a pilot set of about 20 rational subgroups), and A_2 is a multiplier obtained from the following table:

n	2	3	4	5	6	7
A_2	1.880	1.023	0.729	0.577	0.483	0.419

Control lines for the R chart

$$LCL_R = D_3 \bar{R}$$
$$UCL_R = D_4 \bar{R}$$

where $\bar{R}$ is the average of ranges taken from a pilot set (about 20 rational subgroups), and D_3 and D_4 are multipliers obtained from the following table:

n	2	3	4	5	6	7
D_3	0	0	0	0	0	0.076
D_4	3.267	2.574	2.282	2.114	2.004	1.924

Control lines for the s chart

$$LCL_s = B_3 \bar{s}$$
$$UCL_s = B_4 \bar{s}$$

where $\bar{s}$ is the average of all the subgroup standard deviations taken from a pilot set (about 20 rational subgroups) and B_3 and B_4 are determined from the following table:

n	2	3	4	5	6	7	8	9	10
B_3	0	0	0	0	0.030	0.118	0.185	0.239	0.284
B_4	3.267	2.568	2.666	2.089	1.970	1.882	1.815	1.761	1.716

Control lines for the p chart

$$LCL_p = \bar{p} - 3\sqrt{\frac{\bar{p}(1 - \bar{p})}{n}}$$

$$UCL_p = \bar{p} + 3\sqrt{\frac{\bar{p}(1 - \bar{p})}{n}}$$

where $\bar{p}$ is the average proportion defective taken from a pilot set (about 20 rational subgroups) and n is the sample size.

Control lines for the c chart

$$LCL_c = \bar{c} - 3\sqrt{\bar{c}}$$
$$UCL_c = \bar{c} + 3\sqrt{\bar{c}}$$

where $\bar{c}$ is the average number of defects taken from a pilot set (about 20 rational subgroups)

Appendix J

Formulas for hypothesis testing

Test	Assumptions	Null hypothesis H_0	Alternative hypothesis H_A	Test statistics	Decision rules
1. Test concerning a population mean μ	Parent population is normal and standard deviation σ is known	$\mu = \mu_0$ $\mu \leq \mu_0$ $\mu \geq \mu_0$	$\mu \neq \mu_0$ $\mu > \mu_0$ $\mu < \mu_0$	$Z = \dfrac{\bar{X} - \mu_0}{\sigma/\sqrt{n}}$	Reject H_0, if $Z > z_{\alpha/2}$ or $Z < -z_{\alpha/2}$ Reject H_0, if $Z > z_\alpha$ Reject H_0, if $Z < -z_\alpha$
	Parent population is not necessarily normal and standard deviation σ is unknown ($n > 30$)	$\mu = \mu_0$ $\mu \leq \mu_0$ $\mu \geq \mu_0$	$\mu \neq \mu_0$ $\mu > \mu_0$ $\mu < \mu_0$	$Z = \dfrac{\bar{X} - \mu_0}{S/\sqrt{n}}$	Reject H_0, if $Z > z_{\alpha/2}$ or $Z < -z_{\alpha/2}$ Reject H_0, if $Z > z_\alpha$ Reject H_0, if $Z < -z_\alpha$
	Parent population is normal and standard deviation σ is unknown	$\mu = \mu_0$ $\mu \leq \mu_0$ $\mu \geq \mu_0$	$\mu \neq \mu_0$ $\mu > \mu_0$ $\mu < \mu_0$	$t = \dfrac{\bar{X} - \mu_0}{S/\sqrt{n}}$	Reject H_0, if $t > t_{\alpha/2,(n-1)}$ or $t < -t_{\alpha/2,(n-1)}$ Reject H_0, if $t > t_{\alpha,(n-1)}$ Reject H_0, if $t < -t_{\alpha,(n-1)}$
2. Test concerning a population variance σ^2	Parent population is normal and the mean μ is unknown	$\sigma^2 = \sigma_0^2$ $\sigma^2 \leq \sigma_0^2$ $\sigma^2 \geq \sigma_0^2$	$\sigma^2 \neq \sigma_0^2$ $\sigma^2 > \sigma_0^2$ $\sigma^2 < \sigma_0^2$	$\chi^2 = \dfrac{(n-1)S^2}{\sigma_0^2}$	Reject H_0, if $\chi^2 > \chi_{\alpha/2,(n-1)}^2$ or $\chi^2 < \chi_{1-\alpha/2,(n-1)}^2$ Reject H_0, if $\chi^2 > \chi_{\alpha,(n-1)}^2$ Reject H_0, if $\chi^2 < \chi_{1-\alpha,(n-1)}^2$
3. Test concerning a population proportion p	Parent population is Bernoulli ($n > 30$)	$p = p_0$ $p \leq p_0$ $p \geq p_0$	$p \neq p_0$ $p > p_0$ $p < p_0$	$Z = \dfrac{\bar{p} - p_0}{\sqrt{p_0(1 - p_0)/n}}$	Reject H_0, if $Z > z_{\alpha/2}$ or $Z < -z_{\alpha/2}$ Reject H_0, if $Z > z_\alpha$ Reject H_0, if $Z < -z_\alpha$
4. Test concerning a population mean λ	Parent population is Poisson ($n > 30$)	$\lambda = \lambda_0$ $\lambda \leq \lambda_0$ $\lambda \geq \lambda_0$	$\lambda \neq \lambda_0$ $\lambda > \lambda_0$ $\lambda < \lambda_0$	$Z = \dfrac{\bar{X} - \lambda_0}{\sqrt{\lambda_0/n}}$	Reject H_0, if $Z > z_{\alpha/2}$ or $Z < -z_{\alpha/2}$ Reject H_0, if $Z > z_\alpha$ Reject H_0, if $Z < -z_\alpha$

(Continued)

Test	Assumptions	Null hypothesis H_0	Alternative hypothesis H_A	Test statistics	Decision rules
5. Test concerning the difference between two population means $(\mu_1 - \mu_2)$	Parent populations are normal and standard deviations $(\sigma_1$ and $\sigma_2)$ are known	$\mu_1 = \mu_2$ $\mu_1 \leq \mu_2$ $\mu_1 \geq \mu_2$	$\mu_1 \neq \mu_2$ $\mu_1 > \mu_2$ $\mu_1 < \mu_2$	$Z = \dfrac{\bar{X}_1 - \bar{X}_2}{\sqrt{(\sigma_1^2/n_1) + (\sigma_2^2/n_2)}}$	Reject H_0, if $Z > z_{\alpha/2}$ or $Z < -z_{\alpha/2}$ Reject H_0, if $Z > z_\alpha$ Reject H_0, if $Z < -z_\alpha$
	Parent populations are normal and standard deviations $(\sigma_1$ and $\sigma_2)$ are unknown but assumed equal	$\mu_1 = \mu_2$ $\mu_1 \leq \mu_2$ $\mu_1 \geq \mu_2$	$\mu_1 \neq \mu_2$ $\mu_1 > \mu_2$ $\mu_1 < \mu_2$	$t = \dfrac{\bar{X}_1 - \bar{X}_2}{S_p \sqrt{(1/n_1) + (1/n_2)}}$ where $S_p = \sqrt{\dfrac{(n_1 - 1)S_1^2 + (n_2 - 1)S_2^2}{n_1 + n_2 - 2}}$	Reject H_0, if $t > t_{\alpha/2,\nu}$ or $t < -t_{\alpha/2,\nu}$ Reject H_0, if $t > t_{\alpha,\nu}$ Reject H_0, if $t < -t_{\alpha,\nu}$ where $\nu = n_1 + n_2 - 2$
	Parent populations are normal and standard deviations $(\sigma_1$ and $\sigma_2)$ are unknown and unequal	$\mu_1 = \mu_2$ $\mu_1 \leq \mu_2$ $\mu_1 \geq \mu_2$	$\mu_1 \neq \mu_2$ $\mu_1 > \mu_2$ $\mu_1 < \mu_2$	$t = \dfrac{\bar{X}_1 - \bar{X}_2}{\sqrt{(S_1^2/n_1) + (S_2^2/n_2)}}$	Reject H_0, if $t > t_{\alpha/2,\nu}$ or $t < -t_{\alpha/2,\nu}$ Reject H_0, if $t > t_{\alpha,\nu}$ Reject H_0, if $t < -t_{\alpha,\nu}$ where $\nu = \dfrac{\left[(s_1^2/n_1) + (s_2^2/n_2)\right]^2}{(s_1^2/n_1)^2/(n_1 - 1) + (s_2^2/n_2)^2/(n_2 - 1)}$
	Parent populations are not necessarily normal and standard deviations $(\sigma_1$ and $\sigma_2)$ are unknown $(n_1 > 30, n_2 > 30)$	$\mu_1 = \mu_2$ $\mu_1 \leq \mu_2$ $\mu_1 \geq \mu_2$	$\mu_1 \neq \mu_2$ $\mu_1 > \mu_2$ $\mu_1 < \mu_2$	$Z = \dfrac{\bar{X}_1 - \bar{X}_2}{\sqrt{(S_1^2/n_1) + (S_2^2/n_2)}}$	Reject H_0, if $Z > z_{\alpha/2}$ or $Z < -z_{\alpha/2}$ Reject H_0, if $Z > z_\alpha$ Reject H_0, if $Z < -z_\alpha$

#	Description	Assumptions	H_0	H_1	Test statistic	Rejection region
6.	Test concerning the difference between population means of paired observations (μ_d)	Parent population is bivariate normal and standard deviation σ_d is known	$\mu_d = \mu_{d_0}$ $\mu_d \leq \mu_{d_0}$ $\mu_d \geq \mu_{d_0}$	$\mu_d \neq \mu_{d_0}$ $\mu_d > \mu_{d_0}$ $\mu_d < \mu_{d_0}$	$Z = \dfrac{\bar{d} - \mu_{d_0}}{\sigma_d/\sqrt{n}}$	Reject H_0, if $Z > z_{\alpha/2}$ or $Z < -z_{\alpha/2}$ Reject H_0, if $Z > z_\alpha$ Reject H_0, if $Z < -z_\alpha$
		Parent population is bivariate normal and standard deviation σ_d is unknown	$\mu_d = \mu_{d_0}$ $\mu_d \leq \mu_{d_0}$ $\mu_d \geq \mu_{d_0}$	$\mu_d \neq \mu_{d_0}$ $\mu_d > \mu_{d_0}$ $\mu_d < \mu_{d_0}$	$t = \dfrac{\bar{d} - \mu_{d_0}}{S_d/\sqrt{n}}$ where $\bar{d}$ is the mean of the difference between sample paired observations and S_d is its standard deviation	Reject H_0, if $t > t_{\alpha/2,(n-1)}$ or $t < -t_{\alpha/2,(n-1)}$ Reject H_0, if $t > t_{\alpha,(n-1)}$ Reject H_0, if $t < -t_{\alpha,(n-1)}$
7.	Test concerning the ratio between two population variances (σ_1^2/σ_2^2)	Parent populations are normal and their means (μ_1 and μ_2) are unknown	$\sigma_1^2 = \sigma_2^2$ $\sigma_1^2 \leq \sigma_2^2$ $\sigma_1^2 \geq \sigma_2^2$	$\sigma_1^2 \neq \sigma_2^2$ $\sigma_1^2 > \sigma_2^2$ $\sigma_1^2 < \sigma_2^2$	$F = \dfrac{S_1^2}{S_2^2}$	Reject H_0, if $F > F_{\nu_1,\nu_2,\alpha/2}$ or $F < F_{\nu_1,\nu_2,1-\alpha/2}$ Reject H_0, if $F > F_{\nu_1,\nu_2,\alpha}$ Reject H_0, if $F < F_{\nu_1,\nu_2,1-\alpha}$ where $\nu_1 = n_1 - 1$ and $\nu_2 = n_2 - 1$
8.	Test concerning the difference between two population proportions ($p_1 - p_2$)	Parent populations are Bernoulli ($n_1 > 30$, $n_2 > 30$)	$p_1 = p_2$ $p_1 \leq p_2$ $p_1 \geq p_2$	$p_1 \neq p_2$ $p_1 > p_2$ $p_1 < p_2$	$Z = \dfrac{\bar{p}_1 - \bar{p}_2}{\sqrt{\hat{p}(1 - \hat{p})(1/n_1 + 1/n_2)}}$ where $\hat{p} = \dfrac{n_1\bar{p}_1 + n_2\bar{p}_2}{n_1 + n_2}$	Reject H_0, if $Z > z_{\alpha/2}$ or $Z < -z_{\alpha/2}$ Reject H_0, if $Z > z_\alpha$ Reject H_0, if $Z < -z_\alpha$
9.	Test concerning the difference between two population means ($\lambda_1 - \lambda_2$)	Parent populations are Poisson ($n_1 > 30$, $n_2 > 30$)	$\lambda_1 = \lambda_2$ $\lambda_1 \leq \lambda_2$ $\lambda_1 \geq \lambda_2$	$\lambda_1 \neq \lambda_2$ $\lambda_1 > \lambda_2$ $\lambda_1 < \lambda_2$	$Z = \dfrac{\bar{X}_1 - \bar{X}_2}{S\sqrt{(1/n_1 + 1/n_2)}}$ where $S = \sqrt{\dfrac{n_1\bar{X}_1 + n_2\bar{X}_2}{n_1 + n_2}}$	Reject H_0, if $Z > z_{\alpha/2}$ or $Z < -z_{\alpha/2}$ Reject H_0, if $Z > z_\alpha$ Reject H_0, if $Z < -z_\alpha$

Appendix K

Formulas for confidence intervals

Confidence Interval for a Population Mean μ

When parent population is normal and σ^2 is known $\qquad \bar{X} \pm z_{\alpha/2}\dfrac{\sigma}{\sqrt{n}}$

When parent population is normal, σ^2 is unknown, and sample is small $\qquad \bar{X} \pm t_{n-1,\alpha/2}\dfrac{S}{\sqrt{n}}$

When parent population is not necessarily normal, σ^2 is unknown, and sample is large $\qquad \bar{X} \pm z_{\alpha/2}\dfrac{S}{\sqrt{n}}$

Sample size for the confidence interval of a population mean μ with estimation error e $\qquad n = \dfrac{(z_{\alpha/2})^2 \sigma^2}{e^2}$

Confidence Interval of a Population Proportion p

When parent population is Bernoulli and sample is large $\qquad \bar{p} \pm z_{\alpha/2}\sqrt{\dfrac{\bar{p}(1-\bar{p})}{n}}$

Sample size for the confidence interval of a population proportion p with estimation error e $\qquad n = \dfrac{z_{\alpha/2}^2 \bar{p}(1-\bar{p})}{e^2}$

Confidence Interval for a Population Variance σ^2

When parent population is normal and the mean μ is unknown $\qquad \dfrac{(n-1)S^2}{\chi^2_{n-1,\alpha/2}} \leq \sigma^2 \leq \dfrac{(n-1)S^2}{\chi^2_{n-1,1-\alpha/2}}$

Confidence Interval for the Difference of Two Population Means $(\mu_1 - \mu_2)$

When parent populations are normal and σ_1^2 and σ_2^2 are known $\qquad (\bar{X}_1 - \bar{X}_2) \pm z_{\alpha/2}\sqrt{\left(\dfrac{\sigma_1^2}{n_1} + \dfrac{\sigma_2^2}{n_2}\right)}$

When parent populations are not necessarily normal, σ_1^2 and σ_2^2 are unknown, and samples are large $\qquad (\bar{X}_1 - \bar{X}_2) \pm z_{\alpha/2}\sqrt{\left(\dfrac{S_1^2}{n_1} + \dfrac{S_2^2}{n_2}\right)}$

When parent populations are normal, σ_1^2 and σ_2^2 are unknown, $\sigma_1^2 = \sigma_2^2$, and samples are small $\qquad (\bar{X}_1 - \bar{X}_2) \pm t_{\alpha/2,\nu} S_p\sqrt{\left(\dfrac{1}{n_1} + \dfrac{1}{n_2}\right)}$

$$\text{where } S_p = \sqrt{\dfrac{(n_1 - 1)S_1^2 + (n_2 - 1)S_2^2}{n_1 + n_2 - 2}}$$

$$\text{and } \nu = n_1 + n_2 - 2$$

When parent populations are normal, σ_1^2 and σ_2^2 are unknown, $\sigma_1^2 \neq \sigma_2^2$ and samples are small

$$(\bar{X}_1 - \bar{X}_2) \pm t_{\alpha/2,\nu} \sqrt{\left(\frac{S_1^2}{n_1} + \frac{S_2^2}{n_2}\right)}$$

$$\text{where } \nu = \frac{\left(\frac{s_1^2}{n_1} + \frac{s_2^2}{n_2}\right)^2}{\frac{\left(s_1^2/n_1\right)^2}{n_1-1} + \frac{\left(s_2^2/n_2\right)^2}{n_2-1}}$$

Confidence intervals for the difference μ_d between Two Population Means of a Paired Sample of Size n ($\mu_d = \mu_1 - \mu_2$)

When parent population is bivariate normal and standard deviation σ_d is known

$$\bar{d} \pm z_{\alpha/2} \frac{\sigma_d}{\sqrt{n}}$$

When parent population is bivariate normal and standard deviation σ_d is unknown

$$\bar{d} \pm t_{\alpha/2,(n-1)} \frac{S_d}{\sqrt{n}}$$

Confidence Interval for the Difference between Two Population Proportions ($p_1 - p_2$)

When parent populations are Bernoulli and samples are large

$$(\bar{p}_1 - \bar{p}_2) \pm z_{\alpha/2} \sqrt{\frac{\bar{p}_1(1 - \bar{p}_1)}{n_1} + \frac{\bar{p}_2(1 - \bar{p}_2)}{n_2}}$$

Confidence Interval for the Ratio of Two Population Variances (σ_1^2/σ_2^2)

When parent populations are normal and their means (μ_1 and μ_2) are unknown

$$\frac{S_1^2/S_2^2}{F_{\nu_1,\nu_2;\alpha/2}} \leq \frac{\sigma_1^2}{\sigma_2^2} \leq \frac{S_1^2/S_2^2}{F_{\nu_1,\nu_2;1-\alpha/2}}$$

$$\text{where } \nu_1 = n_1 - 1 \text{ and } \nu_2 = n_2 - 1$$

Appendix L

Relations between moments and cumulants[*]

Expressions for Moments about Origin in Terms of Cumulants

The following expressions give the first 10 moments about the origin in terms of cumulants of a probability distribution:

$$\mu_1' = \kappa_1$$

$$\mu_2' = \kappa_2 + \kappa_1^2$$

$$\mu_3' = \kappa_3 + 3\kappa_2\kappa_1 + \kappa_1^3$$

$$\mu_4' = \kappa_4 + 4\kappa_3\kappa_1 + 3\kappa_2^2 + 6\kappa_2\kappa_1^2 + \kappa_1^4$$

$$\mu_5' = \kappa_5 + 5\kappa_4\kappa_1 + 10\kappa_3\kappa_2 + 10\kappa_3\kappa_1^2 + 15\kappa_2^2\kappa_1 + 10\kappa_2\kappa_1^3 + \kappa_1^5$$

$$\mu_6' = \kappa_6 + 6\kappa_5\kappa_1 + 15\kappa_4\kappa_2 + 15\kappa_4\kappa_1^2 + 10\kappa_3^2 + 60\kappa_3\kappa_2\kappa_1 + 20\kappa_3\kappa_1^3 + 15\kappa_2^3$$
$$+ 45\kappa_2^2\kappa_1^2 + 15\kappa_2\kappa_1^4 + \kappa_1^6,$$

$$\mu_7' = \kappa_7 + 7\kappa_6\kappa_1 + 21\kappa_5\kappa_2 + 21\kappa_5\kappa_1^2 + 35\kappa_4\kappa_3 + 105\kappa_4\kappa_2\kappa_1 + 35\kappa_4\kappa_1^3 + 70\kappa_3^2\kappa_1$$
$$+ 105\kappa_3\kappa_2^2 + 210\kappa_3\kappa_2\kappa_1^2 + 35\kappa_3\kappa_1^4 + 105\kappa_2^2\kappa_1^3 + 105\kappa_2^3\kappa_1 + 21\kappa_2\kappa_1^5 + \kappa_1^7$$

$$\mu_8' = \kappa_8 + 8\kappa_7\kappa_1 + 28\kappa_6\kappa_2 + 28\kappa_6\kappa_1^2 + 56\kappa_5\kappa_3 + 168\kappa_5\kappa_2\kappa_1 + 56\kappa_5\kappa_1^3 + 35\kappa_4^2$$
$$+ 280\kappa_4\kappa_3\kappa_1 + 210\kappa_4\kappa_2^2 + 420\kappa_4\kappa_2\kappa_1^2 + 70\kappa_4\kappa_1^4 + 280\kappa_3^2\kappa_2 + 280\kappa_3^2\kappa_1^2$$
$$+ 840\kappa_3\kappa_2^2\kappa_1 + 560\kappa_3\kappa_2\kappa_1^3 + 56\kappa_3\kappa_1^5 + 105\kappa_2^4 + 420\kappa_2^3\kappa_1^2 + 210\kappa_2^2\kappa_1^4$$
$$+ 28\kappa_2\kappa_1^6 + \kappa_1^8$$

$$\mu_9' = \kappa_9 + 9\kappa_8\kappa_1 + 36\kappa_7\kappa_2 + 36\kappa_7\kappa_1^2 + 84\kappa_6\kappa_3 + 252\kappa_6\kappa_2\kappa_1 + 84\kappa_6\kappa_1^3 + 126\kappa_5\kappa_4$$
$$+ 504\kappa_5\kappa_3\kappa_1 + 378\kappa_5\kappa_2^2 + 756\kappa_5\kappa_2\kappa_1^2 + 126\kappa_5\kappa_1^4 + 315\kappa_4^2\kappa_1 + 1260\kappa_4\kappa_3\kappa_2$$
$$+ 1260\kappa_4\kappa_3\kappa_1^2 + 1890\kappa_4\kappa_2^2\kappa_1 + 1260\kappa_4\kappa_2\kappa_1^3 + 126\kappa_4\kappa_1^5 + 280\kappa_3^3 + 2520\kappa_3^2\kappa_2\kappa_1$$
$$+ 840\kappa_3^2\kappa_1^3 + 1260\kappa_3\kappa_2^3 + 3780\kappa_3\kappa_2^2\kappa_1^2 + 1260\kappa_3\kappa_2\kappa_1^4 + 84\kappa_3\kappa_1^6 + 945\kappa_2^4\kappa_1$$
$$+ 1260\kappa_2^3\kappa_1^3 + 378\kappa_2^2\kappa_1^5 + 36\kappa_2\kappa_1^7 + \kappa_1^9$$

---

[*]The results given in this appendix are adapted from *Kendall's Advanced Theory of Statistics*, 6th ed., Vol. 1 (Chap. 3) by A. Stuart and K. Ord (Arnold, London, 1994).

$$\mu'_{10} = \kappa_{10} + 10\kappa_9\kappa_1 + 45\kappa_8\kappa_2 + 45\kappa_8\kappa_1^2 + 120\kappa_7\kappa_3 + 360\kappa_7\kappa_2\kappa_1 + 120\kappa_7\kappa_1^3 + 210\kappa_6\kappa_4$$
$$+ 840\kappa_6\kappa_3\kappa_1 + 630\kappa_6\kappa_2^2 + 1260\kappa_6\kappa_2\kappa_1^2 + 210\kappa_6\kappa_1^4 + 126\kappa_5^2 + 1260\kappa_5\kappa_4\kappa_1$$
$$+ 2520\kappa_5\kappa_3\kappa_2 + 2520\kappa_5\kappa_3\kappa_1^2 + 3780\kappa_5\kappa_2^2\kappa_1 + 2520\kappa_5\kappa_2\kappa_1^3 + 252\kappa_5\kappa_1^5$$
$$+ 1575\kappa_4^2\kappa_2 + 1575\kappa_4^2\kappa_1^2 + 2100\kappa_4\kappa_3^2 + 12{,}600\kappa_4\kappa_3\kappa_2\kappa_1 + 4200\kappa_4\kappa_3\kappa_1^3$$
$$+ 3150\kappa_4\kappa_2^3 + 9450\kappa_4\kappa_2^2\kappa_1^2 + 3150\kappa_4\kappa_2\kappa_1^4 + 210\kappa_4\kappa_1^6 + 2800\kappa_3^3\kappa_1 + 6300\kappa_3^2\kappa_2^2$$
$$+ 12{,}600\kappa_3^2\kappa_2\kappa_1^2 + 2100\kappa_3^2\kappa_1^4 + 12{,}600\kappa_3\kappa_2^3\kappa_1 + 12{,}600\kappa_3\kappa_2^2\kappa_1^3 + 2520\kappa_3\kappa_2\kappa_1^5$$
$$+ 120\kappa_3\kappa_1^7 + 945\kappa_2^5 + 4725\kappa_2^4\kappa_1^2 + 3150\kappa_2^3\kappa_1^4 + 630\kappa_2^2\kappa_1^6 + 45\kappa_2\kappa_1^8 + \kappa_1^{10}$$

Expressions for Central Moments in Terms of Cumulants

The following expressions give the first 10 central moments in terms of cumulants of a probability distribution:

$$\mu_2 = \kappa_2$$
$$\mu_3 = \kappa_3$$
$$\mu_4 = \kappa_4 + 3\kappa_2^2$$
$$\mu_5 = \kappa_5 + 10\kappa_3\kappa_2$$
$$\mu_6 = \kappa_6 + 15\kappa_4\kappa_2 + 10\kappa_3^2 + 15\kappa_2^3$$
$$\mu_7 = \kappa_7 + 21\kappa_5\kappa_2 + 35\kappa_4\kappa_3 + 105\kappa_3\kappa_2^2$$
$$\mu_8 = \kappa_8 + 28\kappa_6\kappa_2 + 56\kappa_5\kappa_3 + 35\kappa_4^2 + 210\kappa_4\kappa_2^2 + 280\kappa_3^2\kappa_2 + 105\kappa_2^4$$
$$\mu_9 = \kappa_9 + 36\kappa_7\kappa_2 + 84\kappa_6\kappa_3 + 126\kappa_5\kappa_4 + 378\kappa_5\kappa_2^2 + 1260\kappa_4\kappa_3\kappa_2 + 280\kappa_3^3 + 1260\kappa_3\kappa_2^3$$
$$\mu_{10} = \kappa_{10} + 45\kappa_8\kappa_2 + 120\kappa_7\kappa_3 + 210\kappa_6\kappa_4 + 630\kappa_6\kappa_2^2 + 126\kappa_5^2 + 2520\kappa_5\kappa_3\kappa_2$$
$$+ 1575\kappa_4^2\kappa_2 + 2100\kappa_4\kappa_3^2 + 3150\kappa_4\kappa_2^3 + 6300\kappa_3^2\kappa_2^2 + 945\kappa_2^5$$

Expressions for Cumulants in Terms of Moments about Origin

The following expressions give the first 10 cumulants in terms of moments about the origin of a probability distribution:

$$\kappa_1 = \mu'_1$$
$$\kappa_2 = \mu'_2 - \mu_1'^2$$
$$\kappa_3 = \mu'_3 - 3\mu'_2\mu'_1 + 2\mu_1'^3$$
$$\kappa_4 = \mu'_4 - 4\mu'_3\mu'_1 - 3\mu_2'^2 + 12\mu'_2\mu_1'^2 - 6\mu_1'^4$$
$$\kappa_5 = \mu'_5 - 5\mu'_4\mu'_1 - 10\mu'_3\mu'_2 + 20\mu'_3\mu_1'^2 + 30\mu_2'^2\mu'_1 - 60\mu'_2\mu_1'^3 + 24\mu_1'^5$$
$$\kappa_6 = \mu'_6 - 6\mu'_5\mu'_1 - 15\mu'_4\mu'_2 + 30\mu'_4\mu_1'^2 - 10\mu_3'^2 + 120\mu'_3\mu'_2\mu'_1 - 120\mu'_3\mu_1'^3$$
$$+ 30\mu_2'^3 - 270\mu_2'^2\mu_1'^2 + 360\mu'_2\mu_1'^4 - 120\mu_1'^6$$
$$\kappa_7 = \mu'_7 - 7\mu'_6\mu'_1 - 21\mu'_5\mu'_2 + 42\mu'_5\mu_1'^2 - 35\mu'_4\mu'_3 + 210\mu'_4\mu'_2\mu'_1$$
$$- 210\mu'_4\mu_1'^3 + 140\mu_3'^2\mu'_1 + 210\mu'_3\mu_2'^2 - 1260\mu'_3\mu'_2\mu_1'^2 + 840\mu'_3\mu_1'^4$$
$$- 630\mu_2'^3\mu'_1 + 2520\mu_2'^2\mu_1'^3 - 2520\mu'_2\mu_1'^5 + 720\mu_1'^7$$
$$\kappa_8 = \mu'_8 - 8\mu'_7\mu'_1 - 28\mu'_6\mu'_2 + 56\mu'_6\mu_1'^2 - 56\mu'_5\mu'_3 + 336\mu'_5\mu'_2\mu'_1$$
$$- 336\mu'_5\mu_1'^3 - 35\mu_4'^2 + 560\mu'_4\mu'_3\mu'_1 + 420\mu'_4\mu_2'^2 - 2520\mu'_4\mu'_2\mu_1'^2$$
$$+ 1680\mu'_4\mu_1'^4 + 560\mu_3'^2\mu'_2 - 1680\mu_3'^2\mu_1'^2 - 5040\mu'_3\mu_2'^2\mu'_1$$
$$+ 13{,}440\mu'_3\mu'_2\mu_1'^3 - 6720\mu'_3\mu_1'^5 - 630\mu_2'^4 + 10{,}080\mu_2'^3\mu_1'^2$$
$$- 25{,}200\mu_2'^2\mu_1'^4 + 20{,}160\mu'_2\mu_1'^6 - 5040\mu_1'^8$$

$$\kappa_9 = \mu'_9 - 9\mu'_8\mu'_1 - 36\mu'_7\mu'_2 + 72\mu'_7\mu'^2_1 - 84\mu'_6\mu'_3 + 504\mu'_6\mu'_2\mu'_1$$
$$- 504\mu'_6\mu'^3_1 - 126\mu'_5\mu'_4 + 1008\mu'_5\mu'_3\mu'_1 + 756\mu'_5\mu'^2_2 - 4536\mu'_5\mu'_2\mu'^2_1$$
$$+ 3024\mu'_5\mu'^4_1 + 630\mu'^2_4\mu'_1 + 2520\mu'_4\mu'_3\mu'_2 - 7560\mu'_4\mu'_3\mu'^2_1$$
$$- 11,340\mu'_4\mu'^2_2\mu'_1 + 30,240\mu'_4\mu'_2\mu'^3_1 - 15,120\mu'_4\mu'^5_1 + 560\mu'^3_3$$
$$- 15,120\mu'^2_3\mu'_2\mu'_1 + 20,160\mu'^2_3\mu'^3_1 - 7560\mu'_3\mu'^3_2 + 90,720\mu'_3\mu'^2_2\mu'^2_1$$
$$- 151,200\mu'_3\mu'_2\mu'^4_1 + 60,480\mu'_3\mu'^6_1 + 22,680\mu'^4_2\mu'_1 - 151,200\mu'^3_2\mu'^3_1$$
$$+ 272,160\mu'^2_2\mu'^5_1 - 181,440\mu'_2\mu'^7_1 + 40,320\mu'^9_1$$

$$\kappa_{10} = \mu'_{10} - 10\mu'_9\mu'_1 - 45\mu'_8\mu'_2 + 90\mu'_8\mu'^2_1 - 120\mu'_7\mu'_3 + 720\mu'_7\mu'_2\mu'_1$$
$$- 720\mu'_7\mu'^3_1 - 210\mu'_6\mu'_4 + 1680\mu'_6\mu'_3\mu'_1 + 1260\mu'_6\mu'^2_2$$
$$- 7560\mu'_6\mu'_2\mu'^2_1 + 5040\mu'_6\mu'^4_1 - 126\mu'^2_5 + 2520\mu'_5\mu'_4\mu'_1$$
$$+ 5040\mu'_5\mu'_3\mu'_2 - 15,120\mu'_5\mu'_3\mu'^2_1 - 22,680\mu'_5\mu'^2_2\mu'_1 + 60,480\mu'_5\mu'_2\mu'^3_1$$
$$- 30,240\mu'_5\mu'^5_1 + 3150\mu'^2_4\mu'_2 - 9450\mu'^2_4\mu'^2_1 + 4200\mu'_4\mu'^2_3$$
$$- 75,600\mu'_4\mu'_3\mu'_2\mu'_1 + 100,800\mu'_4\mu'_3\mu'^3_1 - 18,900\mu'_4\mu'^3_2$$
$$+ 226,800\mu'_4\mu'^2_2\mu'^2_1 - 378,000\mu'_4\mu'_2\mu'^4_1 + 151,200\mu'_4\mu'^6_1 - 16,800\mu'^3_3\mu'_1$$
$$- 37,800\mu'^2_3\mu'^2_2 + 302,400\mu'^2_3\mu'_2\mu'^2_1 - 252,000\mu'^2_3\mu'^4_1 + 302,400\mu'_3\mu'^3_2\mu'_1$$
$$- 1,512,000\mu'_3\mu'^2_2\mu'^3_1 + 1,814,400\mu'_3\mu'_2\mu'^5_1 - 604,800\mu'_3\mu'^7_1$$
$$+ 22,680\mu'^5_2 - 567,000\mu'^4_2\mu'^2_1 + 2,268,000\mu'^3_2\mu'^4_1 - 3,175,200\mu'^2_2\mu'^6_1$$
$$+ 1,814,400\mu'_2\mu'^8_1 - 362,880\mu'^{10}_1$$

Expressions for Cumulants in Terms of Central Moments

The following expressions give the first 10 cumulants in terms of central moments of a probability distribution:

$$\kappa_2 = \mu_2$$
$$\kappa_3 = \mu_3$$
$$\kappa_4 = \mu_4 - 3\mu^2_2$$
$$\kappa_5 = \mu_5 - 10\mu_3\mu_2$$
$$\kappa_6 = \mu_6 - 15\mu_4\mu_2 - 10\mu^2_3 + 30\mu^3_2$$
$$\kappa_7 = \mu_7 - 21\mu_5\mu_2 - 35\mu_4\mu_3 + 210\mu_3\mu^2_2$$
$$\kappa_8 = \mu_8 - 28\mu_6\mu_2 - 56\mu_5\mu_3 - 35\mu^2_4 + 420\mu_4\mu^2_2 + 560\mu^2_3\mu_2 - 630\mu^4_2$$
$$\kappa_9 = \mu_9 - 36\mu_7\mu_2 - 84\mu_6\mu_3 - 126\mu_5\mu_4 + 756\mu_5\mu^2_2 + 2520\mu_4\mu_3\mu_2$$
$$+ 560\mu^3_3 - 7560\mu_3\mu^3_2$$
$$\kappa_{10} = \mu_{10} - 45\mu_8\mu_2 - 120\mu_7\mu_3 - 210\mu_6\mu_4 + 1260\mu_6\mu^2_2 - 126\mu^2_5$$
$$+ 5040\mu_5\mu_3\mu_2 + 3150\mu^2_4\mu_2 + 4200\mu_4\mu^2_3 - 18,900\mu_4\mu^3_2$$
$$- 37,800\mu^2_3\mu^2_2 + 22,680\mu^5_2$$

Appendix M

First occurrence of some commonly used terms in probability and statistics

This appendix lists the first occurrence in print of some selected terms defined in this dictionary. For further details and the first occurrence of some other commonly used terms in probability and statistics, the reader is referred to the papers H. A. David given in the footnote to the following table and references cited therein.

Term	Author(s)	Year
additivity (in ANOVA)	Eisenhart, C.	1947
alias	Finney, D. J.	1945
alternative hypothesis	Neyman, J., and Pearson, E. S.	1933
analysis of covariance	Bailey, A. L.	1931
analysis of variance	Fisher, R. A.	1918
association	Yule, G. U.	1900
asymptotic efficiency	Wald, A.	1948
autocorrelation	Wold, H.	1938
autoregression	Wold, H.	1938
average sample number function	Wald, A.	1947
balanced incomplete blocks	Fisher, R. A., and Yates, F.	1938
bar chart	Brinton, W. C.	1914
Bayes' theorem	Todhunter, I.	1865
Bayes' theorem (regle de Bayes)	Cournot, A. A.	1843
bayesian	Fisher, R. A.	1950
bell-shaped curve	Galton, F.	1876
best linear unbiased estimate	David, F. N., and Neyman, J.	1938
beta distribution (distribuzione β)	Gini, C.	1911
biased (errors)	Bowley, A. L.	1897
bimodal	Williams, S. R.	1903
binomial distribution	Yule, G. U.	1911
bioassay	Wood, H. C.	1912
biometry	Whewell, W.	1831
biostatistics	Webster's Dictionary	1890
Bonferroni inequalities	Feller, W.	1950
bootstrap	Efron, B.	1979

(*Continued*)

Term	Author(s)	Year
box plot	Tukey, J. W.	1970
censoring	Hald, A.	1949
central limit theorem (zentraler Grenzwetsatz)	Cramér, H.	1937
central limit theorem (zentraler Grenzwetsatz)	Pólya, G.	1920
characteristic function (fonction caracteristique)	Poincare, H.	1912
characteristic function (fonction caracteristique)	Kullback, S.	1934
chi-squared (χ^2)	Pearson, K.	1900
cluster analysis	Tryon, R. C.	1939
coefficient of correlation	Pearson, K.	1896
coefficient of variation	Pearson, K.	1896
composite hypothesis	Neyman, J., and Pearson, E. S.	1933
computer-intensive	Diaconis, P., and Efron, B.	1983
confidence coefficient	Neyman, J.	1934
confidence interval	Neyman, J.	1934
confounding	Fisher, R. A.	1926
consistency	Fisher, R. A.	1922
consistency (of a test)	Wald, A., and Wolfowitz, J.	1940
contingency table	Pearson, K.	1904
convolution	Winter, A.	1934
correlated	Galton, F.	1875
correlation	Galton, F.	1888
correlation coefficient	Pearson, K.	1896
correlogram	Wold, H.	1938
covariance	Fisher, R. A.	1930
Cramér–Rao inequality	Neyman, J., and Scott, E. L.	1948
critical region	Neyman, J., and Pearson, E. S.	1933
cumulant	Fisher, R. A., and Wishart, J.	1931
cumulative distribution function (cdf)	Wilks, S. S.	1943
decile, upper and lower	Galton, F.	1882
decision theory	Ghosh, M. N.	1952
degrees of freedom	Fisher, R. A.	1922
deviance	Nelder, J. A., and Wedderburn, R. W. M.	1972
deviate (normal)	Galton, F.	1907
discriminant function	Fisher, R. A.	1936
dispersion	Edgeworth, F. Y.	1892
distribution function, cumulative (cdf)	Wilks, S. S.	1943
distribution function	von Mises, R.	1919
distribution function (verteilungsfunktion)	Doob, J. L.	1935
double exponential (laplace)	Fisher, R. A.	1920
econometrics	Frisch, R.	1933
efficiency	Fisher, R. A.	1922
empirical bayes	Robbins, H.	1956
errors of first and second kind	Neyman, J., and Pearson, E. S.	1933
estimator	Pitman, E. J. G.	1938
exploratory data analysis	Tukey, J. W.	1970
exponential (negative exponential)	Pearson, K.	1895
exponential family	Girshick, M. A., and Savage, L. J.	1951
extreme value distribution	Lieblein, J.	1953
factor analysis	Thurstone, L. L.	1931
factorial design	Fisher, R. A.	1935

Term	Author(s)	Year
factorial moment	Steffensen, J. F.	1923
fiducial	Fisher, R. A.	1930
fixed effects	Eisenhart, C.	1947
fixed model	Scheffé, H.	1946
fractional replication	Finney, D. J.	1945
game theory	Williams, J. D.	1954
gamma distribution	Weatherburn, C. E.	1946
Gauss–Markov theorem	Scheffe, H.	1959
geometric distribution	Feller, W.	1950
goodness of fit	Pearson, K.	1900
Graeco–Latin square	Fisher, R. A., and Yates, F.	1934
hazard rate	Barlow, R. E., Marshall, A. W., and Proschan, F.	1963
heteroscedastic	Pearson, K.	1905
heteroskedastic	Valavanis, S.	1959
hierarchical bayes	Good, I. J.	1980
histogram	Pearson, K.	1895
homoscedastic	Pearson, K.	1905
homoskedastic	Valavanis, S.	1959
Hotelling's T^2	Simaika, J. B.	1941
index number	Jevons, W. S.	1875
interaction	Fisher, R. A.	1926
interquartile range	Galton, F.	1882
interval estimation	Mood, A. M.	1950
jackknife	Miller, R. G.	1964
j-shaped	Yule, G. U.	1911
kurtosis	Pearson, K.	1905
Latin square (carré Latin)	Euler, L.	1782
Latin square (carré Latin)	Cayley, A.	1890
lattice (design)	Yates, F.	1937
law of large numbers (la loi des grands nombres)	Poisson, S. D.	1835
level of significance	Fisher, R. A.	1925
likelihood ratio	Neyman, J., and Pearson, E. S.	1931
linear model, generalized	Nelder, J. A., and Wedderburn, R. W. M.	1972
linear model	Anderson, R. L., and Bancroft, T. A.	1952
linear programming	Dantzig, G. B.	1949
location	Fisher, R. A.	1922
location parameter	Pitman, E. J. G.	1938
logit	Berkson, J.	1944
log–linear model	Bishop, Y. M. M., and Fienberg, S. E.	1969
lognormal distribution	Gaddum, J. H.	1945
Markov chain	Doob, J. L.	1942
Markov chain (chaines de Markoff)	Doeblin, W.	1937
maximum likelihood	Fisher, R. A.	1922
mean square (of errors)	Edgeworth, F. Y.	1885
median	Galton, F.	1882
median (valeur mediane)	Cournot, A. A.	1843
median absolute deviation	Andrews, D. F., Bickel, P. J., Hampel, F. R., Huber, P. J., Rogers, W. H., and Tukey, J. W.	1972

(Continued)

Term	Author(s)	Year
median-unbiased	Brown, G. W.	1947
meta-analysis	Glass, G. V.	1976
method of maximum likelihood	Fisher, R. A.	1922
method of moments	Pearson, K.	1902
method of least squares (méthode des moindres quarres)	Legendre, A. M.	1805
method of least squares (méthode des moindres quarres)	Ivory, J.	1825
minimax (solution, strategy)	Wald, A.	1947
minimum chi-squared	Fisher, R. A.	1928
mixed model	Mood, A. M.	1950
mode	Pearson, K.	1895
Model I, II (in ANOVA)	Eisenhart, C.	1947
model, linear	Anderson, R. L., and Bancroft, T. A.	1952
model, mixed	Mood, A. M.	1950
model, random effects	Scheffé, H.	1956
model, components of variance	Mood, A. M.	1950
moment	Pearson, K.	1893
moment generating function	Craig, C. C.	1936
Monte Carlo methods	von Neumann, J., and Ulam, S. M.	1940
moving average	Yule, G. U.	1921
multiple comparisons	Duncan, D. B.	1951
multiple correlation coefficient	Pearson, K.	1914
negative binomial distribution	Greenwood, M., and Yule, G. U.	1920
noncentral	Fisher, R. A.	1928
nonparametric	Wolfowitz, J.	1942
normal (distribution)	Galton, F.	1889
normal score	Fisher, R. A., and Yates, F.	1938
nuisance parameter	Hotelling, H.	1940
null hypothesis	Fisher, R. A.	1935
odds ratio	Gart, J. J.	1962
order statistic	Wilks, S. S.	1942
p value	Deming, W. E.	1943
parameter	Czuber, E.	1914
parameter	Fisher, R. A.	1922
Pareto distribution	Pigou, A. C.	1920
partial correlation	Yule, G. U.	1907
partial regression	Yule, G. U.	1897
percentile	Galton, F.	1885
permutation test	Box, G. E. P., and Andersen, S. L.	1955
pie chart	Haskell, A. C.	1922
point estimation	Wilks, S. S.	1943
Poisson distribution (essentially)	Soper, H. E.	1914
posterior probability	Wrinch, D., and Jeffreys, H.	1921
power function	Neyman, J., and Pearson, E. S.	1936
power (of a test)	Neyman, J., and Pearson, E. S.	1933
principal components	Hotelling, H.	1933
prior probability	Wrinch, D., and Jeffreys, H.	1921
probability density	von Mises, R.	1919
probability density function	Wilks, S. S.	1943

Term	Author(s)	Year
probability function	Aitken, A. C.	1939
probability generating function	Seal, H. L.	1949
probability paper	Hazen, A.	1914
probit analysis	Finney, D. J.	1944
product-limit estimate	Kaplan, E. L., and Meier, P.	1958
quantile	Kendall, M. G.	1940
quartile, upper and lower	Galton, F.	1882
random effects	Eisenhart, C.	1947
random model	Scheffé, H.	1956
random sampling	Pearson, K.	1900
random variable	Winter, A.	1934
random variable (variabile casuale)	Cantelli, F. P.	1916
random walk	Pearson, K.	1905
randomization	Fisher, R. A.	1926
randomization test	Box, G. E. P., and Andersen, S. L.	1955
randomized blocks	Fisher, R. A.	1926
randomized response	Warner, S. L.	1965
range	Lloyd, H.	1848
regression	Galton, F.	1897
regression, partial	Yule, G. U.	1979
resampling	Efron, B.	1979
response surface	Box, G. E. P., and Wilson, K. B.	1951
ridge regression	Hoerl, A. E., and Kennard, R.W.	1970
robustness	Box, G. E. P.	1953
sampling distribution	Fisher, R. A.	1928
scale parameter	Pitman, E. J. G.	1938
scatter-plot	Kurtz, A. K., and Edgerton, H. A.	1939
sequential analysis	Wald, A.	1945
serial correlation	Yule, G. U.	1926
Sheppard's corrections	Pearson, K.	1901
sign test	Stewart, W. M.	1941
significance, level of	Fisher, R. A.	1925
simple hypothesis	Neyman, J., and Pearson, E. S.	1933
simple random sampling	Cochran, W. G.	1953
skewness	Pearson, K.	1895
split plot	Yates, F.	1935
standard deviation (σ)	Pearson, K.	1894
standard error	Yule, G. U.	1897
statistic	Fisher, R. A.	1922
statistics	Hooper, W.	1770
stem-and-leaf displays	Tukey, J. W.	1972
Student's t (essentialy)	Fisher, R. A.	1924
studentized range	Pearson, E. S., and Hartley, H. O.	1943
subjective probability	Keynes, J. M.	1921
sufficient statistic	Fisher, R. A.	1925
survival function	Kaplan, E. L., and Meier, P.	1958
test of hypothesis	Neyman, J., and Pearson, E. S.	1928
test of significance	Fisher, R. A.	1925
time series	Persons, W. M.	1919
tolerance limits (statistical)	Wilks, S. S.	1941

(Continued)

Term	Author(s)	Year
treatment effect	Wilks, S. S.	1943
trend	Hooker, R. H.	1901
type I and type II errors	Neyman, J., and Pearson, E. S.	1933
uniform distribution	Uspensky, J. V.	1937
uniformly most powerful test	Neyman, J., and Pearson, E. S.	1936
unimodal	De Helguero, F.	1904
U shaped	Yule, G. U.	1911
variance	Fisher, R. A.	1918
variance components	Daniels, H. E.	1939
varitate	Fisher, R. A.	1925
Weibull distribution	Lieblein, J.	1955
Yates' correction for continuity	Fisher, R. A.	1936
Youden square	Fisher, R. A.	1938
z distribution	Fisher, R. A.	1924
zero-sum game	Von Neumann, J., and Morgenstern, O.	1944

Adapted from H. A. David (1995), "First (?) Occurrence of Common Terms in Mathematical Statistics."
The American Statistician, Vol. 49, No. 2, pp. 121–133, and H. A. David (1998), "First (?) occurrence of Common Terms in Probability and Statistics," *The American Statistician,* Vol. 52, No. 1, pp. 36–40. With permission.

Appendix N

A selected bibliography for further reading

Readers who wish to obtain additional information about the entries defined in this dictionary have hundreds and thousands of other works from which to choose. In this appendix, we provide a selected list of books and references that are representative of dozens of other publications available on a particular topic of interest. The books are grouped into a number of categories covering all important areas of statistical theory and methodology:

1. General Statistics	2. Applied Statistics and Data Analysis	3. Exploratory and Graphical Data Analysis
4. Agricultural and Biological Statistics	5. Business Statistics	6. Chemical and Physical Sciences and Engineering Statistics
7. Economic Statistics and Econometrics	8. Medical and Health Statistics	9. Statistics in Ecology and Environmental Sciences
10. Statistics for Social and Behavioral Sciences	11. Statistical Methods	12. Mathematical Statistics/ Statistical Theory
13. Advanced Statistical Theory	14. Probability Theory	15. Statistical Distributions
16. Categorical Data and Contingency Table Analysis	17. Linear Statistical Models	18. Nonparametric Regression and Generalized Linear Models
19. Regression Analysis	20. Nonlinear Regression	21. Log–Linear Models and Logistic Regression
22. Analysis of Variance	23. Design and Analysis of Experiments	24. Response Surface Methodology
25. Repeated Measures Analysis	26. Nonparametric Statistics	27. Sampling and Sample Surveys
28. Time Series Analysis and Forecasting	29. Multivariate Statistical Analysis	30. Stochastic Processes
31. Monte Carlo Methods and Simulation	32. Resampling Methods: Jackknife and Bootstrap	33. Statistical Quality Control and Related Methods
34. Statistical Reliability	35. Bayesian Statistics	36. Clinical Trials
37. Epidemiologic Methods	38. Statistical Epidemiology	39. Kaplan–Meier Method and Survival Analysis
40. Meta-Analysis and Other Methods for Quantitative Synthesis	41. Structural Equation Modeling	42. Statistical Consulting and Training
43. Statistical Computing	44. Statistical Software Packages	45. Probability and Statistics Literacy

(*Continued*)

46. Probability and Statistics for Lay Readers	47. Handbooks and Encyclopedias	48. Calculus, Matrix Algebra, and Numerical Analysis Useful in Statistics
49. Statistical Tables	50. Dictionaries, Quotations, and Other References	51. History of Statistics/Probability and Leading Personalities

1. General Statistics

Aczel, A. D. (1995). *Statistics: Concepts and Applications.* Irwin, Burr Ridge, Illinois.

Frank, H., and Althon, S. C. (1994). *Statistics: Concepts and Applications.* Cambridge University Press, New York.

Freedman, D., Pisani, R., Purves, R., and *Adhikari, A.* (1997). *Statistics,* 3rd ed. Norton, New York.

Mann, P. S. (2001). *Introductory Statistics,* 4th ed. John Wiley, New York.

Moore, D. S., and McCabe, G. P. (1998). *Introduction to the Practice of Statistics,* 3rd ed. W. H. Freeman, New York.

2. Applied Statistics and Data Analysis

Cox, D. R., and Snell, E. J. (1981). *Applied Statistics: Principles and Examples.* Chapman & Hall, London.

Hamilton, L. C. (1990). *Modern Data Analysis: A First Course in Applied Statistics.* Duxbury Press, Belmont, California.

Iman, R. L. (1994). *A Data-Based Approach to Statistics.* Duxbury Press, Belmont, California.

Sprent, P. (1998). *Data Driven Statistical Models.* Chapman & Hall, London.

Yandell, B. S. (1997). *Practical Data Analysis and Designed Experiments.* Chapman & Hall, London.

3. Exploratory and Graphical Data Analysis

Basford, K. E., and Tukey, J. W. (1999). *Graphical Analysis of Multiresponse Data.* CRC Press, Boca Raton, Florida.

Chambers, J. M., Cleveland, W. S., Kleiner, B., and Tukey, P. A. (1983). *Graphical Methods for Data Analysis.* Wadsworth, Pacific Grove, California.

Jacoby, W. G. (1998). *Statistical Graphs for Visualizing Multivariate Data.* Sage, Thousand Oaks, California.

Tukey, J. W. (1977). *Exploratory Data Analysis.* Addison–Wesley, Reading, Massachusetts.

Velleman, P. F., and Hoaglin, D. C. (1981). *Applications, Basics and Computing of Exploratory Data Analysis.* Duxbury Press, Boston.

4. Agricultural and Biological Statistics

Mead, R., Curnow, R. N., and Hasted, A. M. (1993). *Statistical Models in Agriculture and Experimental Biology,* 2nd ed. Chapman & Hall, London.

Petersen, R. G. (1994). *Agricultural Field Experiments: Design and Analysis.* Marcel Dekker, New York.

Watt, T. A. (1997). *Introductory Statistics for Biology Students,* 2nd ed. Chapman & Hall/CRC, Boca Raton, Florida.

Williams, B. G. (1993). *Biostatistics: Concepts and Applications for Biologists.* Chapman & Hall, London.

Zar, J. H. (1999). *Biostatistical Analysis,* 4th ed. Prentice–Hall, Upper Saddle River, New Jersey.

5. Business Statistics

Berenson, M. L., and Levine, D. M. (1996). *Basic Business Statistics: Concepts and Applications,* 6th ed. Prentice–Hall, Englewood Cliffs, New Jersey.

Foster, D. P., Stine, R. A., and Waterman, R. P. (1998). *Business Analysis Using Regression: A Casebook.* Springer–Verlag, New York.

Letchford, S. (1994). *Statistics for Accountants.* Chapman & Hall, London.

Mendenhall, W., Beaver, R. J., and Beaver, B. M. (1996). *A Course in Business Statistics,* 4th ed. Duxbury Press, Belmont, California.

Siegel, A. F. (2000). *Practical Business Statistics,* 4th ed. Irwin/McGraw–Hill, Burr Ridge, Illinois.

6. Chemical and Physical Sciences and Engineering Statistics

Devore, J. L., and Farnum, N. (1999). *Applied Statistics for Engineers and Scientists.* Duxbury Press, Belmont, California.

Metcalfe, A. V. (1997). *Statistics in Civil Engineering.* Arnold, London.

Rosenkrantz, W. A. (1997). *Introduction to Probability and Statistics for Scientists and Engineers.* McGraw–Hill, New York.

Sincich, T., and Mendenhall, W. (1995). *Statistics for Engineering and the Sciences,* 4th ed. Prentice–Hall, Englewood Cliffs, New Jersey.

Smith, P. J. (1998). *Into Statistics: A Guide to Understanding Statistical Concepts in Engineering and the Sciences,* 2nd ed. Springer–Verlag, New York.

7. Economic Statistics and Econometrics

Baltagi, B. H. (1999). *Econometrics,* 2nd revised ed. Springer–Verlag, New York.

Davidson, R., and MacKinnon, J. G. (1993). *Estimation and Inference in Econometrics.* Oxford University Press, New York.

Greene, W. H. (1999). *Econometric Analysis,* 4th ed. Prentice–Hall, Englewood Cliffs, New Jersey.

Johnston, J., and DiNardo, J. (1997). *Econometric Methods,* 4th ed. McGraw–Hill, New York.

Mittelhammer, R. C. (1996). *Mathematical Statistics for Economics and Business.* Springer–Verlag, New York.

8. Medical and Health Statistics

Altman, D. G. (2001). *Practical Statistics for Medical Research,* 2nd ed. Chapman & Hall/CRC, Boca Raton, Florida.

Armitage, P., and Berry, G. (1994). *Statistical Methods in Medical Research,* 3rd ed. Blackwell Scientific, London.

Dawson–Saunders, B., and Trapp, R. G. (1994). *Basic and Clinical Biostatistics,* 2nd ed. Appleton & Lange, Norwalk, Connecticut.

Forthofer, R. N., and Lee, E. S. (1995). *Introduction to Biostatistics.* Academic Press, San Diego, California.

Rosner, B. (2000). *Fundamentals of Biostatistics,* 5th ed. Duxbury Press, Belmont, California.

9. Statistics in Ecology and Environmental Sciences

Gilbert, R. O. (1987). *Statistical Methods for Environmental Pollution Monitoring.* Van Nostrand Reinhold, New York.

Manly, B. F. J. (2000). *Statistics for Environmental Science and Management.* Chapman & Hall/CRC, Boca Raton, Florida.

Millard, S. P., and Neerchal, N. K. (2000). *Environmental Statistics with S-Plus.* CRC Press, Boca Raton, Florida.

Ott, W. R. (1995). *Environmental Statistics and Data Analysis.* CRC Press, Boca Raton, Florida.

Pearson, J. C. G., and Turton, A. (1993). *Statistical Methods in Environmental Health.* Chapman & Hall, London.

10. Statistics for Social and Behavioral Sciences

Howell, D. C. (1999). *Fundamental Statistics for the Behavioral Sciences with CDRom,* 4th ed. Duxbury Press, Belmont, California.

Hutcheson, G. D., and Sofroniou, N. (1999). *The Multivariate Social Statistics: Introductory Statistics Using Generalized Linear Models.* Sage, Thousand Oaks, California.

Lockhart, R. S. (1998). *Introduction to Statistics and Data Analysis for the Behavioral Sciences.* Freeman, New York.

Lomax, R. G. (1998). *Statistical Concepts: A Second Course for Education and the Behavioral Sciences.* Laurence-Erlbaum, Mahwah, New Jersey.

Ott, R. L., Larson, R. F., Rexroat, C., and Mendenhall, W. (1992). *Statistics: A Tool for the Social Sciences,* 5th ed. Duxbury Press, Belmont, California.

11. Statistical Methods

Freund, R. J., and Wilson, W. J. (1996). *Statistical Methods,* revised ed. Academic Press, New York.

Ott, R. L. (1993). *An Introduction to Statistical Methods and Data Analysis,* 4th ed. Duxbury Press, Belmont, California.

Rustagi, J. S. (1991). *Introduction to Statistical Methods,* Vols. I and II. Rowman & Allanheld, Totowa, New Jersey.

Snedecor, G. W., and Cochran, W. G. (1989). *Statistical Methods,* 8th ed. Iowa State University Press, Ames, Iowa.

Steel, G. D., Torrie, J. H., and Dickey, D. A. (1997). *Principles and Procedures of Statistics: A Biometrical Introduction,* 3rd ed. McGraw–Hill, New York.

12. Mathematical Statistics/Statistical Theory

Hogg, R. V., and Craig, A. T. (1995). *Introduction to Mathematical Statistics,* 5th ed. Prentice–Hall, Englewood Cliffs, New Jersey.

Lindgren, B. W. (1993). *Statistical Theory,* 4th ed. Chapman & Hall, New York.

Mendenhall, W., Wackerly, D. D., and Scheaffer, R. L. (2001). *Mathematical Statistics with Applications,* 6th ed. Duxbury Press, Boston.

Mood, A. M., Graybill, F. A., and Boes, D. C. (1974). *Introduction to the Theory of Statistics.* McGraw–Hill, New York.

Rice, J. A. (1995). *Mathematical Statistics and Data Analysis,* 2nd ed. Duxbury Press, Boston.

13. Advanced Statistical Theory

Cox, D. R., and Hinkley, D. V. (1974). *Theoretical Statistics.* Chapman & Hall, London. (Softbound edition, 1986.)

Lehmann, E. L. (1997). *Testing Statistical Hypothesis,* 2nd ed. Springer–Verlag, New York.

Lehmann, E. L., and Casella, G. (1998). *Theory of Point Estimation,* 2nd ed. Springer–Verlag, New York.

Rao, C. R. (1973). *Linear Statistical Inference and Its Applications,* 2nd ed. John Wiley, New York.

Stuart, A., and Ord, K. (1991, 1994). *Kendall's Advanced Theory of Statistics,* Vol. 1, 6th ed., Vol. 2, 5th ed. Arnold, London.

14. Probability Theory

Feller, W. (1968). *An Introduction to Probability Theory and Its Applications,* Vol. 1, 3rd ed.; Vol. 2, 1966. John Wiley, New York.

Fridett, B., and Gray, L. (1997). *A Modern Approach to Probability Theory.* Birkhäuser, Boston.

Gut, A. (1995). *An Intermediate Course in Probability.* Springer–Verlag, New York.

Ross, S. M. (1999). *Introduction to Probability Models,* 6th ed. Academic Press, Orlando, Florida.

Stirzaker, D. (1999). *Probability and Random Variables.* Cambridge University Press, Cambridge, U.K.

15. Statistical Distributions

Evans, M., Hastings, N., and Peacock, B. (2000). *Statistical Distributions,* 3rd ed. John Wiley, New York.

Johnson, N. L., Kotz, S., and Balakrishnan, N. (1994, 1995). *Continuous Univariate Distributions,* Vols. 1 and 2, 2nd ed. John Wiley, New York.

Johnson, N. L., Kotz, S., and Balakrishnan, N. (1997). *Discrete Multivariate Distributions,* 2nd ed. John Wiley, New York.

Johnson, N. L., Kotz, S., and Kemp, A. W. (1992). *Univariate Discrete Distributions,* 2nd ed. John Wiley, New York.

Patel, J. K., and Read, C. B. (1996). *Handbook of the Normal Distribution,* 2nd ed. Marcel Dekker, New York.

16. Categorical Data and Contingency Table Analysis

Agresti, A. (1996). *An Introduction to Categorical Data Analysis.* John Wiley, New York.

Andersen, E. B. (1997). *Introduction to the Statistical Analysis of Categorical Data.* Springer–Verlag, New York.

Everitt, B. S. (1992). *The Analysis of Contingency Tables,* 2nd ed. Chapman & Hall, New York.

Freedman, D. H., Jr. (1987). *Applied Categorical Data Analysis.* Marcel Dekker, New York.

Lloyd, C. J. (1999). *Statistical Analysis of Categorical Data.* John Wiley, New York.

17. Linear Statistical Models

Bowerman, B. L., O'Connell, R. T., and Dickey, D. A. (1990). *Linear Statistical Models: An Applied Approach,* 2nd ed. Duxbury Press, Boston.

Hocking, R. R. (1996). *Methods and Applications of Linear Models: Regression and the Analysis of Variance.* John Wiley, New York.

Jorgensen, B. (1993). *The Theory of Linear Models.* Chapman & Hall, London.

Neter, J., Kutner, M. H., Nachtsheim, C. J., and Wasserman, W. (1996). *Applied Linear Statistical Models,* 4th ed. Irwin, Burr Ridge, Illinois.

Stapleton, J. H. (1995). *Linear Statistical Models.* John Wiley, New York.

18. Nonparametric Regression and Generalized Linear Models

Dobson, A. J. (2001). *An Introduction to Generalized Linear Models,* 2nd ed. Chapman & Hall/CRC, Boca Raton, Florida.

Green, P. J., and Silverman, B. W. (1993). *Nonparametric Regression and Generalized Linear Models.* Chapman & Hall, London.

Hardle, W. (1992). *Applied Nonparametric Regression.* Cambridge University Press, New York.

Hastie, T. J., and Tibshirani, R. J. (1990). *Generalized Additive Models.* Chapman & Hall, London.

McCullagh, P., and Nelder, J. A. (1989). *Generalized Linear Models,* 2nd ed. Chapman & Hall, London.

19. Regression Analysis

Chatterjee, S., Hadi, A. S., and Price, B. (2000). *Regression Analysis by Example,* 3rd ed. John Wiley, New York.

Cook, R. D., and Weisberg, S. (1999). *Applied Regression Including Computing and Graphics.* John Wiley, New York.

Draper, N. R., and Smith, H. (1998). *Applied Regression Analysis,* 3rd ed. John Wiley, New York.

Rawlings, J. O., Pantula, S. G., and Dickey, D. A. (1998). *Applied Regression Analysis: A Research Tool,* 2nd ed. Springer–Verlag, New York.

Ryan, T. P. (1997). *Modern Regression Methods.* John Wiley, New York.

20. Nonlinear Regression

Bates, D. M., and Watts, D. G. (1988). *Nonlinear Regression Analysis and Its Applications.* John Wiley, New York.

Gallant, A. R. (1987). *Nonlinear Statistical Models.* John Wiley, New York.

Huet, S., Bouvier, A., Gruet, M-A., and Jolivet, E. (1996). *Statistical Tools for Nonlinear Regression.* Springer–Verlag, New York.

Ratkowsky, D. A. (1983). *Nonlinear Regression Modeling.* Marcel Dekker, New York.

Seber, G. A. F., and Wild, C. J. (1989). *Nonlinear Regression.* John Wiley, New York.

21. Log–Linear Models and Logistic Regression

Christensen, R. (1997). *Log–linear Models and Logistic Regression,* 2nd ed. Springer–Verlag, New York.

Collett, D. (1991). *Modeling Binary Data.* Chapman & Hall, London.

Hosmer, D. W., and Lemeshow, S. (2000). *Applied Logistic Regression,* 2nd ed. John Wiley, New York.

Kleinbaum, D. G. (1997). *Logistic Regression: A Self-Learning Text.* Springer–Verlag, New York.

Lindsey, J. K. (1995). *Modelling Frequency and Count Data.* Oxford University Press, Oxford.

22. Analysis of Variance

Hoaglin, D. C., Mosteller, F., and Tukey, J. W. (eds.) (1991). *Fundamentals of Exploratory Analysis of Variance.* John Wiley, New York.

Lindman, H. R. (1991). *Analysis of Variance in Experimental Design.* Springer–Verlag, New York.

Sahai, H., and Ageel, M. I. (2000). *The Analysis of Variance: Fixed, Random and Mixed Models.* Birkhäuser, Boston.

Scheffé, H. (1959). *The Analysis of Variance.* John Wiley, New York.

Turner, J. R., and Thayer, J. F. (2001). *Introduction to Analysis of Variance: Design, Analysis and Interpretation.* Sage, Thousand Oaks, California.

23. Design and Analysis of Experiments

Clarke, G. M., and Kempson, R. E. (1997). *Introduction to the Design and Analysis of Experiments.* Arnold, London.

Cobb, G. W. (1998). *Introduction to Design and Analysis of Experiments.* Springer–Verlag, New York.

Cox, D. R., and Reid, N. (2000). *The Theory of the Design of Experiments.* Chapman & Hall/CRC, Boca Raton, Florida.

Dean, A. M., and Voss, D. (1998). *Design and Analysis of Experiments.* Springer–Verlag, New York.

Montgomery, D. C. (2001). *Design and Analysis of Experiments,* 5th ed. John Wiley, New York.

24. Response Surface Methodology

Box, G. E. P., and Draper, N. R. (1986). *Empirical Model Building and Response Surfaces.* John Wiley, New York.

Cornell, J. A. (1990). *How to Apply Response Surface Methodology,* revised ed. American Society for Quality Control, Wisconsin.

Daniel, C., and Wood, F. S. (1980). *Fitting Equations to Data,* 2nd ed. John Wiley, New York.

Khuri, A. I., and Cornell, J. (1996). *Response Surface: Design and Analysis,* 2nd ed. Marcel Dekker, New York.

Myers, R. H., and Montgomery, D. C. (1995). *Response Surface Methodology: Process and Product Optimization Using Designed Experiments.* John Wiley, New York.

25. Repeated Measures Analysis

Crowder, M. J., and Hand, D. J. (1990). *Analysis of Repeated Measures.* Chapman & Hall, London.

Davidian, M., and Giltinan, D. M. (1995). *Nonlinear Models for Repeated Measurement Data.* Chapman & Hall, London.

Hand, D. J., and Taylor, C. C. (1987). *Multivariate Analysis of Variance and Repeated Measures: A Practical Approach for Behavioral Scientists.* Chapman & Hall, London.

Kenward, M. G. (1996). *Analysis of Repeated Measurements.* Oxford University Press, New York.

Lindsey, J. K. (1999). *Models for Repeated Measurements,* 2nd ed. Oxford University Press, Oxford.

26. Nonparametric Statistics

Conover, W. J. (1999). *Practical Nonparametric Statistics,* 3rd ed. John Wiley, New York.

Daniel, W. W. (1990). *Applied Nonparametric Statistics,* 2nd ed. Brooks/Cole, Belmont, California.

Hollander, M., and Wolfe, D. A. (1998). *Nonparametric Statistical Methods,* 2nd ed. John Wiley, New York.

Maritz, J. S. (1995). *Distribution Free Statistical Methods.* Chapman & Hall, London.

Sprent, P., and Smeeton, N. (2000). *Applied Nonparametric Statistical Methods,* 3rd ed. Chapman & Hall/CRC, Boca Raton, Florida.

27. Sampling and Sample Surveys

Cochran, W. G. (1977). *Sampling Techniques,* 3rd ed. John Wiley, New York.

Lehtonen, R., and Pahkinen, E. J. (1995). *Practical Methods for Design and Analysis of Complex Surveys.* John Wiley, New York.

Levy, P. S., and Lemeshow, S. (1999). *Sampling of Populations: Methods and Applications,* 3rd ed. John Wiley, New York.

Singh, R., and Singh, N. (1996). *Elements of Survey Sampling.* Kulwer, Dordrecht.
Som, R. K. (1995). *Practical Sampling Techniques,* 2nd ed. Marcel Dekker, New York.

28. Time Series Analysis and Forecasting
Bowerman, B. L., and O'Connell, R. T. (1993). *Forecasting and Time Series: An Applied Approach,* 3rd ed. Duxbury Press, Boston.
Brockwell, P. J., and Davis, R. A. (1997). *An Introduction to Time Series and Forecasting.* Springer–Verlag, New York.
Chatfield, C. (1996). *The Analysis of Time Series,* 5th ed. Chapman & Hall/CRC, Boca Raton, Florida.
Franses, P. H. (1998). *Time Series Models for Business and Economic Forecasting.* Cambridge University Press, New York.
Pole, A., West, M., and Harrison, J. (1994). *Applied Bayesian Forecasting and Time Series Analysis.* Chapman & Hall/CRC, Boca Raton, Florida.

29. Multivariate Statistical Analysis
Afifi, A. A., and Clark, V. (1996). *Computer-Aided Multivariate Analysis,* 3rd ed. Chapman & Hall, London.
Chatfield, C., and Collins, A. J. (2000). *Introduction to Multivariate Analysis.* Chapman & Hall/CRC, Boca Raton, Florida.
Flury, B. (1997). *A First Course in Multivariate Statistics.* Springer–Verlag, New York.
Gnanadesikan, R. (1997). *Methods for Statistical Data Analysis of Multivariate Observations,* 2nd ed. John Wiley, New York.
Manly, B. F. J. (1994). *Multivariate Statistical Methods: A Primer,* 2nd ed. Chapman & Hall, London.

30. Stochastic Processes
Durrett, R. (1999). *Essentials of Stochastic Processes.* Springer–Verlag, New York.
Karlin, S., and Taylor, H. M. (1981). *A Second Course in Stochastic Processes.* Academic Press, New York.
Kulkarni, V. G. (1995). *Modeling and Analysis of Stochastic System.* Chapman & Hall, London.
Lawler, G. F. (1995). *Introduction to Stochastic Processes.* Chapman & Hall, London.
Ross, S. (1996). *Stochastic Processes,* 2nd ed. John Wiley, New York.

31. Monte Carlo Methods and Simulation
Fishman, G. (1996). *Monte Carlo: Concepts, Algorithms, and Applications.* Springer–Verlag, New York.
Gentle, J. E. (2000). *Random Number Generation and Monte Carlo Methods.* Springer–Verlag, Berlin/Heidelberg.
Robert, C. P., and Casella, G. (2000). *Monte Carlo Statistical Methods.* Springer–Verlag, Berlin/Heidelberg.
Ross, S. M. (1997). *Simulation,* 2nd ed. Academic Press, San Diego, California.
Rubinstein, R. Y., and Melamed, B. (1998). *Modern Simulation and Modeling.* John Wiley, New York.

32. Resampling Methods: Jackknife and Bootstrap
Chernick, M. R. (1999). *Bootstrap Methods: A Practitioner's Guide.* John Wiley, New York.
Davison, A. C., and Hinkley, D. V. (1997). *Bootstrap Methods and Their Applications.* Cambridge University Press, Cambridge.

Efron, B., and Tibshirani, R. J. (1994). *An Introduction to the Bootstrap.* Chapman & Hall, London.

Good, P. I. (1999). *Resampling Methods.* Birkhäuser, Boston.

Shao, J., and Tu, D. (1996). *The Jackknife and Bootstrap.* Springer–Verlag, New York.

33. Statistical Quality Control and Related Methods

Bissell, D. (1994). *Statistical Methods for SPC and TQM.* Chapman & Hall, London.

Drain, D. (1997). *Statistical Methods for Industrial Process Control.* Chapman & Hall, London.

Mittag, H. J., and Rinne, H. (1993). *Statistical Methods of Quality Assurance.* Chapman & Hall, London.

Montgomery, D. C. (2001). *Introduction to Statistical Quality Control,* 4th ed. John Wiley, New York.

Thompson, J. R., and Koronacki, J. (1993). *Statistical Process Control for Quality Improvement.* Chapman & Hall, London.

34. Statistical Reliability

Ansell, J. I., and Phillips, M. J. (1994). *Practical Methods for Reliability Data Analysis.* Clarendon Press, Oxford.

Aven, T., and Jensen, U. (1999). *Stochastic Models in Reliability.* Springer–Verlag, Berlin.

Crowder, M. J., Kimber, A. C., Sweeting, T. J., and Smith, R. A. (1991). *Statistical Analysis of Reliability Data.* Chapman & Hall, London.

Meeker, W. Q., and Escobar, L. A. (1998). *Statistical Methods for Reliability Data.* John Wiley, New York.

Tobias, P. A., and Trindade, D. C. (1995). *Applied Reliability,* 2nd ed. Chapman & Hall, London.

35. Bayesian Statistics

Carlin, B. P., and Louis, T. A. (2000). *Bayes and Empirical Bayes Methods for Data Analysis,* 2nd ed. Chapman & Hall/CRC, Boca Raton, Florida.

Gelman, A., Carlin, J. B., Stern, H. S., and Rubin, D. B. (1995). *Bayesian Data Analysis.* Chapman & Hall, London.

Lee, P. M. (1997). *Bayesian Statistics,* 2nd ed. Arnold, London.

Leonard, T., and Hsu, J. S. J. (1999). *Bayesian Methods: An Analysis for Statisticians and Interdisciplinary Researchers.* Cambridge University Press, Cambridge.

O'Hagan, A. (1994). *Kendall's Advanced Theory of Statistics,* Vol. 2B: *Bayesian Inference.* Arnold, London.

36. Clinical Trials

Chow, S. C., and Liu, J. P. (1998). *Design and Analysis of Clinical Trials: Concepts and Methodologies.* John Wiley, New York.

Green, S., Benedetti, J., and Crowley, J. (1997). *Clinical Trials in Oncology.* Chapman & Hall, London.

Meinert, C. (1986). *Clinical Trials: Design, Conduct and Analysis.* Oxford University Press, New York.

Piantadosi, S. (1997). *Clinical Trials: A Methodological Perspective.* John Wiley, New York.

Wooding, W. M. (1994). *Planning Pharmaceutical Clinical Trials: Basic Statistical Principles.* John Wiley, New York.

37. Epidemiologic Methods

Clayton, D., and Hills, M. (1993). *Statistical Models in Epidemiology.* Oxford University Press, Oxford.

Kleinbaum, D. G., Kupper, L. L., and Morgenstern, H. (1982). *Epidemiologic Research: Principles and Quantitative Methods.* Van Nostrand Reinhold, New York.

McNeil, D. (1996). *Epidemiological Research Methods.* John Wiley, New York.

Rothman, K. J., and Greenland, S. (1998). *Modern Epidemiology,* 2nd ed. Lippincott–Raven, Philadelphia, Pennsylvania.

Schlesselman, J. J. (1982). *Case-Control Studies: Design, Conduct and Analysis.* Oxford University Press, New York.

38. Statistical Epidemiology

Breslow, N. E., and Day, N. E. (1980, 1987). *Statistical Methods in Cancer Research,* Vol. I: *The Analysis of Case Control Studies,* Vol. II: *The Design and Analysis of Cohort Studies.* Oxford University Press, New York.

Kahn, H. A., and Sempos, C. T. (1989). *Statistical Methods in Epidemiology.* Oxford University Press, New York.

Sahai, H., and Khurshid, A. (1996). *Statistics in Epidemiology: Methods, Techniques and Applications.* CRC Press, Boca Raton, Florida.

Selvin, S. (1995). *Statistical Analysis of Epidemiologic Data,* 2nd ed. Oxford University Press, New York.

Woodward, M. (1999). *Epidemiology: Study Design and Data Analysis.* Chapman & Hall, London.

39. Kaplan–Meier Method and Survival Analysis

Collett, D. (1994). *Modeling Survival Data in Medical Research.* Chapman & Hall, London.

Hosmer, D. W., and Lemeshow, S. (1999). *Applied Survival Analysis: Regression Modeling of Time to Event Data.* John Wiley, New York.

Le, C. T. (1997). *Applied Survival Analysis.* John Wiley, New York.

Marubini, E., and Valsecchi, M. G. (1995). *Analyzing Survival Data from Clinical Trials.* John Wiley, New York.

Parmar, M. K. B., and Machin, D. (1995). *Survival Analysis: A Practical Approach.* John Wiley, New York.

40. Meta-Analysis and Other Methods for Quantitative Synthesis

Glass, G. V., McGaw, B., and Smith, M. L. (1981). *Meta-Analysis in Social Research.* Sage, Thousand Oaks, California.

Hedges, L. V., and Olkin, I. (1985). *Statistical Methods for Meta-Analysis.* Academic Press, Orlando, Florida.

Lipsey, M. W., and Wilson, D. B. (2000). *Practical Meta-Analysis.* Sage, Thousand Oaks, California.

Petitti, D. B. (2000). *Meta-Analysis, Decision Analysis, and Cost-Effectiveness Analysis: Methods for Quantitative Synthesis in Medicine.* Oxford University Press, New York.

Sutton, A. J., Abrams, K. R., Jones, D. R., Sheldon, T. A., and Song, F. (2000). *Methods for Meta-Analysis in Medical Research.* John Wiley, New York.

41. Structural Equation Modeling

Bartholomew, D. J., and Knott, M. (1999). *Latent Variable Models and Factor Analysis,* 2nd ed. Oxford University Press, New York.

Kline, R. B. (1998). *Structural Equation Modeling.* Guilford Press, New York.

Maruyama, G. M. (1997). *Basics of Structural Equations Modeling.* Sage, Thousand Oaks, California.

Mueller, R. O. (1996). *Basic Principles of Structural Equation Modeling.* Springer–Verlag, New York.

Raykov, T., and Marcoulides, G. A. (2000). *A First Course in Structural Equation Modeling.* Lawrence–Erlbaum, Mahwah, New Jersey.

42. Statistical Consulting and Training

Derr, J. (2000). *Statistical Consulting: A Guide to Effective Communication.* Duxbury Press, Belmont, California.

Chatfield, C. (1995). *Problem Solving: A Statistician's Guide,* 2nd ed. Chapman & Hall, London.

Hand, D. J., and Everitt, B. (eds.) (1987). *The Statistical Consultant in Action.* Cambridge University Press, Cambridge, U.K.

Loynes, R. M. (ed.) (1987). *The Training of Statisticians Round the World.* International Statistical Institute, Voorburg, The Netherlands.

Newton, R. R., and Rudestam, K. E. (1999). *Your Statistical Consultant: Answer to Your Data Analysis Questions.* Sage, Thousand Oaks, California.

43. Statistical Computing

Chambers, J. M. (1977). *Computational Methods for Data Analysis.* John Wiley, New York.

Gelfand, A. E. G., and Smith, A. F. M. (1997). *Bayesian Computation.* John Wiley, New York.

Kennedy, W. J., Jr., and Gentle, J. E. (1980). *Statistical Computing.* Marcel Dekker, New York.

Noreen, E. W. (1989). *Computer Intensive Methods for Testing Hypotheses: An Introduction.* John Wiley, New York.

Thisted, R. A. (1988). *Elements of Statistical Computing: Numerical Computation.* Chapman & Hall, London.

44. Statistical Software Packages

Dixon, W. J. (ed.) (1992). *BMDP Statistical Software Manual,* Vols. I, II, and III. University of California Press, Los Angeles.

Minitab, Inc. (2000). *MINITAB Reference Manual,* Release 13. Minitab, Inc., State College, Pennsylvania.

SAS Institute (2000). *SAS/STAT User's Guide,* Version 8.0, Vols. I, II, and III. SAS Institute, Inc., Cary, North Carolina.

SPSS, Inc. (2001). *SPSS Base 10.1 for Windows User's Guide.* SPSS, Inc., Chicago, Illinois.

STATA, Inc. (2000). *STATA Reference Manual,* Release 7.0. Stata Corporation, College Station, Texas.

45. Probability and Statistics Literacy

David, F. N. (1962). *Games, Gods and Gambling.* Griffin, London.

Isaac, R. (1995). *The Pleasures of Probability.* Springer–Verlag, New York.

Maxwell, N. (1998). *Statistics Literacy.* Springer–Verlag, New York.

Rao, C. R. (1997). *Statistics and Truth,* 2nd ed. World Scientific, Singapore.

Zeisel, H., and Kaye, D. (1997). *Prove It with Figures.* Springer–Verlag, New York.

46. Probability and Statistics for Lay Readers

Hooke, R. (1983). *How to Tell the Liars from the Statisticians.* Marcel Dekker, New York.

Huff, D., and Geis, I. (1993). *How to Lie with Statistics,* reissue edition, Norton, New York.

Lowry, R. (1989). *The Architecture of Chance.* Oxford University Press, New York.

Salkind, N. J. (2000). *Statistics for People Who (Think They) Hate Statistics.* Sage, Thousand Oaks, California.

Weaver, J. H. (1997). *Conquering Statistics: Numbers without the Crunch.* Plenum Press, New York.

47. Handbooks and Encyclopedias

Armitage, P., and Colton, T. (1998). *Encyclopedia of Biostatistics,* 6 vol. set. John Wiley, New York.

Kotz, S., and Johnson, N. L. (eds.) (1982–1988). *Encyclopedia of Statistical Sciences,* 9 vol. set, John Wiley, New York.

Kruskal, W. H., and Tanur, J. M. (1978). *An International Encyclopedia of Statistics,* 2 vol. set. Free Press, New York.

Sachs, L., and Reynarowych, Z. (1984). *Applied Statistics: A Handbook of Techniques,* 2nd ed. Springer–Verlag, New York.

Sheskin, D. J. (1997). *Handbook of Parametric and Nonparametric Statistical Procedures.* CRC Press, Boca Raton, Florida.

48. Calculus, Matrix Algebra, and Numerical Analysis Useful in Statistics

Gentle, J. E. (1998). *Numerical Linear Algebra for Applications in Statistics.* Springer–Verlag, New York.

Harville, D. A. (1997). *Matrix Algebra from a Statistician's Perspective.* Springer–Verlag, New York.

Healy, M. (2000). *Matrices for Statistics,* 2nd ed. Oxford University Press, New York.

Khuri, A. I. (1993). *Advanced Calculus with Applications in Statistics.* John Wiley, New York.

Lange, K. (1999). *Numerical Analysis for Statisticians.* Springer–Verlag, New York.

49. Statistical Tables

Beyer, W. H. (2000). *Standard Probability and Statistics: Tables and Formulae,* 2nd ed. CRC Press, Boca Raton, Florida.

Fisher, R. A., and Yates, F. (1963). *Statistical Tables for Biological, Agriculture, and Medical Research,* 6th ed. Hafner, New York (4th ed., 1953, 5th ed., 1957).

Kokoska, S., and Nevison, C. (1990). *Statistical Tables and Formulae,* 2nd ed. Springer–Verlag, New York.

Lentner, C. (1982). *Geigy Scientific Tables,* Vol. 2: *Introduction to Statistics, Statistical Tables, and Mathematical Formulae.* Ciba–Geigy, Basel, Switzerland.

Pearson, E. S., and Hartley, H. O. (1970, 1973). *Biometrika Tables for Statisticians,* Vols. I and II, 3rd ed. Cambridge University Press, Cambridge.

50. Dictionaries, Quotations, and Other References

Everitt, B. S. (1998). *The Cambridge Dictionary of Statistics.* Cambridge University Press, Cambridge.

Gaither, C. C., and Cavazos–Gaither, A. E. (1996). *Statistically Speaking: A Collection of Quotes and Quips from the Improbable to the Infinite.* Institute of Physics, Bristol, U.K.

Marriott, F. H. C. (1990). *A Dictionary of Statistical Terms,* 5th ed. Longman, Essex, England. (1st ed. 1957, 2nd ed. 1960, 3rd ed. 1971, 4th ed. 1982 by M. G. Kendall and W. R. Buckland).

Preira–Maxwell, F. (1998). *A–Z of Medical Statistics.* Arnold, London.

Vogt, W. P. (1993). *Dictionary of Statistics and Methodology.* Sage, Thousand Oaks, California.

51. History of Statistics/Probability and Leading Personalities

Hald, A. (1990). *A History of Probability and Statistics: Before 1750.* John Wiley, New York.

Hald, A. (1998). *A History of Mathematical Statistics: From 1750 to 1930.* John Wiley, New York.

Johnson, N. L., and Kotz, S. (eds.) (1997). *Leading Personalities in Statistical Sciences: From the Seventeenth Century to Present.* John Wiley, New York.

Stigler, S. M. (1986). *The History of Statistics: The Measurement of Uncertainty Before 1900.* Belknap Press, Cambridge, Massachusetts.

Stigler, S. M. (1999). *Statistics on the Table: The History of Statistical Concepts.* Harvard University Press, Cambridge, Massachusetts.

BAKER & TAYLOR